D0918883

Romantic Bards and British Reviewers

Romantic Bards and British Reviewers

A Selected Edition of the Contemporary Reviews of the Works of Wordsworth, Coleridge, Byron, Keats and Shelley

Edited by

JOHN O. HAYDEN

UNIVERSITY OF NEBRASKA PRESS · LINCOLN

Publishers on the Plains
UNP

First published in the United States of America 1971
by The University of Nebraska Press
Lincoln, Nebraska 68508
Printed in Great Britain

Library of Congress Catalog Card No. 71-125670
International Standard Book Number 0-8032-0773-5

Contents

IV   Keats

V   Shelley

Introduction

It is widely known that what is called the Romantic revolution in England in the early nineteenth century was marked by a phenomenal number of distinguished works of literature. And yet it is known mainly to specialists that this literary revolution was accompanied by a similar movement in criticism, an equally phenomenal outburst of periodical criticism, even though evidence of the accompanying critical movement can be found without delving very deeply into the literary background of the period—in passages and chapters of well-known prose works, in the correspondence of most of the writers, in defensive or provoking prefaces to volumes of poetry, and even in the poetry itself.

The early nineteenth century indeed stands out as a great age of literary reviewing. In 1800, about a dozen periodicals—a few monthly Reviews (periodicals wholly devoted to criticism) and the rest monthly magazines with critical departments—carried literary reviews as a regular feature. By the second decade of the 1800s the number of reviewing periodicals in circulation had risen to an average of twenty-five, many of them quarterly, monthly, and weekly Reviews. A peak of at least thirty-one was reached in the early 1820s, but by the end of 1826 the number was quickly dwindling again to a mere dozen or so. All of this critical activity—some sixty or more periodicals were involved—has, however, been largely ignored, with the exception of a few infamous reviews of the works of Wordsworth and Keats, which have received more attention than they deserve, especially in terms of their critical merit.

The overlooking of this important mass of critical effort is in any case less difficult to explain than why reviewing was then more popular than it ever was before or has been since. Probably the most significant factor was the growth of the reading public. Through industrial and commercial expansion the middle class had become larger and more powerful and desired the polish and taste of their superiors on the social scale. Lending libraries and advances in printing techniques were making more books available, but how was one to know which were the 'right' books to read? The answer was obvious: in Thomas Love Peacock's novel *Nightmare Abbey*, a parcel arrived for one of the guests at the abbey—'a new novel, and a new poem, . . . and the last number of a popular Review'.

Nightmare Abbey, as well as showing the popularity of the Reviews at the time it was published (1817), testifies to the contemporary con-suming interest in literature. Most of the characters represent satirically either contemporary literary figures or attitudes. A later novel by Peacock, *Crotchet Castle* (1831), has but a few such literary figures; most of the characters are involved instead with social or economic satire. In little more than a decade a shift in interest had apparently taken place, and it explains in part the waning of literary reviewing after the first quarter of the century. Almost all the poetry of the major Romantic poets had already been published; Byron, Keats, and Shelley were dead. By 1830 the Romantic period was over, in terms of both its literature and its criticism.

Explanations aside, the facts are clear: the public did patronize Reviews generously in the early nineteenth century. These periodicals must have been of some importance in establishing tastes and reputa-tions; the great variety of kinds alone would indicate this. At least some data suggest that each kind of periodical—quarterlies, monthlies, magazines, and weeklies—had its own era of special impact in the years between 1800 and 1825, and an idea of their probable influence can be obtained from evidence of contemporary notoriety, longevity and such circulation figures as are extant.

Of the sixty-odd periodicals that carried reviews, twenty-five or so were sufficiently significant to be represented in this edition. Of these the monthly Reviews, many of which were survivors of the eighteenth century, were most influential in the early years of the following century. The *Monthly Review* (1749–1845) and the *Critical Review* (1756–1817) were the two oldest and most important, but there were also the *British Critic* (1793–1826) and the *Antijacobin Review* (1798–1821), the last being from all indications the least respected of the four. Of those monthlies founded after 1800, the *Eclectic Review* (1805–68) is the only one worth serious mention. The *Christian Observer* (1802–74) lasted a considerable time, but its literary reviewing was only sporadic.

The quarterlies, the *Edinburgh Review* (1802–1929) and the *Quarterly Review* (1809–1968), were unquestionably the most powerful critical organs from their founding right through the period. They are the two periodicals most spoken of, most praised and blamed, at the time; it was an honor to be discovered to be a contributor to either. Another quarterly, the *British Review* (1811–25), was probably only as influential as the monthlies. The *Annual Review* (1802–08) was, as its title indicates, a yearly publication; because of its design, its critical voice was heard mainly in the Colonies.

Like the monthly Reviews, many of the monthly magazines that carried literary criticism were relics of the eighteenth century. This is particularly true of the venerable *Gentleman's Magazine* (1731–1868) and the *Scots Magazine* (1739–1826). Several were established later in the eighteenth century: the *European Magazine and London Review* (1782–1826) and the *Monthly Magazine* (1796–1826). None of these older magazines, however, nor the fashionable magazines like the *British Lady's Magazine* (1815–19) and the *Monthly Literary Recreations* (1806–07) are likely to have made much of a critical impression on the age. The reviews they carried were shorter, often no more than a paragraph, and vied for the reader's attention with many other features, such as original articles, correspondence, and chronicles. Reviews were only one of their regular, titled departments.

In 1817, *Blackwood's* (1817–   ) initiated a transformation of the magazines. After a few issues in the old style, its layout was substantially altered to make it more readable: all the formal departments were dropped, and the literary reviews were intermingled with the other articles and, perhaps even more important, were much longer. Most of the magazines continued in the old rut, but the *Scots Magazine* (which changed its name to the *Edinburgh Magazine* in 1817) and the *New Monthly Magazine* (1814–36) soon followed the lead of *Blackwood's*; and Baldwin's *London Magazine* (1820–29) and Gold's *London Magazine* (1820–21) began as imitations. From all indications these magazines, especially *Blackwood's*, were much more popular and influential as critical organs than their stodgy predecessors.

The weekly journals were even slower than the magazines in establishing their critical importance. Although the *Examiner* (1808–81) had begun a regular reviewing section in 1816, as did the *Champion* (1814–22) at its inception, the critical influence of these journals, like that of the magazines, must have been dissipated to some extent by their other features, especially their political columns. It was probably not until the *Literary Gazette* (1817–62) and its imitators, such as the *Literary Chronicle* (1819–29), took hold in the early 1820s that the weekly journals became a critical force. These later weeklies were, as their titles would seem to warrant, concerned more strictly with literature; and reviews were a prominent feature.

Thus there was a sort of build-up of critical power in the Romantic period, with more and more different types of periodicals entering the critical arena and reaching their peak of influence in the early 1820s. Yet a discussion of their influence must be qualified, since the political forces of the time would have limited the audience for any one periodical. The Romantic age was a time of war and depressions, of political, social, and economic ferment. Political feelings ran high, and because of the importance of the Reviews they were naturally affected.

Some of the political undertow in which the Reviews were caught was partisan, but even so it was seldom merely a question of the Tories versus the Whigs (and Radicals), for both the Tories and Whigs are better seen as factions with a shared conception of aristocratic government. The Whigs, or the Opposition, and the Tories, or the Government, both had some members who were liberal and some who were conservative. Of the two major Reviews, the *Edinburgh*, which had on its cover the buff and blue of the Foxite Whigs, seems to have been liberal because its founders and main contributors were liberal, while those of the Tory *Quarterly* were mostly conservative and gave it such a bias accordingly. They were, then, not strictly speaking partisan organs, but reflected the actual political cleavage of the times: liberal and conservative. In the wake of the French Revolution and with the Radicals clamoring for reform of Parliament, political ideology was much more important than partisan affiliation. Partisan bickering is a luxury reserved for peaceful times. All political principles were being called into question; nothing was sacred.

In these terms of liberal and conservative, the probable influence of the Romantic reviewing periodicals was split approximately down the middle. Much of the liberal power lay in periodicals run by Dissenters, who, outside of the Establishment, had less reason to hold back their political views and more to gain from change. Such were the *Monthly Review*, the *Critical Review*, the *Monthly Magazine*, the *Eclectic Review*, and the *Annual Review*. Radical periodicals like Leigh Hunt's *Examiner* should also be considered in the liberal line-up. On the other side, were the *British Critic* and the *Antijacobin Review*, both of which were connected with the Established Church and were founded to counteract the influence of the *Monthly Review* and the *Critical*. The *New Monthly Magazine* was likewise established to counteract a liberal periodical, the

Radical *Monthly Magazine*, but later became more liberal. Other more powerful conservative periodicals were the *Literary Gazette* and *Blackwood's Magazine*, although the latter was often so maverick as to defy political categorization.

The general political bias of the Romantic periodicals has in the past probably been exaggerated. There were, for one thing, many contributors who were shared by periodicals of differing political persuasion, and whatever the amount of bias, there is little evidence that it seriously affected the reviewing of literature as long as the literature under review was not itself politically volatile. Light partisan satire of the sort written by Thomas Moore met with considerable indulgence from the other side; and there were occasional instances of the crossing of political lines even in reviews of political works, as in the unfavorable reviews of *Queen Mab* in the *Monthly Magazine* and of Southey's *A Vision of Judgement* in the *Literary Gazette*. These examples make it difficult to accept the customary simple view that an unfavorable review of a liberal writer in a reactionary periodical was necessarily a matter of political prejudice.

There were of course instances of politically biased reviews of literature. The worst cases occurred in conservative periodicals, the *Quarterly*, *Blackwood's*, and the *Literary Gazette*, all three of which at times subjected writers to scathing attacks—termed 'personality'—on their private lives. And yet the writers mainly involved, Byron, Shelley, Keats and Hazlitt, were more than merely liberal; they often obtruded into their works jacobinical or unpatriotic sentiments that were considered dangerous enough to call forth any kind of attack. It is also worth noting that rabid attacks make good copy, and good copy sells periodicals. The last point may sound cynical; it is, however, intended as an additional explanation, not an excuse.

To be sure, some of the attacks, such as *Blackwood's* abuse of Keats, were inexcusable; but some of the strong but less abusive criticism deserves more indulgence than it usually receives. There was a tradition of bluntness and even acrimony in the periodical criticism of the time, and although it may occasionally shock the reader new to that criticism, it is surely pointless to become more upset at it than those living at the time. Moreover, political prejudices may sometimes have helped writers, especially those in the liberal camp. Perhaps for this reason, for example, the reception of Keats's first volume was on the whole favorable in excess of its merits. But whether a help or a hindrance, political bias is seldom easy to discriminate from legitimate criticism, since valid critical principles are often brought forward in the judgments. To leave them out of account is an act of bias itself.

The customary view of the Reviews as citadels of political reaction, with reviewers making sorties against any inoffensive poet who happened by, would be less questionable if the anonymous marauding reviewers were today either totally unknown or known to be hired hacks. Unfortunately for that view, many of the literary reviewers have been identified, and they do not fit the role written for them by later commentators. Rather they are generally men who made their mark on the period for a diversity of talents.

One of the main reasons for this high quality is that, following a policy initiated by the *Edinburgh Review*, many of the periodicals paid their contributors well. In the case of the great quarterlies, there was also the incentive of the honor of being known to be a contributor; one was always in the best of company. Francis Jeffrey, the editor of the *Edinburgh* for the first twenty-seven years and later a Judge of the Court of Session in Scotland (an office which brought with it the title 'Lord'), held a virtual monopoly of the important literary reviewing for that periodical, although two of its important literary reviews were written by Henry, later Lord, Brougham and by William Hazlitt. The *Quarterly*, edited by William Gifford, a literary satirist and classical translator, retained the services of Walter Scott and Robert Southey. Southey wrote few reviews of literature, but Scott was active in this regard. Other noted contributors to the *Quarterly* included Charles Lamb; John Taylor Coleridge, nephew of the poet; John Wilson Croker, long the First Secretary of the Admiralty, as well as a poet and a scholar of some note; and William Lyall, a churchman who later became Dean of Canterbury.

The literary reviewers for the monthlies, magazines, and weeklies add to the impressive list provided by the quarterlies. Hazlitt, Southey, and Lamb, in fact, also wrote for the other, lesser periodicals. In addition, Lord Byron, William Taylor of Norwich, John Scott, P. G. Patmore, Leigh Hunt, James Montgomery, John Foster, and John Hamilton Reynolds—all literary men of considerable reputation in the period—were involved in reviewing. There was, furthermore, a close connection between law and literature in the early nineteenth century; the list of lawyers, some of whom were also authors as well as reviewers, includes John Gibson Lockhart, John Wilson, William Roberts, Thomas Denman, and Thomas Noon Talfourd. This enumeration of reviewers could easily be extended with names of distinguished physicians, journalists, ministers, and university professors.

The reviews were with few exceptions anonymous. Only one journal, the *London Review* (1809), broke with the tradition and listed the authors of its reviews; it lasted only four numbers. Although many of the

Romantic reviewers have been identified, especially those writing for the *Edinburgh*, the *Quarterly*, the *Eclectic*, and the *Monthly Review*, *Blackwood's*, and the *London Magazine*, many others have eluded scholars, and so it is possible that the reviewers named above worked side by side with reviewers of a strictly mercenary and malicious nature. It is possible, but not probable; it is much more likely that they were all, or almost all, of a kind; and from the evidence of known contributors they would hardly seem to fall into the category of hired hacks.

The reasons for the anonymity provide a rich subject for speculation. The most obvious are that there was a tradition of reviewing anonymity coming down from the eighteenth century and that the anonymity afforded the reviewers a freedom they would otherwise have lacked. The literary world of the time was relatively small and was concentrated, along with the reviewing periodicals, in two large metropolitan centers, London and Edinburgh; and thus reviewers might easily have been acquainted with the writers they were reviewing and have felt an added strain to their objectivity if the reviews had been signed. And yet these reasons do not really explain why the anonymity was abandoned for the most part later in the century. It seems more than likely that literary anonymity held a peculiar fascination for Romantic writers as a whole. In the literature of the time it was more prevalent than usual: not only did the 'Great Unknown', Scott, go to great lengths to cover up his authorship of the Waverley novels, but some of Scott's poetry, as well as works by Jane Austen, Wordsworth, Byron, Hazlitt, Moore, and Rogers, were cloaked in anonymity.

The reviewers, I believe, seldom abused their own anonymity. They saw a definite connection between literature and society, a connection which, owing to the large reading public for serious literature, was probably much clearer and more direct than it is today. Literature, in the reviewers' opinion, could affect men's lives in many ways, and many reviewers felt themselves to be the guardians of those lives. Thus, the tone of the reviews was almost always serious, and occasionally even solemn or pompous. William Roberts in the *British Review* was often guilty of such a pose; and, coupled with an incredible gullibility, it earned his Review the nickname (dispensed by Byron) of 'my Grandmother's Review, the British'. At times, too, the reviews could be farcical or tongue-in-cheek, like the review of Byron's *Hours of Idleness* in the *Edinburgh Review*, but overall their most pervasive qualities are their vigor and concern.

There were, however, some general reviewing policies current in the period that acted as restraints on the reviewers' vigor. Many of the quarterly and monthly Reviews attempted to maintain a consistent critical opinion; if a contributor deviated from it, he most likely would have his review heavily edited or rejected. The magazines did not share such a policy, allowing their reviewers greater freedom. This fact goes far to explain the gross inconsistencies so often found in *Blackwood's*.

Many of the secondary reviewing periodicals, moreover, saw their critical task as a simple function; they attempted merely to describe, give illustrative quotations from, and evaluate the works under review. Since they were trying to inform the public of which new books were worth purchasing, there was an unwritten law that collected and second editions were passed by, except to warn the public of 'bookmaking'— the reprinting of works previously published in periodicals or in other editions with other titles. ('Bookmaking' also referred to the publication of expensive limited editions and fairly short poems eked out with copious notes or a combination of the two.) Although the Reviews did not always follow this rule, it does explain the scanty reception of such works as Wordsworth's collected *Poems* of 1815.

The quarterlies, on the other hand, did not see their function as quite so simple. The *Edinburgh* instituted at its founding a policy of greater selectivity in the books to be reviewed than was the case with the monthly Reviews. The *Monthly Review* had already announced a cutback in scope in 1790 owing to the increase in publications, but it still tried to review as many new books as possible, if only in brief notices at the end of its volumes. The reviews in the *Edinburgh* and its imitator, the *Quarterly*, were fewer and thus longer and could therefore accommodate digressions, theorizing, and longer quotations. Sometimes they even became essays or polemical tracts, almost ignoring the works under review; but this tendency was usually held in check in the critiques of literature. When controlled, such reviews made more interesting reading, and part of the success and influence of the quarterlies probably derives from this cause.

Influence is one thing, critical worth another. The secondary reviewing periodicals often contain, I believe, better criticism than the two giants, if only because reviews in the second-string periodicals are often more disinterested and less diffuse. The *Edinburgh* and the *Quarterly*, falling back on the security of their popularity, sometimes indulged themselves, the *Edinburgh* in disingenuously favorable reviews of Jeffrey's friends, the *Quarterly* in political 'personality'. *Blackwood's*, the most influential of the magazines, has undoubtedly the worst history of shoddy criticism; it frequently dealt out prejudiced, indiscriminate, and slack critical judgments.

All of the reviewing periodicals shared the same general critical values, whether they abused them or not. They were all working in the Aristotelian critical tradition, which has been termed the Classical tradition by Walter Jackson Bate (in his *Prefaces to Criticism* [New York, 1959]) to distinguish it from the rule-ridden tradition of Neo-classical rationalism, typified by Thomas Rymer. The Aristotelian tradition had come down to the Romantic reviewers through Dryden and Dr Johnson, and, as Bate has pointed out, it became more rather than less flexible in the eighteenth century.

Because of the flexibility, the critical values of the reviewers cannot be set down in a formal list. And yet this is not to say that they were capricious. They were based on reason, experience, and knowledge of human nature, and thus could be adapted as the occasion demanded. Language was considered as a communicative art and was required to be grammatical and to make sense. Badly written poetry, it was thought, could corrupt the language; Byron, Scott, and Shelley were especially arraigned in this regard. Since literature was seen as mimetic —as having strong ties with objective reality—diction, imagery, and characterization were likewise subjected to the scrutiny of reason and experience. In applying such standards, of course, the reviewers were occasionally too strict, unimaginative, even sometimes obtuse, but they seldom became hyper-rational and in fact often went overboard in their praise of the emotional content of Romantic literature.

Also in the Aristotelian tradition, the Romantic reviewers accepted the Horatian formula that literature teaches as well as pleases, that it is at least in some general sense moral. Sometimes, as in the *British Critic*'s review of *Don Juan* I–II, the moral criticism was puritanical, a fact which is not surprising when the religious affiliation of so many of the periodicals is taken into account. Most of the puritanical remarks— and their frequency should not be exaggerated—concerned sexual morality; but although adverse criticism of offenses of that nature was the largest single item of moral comment, the majority of moral objections were directed at offenses of other kinds. The presentation of vicious heroes whose virtues might make their vices seem attractive was one; Scott and Byron came in for a good deal of adverse criticism on this score.

That the Romantic reviewers belonged to the Aristotelian critical tradition will not, I suppose, be a matter of wonder. It was the central tradition in English criticism down at least to Matthew Arnold; and it is still being practiced in the United States and especially in England, although its philosophical underpinnings are often shaky today. Critical relativism and its natural concomitant, critical impressionism, although they were already evident in the early 1820s in reviews by

P. G. Patmore and John Wilson, had to wait to come into their own later with the art-for-art's-sake pronouncements of Pater and Wilde.

The extent of the Romantic literary revolution is often exaggerated. In the literature produced there is a great deal of experimentation but no definite break with the past; and there are in it as many elements of the old as of the new. In literary criticism, there was likewise no break: there was a new emphasis on creative theory—in terms of M. H. Abrams's *The Mirror and the Lamp* (New York, 1953), emphasis on the lamp—in the writings of Wordsworth, Coleridge, Shelley, and Keats, but they did not discard older literary theory that was concerned with the relationship of literature to objective reality—Abrams's mirror. Wordsworth's Preface to the *Lyrical Ballads* and Coleridge's *Biographia Literaria* in fact were in many respects reactionary documents —the former laments new trends in literature—and even Shelley in his *Defense of Poetry* comes out strongly for a purpose in poetry. There was little room for quarrel, at least in broad literary theory, between the Romantic poets and the Romantic reviewers.

Contrary to the popular view, the Romantic reviewers were on the whole very much in favor of the literature with which they were dealing. They had some serious qualifications to that approval, as well they might have in an age of so much literary experimentation. They also provided an atmosphere of concern and interest which may have been an important stimulus to English Romantic literature. Just how much causal connection there was between that literature and its contemporary critics will never be known with any accuracy, but it must surely have existed. The Romantic reviewers, in any event, had a great deal to say about literature, and they deserve a fair, unprejudiced reading, the kind that they are commonly supposed to have denied to the works with which they were dealing and that, ironically, they have never yet received themselves.

The reviews in this edition were selected to present the best criticism of the best-known works of the major poets. When I have departed from that policy it was to include famous, or rather more often infamous, reviews or reviewers, as well as reviews that are representative of either critical trends or of a particular type of review or periodical. The most important distinction between this and the policies of previous editions is that the poets are not emphasized to the neglect of the reviewers. The poets receive their due, but it should be kept in mind that in spite of the attempt to be as representative as possible, the selections were made from many hundreds of reviews and that, from those given, it is impossible to generalize about the overall reception of a particular work or the reputation of a poet as a whole.

Within the reviews selected, quotations and plot summaries have been shortened or omitted altogether to conserve space wherever it was possible without losing the point for which quotations were given or wherever the plot summaries contained no critical comment. Such editing is always noted in brackets. Line numbers of the latest editions are given for omitted quotations, and so there should be little difficulty in locating the passages in question. (In the case of omitted quotations from works by Wordsworth, who revised his poems extensively, sometimes only approximate line numbers of modern editions could be given.) The reviews otherwise stand as they appeared in the periodicals; spelling and punctuation have not been amended except for obvious typographical errors, and the reviewers' footnotes have been marked as such and placed in brackets.

I
Wordsworth

Reviews of
Wordsworth's (and Coleridge's)
'Lyrical Ballads'

Critical Review

2d ser. XXIV (Oct. 1798), 197–204. The author was Robert Southey: see Jack Simmons, Southey (*London, 1945), p. 78.*

The majority of these poems, we are informed in the advertisement, are to be considered as experiments.

'They were written chiefly with a view to ascertain how far the language of conversation in the middle and lower classes of society is adapted to the purposes of poetic pleasure.' p. i.

Of these experimental poems, the most important is the Idiot Boy, the story of which is simply this.

[The story is briefly summarized, and lines 312–91 are quoted.]

No tale less deserved the labour that appears to have been bestowed upon this. It resembles a Flemish picture in the worthlessness of its design and the excellence of its execution. From Flemish artists we are satisfied with such pieces: who would not have lamented, if Corregio or Rafaelle had wasted their talents in painting Dutch boors or the humours of a Flemish wake?

The other ballads of this kind are as bald in story, and are not so highly embellished in narration. With that which is entitled the Thorn, we were altogether displeased. The advertisement says, it is not told in the person of the author, but in that of some loquacious narrator. The author should have recollected that he who personates tiresome loquacity, becomes tiresome himself. The story of a man who suffers

3

the perpetual pain of cold, because an old woman prayed that he never might be warm, is perhaps a good story for a ballad, because it is a well-known tale: but is the author certain that it is *well authenti-cated?* and does not such an assertion promote the popular super-stition of witchcraft?

In a very different style of poetry, is the Rime of the Ancyent Marinere; a ballad (says the advertisement) 'professedly written in imitation of the *style*, as well as of the spirit of the elder poets.' We are tolerably conversant with the early English poets; and can dis-cover no resemblance whatever, except in antiquated spelling and a few obsolete words. This piece appears to us perfectly original in style as well as in story. Many of the stanzas are laboriously beautiful; but in connection they are absurd or unintelligible. Our readers may exercise their ingenuity in attempting to unriddle what follows.

'The roaring wind! it roar'd far off,
   It did not come anear;
But with its sound it shook the sails
   That were so thin and sere.

The upper air bursts into life,
   And a hundred fire-flags sheen
   To and fro they are hurried about;
And to and fro, and in and out
   The stars dance on between.

The coming wind doth roar more loud;
   The sails do sigh, like sedge:
The rain pours down from one black cloud,
   And the moon is at its edge.

Hark! hark! the thick black cloud is cleft,
   And the moon is at its side:
Like waters shot from some high crag,
The lightning falls with never a jag
   A river steep and wide.

The strong wind reach'd the ship: it roar'd
   And dropp'd down, like a stone!
Beneath the lightning and the moon
   The dead men gave a groan.' P. 27.

We do not sufficiently understand the story to analyse it. It is a Dutch attempt at German sublimity. Genius has here been employed in producing a poem of little merit.

With pleasure we turn to the serious pieces, the better part of the volume. The Foster-Mother's Tale is in the best style of dramatic narrative. The Dungeon and the Lines upon the Yew-tree Seat, are beautiful.[1] The Tale of the Female Vagrant is written in the stanza, not the style, of Spenser. We extract a part of this poem.

[Ten stanzas are quoted. The poem was not republished, but in 1842 it was incorporated into *Guilt and Sorrow*.]

Admirable as this poem is, the author seems to discover still superior powers in the Lines written near Tintern Abbey. On reading this production, it is impossible not to lament that he should ever have condescended to write such pieces as the Last of the Flock, the Convict, and most of the ballads. In the whole range of English poetry, we scarcely recollect any thing superior to a part of the following passage.

[Lines 65–111 are quoted.]

The 'experiment,' we think, has failed, not because the language of conversation is little adapted to 'the purposes of poetic pleasure,' but because it has been tried upon uninteresting subjects. Yet every piece discovers genius; and, ill as the author has frequently employed his talents, they certainly rank him with the best of living poets.

British Critic

XIV (Oct. 1799), 364–69. The reviewer is unknown.

The attempt made in this little volume is one that meets our cordial approbation; and it is an attempt by no means unsuccessful. The endeavour of the author is to recall our poetry, from the fantastical excess of refinement, to simplicity and nature. The account of this design, and its probable effects upon modern readers, is so very sensibly given in the Introduction, that we shall insert the passage at large.

[The first four paragraphs of the Advertisement are quoted.]

We fully agree with the author, that the true notion of poetry must be sought among the poets, rather than the critics; and we will add that, unless a critic is a poet also, he will generally make but indifferent work in judging of the effusions of Genius. In the collection of poems subjoined to this introduction, we do not often find expressions that we esteem too familiar, or deficient in dignity; on the contrary, we

---

[1] 'The Foster-Mother's Tale' and 'The Dungeon' were written by Coleridge.

think that in general the author has succeeded in attaining that judicious degree of simplicity, which accommodates itself with ease even to the sublime. It is not by pomp of words, but by energy of thought, that sublimity is most successfully achieved; and we infinitely prefer the simplicity, even of the most unadorned tale in this volume, to all the meretricious frippery of the *Darwinian* taste.[1]

The Poem of 'the Ancyent Marinere,' with which the collection opens, has many excellencies, and many faults; the beginning and the end are striking and well-conducted; but the intermediate part is too long, and has, in some places, a kind of confusion of images, which loses all effect, from not being quite intelligible. The author, who is confidently said to be Mr. Coleridge, is not correctly versed in the old language, which he undertakes to employ. 'Noises of a *swound*,' p. 9, and 'broad as a *weft*,' p. 11, are both nonsensical; but the ancient style is so well imitated, while the antiquated words are so very few, that the latter might with advantage be entirely removed without any detriment to the effect of the Poem. The opening of the Poem is admirably calculated to arrest the reader's attention, by the well-imagined of the idea Wedding Guest, who is held to hear the tale, in spite of his efforts to escape. The beginning of the second canto, or fit, has much merit, if we except the very unwarrantable comparison of the Sun to that which no man can conceive:—'like God's own head,' a simile which makes a reader shudder; not with poetic feeling, but with religious disapprobation. The following passage is eminently good.

[Lines 103–22 are quoted.]

The conclusion, as we remarked before, is very good, particularly the idea that the Marinere has periodical fits of agony, which oblige him to relate his marvellous adventure; and this,

> 'I pass, like night, from land to land,
> I have strange power of speech;
> The moment that his face I see,
> I know the man that must hear me;
> To him my tale I teach.' P. 49.

Whether the remaining poems of the volume are by Mr. Coleridge, we have not been informed; but they seem to proceed from the same mind; and in the Advertisement, the writer speaks of himself as of a single person accountable for the whole. It is therefore reasonable to

---

[1] Erasmus Darwin, a late eighteenth-century poet, wrote in the didactic mode and in the heroic couplets of earlier eighteenth-century poets.

conclude, that this is the fact. They all have merit, and many among them a very high rank of merit, which our feelings respecting some parts of the supposed author's character do not authorize or incline us to deny. The Poem on the Nightingale, which is there styled *a conversational Poem*, is very good; but we do not perceive it to be more conversational than Cowper's Task, which is the best poem in that style that our language possesses.[1] 'The Female Vagrant,' is a composition of exquisite beauty, nor is the combination of events, related in it, out of the compass of possibility; yet we perceive, with regret, the drift of the author in composing it; which is to show the worst side of civilized society, and thus to form a satire against it. But let fanciful men rail as they will at the evils which no care can always prevent, they can have no dream more wild than the supposition, that any human wisdom can possibly exclude all evils from a state which divine Providence has decreed, for reasons the most wise, to be a state of suffering and of trial. The sufferers may be changed, by infinite revolutions, but sufferers there will be, till Heaven shall interfere to change the nature of our tenure upon earth. From this beautiful Poem, partly on account of its apparent design, and partly because the loss of the connection would destroy much of its effect, we shall make no extract.

The story of 'Goody Blake and Harry Gill,' is founded, the Introduction tells us, 'on a well-authenticated fact which happened in Warwickshire.' Yet it is a miracle; and modern miracles can seldom be admitted, without some degree of credulity, or a very uncommon weight of evidence. One of the simplest stories in the book, is that entitled 'We are Seven,' yet he must be a very fastidious reader who will deny that it has great beauty and feeling.

The tale of 'the Thorn' has many beauties; nor can we pass without notice 'the Mad Mother,' or the long and familiar tale of 'the Idiot Boy,' which, though it descends quite to common life, is animated by much interest, and told with singular felicity. One more Poem we shall particularly notice for its pathos, and shall indeed insert the whole. The imagery of it is in many instances new, and is introduced with admirable effect.

['The Complaint of a Forsaken Indian Woman', as well as its headnote, is quoted in full.]

The purchasers of this little volume will find that, after all we have said, there are poems, and passages of poems, which we have been obliged to pass over, that well deserve attention and commendation; nor does there appear any offensive mixture of enmity to present

---

[1] 'The Nightingale' was written by Coleridge.

institutions, except in one or two instances, which are so unobtrusive as hardly to deserve notice.

Antijacobin Review

V (April 1800), 334. The author was Rev. William Heath. The authority for this attribution is a manuscript note in the staff copy of the Review *now in the British Museum.*

This is a volume of a very different description from the above.[1] It has genius, taste, elegance, wit, and imagery of the most beautiful kind. 'The ancyent Marinere' is an admirable 'imitation of the style as well as of the spirit of the elder poets.' The softer 'Mother's Tale'[2] is pathetic, and pleasing in the extreme—'Simon Lee the old Huntsman' —'The idiot Boy,' and the tale of 'Goody Blake, and Harry Gill' are all beautiful in their kind; indeed the whole volume convinces us that the author possesses a mind at once classic and accomplished, and we, with pleasure, recommend it to the notice of our readers as a production of no ordinary merit.

[1] The preceding volume reviewed was R. J. Thorne's *Lodon and Miranda,* a tale in blank verse heavily criticized by the reviewer.

[2] 'The Foster-Mother's Tale' was written by Coleridge.

Reviews of Wordsworth's 'Poems in Two Volumes'

Monthly Literary Recreations

III (*July 1807*), *65–66. The author was Lord Byron: see* R. E. Prothero, *ed.,* The Works of Lord Byron: Letters and Journals (*London, 1898–1901*), *V, 452.*

The volumes before us are by the author of Lyrical Ballads, a collection which has not undeservedly met with a considerable share of public applause. The characteristics of Mr. W.'s muse are simple and flowing, though occasionally inharmonious verse, strong, and sometimes irresistible appeals to the feelings, with unexceptionable sentiments. Though the present work may not equal his former efforts, many of the poems possess a native elegance, natural and unaffected, totally devoid of the tinsel embellishments and abstract hyperboles of several cotemporary sonneteers. The last sonnet in the first volume, p. 152, is perhaps the best, without any novelty in the sentiments, which we hope are common to every Briton at the present crisis; the force and expression is that of a genuine poet, feeling as he writes:

'Another year! another deadly blow!
Another mighty empire overthrown!
And we are left, or shall be left, alone—
The last that dares to struggle with the foe.
'Tis well!—from this day forward we shall know
That in ourselves our safety must be sought,
That by our own right-hands it must be wrought;
That we must stand unprop'd, or be laid low.
O dastard! whom such foretaste doth not cheer!
We shall exult, if they who rule the land

> Be men who hold its many blessings dear,
> Wise, upright, valiant, not a venal band,
> Who are to judge of danger which they fear,
> And honor which they do not understand.'

The song at the Feast of Brougham Castle, the Seven Sisters, the Affliction of Margaret ——— of ——— possess all the beauties, and few of the defects of this writer; the following lines from the last are in his first style:

> 'Ah! little doth the young one dream
> When full of play and childish cares,
> What power hath e'en his wildest scream,
> Heard by his mother unawares:
> He knows it not, he cannot guess:
> Years to a mother bring distress,
> But do not make her love the less.'

The pieces least worthy of the author are those entitled 'Moods of my own Mind,' we certainly wish these 'Moods' had been less frequent, or not permitted to occupy a place near works, which only make their deformity more obvious; when Mr. W. ceases to please, it is by 'abandoning' his mind to the most commonplace ideas, at the same time clothing them in language not simple, but puerile: what will any reader or auditor, out of the nursery, say to such namby-pamby as 'Lines written at the foot of Brother's Bridge.'[1]

> 'The cock is crowing,
> The stream is flowing,
> The small birds twitter,
> The lake doth glitter.
> The green field sleeps in the sun;
> The oldest and youngest
> Are at work with the strongest,
> The cattle are grazing,
> Their heads never raising,
> There are forty feeding like one,
> Like any army defeated,
> The snow hath retreated,
> And now doth fare ill,
> On the top of the bare hill.'

[1] The title of the poem was 'Written in March'.

'The plough-boy is whooping anon, anon,'[1] &c. &c. is in the same exquisite measure; this appears to us neither more or less than an imitation of such minstrelsy as soothed our cries in the cradle, with the shrill ditty of

> 'Hey de diddle,
> The cat and the fiddle:
> The cow jump'd over the moon,
> The little dog laugh'd to see such sport,
> And the dish ran away with the spoon.'

On the whole, however, with the exception of the above, and other INNOCENT odes of the same cast, we think these volumes display a genius worthy of higher pursuits, and regret that Mr. W. confines his muse to such trifling subjects; we trust his motto will be in future, 'Paulo majora canamus.'[2] Many, with inferior abilities, have acquired a loftier seat on Parnassus, merely by attempting strains in which Mr. W. is more qualified to excel.

Edinburgh Review

XI (Oct. 1807), 214–31. The author was Francis Jeffrey: see Walter E. Houghton (ed.), The Wellesley Index to Victorian Periodicals (Toronto, 1966), p. 442.

This author is known to belong to a certain brotherhood of poets, who have haunted for some years about the Lakes of Cumberland; and is generally looked upon, we believe, as the purest model of the excellences and peculiarities of the school which they have been labouring to establish. Of the general merits of that school, we have had occasion to express our opinion pretty fully, in more places than one, and even to make some allusion to the former publications of the writer now before us.[3] We are glad, however, to have found an opportunity of attending somewhat more particularly to his pretensions.

The Lyrical Ballads were unquestionably popular; and, we have no hesitation in saying, deservedly popular; for in spite of their occasional vulgarity, affectation, and silliness, they were undoubtedly characterised

---

[1] A continuation of the poem 'Written in March'.

[2] 'Let us sing a little higher'—the motto to the 'Ode' ['Intimations of Immortality'].

[3] See note on p. 13 below.

by a strong spirit of originality, of pathos, and natural feeling; and recommended to all good minds by the clear impression which they bore of the amiable dispositions and virtuous principles of the author. By the help of these qualities, they were enabled, not only to recommend themselves to the indulgence of many judicious readers, but even to beget among a pretty numerous class of persons, a sort of admiration of the very defects by which they were attended. It was upon this account chiefly, that we thought it necessary to set ourselves against this alarming innovation. Childishness, conceit, and affectation, are not of themselves very popular or attractive; and though mere novelty has sometimes been found sufficient to give them a temporary currency, we should have had no fear of their prevailing to any dangerous extent, if they had been graced with no more seductive accompaniments. It was precisely because the perverseness and bad taste of this new school was combined with a great deal of genius and of laudable feeling, that we were afraid of their spreading and gaining ground among us, and that we entered into the discussion with a degree of zeal and animosity which some might think unreasonable towards authors, to whom so much merit had been conceded. There were times and moods indeed, in which we were led to suspect ourselves of unjustifiable severity, and to doubt, whether a sense of public duty had not carried us rather too far in reprobation of errors, that seemed to be atoned for, by excellences of no vulgar description. At other times, the magnitude of these errors—the disgusting absurdities into which they led their feebler admirers, and the derision and contempt which they drew from the more fastidious, even upon the merits with which they were associated, made us wonder more than ever at the perversity by which they were retained, and regret that we had not declared ourselves against them with still more formidable and decided hostility.

In this temper of mind, we read the *annonce* of Mr Wordsworth's publication with a good deal of interest and expectation, and opened his volumes with greater anxiety, than he or his admirers will probably give us credit for. We have been greatly disappointed certainly as to the quality of the poetry; but we doubt whether the publication has afforded so much satisfaction to any other of his readers:—it has freed us from all doubt or hesitation as to the justice of our former censures, and has brought the matter to a test, which we cannot help hoping may be convincing to the author himself.

Mr Wordsworth, we think, has now brought the question, as to the merit of his new school of poetry, to a very fair and decisive issue. The volumes before us are much more strongly marked by all its peculiarities than any former publication of the fraternity. In our apprehension, they are, on this very account, infinitely less interesting or meritorious; but it belongs to the public, and not to us, to decide upon their merit, and we will confess, that so strong is our conviction of their obvious inferiority, and the grounds of it, that we are willing for once to waive our right of appealing to posterity, and to take the judgment of the present generation of readers, and even of Mr Wordsworth's former admirers, as conclusive on this occasion. If these volumes, which have all the benefit of the author's former popularity, turn out to be nearly as popular as the lyrical ballads—if they sell nearly to the same extent—or are quoted and imitated among half as many individuals, we shall admit that Mr Wordsworth has come much nearer the truth in his judgment of what constitutes the charm of poetry, than we had previously imagined—and shall institute a more serious and respectful inquiry into his principles of composition than we have yet thought necessary. On the other hand,—if this little work, selected from the compositions of five maturer years, and written avowedly for the purpose of exalting a system, which has already excited a good deal of attention, should be generally rejected by those whose prepossessions were in its favour, there is room to hope, not only that the system itself will meet with no more encouragement, but even that the author will be persuaded to abandon a plan of writing, which defrauds his industry and talents of their natural reward.

Putting ourselves thus upon our country, we certainly look for a verdict against this publication; and have little doubt indeed of the result, upon a fair consideration of the evidence contained in these volumes.—To accelerate that result, and to give a general view of the evidence, to those into whose hands the record may not have already fallen, we must now make a few observations and extracts.

We shall not resume any of the particular discussions by which we formerly attempted to ascertain the value of the improvements which this new school has effected in poetry;[1] but shall lay the grounds of our opposition, for this time, a little more broadly. The end of poetry, we take it, is to please—and the name, we think, is strictly applicable to every metrical composition from which we receive pleasure, without any laborious exercise of the understanding. This pleasure, may, in general, be analyzed into three parts—that which we receive from the excitement of Passion or emotion—that which is derived from the play of Imagination, or the easy exercise of Reason—and that which depends on the character and qualities of the Diction. The two first are the vital and primary springs of poetical delight, and can scarcely require explanation to any one. The last has been alternately overrated

[1] [See Vol. I, p. 63, &c.—Vol. VII. p. 1, &c.—Reviewer's note.]

and undervalued by the professors of the poetical art, and is in such low estimation with the author now before us and his associates, that it is necessary to say a few words in explanation of it.

One great beauty of diction exists only for those who have some degree of scholarship or critical skill. This is what depends on the exquisite *propriety* of the words employed, and the delicacy with which they are adapted to the meaning which is to be expressed. Many of the finest passages in Virgil and Pope derive their principal charm from the fine propriety of their diction. Another source of beauty, which extends only to the more instructed class of readers, is that which consists in the judicious or happy application of expressions which have been sanctified by the use of famous writers, or which bear the stamp of a simple or venerable antiquity. There are other beauties of diction, however, which are perceptible by all—the beauties of sweet sound and pleasant associations. The melody of words and verses is indifferent to no reader of poetry; but the chief recommendation of poetical language is certainly derived from those general associations, which give it a character of dignity or elegance, sublimity or tenderness. Every one knows that there are low and mean expressions, as well as lofty and grave ones; and that some words bear the impression of coarseness and vulgarity, as clearly as others do of refinement and affection. We do not mean, of course, to say any thing in defence of the hackneyed common-places of ordinary versemen. Whatever might have been the original character of these unlucky phrases, they are now associated with nothing but ideas of schoolboy imbecility and vulgar affectation. But what we do maintain is, that much of the most popular poetry in the world owes its celebrity chiefly to the beauty of its diction; and that no poetry can be long or generally acceptable, the language of which is coarse, inelegant, or infantine.

From this great source of pleasure, we think the readers of Mr Wordsworth are in a great measure cut off. His diction has no where any pretensions to elegance or dignity; and he has scarcely ever con-descended to give the grace of correctness or melody to his versifica-tion. If it were merely slovenly and neglected, however, all this might be endured. Strong sense and powerful feeling will ennoble any ex-pressions; or, at least, no one who is capable of estimating those higher merits, will be disposed to mark these little defects. But, in good truth, no man, now-a-days, composes verses for publication with a slovenly neglect of their language. It is a fine and laborious manu-facture, which can scarcely ever be made in a hurry; and the faults which it has, may, for the most part, be set down to bad taste or incapacity, rather than to carelessness or oversight. With Mr Wordsworth and his friends, it is plain that their peculiarities of diction are things of choice, and not of accident. They write as they do, upon principle and system; and it evidently costs them much pains to keep *down* to the standard which they have proposed to themselves. They are, to the full, as much mannerists, too, as the poetasters who ring changes on the common-places of magazine versification; and all the difference between them is, that they borrow their phrases from a different and a scantier *gradus ad Parnassum*. If they were, indeed, to discard all imitation and set phraseology, and to bring in no words merely for show or for metre,—as much, perhaps, might be gained in freedom and originality, as would infallibly be lost in allusion and authority; but, in point of fact, the new poets are just as great borrowers as the old; only that, instead of borrowing from the more popular passages of their illustrious predecessors, they have preferred furnishing themselves from vulgar ballads and plebeian nurseries.

Their peculiarities of diction alone, are enough, perhaps, to render them ridiculous; but the author before us really seems anxious to court this literary martyrdom by a device still more infallible,—we mean, that of connecting his most lofty, tender, or impassioned conceptions, with objects and incidents, which the greater part of his readers will probably persist in thinking low, silly, or uninteresting. Whether this is done from affectation and conceit alone, or whether it may not arise, in some measure, from the self-illusion of a mind of extraordinary sensibility, habituated to solitary meditation, we cannot undertake to determine. It is possible enough, we allow, that the sight of a friend's garden-spade, or a sparrow's nest, or a man gathering leeches, might really have suggested to such a mind a train of powerful impressions and interesting reflections; but it is certain, that, to most minds, such associations will always appear forced, strained, and unnatural; and that the composition in which it is attempted to exhibit them, will always have the air of parody, or ludicrous and affected singularity. All the world laughs at Elegiac stanzas to a sucking-pig—a Hymn on Washing-day—Sonnets to one's grandmother—or Pindarics on goose-berry-pye; and yet, we are afraid, it will not be quite easy to convince Mr Wordsworth, that the same ridicule must infallibly attach to most of the pathetic pieces in these volumes. To satisfy our readers, however, as to the justice of this and our other anticipations, we shall proceed, without further preface, to lay before them a short view of their contents.

The first is a kind of ode 'to the Daisy,'—very flat, feeble, and affected; and in a diction as artificial, and as much encumbered with heavy expletives, as the theme of an unpractised schoolboy. The two following stanzas will serve as a specimen.

> 'When soothed a while by milder airs,
> Thee Winter in the garland wears
> That thinly shades his few grey hairs;
> *Spring cannot shun thee;*
> Whole summer fields are thine by right;
> And Autumn, melancholy Wight!
> Doth in thy crimson head delight
> When rains are on thee.
> In shoals and bands, a morrice train,
> Thou greet'st the Traveller in the lane;
> If welcome once thou count'st it gain;
> *Thou art not daunted,*
> Nor car'st if thou be set at naught;
> And oft alone in nooks remote
> We meet thee, like a pleasant thought,
> *When such are wanted.'* I. p. 2.

The scope of the piece is to say, that the flower is found every where; and that it has suggested many pleasant thoughts to the author —some chime of fancy *'wrong or right'*—some feeling of devotion *'more or less'*—and other elegancies of the same stamp. It ends with this unmeaning prophecy.

> 'Thou long the poet's praise shalt gain;
> Thou wilt be more beloved by men
> In times to come; thou not in vain
> Art Nature's favourite.' I. 6.

The next is called 'Louisa,' and begins in this dashing and affected manner.

> 'I met Louisa in the shade;
> And, having seen that lovely maid,
> *Why should I fear to say*
> That she is ruddy, fleet, and *strong*;
> *And down the rocks can leap* along,
> Like rivulets in May?' I. 7.

Does Mr Wordsworth really imagine that this is at all more natural or engaging than the ditties of our common song writers?

A little farther on we have another original piece, entitled, 'The Redbreast and the Butterfly,' of which our readers will probably be contented with the first stanza.

'Art thou the bird whom man loves best,
The pious bird with the scarlet breast,
        Our little English Robin;
The bird that comes about our doors
When autumn winds are sobbing?
Art thou the Peter of Norway Boors?
        Their Thomas in Finland,
        And Russia far inland?
The bird, whom *by some name or other*
All men who know thee call their brother,
The darling of children and men?
Could Father Adam open his eyes,
And see this sight, beneath the skies,
He'd wish to close them again.' I. 16.

This, it must be confessed, is 'Silly Sooth' in good earnest. The three last lines seem to be downright raving.

By and by, we have a piece of namby-pamby 'to the Small Celandine,' which we should almost have taken for a professed imitation of one of Mr Philips's prettyisms. Here is a page of it.

'Comfort have thou of thy merit,
Kindly, unassuming spirit!
Careless of thy neighbourhood,
Thou dost show thy pleasant face
On the moor, and in the wood,
In the lane;—there's not a place,
Howsoever mean it be,
But 'tis good enough for thee.
Ill befal the yellow flowers,
Children of the flaring hours!
Buttercups, that will be seen,
Whether we will see or no;
Others, too, of lofty mien;
They have done as wordlings do,
Taken praise that should be thine,
Little, humble Celandine!' I. 25.

After talking of its 'bright coronet,'

'And its arch and wily ways,
And its store of other praise,'

the ditty is wound up with this piece of babyish absurdity.

'Thou art not beyond the moon,
But a thing "beneath our shoon;"
Let, as old Magellan did,
Others roam about the sea;
Build who will a pyramid;
Praise it is enough for me,
If there be but three or four
Who will love my little flower.' I. 30.

After this come some more manly lines on 'The Character of the Happy Warrior,' and a chivalrous legend on 'The Horn of Egremont Castle,' which, without being very good, is very tolerable, and free from most of the author's habitual defects. Then follow some pretty, but professedly childish verses, on a kitten playing with the falling leaves. There is rather too much of Mr Ambrose Philips here and there in this piece also; but it is amiable and lively.

Further on, we find an 'Ode to Duty,' in which the lofty vein is very unsuccessfully attempted. This is the concluding stanza.

'Stern lawgiver! yet thou dost wear
The Godhead's most benignant grace;
Nor know we any thing so fair
As is the smile upon thy face;
Flowers laugh before thee on their beds;
And fragrance in thy footing treads;
Thou dost preserve the stars from wrong;
And the most ancient heavens through thee are fresh and strong.' I. 73.

The two last lines seem to be utterly without meaning; at least we have no sort of conception in what sense *Duty* can be said to keep the old skies *fresh*, and the stars from wrong.

The next piece, entitled 'The Beggars,' may be taken, we fancy, as a touchstone of Mr Wordsworth's merit. There is something about it that convinces us it is a favourite of the author's; though to us, we will confess, it appears to be a very paragon of silliness and affectation. Our readers shall have the greater part of it. It begins thus.

[The first, third, and two final stanzas (later much revised) are quoted with some interlocking (and mildly sarcastic) comments.]

'Alice Fell' is a performance of the same order. The poet, driving into Durham in a postchaise, hears a sort of scream; and, calling to the post-boy to stop, finds a little girl crying on the back of the vehicle.

[Lines 21–28 and 41–60 are quoted with interlocking comment.]

If the printing of such trash as this be not felt as an insult on the public taste, we are afraid it cannot be insulted.

After this follows the longest and most elaborate poem in the volume, under the title of 'Resolution and Independence.' The poet, roving about on a common one fine morning, falls into pensive musings on the fate of the sons of song, which he sums up in this fine distich.

> 'We poets in our youth begin in gladness;
> But thereof comes in the end despondency and madness.' I. p. 92.

[A summary of the story with some sarcastic comments is given. The following lines are quoted: 55–56, 75–84, 88–91, 99–105, 116–26, and 139–40. (Some of these lines were later revised.) Many phrases are italicized by the reviewer.]

We defy the bitterest enemy of Mr Wordsworth to produce any thing at all parallel to this from any collection of English poetry, or even from the specimens of his friend Mr Southey. The volume ends with some sonnets, in a very different measure, of which we shall say something by and by.

The first poems in the second volume were written during a tour in Scotland. The first is a very dull one about Rob Roy; but the title that attracted us most was 'an Address to the Sons of *Burns*, after visiting their Father's Grave.' Never was any thing, however, more miserable. This is one of the four stanzas.

> 'Strong bodied if ye be to bear
> Intemperance with less harm, beware!
> But if your father's wit ye share,
>   Then, then indeed,
> Ye sons of Burns! for watchful care
>   There will be need.' II. p. 29.

The next is a very tedious, affected performance, called 'the Yarrow Unvisited.' The drift of it is, that the poet refused to visit this cele-brated stream, because he had a 'vision of his own' about it, which the reality might perhaps undo; and, for this no less fantastical reason—

> 'Should life be dull, and spirits low,
> "Twill soothe us in our sorrow,
> 'That earth has something yet to show,
> 'The bonny holms of Yarrow!' II. p. 35.

19

After this we come to some ineffable compositions, which the poet has simply entitled, 'Moods of my own Mind.' One begins—

> 'O Nightingale! thou surely art
> A creature of a fiery heart—
> Thou sing'st as if the god of wine
> Had help'd thee to a valentine.' II. p. 42.

This is the whole of another—

['My heart leaps up' is printed in full.]

A third, 'on a Sparrow's Nest,' runs thus—

> 'Look, five blue eggs are gleaming there!
> *Few visions have I seen more fair,*
> *Nor many prospects of delight*
> More pleasing than that simple sight.' II. p. 53.

The charm of this fine prospect, however, was, that it reminded him of another nest which his sister Emmeline and he had visited in their childhood.

> 'She look'd at it as if she fear'd it;
> Still wishing, dreading to be near it:
> Such heart was in her, being then
> A little prattler among men.' &c. &c. II. p. 54.

We have then a rapturous mystical ode to the Cuckoo; in which the author, striving after force and originality, produces nothing but absurdity.

> 'O Cuckoo! Shall I call thee bird,
> Or but a wandering voice?' II. p. 57.

And then he says, that the said voice seemed to pass from hill to hill, 'about, and all about!'—Afterwards he assures us, it tells him 'in the vale of visionary hours,' and calls it a darling; but still insists, that it is

> 'No bird; but an invisible thing,
> A voice,—a mystery.' II. p. 58.

It is afterwards 'a hope;' and 'a love;' and, finally,

20

'O blessed *bird*! the earth we pace
Again appears to be
An unsubstantial, faery place,
That is fit home for thee!' II. p. 59.

After this there is an address to a butterfly, whom he invites to visit him, in these simple strains—

'This plot of orchard-ground is ours;
My trees they are, my sister's flowers;
Stop here whenever you are weary.' II. p. 61.

We come next to a long story of a 'Blind Highland Boy,' who lived near an arm of the sea, and had taken a most unnatural desire to venture on that perilous element. His mother did all she could to prevent him; but one morning, when the good woman was out of the way, he got into a vessel of his own, and pushed out from the shore:

'In such a vessel ne'er before
Did human creature leave the shore.' II. p. 72.

And then we are told, that if the sea should get rough, 'a beehive would be ship as safe.' 'But say, what was it?' a poetical interlocutor is made to exclaim most naturally; and here followeth the answer, upon which all the pathos and interest of the story depend.

'A HOUSEHOLD TUB, like one of those
Which women use to wash their clothes!!' II. p. 72.

This, it will be admitted, is carrying the matter as far as it will well go; nor is there any thing,—down to the wiping of shoes, or the evisceration of chickens,—which may not be introduced in poetry, if this is tolerated. A boat is sent out and brings the boy ashore, who being tolerably frightened we suppose, promises to go to sea no more; and so the story ends.

Then we have a poem, called 'the Green Linnet,' which opens with the poet's telling us,

'A whispering leaf is now my joy,
And then a bird will be the *toy*
    That doth my fancy *tether*.' II. p. 79.

21

and closes thus—

> 'While thus before my eyes he gleams,
> A brother of the leaves he seems;
> When in a moment forth *he teems*
>   His little song in gushes:
> As if it pleas'd him to disdain
> And mock the form which he did feign,
> While he was dancing with the train
>   Of leaves among the bushes.' II. p. 81.

The next is called 'Star Gazers.' A set of people peeping through a telescope, all seem to come away disappointed with the sight; whereupon Thus sweetly moraliseth our poet.

[Lines 8–12 and 17–20 are quoted.]

There are then some really sweet and amiable verses on a French lady, separated from her own children, fondling the baby of a neighbouring cottager;—after which we have this quintessence of unmeaningness, entitled, 'Foresight.'

> 'That is work which I am rueing—
> Do as Charles and I are doing!
> Strawberry-blossoms, one and all,
> We must spare them—here are many:
> Look at it—the flower is small,
> Small and low, though fair as any:
> Do not touch it! summers two
> I am older, Anne, than you.
> Pull the primrose, sister Anne!
> Pull as many as you can.
>
> Primroses, the spring may love them—
> Summer knows but little of them:
> Violets, do what they will,
> Wither'd on the ground must lie;
> Daisies will be daisies still;
> Daisies they must live and die:
> Fill your lap, and fill your bosom,
> Only spare the strawberry-blossom!' II. p. 115, 116.

Afterwards come some stanzas about an echo repeating a cuckoo's voice; here is one for a sample—

'Whence the voice? from air or earth?
This the cuckoo cannot tell;
But a startling sound had birth,
As the bird must know full well.' II. p. 123.

Then we have Elegiac stanzas 'to the Spade of a friend,' beginning—

'Spade! with which Wilkinson hath till'd his lands,'

—but too dull to be quoted any further.

After this there is a Minstrel's Song, on the Restoration of Lord Clifford the Shepherd, which is in a very different strain of poetry; and then the volume is wound up with an 'Ode,' with no other title but the motto, *Paulo majora canamus*.[1] This is, beyond all doubt, the most illegible and unintelligible part of the publication. We can pretend to give no analysis or explanation of it;—our readers must make what they can of the following extracts.

[Lines 51–57 and 133–71 of 'Ode: Intimations of Immortality' are quoted.]

We have thus gone through this publication, with a view to enable our readers to determine, whether the author of the verses which have now been exhibited, is entitled to claim the honours of an improver or restorer of our poetry, and to found a new school to supersede or new-model all our maxims on the subject. If we were to stop here, we do not think that Mr Wordsworth, or his admirers, would have any reason to complain; for what we have now quoted is undeniably the most peculiar and characteristic part of his publication, and must be defended and applauded if the merit or originality of his system is to be seriously maintained. In our own opinion, however, the demerit of that system cannot be fairly appreciated, until it be shown, that the author of the bad verses which we have already extracted, can write good verses when he pleases; and that, in point of fact, he does always write good verses, when, by any accident, he is led to abandon his system, and to transgress the laws of that school which he would fain establish on the ruin of all existing authority.

The length to which our extracts and observations have already extended, necessarily restrains us within more narrow limits in this part

[1] The 'Ode: Intimations of Immortality' was entitled merely 'Ode' in the *Poems in Two Volumes* and carried no motto poem. The lack of these aids to understanding may partly explain the difficulties which Jeffrey, as well as other reviewers, found in the poem.

of our citations; but it will not require much labour to find a pretty decided contrast to some of the passages we have already detailed. The song on the restoration of Lord Clifford[1] is put into the mouth of an ancient minstrel of the family; and in composing it, the author was led, therefore, almost irresistibly to adopt the manner and phraseology that is understood to be connected with that sort of composition, and to throw aside his own babyish incidents and fantastical sensibilities. How he has succeeded, the reader will be able to judge from the few following extracts. The poem opens in this spirited manner—

> 'High in the breathless hall the Minstrel sate,
> And Emont's murmur mingled with the song.—
> The words of ancient time I thus translate,
> A festal strain that hath been silent long.
> "From town to town, from tower to tower,
> The red rose is a gladsome flower.
> Her thirty years of winter past,
> The red rose is revived at last;
> She lifts her head for endless Spring,
> For everlasting blossoming!" ' II. pp. 128–29.

After alluding, in a very animated manner, to the troubles and perils which drove the youth of the hero into concealment, the minstrel proceeds—

[Lines 87–101 and 138–72 are quoted.]

All English writers of sonnets have imitated Milton; and, in this way, Mr Wordsworth, when he writes sonnets, escapes again from the trammels of his own unfortunate system; and the consequence is, that his sonnets are as much superior to the greater part of his other poems, as Milton's sonnets are superior to his. We give the following 'On the Extinction of the Venetian Republic.'

[The entire sonnet is quoted.]

The following is entitled 'London.'

[The entire sonnet is quoted.]

We make room for this other; though the four first lines are bad, and 'week-day man' is by no means a Miltonic epithet.

['I grieved for Bounaparte' is quoted in full.]

---

[1] 'Song at the Feast of Brougham Castle.'

24

When we look at these, and many still finer passages, in the writings of this author, it is impossible not to feel a mixture of indignation and compassion, at that strange infatuation which has bound him up from the fair exercise of his talents, and withheld from the public the many excellent productions that would otherwise have taken the place of the trash now before us. Even in the worst of these productions: there are, no doubt, occasional little traits of delicate feeling and original fancy; but these are quite lost and obscured in the mass of childishness and insipidity with which they are incorporated; nor can any thing give us a more melancholy view of the debasing effects of this miserable theory, than that it has given ordinary men a right to wonder at the folly and presumption of a man gifted like Mr Wordsworth, and made him appear, in his second avowed publication, like a bad imitator of the worst of his former productions.

We venture to hope, that there is now an end of this folly; and that, like other follies, it will be found to have cured itself by the extravagances resulting from its unbridled indulgence. In this point of view, the publication of the volumes before us may ultimately be of service to the good cause of literature. Many a generous rebel, it is said, has been reclaimed to his allegiance by the spectacle of lawless outrage and excess presented in the conduct of the insurgents; and we think there is every reason to hope, that the lamentable consequences which have resulted from Mr Wordsworth's open violation of the established laws of poetry,[1] will operate as a wholesome warning to those who might otherwise have been seduced by his example, and be the means of restoring to that antient and venerable code its due honour and authority.

Eclectic Review

IV (Jan. 1808), 35–43. The author was James Montgomery, a minor poet, see John Holland and James Everett, Life of James Montgomery (London 1854–56), II, 183.

In this age of poetical experiment, Mr. Wordsworth has distinguished himself, by his 'Lyrical Ballads,' as one of the boldest and most fortunate adventurers in the field of innovation. Casting away, at once and entirely, all the splendid artifices of style, invented in the earliest ages

---

[1] Note that the mention of 'the established laws of poetry' occurs in an extended metaphor of law and disorder.

by the fathers of poetry, and perpetuated among all classes and generations of their successors, he avowed, in his Preface to that work, that
'his principal object was to chuse incidents and situations from common
life, and to relate and describe them throughout, as far as was possible,
in a selection of language really used by men; and at the same time
to throw upon them a certain colouring of imagination, whereby
ordinary things should be presented to the mind in an unusual way;
and further, and above all, to make these incidents and situations interesting by tracing in them, truly, though not ostentatiously, the
primary laws of our nature; chiefly as far as regards the manner in
which we associate ideas in a state of excitement.' Pref. p. vii. Were
these volumes (the *Lyrical Ballads*, &c.) now before us for criticism,
however we might admire and commend Mr. Wordsworth's ingenuity
in the advancement and vindication of his theory of poetical phraseology; and however we might agree with him, so far as his system
would restrict the multitude of epithets that frequently render verse
too heavy for endurance,—we would certainly protest against the unqualified rejection of those embellishments of diction, suited to the
elevation of enthusiastic thoughts equally above ordinary discourse
and ordinary capacities, which essentially distinguish Poetry from
Prose, and have been sanctioned by the successful usage of Bards in
every age and nation, civilized or barbarous, on which the light of
Song has shed its quickening, ennobling, and ameliorating beams.
In dramatic verse, assuredly, the writer, through all his characters,
should speak the truth of living nature: the language of violent passions
should be simple, abrupt, impetuous, and sublime; that of the gentler
affections, ardent, flowing, figurative, and beautifully redundant; while,
in both instances, every colour of expression, every form of thought,
which appeals only to the imagination, and touches not the heart,
should be rigorously proscribed. But in narrative, descriptive, and
ethic poetry, we know no law of nature, and we will acknowledge
none of art, that forbids Genius to speak his mother-tongue,—a
language which, in sound and structure, as well as in character
and sentiment, exalts itself far above the models of common
speech.

A Poet—we speak of him who is really such—is no ordinary man;
(Mr. Wordsworth allows him *'more than usual organic sensibility'*;)—nor
are his compositions the prompt and spontaneous expressions of his
own every-day feelings; (Mr. W. declares, that 'he must have thought
long and deeply, to produce poems to which any value can be attached':)
—No! they are the most hidden ideas of his soul, discovered in his
happiest moments, and appareled in his selectest language. Will such a

man array the most pure, sublime, and perfect conceptions of his superior mind in its highest fervour, only with 'the real language of men in a
state of vivid excitement'? Compare the heroic narratives of Milton,
the magnificent descriptions of Thomson, the solemn musings of
Young, nay even the soliloquies, and frequently the speeches of
Shakspeare, in which characters and passions are pourtrayed with un-
paralleled force and feeling; compare these with 'the real language of
men' on the very same subjects, or in the same situations, however
animated, interested, or excited they may be. The fact is, that poetical
sensibility will, on all occasions, except perhaps in the simple expression
of the highest degree of agony or rapture, suggest language more lively,
affecting, and fervent, than passion itself can inspire in minds less
tremblingly alive to every touch of pain or pleasure. Hence the delight
communicated by true poetry is generally more deeply transporting,
than any that could be derived from the unassisted contemplation of
the objects themselves, which are presented to us by the magic of the
author's art: of this art his *language* is the master-secret; for by that charm
he transfuses into frigid imaginations his warmer feelings, and his
brighter views, on subjects and of things that would only indifferently
affect them in nature and reality.

Mr. Wordsworth is himself a living example of the power which a
man of genius possesses, of awakening unknown and ineffable sensations in the hearts of his fellow-creatures. His *Cumberland Beggar*,
Tintern Abbey, his *Verses on the naming of Places*, and some other pieces
in his former volumes, have taught us new sympathies, the existence
of which in our nature had scarcely been intimated to us by any preceding poet. But Mr. Wordsworth must be reminded, that in these, his
most successful pieces, he has attired his thoughts in diction of trans-
cendent beauty. We will quote two brief passages from *Tintern Abbey*.

[Lines 88–102 and 134–45 are quoted.]

This is no more the language, than these are the thoughts, of men in
general in a state of excitement: language more exquisitely elaborate,
and thoughts more patiently worked out of the very marble of the
mind, we rarely meet with in any writer either of verse or prose. For
such tales as *Andrew Jones, The last of the Flock, Goody Blake and Harry
Gill*, &c. 'the real language of men' may be employed with pleasing
effect; but when Mr. Wordsworth would 'present *ordinary* things in an
unusual way, by casting over them a certain colouring of imagination,'
he is compelled very frequently to resort to splendid, figurative, and
amplifying language. The following, among innumerable examples
from the volumes before us, to which we are compelled reluctantly

to turn, will prove that he sometimes succeeds admirably, and sometimes indifferently, in using this poetical language.

'This tiresome night, O Sleep! thou art to me
A fly, that up and down himself doth shove
Upon a fretful rivulet, now *above*,
Now *on the water* vex'd with mockery.' Vol. I. p. 109.

'The winds that will be howling at all hours,
And are *up gather'd* now, *like sleeping flowers*.' Vol. I. p. 122.

'It is a beauteous evening, calm and free;
The holy time is *quiet as a nun*
Breathless with adoration.' Vol. I. p. 123.

'Dear Child! dear Girl! that walkest with me here,
If thou appear'st untouch'd by solemn thought,
Thy nature is not therefore less divine:
Thou liest in Abraham's bosom all the year,
And worshipp'st at the Temple's inner shrine,
God being with thee when we know it not.' Vol. I. p. 123.

'*Flowers laugh before thee in their beds,*
And Fragrance in thy footing treads.' Vol. I. p. 73.

'The *cataracts blow their trumpets* from the steep;
The *winds* come to me *from the fields of sleep*.' Vol. II. p. 148.

We need insist no more on the necessity of using, in poetry, a
language different from and superior to 'the real language of men,'
since Mr. Wordsworth himself is so frequently compelled to employ it,
for the expression of thoughts which without it would be incom-
municable.

These volumes are distinguished by the same blemishes and beauties
as were found in their predecessors, but in an inverse proportion: the
defects of the poet, in this performance, being as much greater than his
merits, as they were less in his former publication. It is remarkable
that we have not, among all the piebald miscellanies before us, a single
example of that species of poetry, for which the author's theory of
diction and his habits of thinking peculiarly qualify him. The *blank
verse* was the glory of his former volumes; in these there is not a trace
of it. But songs instead we have, and sonnets, and stories, of every
length and form of versification, and of every style and character from
sublimity to silliness. Most of these are mere reveries in rhyme, in
which the Poet's mind seems to be delightfully dreaming, while his

thoughts are romping at random, and playing all manner of mischievous pranks about him; assuming at pleasure the most antic shapes, tricking themselves with the gaudiest colours, sporting at large in every field of fancy, and spurning with gallant independence every rule of art and every sanction of precedent for the government of licentious genius. It would be in vain to attempt to characterize all the contents of these incomparable, and almost incomprehensible volumes. A more rash and injudicious speculation on the weakness or the depravity of the public taste has seldom been made; and we trust that its inevitable failure will bring back Mr. Wordsworth himself to a sense of his own dignity, as well as of the respect due to his readers. The public may often be wrong in its first judgements, but it is always right at last; and Mr. W. can have no hope in its final decision concerning the greater part of the pieces before us.

To do little things gracefully, is sometimes more difficult than to do great things well; but when done, what *are* they? Trifles, that only please by surprize, and only surprize for a moment. Mr. Wordsworth has attempted many things in these volumes, and few indeed have rewarded him for his trouble. The following is perhaps the best of these.

['A Complaint' is quoted in full.]

It would not be easy to quote the *worst*, as a contrast to the *best* of these trifles; the following is probably as bad as any, and almost as bad as can be written by a man of superior talents.

From '*Moods of my own Mind.*'
'The sun has long been set:
The stars are out by twos and threes;
The little birds are piping yet
Among the bushes and the trees;
There's a cuckoo, and one or two thrushes;
And a noise of wind that rushes,
With a noise of water that gushes;
And the cuckoo's sovereign cry
Fills all the hollow of the sky.

'Who would go "parading"
In London and "masquerading,"
On such a night of June,
With that beautiful soft half-moon,
And all these innocent blisses,
On such a night as this is.'

The stories in these volumes are generally inferior, both in subject and in handling, to those which Mr. Wordsworth formerly gave the public. *Alice Fell* only shews that it is possible to tell in verse what is scarcely worth relating in prose. *The Blind Boy* is younger brother to Mr. W.'s own inimitable *Ideot Boy*, but very far behind him in merits and accomplishments. The tale, entitled *Fidelity*, is on the same subject as Walter Scott's *Helvellyn*, (on the fate of a traveller who perished on that wild mountain, and whose body was found three months afterwards, with his Dog alive and watching beside his dead master;) and it proves that Mr. Wordsworth, when he pleases, can be as much inferior to another as to himself.

The Sonnets, in point of imagery and sentiment, are perhaps the most poetical of all these motley productions; but they are exceedingly unequal, often obscure, and generally heavy in the motion of the verse: the lines too are frequently so intertwisted, that if they were not printed in lengths of ten syllables, it would be difficult to break them into metre at all. The following contains a noble thought, which is carried through to the last word, and is a rare example of excellence either in Mr. Wordsworth or any other English Sonnetteer.

['On the Extinction of the Venetian Republic' is quoted in full.]

In Mr. Wordsworth's poetry, more perhaps than in that of any other man, we frequently find images and sentiments, which we have seen and felt a thousand times, without particularly *reflecting* on them, and which, when presented by him, flash upon us with all the delight and surprize of novelty.

'The Cattle are grazing,
Their heads never raising,
There are *forty feeding like one.*' Vol. II. p. 45.

'The Swan on still St. Mary's lake
Floats double, Swan and Shadow!' Vol. II. p. 34.

'O Cuckoo! shall I call thee bird,
Or but a *wandering voice!*
'Thrice welcome, darling of the Spring!
Even yet thou art to me
No Bird; but *an invisible thing,*
A voice, a mystery.
'The same whom in my school-boy days
I listen'd to; *that Cry*
Which made me look a thousand ways;
In bush and tree and sky.' Vol. II. pp. 57-8.

'The grass is bright with rain-drops; on the moors
The Hare is running races in her mirth;
And *with her feet* she from the plashy earth
Raises a mist; which, glittering in the sun,
Runs with her all the way, wherever she doth run.' [Vol. I. p. 90.]

Who, that after long absence has visited the scenes where he spent the days of childhood, and from which he was separated in youth, has not experienced both the expectation and the disappointment described in the following slovenly lines?

' "Beloved Vale!" I said, "when I shall con
Those many records of my childish years,
Remembrance of myself and of my peers
Will press me down: to think of what is gone
Will be an awful thought, if life have one."
But when into the vale I came, no fears
Distress'd me; I look'd round, I shed no tears;
Deep thought, or awful vision, had I none.
By thousand petty fancies I was cross'd,
To see the trees, which I had thought so tall,
Mere dwarfs; the brooks so narrow, fields so small.' Vol. I. p. 119.

A specimen of Mr. Wordsworth's finest talent—that of *personal description*—may be found in a Poem, which we have not room to quote, though we consider it the best in the volume, entitled '*Resolution and Independence.*'

The last piece in this Collection is simply styled '*An Ode,*'[1] and the reader is turned loose into a wilderness of sublimity, tenderness, bombast, and absurdity, to find out the subject as well as he can. The Poet assumes the doctrine of pre-existence, (*a doctrine which religion knows not, and the philosophy of the mind abjures*) and intimates that the happiness of childhood is the reminiscence of blessedness in a former state.[2]

'Our birth is but a sleep and a forgetting.
The Soul that rises with us, our life's star,
Hath had elsewhere its setting,
And cometh from afar;
Not in entire forgetfulness,
And not in utter nakedness,

[1] See note 1 on p. 23 above.⌐

[2] Wordsworth, in his notes dictated to Miss Fenwick, later denied that he was asserting the doctrine of pre-existence.

But trailing clouds of glory do we come
From God, who is our home.' Vol. II. p. 150.

In allusion to these romantic and unwarranted speculations, he says,
in the same Ode, that there are

————'Truths that wake
To perish never;
Which neither listlessness, nor mad endeavour,
Nor man nor boy,
Nor all that is at enmity with joy,
Can utterly abolish or destroy!
Hence, in a season of calm weather,
Though inland far we be,
Our souls have sight of that immortal sea
Which brought us hither,
Can in a moment travel thither,
And see the children sport upon the shore,
And hear the mighty waters rolling evermore.' Vol. II. p. 156.

After our preliminary remarks on Mr. Wordsworth's theory of
poetical language, and the quotations which we have given from these
and his earlier compositions, it will be unnecessary to offer any further
estimate or character of his genius. We shall only add one remark,
which truth compels us to make, in spite of a partiality which we feel
almost for the faults of such a writer as Mr. W. He says, in the preface
to his former volumes, that 'each of the poems' contained therein 'has
a worthy purpose.' Of the pieces now published he has said nothing:
most of them seem to have been written *for* no purpose at all, and
certainly *to* no good one.

Annual Review

*VI (1808), 521–29. The author was Lucy Aikin, a bluestocking and the
sister of the editor: see Edith Morley*, Henry Crabb Robinson on Books
and Their Writers (*London, 1938*), I, 143.

Mr. Wordsworth is a writer whose system and practice of poetry are
both so entirely his own, that in order to appreciate as fairly as we wish
to do, the value of these volumes, it will be necessary for us to enter
somewhat at length into a discussion of the theory of the art. His own
theory of it the author has given in the preface to a former work,

published before this review existed; and as we do not perceive that his style of writing has since undergone any material alteration, we shall refer to it without scruple, as containing the principles upon which the poems immediately before us have been composed.

On glancing the eye over Mr. Wordsworth's poems, the first thing that strikes the reader is, the extreme simplicity of their language: he may peruse page after page without meeting with any of those figures of speech which distinguish we do not say verse from prose, but a plain style from one that may be called cultured, or ornate. Should he however attribute this peculiarity to indolence or deficiency of skill, Mr. W. would complain of injustice, for he has anticipated the charge, and in the preface to 'Lyrical Ballads' has endeavoured to repel it. The highly metaphysical language employed in this preface, and the spirit of mysticism by which it is pervaded, render it somewhat difficult of comprehension, but this, as well as we can collect, is the substance of that portion of it which is to our present purpose.

It was his intention, he says, in his poems to take incidents and situations from humble life, and describe them in the real language of men in that class, only freed from its grosser vulgarisms. He has preferred such incidents and situations, because the feelings of persons in low life are stronger, less complex, and therefore more easy to be developed, than those of persons who move in a wider circle—their language he has preferred for similar reasons, and also because he thought that any departure from nature in this respect must weaken the interest of his poems, both as being a departure from nature, and because the language which the imagination of even the greatest poet suggests to him, must, in liveliness and truth, fall far short of that which is uttered by men in real life, and under the pressure of actual passions. All that is called poetic diction, he therefore despises, and has shunned with the same care that others seek it, convinced that a poet may give all the pleasure he wishes to do without its assistance. At the same time he has 'endeavoured to throw over his draughts a certain colouring of the imagination, whereby ordinary things should be presented to the mind in an unusual way, and further, and above all, to make these incidents and situations interesting by tracing in them, truly though not ostentatiously, the primary laws of our nature chiefly as far as regards the manner in which we associate ideas in a state of excitement.' This last expression savours to us of a jargon with which the public has long been surfeited, and it is evident that not a position is here advanced which might not easily be combated; but as the practical success of a poet is the true test of the justness of his principles, we shall reserve our remarks on this head till we come to extracts. Anticipating an obvious question, why with his sentiments did he write in rhyme and measure? Mr. W. now proceeds sensibly enough to defend his practice in this respect on the ground of the pleasure which the experience of ages has proved these devices to be capable of affording—he adds, that 'from the tendency of metre to divest language in a certain degree of its reality, and throw a kind of half consciousness of unsubstantial existence over the whole composition, there is little doubt that more painfully pathetic incidents and situations may be endured in verse, especially in rhymed verse, than in prose'—He brings in proof, 'the reluctance with which we recur to the more distressing parts of the Gamester and Clarissa Harlow, while Shakespeare's writings in the most pathetic scenes never act upon us as pathetic beyond the bounds of pleasure.' Is not Mr. W. aware that these very arguments might equally be urged in favour of that poetic diction which he is so anxious to banish from his pages, and that the same instances might be adduced in its support that he here brings in favour of metre? [Is it] not poetical diction, much more than mere verse, which produces the difference here pointed out between the writings of Shakespeare, and those of More and Richardson? But Mr. W. is persuaded that he has absolutely established it as a principle that in the dramatic parts of his compositions a poet should employ no other language than such as nature would suggest to his characters, (which after all is a very vague direction, since nature is by no means uniform in her promptings of this kind, and education and local circumstances produce endless diversities of style and expression,) and he endeavours to show that even where the poet speaks in his own character, he should employ no other diction than that of good and select prose. He begins by defining a poet as a man 'endued with more lively sensibilities, more enthusiasm and tenderness, who has a greater knowledge of human nature, and a more comprehensive soul, than are supposed to be common among mankind,' and in fine, as one chiefly distinguished from others, 'by a greater promptness to think and feel without immediate external excitement, and a greater power in expressing such thoughts and feelings as are thus excited in him.' These 'passions and thoughts, and feelings,' he affirms to be the same as those of other men; but even if they were not he proceeds to insist, that as a poet does not write for poets, but for men in general, in order to excite rational sympathy, he must still express himself as other men do. Now it appears to us in the first place, that this definition of a poet is both imperfect and incorrect. It is only that of a person of strong sympathies, who possesses in an unusual degree the power of imagining and describing the feelings of other human beings. A good novel writer must be all this—a descriptive or lyric poet, though perfect in his kind, need not. But one who really deserves the name of a poet, must certainly add another faculty which is not even hinted at in this definition—we scarcely know how to name it, but it is that kind of fancy, akin to wit, which 'glancing from heaven to earth, from earth to heaven,' pervading, as it were, the whole world of nature and of art, snatches from each its beauteous images, combines, adapts, arranges them by a magic of its own, peoples with them its new creations, and at length pours forth in one striking, brilliant, yet harmonious whole.

This faculty, which Mr. W. overlooks, is doubtless the true parent of that diction which he despises; nor will either the frigid reasonings of metaphysicians, or the still more frigid caricaturas and miserable apings of mere versifiers, ever deter the genuine poet from employing it; it is his native tongue, and he must speak it, or be dumb. It is idle and sophistical to contend that because he does not write to poets he must not write like a poet. Many there are who are capable of being moved to rapture by a picture of Raphael or Titian, though they themselves could never guide a pencil—many there are who can follow with their eye the boldest soarings of the Theban eagle, though nature has not lent to them even the rudiments of a wing. If men in general are to be supposed incapable of understanding any expressions but what they would themselves have used in similar circumstances, rich and figurative diction must indeed, on most occasions be proscribed, but let it be remembered that such an interdiction would curtail the eloquence of Burke no less than the poetry of Shakespeare; so sweeping a clause is this, so fatal to the scintillations of wit, and the sports of fancy. Our author afterwards speaks of poetry as a thing too high and sacred to be profaned by the addition of trifling ornaments of style: we cannot well understand what his notion of poetry is, after all, for he here plunges into the very depths of mysticism, but we suppose Virgil and Milton must have had some idea of its power and dignity, and it does appear to us somewhat ridiculous, not to say arrogant, in Mr. Words-worth, to imagine that he has discovered any thing, either in the trivial incidents which he usually makes the subjects of his narrations, or in the moral feelings and deductions which he endeavours to associate with them, too sublime for the admission of such decorations as these masters have not deemed derogatory from the highest themes they ever touched. But we believe one great source of what we consider as the errors of this writer to be his failing to observe the distinction between rhetorical and poetical diction; the former it is that offends; but in his blind zeal he confounds both under the same note of reprobation. He quotes Dr. Johnson's paraphrase of, 'Go to the ant thou sluggard,' and justly stigmatizes it as 'a hubbub of words;' but is this a specimen of poetical diction? Surely not. It contains not one of those figures of speech,—similes, metaphors, allusions, and the like—which take their birth from that inventive, or combining, faculty which we mentioned above, but is tediously lengthened out by that accumulation of idle epithets, frivolous circumstances, and pompous and abstract terms, with which the rhetorician never fails, in prose or verse, to load his feeble and high sounding pages. It is this, this spirit of paraphrase and periphrasis, this idle parade of fine words, that is the bane of modern verse writing; let it be once thoroughly weeded of this, and it will be easy for the pruning hand of taste to lop away any redundancy of metaphor, personification, &c. which may still remain. Thus much for the system of Mr. Wordsworth, which appears to us a frigid and at the same time an extravagant one; we now proceed to examine what its practical application has produced; and whether our author has succeeded according to his intention, by giving us in plain rhymed and measured prose, matter so valuable and interesting as to be capable of affording pleasure equal, or superior, to that usually produced by poems of a similar class composed in a more ornate and polished style. We shall also examine how far the principle of association, on which many of the pieces are composed, appears to have been productive of beauties or defects.

The contents of these volumes may mostly be reduced under the following heads. Ballads, and narratives of incidents apparently from real life. Addresses to various natural objects—the sky-lark, daisy, &c. Sonnets. An ode or two. Certain little pieces entitled, 'Moods of my own mind,' and a few others of the sentimental and descriptive kind. From the narrative pieces we may select the following.

['Fidelity' is quoted in full.]

Here Mr. W. has certainly been fortunate in his subject; the incident is affecting, the scenery picturesque, but has he made a good poem of it, even on his own principles? Surely not. The language is not only prosaic, but generally flat, and in some parts absolutely mean; as in the two last lines of the first verse. The ellipsis, 'For sake of which'[1] is a vulgarism which cannot but offend the cultivated reader; and to call the noise of a fish leaping 'a lonely chear,' is certainly an absurdity which could never pass in prose—but, what is worse still, is the coldness and tameness of the sentiments; on the unfortunate man, scarcely one expression of commiseration is bestowed; and even the dog, the hero of the tale, is presented to the mind in so unimpassioned a manner that

[1] 'For sake of which' in lines 50–51 was changed to read 'for whose sake' in the *Poems* of 1815.

he excites little or no interest. On the whole, in verse or prose, we know not how the tale could have been more flatly related. But let us take another.

['Alice Fell' is quoted in full.]

Mr. W. piques himself upon having had in view an end, a purpose, in all his narratives; but we confess if he has had one here, it is more than we can discover. The same remark applies to the 'Beggars,' and though the 'Sailor's mother,' and the piece termed 'Resolution and Independance,' have a more obvious drift, they still appear to us feeble, unimpressive, and intolerably prolix. The Blind Boy is a pretty tale for children; but little more. We cannot consider Mr. W. as much more fortunate in those addresses to natural objects where he attempts something more fanciful; though still in the same plain language.

['To a Sky-lark' is quoted in full.]

We may here take occasion to remark that these pieces in general are extremely ill rhymed. Forced, imperfect, and double rhymes abounding to an offensive and sometimes ludicrous degree. We may also observe, that one who trusts so much to mere metre, should take a little more pains with it, and not shock our ears with such lines as,

> 'And though little troubled with sloth,
> 'Drunken Lark thou would'st be loth,'

'Louisa,' exhibits some beautiful ideas disguised in quaint and ridiculous language.

['Louisa' is quoted in full.]

The Sonnets, a portion of which are dedicated to liberty, are formed on the model of Milton's and have a certain stiffness—but they hold a severe and manly tone which cannot be in times like these too much listened to—they bear strong traces of feeling and of thought, and convince us that on worthy subjects this man can write worthily.

['It is not to be thought of,' 'There is a bondage worse,' and 'England! the time is come' are quoted in full.]

One of the Odes [,] to Duty, is a meanly written piece, with some good thoughts, the other[1] is a highly mystical effusion, in which the doctrine of pre-existence is maintained. The pieces entitled Moods of my own Mind, are some of them very happy, some quite the reverse.

[1] See notes on pp. 23 and 31 above.

When a man endeavours to make his reader enter into an association that exists in his own mind between daffodils waving in the wind, and laughter—or to teach him to see something very fine in the fancy of crowning a little rock with snow-drops; he fails, and is sure to fail; for it would be strange indeed if any one besides himself ever formed associations so capricious and entirely arbitrary. But when he takes for his theme the youthful feelings connected with the sight of a butter-fly, and the song of the cuckoo, he has struck a right key, and will wake an answering note in the bosoms of all who have mimicked the bird or chaced the insect. There is an exquisiteness of feeling in some of these little poems that disarms criticism.

['To a Butterfly' ('Stay near me') and 'To the Cuckoo' are quoted in full.]

There are likewise some 'Elegiac Stanzas' of great pathos, and a perfectly original turn, which increase our regret at the quantity of mere gossip that this author has allowed to escape him.

We have now bestowed upon these volumes a survey more detailed and laborious than our usual practice, or, in some respects, their importance, might seem to require; but we were anxious to combat a system which appears to us so injurious to its author, and so dangerous to public taste.

Mr. W. doubtless possesses a reflecting mind, and a feeling heart; but nature seems to have bestowed on him little of the fancy of a poet, and a foolish theory deters him from displaying even that little. In addition to this, he appears to us to starve his mind in solitude.—Hence the undue importance he attaches to trivial incidents—hence the mysterious kind of view that he takes of human nature and human life—and hence, finally, the unfortunate habit he has acquired of attaching exquisite emotions to objects which excite none in any other human breast. He says himself in the concluding verse of his volumes,

> 'Thanks to the human heart by which we live,
> 'Thanks to its tenderness, its joys, its fears,
> 'To me the meanest flower that blows doth give,
> 'Thoughts that do often lie too deep for tears.'

This is all very well; these are pleasures that we cannot estimate, and of which we should be sorry to deprive a humble recluse; we only wish to hint, that a lasting poetical reputation is not to be built on foundations so shadowy.

Reviews of Wordsworth's 'Excursion'

Edinburgh Review

XXIV (*Nov. 1814*), *1–30. The author was Francis Jeffrey: see Walter E. Houghton* (*ed.*), The Wellesley Index to Victorian Periodicals (*Toronto, 1966*), *p. 453.*

This will never do. It bears no doubt the stamp of the author's heart and fancy; but unfortunately not half so visibly as that of his peculiar system. His former poems were intended to recommend that system, and to bespeak favour for it by their individual merit;—but this, we suspect, must be recommended by the system—and can only expect to succeed where it has been previously established. It is longer, weaker, and tamer, than any of Mr. Wordsworth's other productions; with less boldness of originality, and less even of that extreme simplicity and lowliness of tone which wavered so prettily, in the Lyrical Ballads, between silliness and pathos. We have imitations of Cowper, and even of Milton here, engrafted on the natural drawl of the Lakers—and all diluted into harmony by that profuse and irrepressible wordiness which deluges all the blank verse of this school of poetry, and lubricates and weakens the whole structure of their style.

Though it fairly fills four hundred and twenty good quarto pages, without note, vignette, or any sort of extraneous assistance, it is stated in the title—with something of an imprudent candour—to be but 'a portion' of a larger work; and in the preface, where an attempt is rather unsuccessfully made to explain the whole design, it is still more rashly disclosed, that it is but 'a part of the second part of a *long* and laborious work'—which is to consist of three parts.

What Mr. Wordsworth's ideas of length are, we have no means of accurately judging; but we cannot help suspecting that they are liberal, to a degree that will alarm the weakness of most modern readers. As far as we can gather from the preface, the entire poem—or one of them, for we really are not sure whether there is to be one or two—is of a biographical nature; and is to contain the history of the author's mind, and of the origin and progress of his poetical powers, up to the period when they were sufficiently matured to qualify him for the great work on which he has been so long employed. Now, the quarto before us contains an account of one of his youthful rambles in the vales of Cumberland, and occupies precisely the period of three days; so that, by the use of a very powerful *calculus*, some estimate may be formed of the probable extent of the entire biography.

This small specimen, however, and the statements with which it is prefaced, have been sufficient to set our minds at rest in one particular. The case of Mr Wordsworth, we perceive, is now manifestly hopeless; and we give him up as altogether incurable, and beyond the power of criticism. We cannot indeed altogether omit taking precautions now and then against the spreading of the malady;—but for himself, though we shall watch the progress of his symptoms as a matter of professional curiosity and instruction, we really think it right not to harass him any longer with nauseous remedies,—but rather to throw in cordials and lenitives, and wait in patience for the natural termination of the disorder. In order to justify this desertion of our patient, however, it is proper to state why we despair of the success of a more active practice.

A man who has been for twenty years at work on such matter as is now before us, and who comes complacently forward with a whole quarto of it after all the admonitions he has received, cannot reasonably be expected to 'change his hand, or check his pride,' upon the suggestion of far weightier monitors than we can pretend to be. Inveterate habit must now have given a kind of sanctity to the errors of early taste; and the very powers of which we lament the perversion, have probably become incapable of any other application. The very quantity too, that he has written, and is at this moment working up for publication upon the old pattern, makes it almost hopeless to look for any change of it. All this is so much capital already sunk in the concern; which must be sacrificed if it be abandoned: and no man likes to give up for lost the time and talent and labour which he has embodied in any permanent production. We were not previously aware of these obstacles to Mr Wordsworth's conversion; and, considering the peculiarities of his former writings merely as the result of certain wanton and capricious experiments on public taste and indulgence, conceived it to be our duty to discourage their repetition by all the means in our power. We now see clearly, however, how the case stands;—and, making up our minds, though with the most sincere pain and reluctance, to consider him as finally lost to the good cause of poetry, shall endeavour to be thankful for the occasional gleams of tenderness and beauty which the natural force of his imagination and affections must still shed over all his production,—and to which we shall ever turn with delight, in spite of the affection and mysticism and prolixity, with which they are so abundantly contrasted.

Long habits of seclusion, and an excessive ambition of originality, can alone account for the disproportion which seems to exist between this author's taste and his genius; or for the devotion with which he has sacrificed so many precious gifts at the shrine of those paltry idols which he has set up for himself among his lakes and his mountains. Solitary musings, amidst such scenes, might no doubt be expected to nurse up the mind to the majesty of poetical conception,—(though it is remarkable, that all the greater poets lived, or had lived, in the full current of society):—But the collision of equal minds,—the admonition of prevailing impressions—seems necessary to reduce its redundancies, and repress that tendency to extravagance or puerility, into which the self-indulgence and self-admiration of genius is so apt to be betrayed, when it is allowed to wanton, without awe or restraint, in the triumph and delight of its own intoxication. That its flights should be graceful and glorious in the eyes of men, it seems almost to be necessary that they should be made in the consciousness that men's eyes are to behold them,—and that the inward transport and vigour by which they are inspired, should be tempered by an occasional reference to what will be thought of them by those ultimate dispensers of glory. An habitual and general knowledge of the few settled and permanent maxims, which form the canon of general taste in all large and polished societies—a certain tact, which informs us at once that many things, which we still love and are moved by in secret, must necessarily be despised as childish, or derided as absurd, in all such societies—though it will not stand in the place of genius, seems necessary to the success of its exertions; and though it will never enable any one to produce the higher beauties of art, can alone secure the talent which does produce them, from errors that must render it useless. Those who have most of the talent, however, commonly acquire this knowledge with the greatest facility;—and if Mr Wordsworth, instead of confining himself almost entirely to the society of the dalesmen and cottagers, and little children, who form the subjects of his book, had condescended to mingle a little more with the people that were to read and judge of it,

41

we cannot help thinking, that its texture would have been considerably improved: At least it appears to us to be absolutely impossible, that any one who had lived or mixed familiarly with men of literature and ordinary judgment in poetry, (of course we exclude the coadjutors and disciples of his own school), could ever have fallen into such gross faults, or so long mistaken them for beauties. His first essays we looked upon in a good degree as poetical paradoxes,—maintained experimentally, in order to display talent, and court notoriety;—and so maintained, with no more serious belief in their truth, than is usually generated by an ingenious and animated defence of other paradoxes. But when we find, that he has been for twenty years exclusively employed upon articles of this very fabric, and that he has still enough of raw material on hand to keep him so employed for twenty years to come, we cannot refuse him the justice of believing that he is a sincere convert to his own system, and must ascribe the peculiarities of his composition, not to any transient affectation, or accidental caprice of imagination, but to a settled perversity of taste or understanding, which has been fostered, if not altogether created, by the circumstances to which we have already alluded.

The volume before us, if we were to describe it very shortly, we should characterize as a tissue of moral and devotional ravings, in which innumerable changes are rung upon a few very simple and familiar ideas:—but with such an accompaniment of long words, long sentences, and unwieldy phrases—and such a hubbub of strained raptures and fantastical sublimities, that it is often extremely difficult for the most skilful and attentive student to obtain a glimpse of the author's meaning—and altogether impossible for an ordinary reader to conjecture what he is about. Moral and religious enthusiasm, though undoubtedly poetical emotions, are at the same time but dangerous inspirers of poetry; nothing being so apt to run into interminable dulness or mellifluous extravagance, without giving the unfortunate author the slightest intimation of his danger. His laudable zeal for the efficacy of his preachments, he very naturally mistakes for the ardour of poetical inspiration;—and, while dealing out the high words and glowing phrases which are so readily supplied by themes of this description, can scarcely avoid believing that he is eminently original and impressive:—All sorts of commonplace notions and expressions are sanctified in his eyes, by the sublime ends for which they are employed; and the mystical verbiage of the methodist pulpit is repeated, till the speaker entertains no doubt that he is the elected organ of divine truth and persuasion. But if such be the common hazards of seeking inspiration from those potent fountains, it may easily be conceived what chance Mr Wordsworth had of escaping their enchantment,—with his natural propensities to wordiness, and his unlucky habit of debasing pathos with vulgarity. The fact accordingly is, that in this production he is more obscure than a Pindaric poet of the seventeenth century; and more verbose 'than even himself of yore;' while the wilfulness with which he persists in choosing his examples of intellectual dignity and tenderness exclusively from the lowest ranks of society, will be sufficiently apparent, from the circumstance of his having thought fit to make his chief prolocutor in this poetical dialogue, and chief advocate of Providence and Virtue, *an old Scotch Pedlar*—retired indeed from business—but still rambling about in his former haunts, and gossiping among his old customers, without his pack on his shoulders. The other persons of the drama are, a retired military chaplain, who has grown half an atheist and half a misanthrope—the wife of an unprosperous weaver—a servant girl with her infant—a parish pauper, and one or two other personages of equal rank and dignity.

The character of the work is decidedly didactic; and more than nine tenths of it are occupied with a species of dialogue, or rather a series of long sermons or harangues which pass between the pedlar, the author, the old chaplain, and a worthy vicar, who entertains the whole party at dinner on the last day of their excursion. The incidents which occur in the course of it are as few and trifling as can be imagined;— and those which the different speakers narrate in the course of their discourses, are introduced rather to illustrate their arguments or opinions, than for any interest they are supposed to possess of their own.— The doctrine which the work is intended to enforce, we are by no means certain that we have discovered. In so far as we can collect, however, it seems to be neither more nor less than the old familiar one, that a firm belief in the providence of a wise and beneficent Being must be our great stay and support under all afflictions and perplexities upon earth —and that there are indications of his power and goodness in all the aspects of the visible universe, whether living or inanimate—every part of which should therefore be regarded with love and reverence, as exponents of those great attributes. We can testify, at least, that these salutary and important truths are inculcated at far greater length, and with more repetitions, than in any ten volumes of sermons that we ever perused. It is also maintained with equal conciseness and originality, that there is frequently much good sense, as well as much enjoyment, in the humbler conditions of life; and that, in spite of great vices and abuses, there is a reasonable allowance both of happiness and goodness in society at large. If there be any deeper or more recondite doctrines in Mr Wordsworth's book, we must confess that they have escaped us;

—and, convinced as we are of the truth and soundness of those to which we have alluded, we cannot help thinking that they might have been better enforced with less parade and prolixity. His effusions on what may be called the physiognomy of external nature, or its moral and theological expression, are eminently fantastic, obscure, and affected.—It is quite time, however, that we should give the reader a more particular account of this singular performance.

[A brief summary of the story with short quotations interspersed is given up to the story of Margaret in Book I.]

We must say, that there is very considerable pathos in the telling of this simple story; and that they who can get over the repugnance excited by the triteness of its incidents, and the lowness of its objects, will not fail to be struck with the author's knowledge of the human heart, and the power he possesses of stirring up its deepest and gentlest sympathies. His prolixity, indeed, it is not so easy to get over. This little story fills about twenty-five quarto pages; and abounds, of course, with mawkish sentiment, and details of preposterous minuteness. When the tale is told, the travellers take their staffs, and end their first day's journey, without further adventure, at a little inn.

[A summary of Book II follows. The retreat of the Solitary is said to be 'most tediously described'.]

The old chaplain, or, as Mr Wordsworth is pleased to call him, the Solitary, tells this dull story at prodigious length; and after giving an inflated description of an effect of mountain-mists in the evening sun, treats his visitors with a rustic dinner—and they walk out to the fields at the close of the second book.

The third makes no progress in the excursion. It is entirely filled with moral and religious conversation and debate, and with a more ample detail of the Solitary's past life, than had been given in the sketch of his friend. The conversation is exceedingly dull and mystical; and the Solitary's confessions insufferably diffuse. Yet there is very considerable force of writing and tenderness of sentiment in this part of the work.

The Fourth book is also filled with dialogues ethical and theological; and, with the exception of some brilliant and forcible expressions here and there, consists of an exposition of truisms, more cloudy, wordy, and inconceivably prolix, than any thing we ever met with.

[The remaining books are summarized with short quotations interspersed.]

—And here the publication somewhat abruptly closes.

Our abstract of the story has been so extremely concise, that it is more than usually necessary for us to lay some specimens of the work itself before our readers. Its grand staple, as we have already said, consists of a kind of mystical morality: and the chief characteristics of the style are, that it is prolix and very frequently unintelligible: and though we are very sensible that no great gratification is to be expected from the exhibition of those qualities, yet it is necessary to give our readers a taste of them, both to justify the sentence we have passed, and to satisfy them that it was really beyond our power to present them with any abstract or intelligible account of those long conversations which we have had so much occasion to notice in our brief sketch of its contents. We need give ourselves no trouble however to select passages for this purpose. Here is the first that presents itself to us on opening the volume; and if our readers can form the slightest guess at its meaning, we must give them credit for a sagacity to which we have no pretension.

[Lines 71–86, 94–99, and 130–37 of Book IV are quoted.]

This is a fair sample of that rapturous mysticism which eludes all comprehension, and fills the despairing reader with painful giddiness and terror. The following, which we meet with on the very next page, is in the same general strain:—though the first part of it affords a good specimen of the author's talent for enveloping a plain and trite observation in all the mock majesty of solemn verbosity. A reader of plain understanding, we suspect, could hardly recognize the familiar remark, that excessive grief for our departed friends is not very consistent with a firm belief in their immortal felicity, in the first twenty lines of the following passage:—In the sequel we do not ourselves pretend to recognize any thing.

[Lines 146–89 of Book IV are quoted.]

If any farther specimen be wanted of the learned author's propensity to deal out the most familiar truths as the oracles of his own inspired understanding, the following wordy paraphrase of the ordinary remark, that the best consolation in distress is to be found in the exercises of piety, and the testimony of a good conscience, may be found on turning the leaf.

[Lines 214–27 of Book IV are quoted.]

We have kept the book too long open, however, at one place, and shall now take a dip in it nearer the beginning. The following account of the pedlar's early training, and lonely meditations among the mountains, is a good example of the forced and affected ecstasies in which this author abounds.

> ———'Nor did he fail,
> While yet a Child, with a Child's eagerness
> Incessantly to turn his ear and eye
> On all things which the moving seasons brought
> To feed such appetite: nor this alone
> Appeased his yearning:—in the after day
> of Boyhood, many an hour in caves forlorn,
> And 'mid the hollow depths of naked crags
> He sate, and even in their fix'd lineaments,
> Or from the power of a peculiar eye,
> Or by creative feeling overborne,
> Or by predominance of thought oppress'd,
> Even in their fix'd and steady lineaments
> He traced an ebbing and a flowing mind.' p. 11.

We should like extremely to know what is meant by tracing an ebbing and flowing mind in the fixed lineaments of naked crags?— but this is but the beginning of the raving fit. The young pedlar's sensations at sunrise are thus naturally recorded.

[Lines 203–18 and 227–36 of Book I are quoted.]

What follows about nature, triangles, stars, and the laws of light, is still more incomprehensible.

[Lines 263–77 and 293–300 of Book I are quoted.]

The whole book, indeed, is full of such stuff. The following is the author's own sublime aspiration after the delight of becoming *a Motion*, or *a Presence*, or *an Energy* among multitudinous streams.

[Lines 508–36 of Book IV are quoted.]

We suppose the reader is now satisfied with Mr Wordsworth's sublimities—which occupy rather more than half the volume:—Of his tamer and more creeping prolixity, we have not the heart to load him with many specimens. The following amplification of the vulgar comparison of human life to a stream, has the merit of adding much obscurity to wordiness; at least, *we* have not ingenuity enough to refer the conglobated bubbles and murmurs, and floating islands to their vital prototypes.

[Lines 967–87 of Book III are quoted.]

The following, however, is a better example of the useless and most tedious minuteness with which the author so frequently details circumstances of no interest in themselves,—of no importance to the story,—and possessing no graphical merit whatsoever as pieces of description. On their approach to the old chaplain's cottage, the author gets before his companion,

[Lines 410–33 of Book II are quoted. In the passage the narrator finds a book.]

And this book, which he

> ———'found to be a work
> In the French Tongue, a Novel of Voltaire,'

leads to no incident or remark of any value or importance, to apologize for this long story of its finding. There is no beauty, we think, it must be admitted, in such passages; and so little either of interest or curiosity in the incidents they disclose, that we can scarcely conceive that any man to whom they had actually occurred, should take the trouble to recount them to his wife and children by his idle fireside:—but, that man or child should think them worth writing down in blank verse, and printing in magnificent quarto, we should certainly have supposed altogether impossible, had it not been for the ample proofs which Mr Wordsworth has afforded to the contrary.

Sometimes their silliness is enhanced by a paltry attempt at effect and emphasis:—as in the following account of that very touching and extraordinary occurrence of a lamb bleating among the mountains. The poet would actually persuade us that he thought the mountains themselves were bleating;—and that nothing could be so grand or impressive. 'List!' cries the old Pedlar, suddenly breaking off in the middle of one of his daintiest ravings—

[Lines 402–11 of Book IV are quoted.]

What we have now quoted will give the reader a notion of the taste and spirit in which this volume is composed; and yet, if it had not contained something a good deal better, we do not know how we should have been justified in troubling him with any account of it. But the truth is, that Mr Wordsworth, with all his perversities, is a person of great powers; and has frequently a force in his moral declamations, and a tenderness in his pathetic narratives, which neither his prolixity nor his affectation can altogether deprive of their effect. We shall venture to give some extracts from the simple tale of the weaver's solitary cottage. Its heroine is the deserted wife; and its chief interest consists in the picture of her despairing despondence and anxiety after his disappearance. The Pedlar, recurring to the well to which he had directed his companion, observes,

[Lines 491–502 and 516–19 of Book I are quoted.]

The bliss and tranquillity of these prosperous years, is well and copiously described;—but at last came sickness, and want of employment;—and the effect on the kind-hearted and industrious mechanic is strikingly delineated.

[Lines 568–74, 585–89, 646–56 and 686–96 of Book I are quoted with interlocking comments.]

The gradual sinking of the spirit under the load of continued anxiety, and the destruction of all the finer springs of the soul, by a course of unvarying sadness, are very feelingly represented in the sequel of this simple narrative.

[Lines 706–22, 734–38, 791–803, 813–21, 829–31, 906–11 and 915–16 of Book I are quoted with interlocking comments.]

The story of the old chaplain, though a little less lowly, is of the same mournful cast, and almost equally destitute of incidents;—for Mr Wordsworth delineates only feelings—and all his adventures are of the heart. The narrative which is given by the sufferer himself, is, in our opinion, the most spirited and interesting part of the poem. He begins thus, and addressing himself, after a long pause, to his ancient countryman and friend the Pedlar—

[Lines 480–87 of Book III are quoted.]

The following account of his marriage and early felicity is written with great sweetness—a sweetness like that of Massinger, in his softer and more mellifluous passages.

[Lines 504–23, 532, 540–49, 597–98, 650–52 and 670–79 of Book III are quoted with interlocking comments.]

The agony of mind into which the survivor was thrown, is described with a powerful eloquence; as well as the doubts and distracting fears which the sceptical speculations of his careless days had raised in his spirit. There is something peculiarly grand and terrible to our feelings in the imagery of these three lines—

'By pain of heart, now checked, and now impelled,
The Intellectual Power, through words and things,
Went sounding on, a dim and perilous way!'

At last he is roused from this dejected mood, by the glorious promises which seemed held out to human nature at the first dawn of the French Revolution;—and it indicates a fine perception of the secret springs of character and emotion, to choose a being so circumstanced as the most ardent votary of that far-spread enthusiasm.

[Lines 734–36, 745–58 and 850–55 of Book III are quoted with interlocking comments.]

We must trespass upon our readers with the fragments of yet another story. It is that of a simple, seduced and deserted girl, told with great sweetness, pathos and indulgence by the Vicar of the parish, by the side of her untimely grave. Looking down on the turf, he says—

[Lines 787–92 and 811–23 of Book VI are quoted.]

Her virgin graces and tenderness are then very beautifully described, and her seduction and lonely anguish passed over very lightly.

[Lines 869–78, 906–10, 916–27, 939–48, 969–87, 1000–01, 1019–23, 1034–37 and 1049–52 of Book VI are quoted with interlocking details.]

These passages, we think, are among the most touching with which the volume presents us; though there are many in a more lofty and impassioned style. The following commemoration of a beautiful and glorious youth, the love and the pride of the valley, is full of warmth and poetry.

[Lines 714 and 717–40 of Book VII are quoted.]

This is lofty and energetic;—but Mr Wordsworth descends, we cannot think very gracefully, when he proceeds to describe how the quoit *whizzed* when his arm launched it—and how the football mounted as high as a lark, at the touch of his toe;—neither is it a suitable catastrophe, for one so nobly endowed, to catch cold by standing too long in the river washing sheep, and die of spasms in consequence. The general reflections on the indiscriminating rapacity of death, though by no means original in themselves, and expressed with too bold a rivalry of the seven ages of Shakespeare, have yet a character of vigour and truth about them that entitles them to notice.

[Lines 946 and 954–75 of Book V are quoted.]

There is a lively and impressive appeal on the injury done to the health, happiness, and morality of the lower orders, by the unceasing and premature labours of our crowded manufactories. The description of night-working is picturesque. In lonely and romantic regions, he says, when silence and darkness incline all to repose—

[Lines 167–85, 262–82, 214–27 of Book VIII and 237–47, 336–54 of Book IX are quoted with interlocking comments.]

There is a good deal of fine description in the course of this work; but we have left ourselves no room for any specimen. The following few lines, however, are a fine epitome of a lake voyage.

[Lines 560–65 of Book IX are quoted.]

We add also the following more elaborate and fantastic picture—which, however, is not without its beauty.

[Lines 437–51 of Book IX are quoted.]

Besides those more extended passages of interest or beauty, which we have quoted, and omitted to quote, there are scattered up and down the book and in the midst of its most repulsive portions, a very great number of single lines and images, that sparkle like gems in the desart, and startle us with an intimation of the great poetic powers that lie buried in the rubbish that has been heaped around them. It is difficult to pick up these, after we have once passed them by; but we shall endeavour to light upon one or two. The beneficial effect of intervals of relaxation and pastime on youthful minds, is finely expressed, we think, in a single line, when it is said to be—

'Like vernal ground to Sabbath sunshine left.'

The following image of the bursting forth of a mountain-spring, seems to us also to be conceived with great elegance and beauty.

'And a few steps may bring us to the spot,
Where haply crown'd with flowrets and green herbs;
The Mountain Infant to the Sun comes forth
Like human life from darkness.'—

The ameliorating effects of song and music on the minds which most delight in them, are likewise very poetically expressed.

————'And when the stream
Which overflowed the soul was passed away,
A consciousness remained that it had left,
Deposited upon the silent shore

> Of Memory, images and precious thoughts,
> That shall not die, and cannot be destroyed.'

Nor is any thing more elegant than the representation of the graceful tranquillity occasionally put on by one of the author's favourites; who, though gay and airy, in general—

> 'Was graceful, when it pleased him, smooth and still
> As the mute Swan that floats adown the stream,
> Or on the waters of th' unruffled lake
> Anchored her placid beauty. Not a leaf
> That flutters on the bough more light than he,
> And not a flower that droops in the green shade,
> More winningly reserved.'—

Nor are there wanting morsels of a sterner and more majestic beauty; as when, assuming the weightier diction of Cowper, he says, in language which the hearts of all readers of modern history must have responded—

> ————'Earth is sick,
> And Heaven is weary of the hollow words
> Which States and Kingdoms utter when they speak
> Of Truth and Justice.'

These examples, we perceive, are not very well chosen—but we have not leisure to improve the selection; and, such as they are, they may serve to give the reader a notion of the sort of merit which we meant to illustrate by their citation.—When we look back to them, indeed, and to the other passages which we have now extracted, we feel half inclined to rescind the severe sentence which we passed on the work at the beginning:—But when we look into the work itself, we perceive that it cannot be rescinded. Nobody can be more disposed to do justice to the great powers of Mr Wordsworth than we are; and, from the first time that he came before us, down to the present moment, we have uniformly testified in their favour, and assigned indeed our high sense of their value as the chief ground of the bitterness with which we resented their perversion. That perversion, however, is now far more visible than their original dignity; and while we collect the fragments, it is impossible not to lament the ruins from which we are condemned to pick them. If any one should doubt of the existence of such a perversion, or be disposed to dispute about the instances we have hastily brought forward, we would just beg leave to refer him to the general plan and the characters of the poem now before us.—Why should Mr Wordsworth have made his hero a superannuated Pedlar? What but the most wretched and provoking perversity of taste and judgment, could induce any one to place his chosen advocate of wisdom and virtue in so absurd and fantastic a condition? Did Mr Wordsworth really imagine, that his favourite doctrines were likely to gain any thing in point of effect or authority by being put into the mouth of a person accustomed to higgle about tape, or brass sleeve-buttons? Or is it not plain that, independent of the ridicule and disgust which such a personification must give to many of his readers, its adoption exposes his work throughout to the charge of revolting incongruity, and utter disregard of probability or nature? For, after he has thus wilfully debased his moral teacher by a low occupation, is there one word that he puts into his mouth, or one sentiment of which he makes him the organ, that has the most remote reference to that occupation? Is there anything in his learned, abstracted, and logical harangues, that savours of the calling that is ascribed to him? Are any of their materials such as a pedlar could possibly have dealt in? Are the manners, the diction, the sentiments, in any, the very smallest degree, accommodated to a person in that condition? or are they not eminently and conspicuously such as could not by possibility belong to it? A man who went about selling flannel and pocket-handkerchiefs in this lofty diction, would soon frighten away all his customers; and would infallibly pass either for a madman, or for some learned and affected gentleman, who, in a frolic, had taken up a character which he was peculiarly ill qualified for supporting.

The absurdity in this case, we think, is palpable and glaring; but it is exactly of the same nature with that which infects the whole substance of the work—a puerile ambition of singularity engrafted on an unlucky predilection for truisms; and an affected passion for simplicity and humble life, most awkwardly combined with a taste for mystical refinements, and all the gorgeousness of obscure phraseology. His taste for simplicity is evinced, by sprinkling up and down his interminable declamations, a few descriptions of baby-houses, and of old hats with wet brims; and his amiable partiality for humble life, by assuring us, that a wordy rhetorician, who talks about Thebes, and allegorizes all the heathen mythology, was once a pedlar—and making him break in upon his magnificent orations with two or three awkward notices of something that he had seen when selling winter raiment about the country—or of the changes in the state of society, which had almost annihilated his former calling.

Quarterly Review

XII (Oct. 1814), 100–11. The author was Charles Lamb, but the review was heavily edited by William Gifford, the editor. See Hill Shine and Helen C. Shine, The Quarterly Review under Gifford *(Chapel Hill, N.C., 1949), p. 44. The issue in which the review was contained was published sometime before Jan. 14, 1815 (ibid).*

The volume before us, as we learn from the Preface, is 'a detached portion of an unfinished poem, containing views of man, nature, and
society;' to be called the Recluse, as having for its principal subject the
'sensations and opinions of a poet living in retirement;' and to be preceded by a 'record in verse of the origin and progress of the author's
own powers, with reference to the fitness which they may be supposed
to have conferred for the task.' To the completion of this plan we look
forward with a confidence which the execution of the finished part is
well calculated to inspire.—Meanwhile, in what is before us there is
ample matter for entertainment: for the 'Excursion' is not a branch (as
might have been suspected) prematurely plucked from the parent tree
to gratify an overhasty appetite for applause; but is, in itself, a complete
and legitimate production.

It opens with the meeting of the poet with an aged man whom he
had known from his school days; in plain words, a Scottish pedlar; a
man who, though of low origin, had received good learning and impressions of the strictest piety from his stepfather, a minister and village
schoolmaster. Among the hills of Athol, the child is described to have
become familiar with the appearances of nature in his occupation as a
feeder of sheep; and from her silent influences to have derived a
character, meditative, tender, and poetical. With an imagination and
feelings thus nourished—his intellect not unaided by books, but those,
few, and chiefly of a religious cast—the necessity of seeking a maintenance in riper years, had induced him to make choice of a profession,
the *appellation* for which has been gradually declining into contempt,
but which formerly designated a class of men, who, journeying in
country places, when roads presented less facilities for travelling, and
the intercourse between towns and villages was unfrequent and
hazardous, became a sort of link of neighbourhood to distant habitations; resembling, in some small measure, in the effects of their periodical returns, the caravan which Thomson so feelingly describes as blessing the cheerless Siberian in its annual visitation, with 'news of human
kind.'

In the solitude incident to this rambling life, power had been given him to keep alive that devotedness to nature which he had imbibed in his childhood, together with the opportunity of gaining such notices of persons and things from his intercourse with society, as qualified him to become a 'teacher of moral wisdom.' With this man, then, in a hale old age, released from the burthen of his occupation, yet retaining much of its active habits, the poet meets, and is by him introduced to a second character—a sceptic—one who had been partially roused from an overwhelming desolation, brought upon him by the loss of wife and children, by the powerful incitement of hope which the French Revolution in its commencement put forth, but who, disgusted with the failure of all its promises, had fallen back into a laxity of faith and conduct which induced at length a total despondence as to the dignity and final destination of his species. In the language of the poet, he

> ———broke faith with those whom he had laid
> In earth's dark chambers.

Yet he describes himself as subject to compunctious visitations from that silent quarter.

> ———Feebly must they have felt,
> Who, in old time, attired with snakes and whips
> The vengeful Furies. Beautiful regards
> Were turned on me—the face of her I loved;
> The wife and mother; pitifully fixing
> Tender reproaches, insupportable!—p. 133.

The conversations with this person, in which the Wanderer asserts the consolatory side of the question against the darker views of human life maintained by his friend, and finally calls to his assistance the experience of a village priest, the third, or rather fourth interlocutor, (for the poet himself is one,) form the groundwork of the 'Excursion.'

It will be seen by this sketch that the poem is of a didactic nature, and not a fable or story; yet it is not wanting in stories of the most interesting kind,—such as the lovers of Cowper and Goldsmith will recognise as something familiar and congenial to them. We might instance the Ruined Cottage, and the Solitary's own story, in the first half of the work; and the second half, as being almost a continued cluster of narration. But the prevailing charm of the poem is, perhaps, that, conversational as it is in its plan, the dialogue throughout is carried on in the very heart of the most romantic scenery which the poet's native hills could supply; and which, by the perpetual references made to it either in the way of illustration or for variety and pleasurable description's sake, is brought before us as we read. We breathe in the fresh air, as we do while reading Walton's Complete Angler; only the country about us is as much bolder than Walton's, as the thoughts and speculations, which form the matter of the poem, exceed the trifling pastime and low-pitched conversation of his humble fishermen. We give the description of the 'two huge peaks,' which from some other vale peered into that in which the Solitary is entertaining the poet and companion.

[Lines 695–725 of Book II are quoted.]

To a mind constituted like that of Mr. Wordsworth, the stream, the torrent, and the stirring leaf—seem not merely to suggest associations of deity, but to be a kind of speaking communication with it. He walks through every forest, as through some Dodona; and every bird that flits among the leaves, like that miraculous one[1] in Tasso, but in language more intelligent, reveals to him far higher love-lays. In his poetry nothing in Nature is dead. Motion is synonymous with life. 'Beside yon spring,' says the Wanderer, speaking of a deserted well, from which, in former times, a poor woman, who died heart-broken, had been used to dispense refreshment to the thirsty traveller,

> ———beside yon spring I stood,
> And eyed its waters, till we seem'd to feel
> One sadness, they and I. For them a bond
> Of brotherhood is broken: time has been
> When every day the touch of human hand
> Dislodged the natural sleep that binds them up
> In mortal stillness.—p. 27.

To such a mind, we say—call it strength or weakness—if weakness, assuredly a fortunate one—the visible and audible things of creation present, not dim symbols, or curious emblems, which they have done at all times to those who have been gifted with the poetical faculty; but

---

[1] [With party-coloured plumes, and purple bill,
A wondrous bird among the rest there flew,
That in plain speech sung love-lays loud and shrill;
Her leden was like human language true;
So much she talk'd, and with such wit and skill,
That strange it seemed how much good she knew.
Fairfax's Translation—Reviewer's note.]

revelations and quick insights into the life within us, the pledge of immortality:—

> ————the whispering air
> Sends inspiration from her shadowy heights,
> And blind recesses of the cavern'd rocks:
> The little rills, and waters numberless,
> Inaudible by day-light.

'I have seen,' the poet says, and the illustration is a happy one:

> ————I have seen
> A curious child, applying to his ear
> The convolutions of a smooth-lipp'd shell
> To which, in silence hush'd, his very soul
> Listen'd intensely, and his countenance soon
> Brighten'd with joy; for murmurings from within
> Were heard—sonorous cadences! whereby,
> To his belief, the monitor express'd
> Mysterious union with its native sea.
> Even such a shell the universe itself
> Is to the ear of faith; and doth impart
> Authentic tidings of invisible things:
> Of ebb and flow, and ever during power;
> And central peace subsisting at the heart
> Of endless agitation.—p. 191.

Sometimes this harmony is imaged to us by an echo; and in one instance, it is with such transcendant beauty set forth by a shadow and its corresponding substance, that it would be a sin to cheat our readers at once of so happy an illustration of the poet's system, and so fair a proof of his descriptive powers.

> Thus having reached a bridge that over-arched
> The hasty rivulet where it lay becalmed
> In a deep pool, by happy chance we saw
> A two-fold image; on a grassy bank
> A snow-white ram, and in the chrystal flood
> Another and the same! most beautiful,
> On the green turf, with his imperial front,
> Shaggy and bold, and wreathed horns superb,
> The breathing creature stood; as beautiful,
> Beneath him, shewed his shadowy counterpart.
> Each had his glowing mountains, each his sky,
> And each seemed centre of his own fair world;

> Antipodes unconscious of each other,
> Yet, in partition, with their several spheres,
> Blended in perfect stillness, to our sight!—p. 407.

Combinations, it is confessed, 'like those reflected in that quiet pool,' cannot be lasting: it is enough for the purpose of the poet, if they are felt.—They are at least his system; and his readers, if they reject them for their creed, may receive them merely as poetry. In him, *faith*, in friendly alliance and conjunction with the religion of his country, appears to have grown up, fostered by meditation and lonely communions with Nature—an internal principle of lofty consciousness, which stamps upon his opinions and sentiments (we were almost going to say) the character of an expanded and generous Quakerism.

From such a creed we should expect unusual results; and, when applied to the purposes of consolation, more touching considerations than from the mouth of common teachers. The finest speculation of this sort perhaps in the poem before us, is the notion of the thoughts which may sustain the spirit, while they crush the frame of the sufferer, who from loss of objects of love by death, is commonly supposed to pine away under a broken heart.

[Lines 165–85 of Book IV are quoted. Lines 174–77 are italicized by the reviewer.]

With the same modifying and incorporating power, he tells us,—

[Lines 1058–77 of Book IV are quoted.]

This is high poetry; though (as we have ventured to lay the basis of the author's sentiments in a sort of liberal Quakerism) from some parts of it, others may, with more plausibility, object to the appearance of a kind of Natural Methodism: we could have wished therefore that the tale of Margaret had been postponed, till the reader had been strengthened by some previous acquaintance with the author's theory, and not placed in the front of the poem, with a kind of ominous aspect, beautifully tender as it is. It is a tale of a cottage, and its female tenant, gradually decaying together, while she expected the return of one whom poverty and not unkindness had driven from her arms. We trust ourselves only with the conclusion—

[Lines 871–916 of Book I are quoted.]

The fourth book, entitled 'Despondency Corrected,' we consider as the most valuable portion of the poem. For moral grandeur; for wide scope of thought and a long train of lofty imagery; for tender personal appeals; and a *versification* which we feel we ought to notice, but feel it also so involved in the poetry, that we can hardly mention it as a distinct excellence; it stands without competition among our didactic and descriptive verse. The general tendency of the argument (which we might almost affirm to be the leading moral of the poem) is to abate the pride of the calculating *understanding*, and to reinstate the *imagination* and the *affections* in those seats from which modern philosophy has laboured but too successfully to expel them.

[Lines 611–21 of Book IV are quoted.]

In the same spirit, those illusions of the imaginative faculty to which the peasantry in solitary districts are peculiarly subject, are represented as the kindly ministers of *conscience*:

> ———with whose service charged
> They come and go, appear and disappear;
> Diverting evil purposes, remorse
> Awakening, chastening an intemperate grief,
> Or pride of heart abating.

Reverting to more distant ages of the world, the operation of that same faculty in producing the several fictions of Chaldean, Persian, and Grecian idolatry, is described with such seductive power, that the Solitary, in good earnest, seems alarmed at the tendency of his own argument.—Notwithstanding his fears, however, there is one thought so uncommonly fine, relative to the spirituality which lay hid beneath the gross material forms of Greek worship, in metal or stone, that we cannot resist the allurement of transcribing it—

[Lines 729–62 of Book IV are quoted. Lines 745–52 are italicized by the reviewer.]

In discourse like this the first day passes away.—The second (for this almost dramatic poem takes up the action of two summer days) is varied by the introduction of the village priest; to whom the Wanderer resigns the office of chief speaker, which had been yielded to his age and experience on the first. The conference is begun at the gate of the church-yard; and after some natural speculations concerning death and immortality—and the custom of funereal and sepulchral observances, as deduced from a feeling of immortality—certain doubts are proposed respecting the quantity of moral worth existing in the world, and in that mountainous district in particular. In the resolution of these doubts, the priest enters upon a most affecting and singular strain of narration, derived from the graves around him. Pointing to hillock after hillock, he gives short histories of their tenants, disclosing their humble virtues, and touching with tender hand upon their frailties.

Nothing can be conceived finer than the manner of introducing these tales. With heaven above his head, and the mouldering turf at his feet—standing betwixt life and death—he seems to maintain that spiritual relation which he bore to his living flock, in its undiminished strength, even with their ashes; and to be in his proper cure, or diocese, among the dead.

We might extract powerful instances of pathos from these tales—the story of Ellen in particular—but their force is in combination, and in the circumstances under which they are introduced. The traditionary anecdote of the Jacobite and Hanoverian, as less liable to suffer by transplanting, and as affording an instance of that finer species of humour, that thoughtful playfulness in which the author more nearly perhaps than in any other quality resembles Cowper, we shall lay (at least a part of it) before our readers.

[A brief summary is given and lines 457-83 and 491-521 of Book VI are quoted.]

The causes which have prevented the poetry of Mr. Wordsworth from attaining its full share of popularity are to be found in the boldness and originality of his genius. The times are past when a poet could securely follow the direction of his own mind into whatever tracts it might lead. A writer, who would be popular, must timidly coast the shore of prescribed sentiment and sympathy. He must have just as much more of the imaginative faculty than his readers, as will serve to keep their apprehensions from stagnating, but not so much as to alarm their jealousy. He must not think or feel too deeply.

If he has had the fortune to be bred in the midst of the most magnificent objects of creation, he must not have given away his heart to them; or if he have, he must conceal his love, or not carry his expressions of it beyond that point of rapture, which the occasional tourist thinks it not overstepping decorum to betray, or the limit which that gentlemanly spy upon Nature, the picturesque traveller, has vouchsafed to countenance. He must do this, or be content to be thought an enthusiast.

If from living among simple mountaineers, from a daily intercourse with them, not upon the footing of a patron, but in the character of an equal, he has detected, or imagines that he has detected, through the cloudy medium of their unlettered discourse, thoughts and apprehensions not vulgar; traits of patience and constancy, love unwearied, and heroic endurance, not unfit (as he may judge) to be made the subject of verse, he will be deemed a man of perverted genius by the philanthropist who, conceiving of the peasantry of his country only as objects of a pecuniary sympathy, starts at finding them elevated to a level of humanity with himself, having their own loves, enmities, cravings, aspirations, &c., as much beyond his faculty to believe, as his beneficence to supply.

If from a familiar observation of the ways of children, and much more from a retrospect of his own mind when a child, he has gathered more reverential notions of that state than fall to the lot of ordinary observers, and, escaping, from the dissonant wranglings of men, has turned his lyre, though but for occasional harmonies, to the milder utterance of that soft age,—his verses shall be censured as infantile by critics who confound poetry 'having children for its subject' with poetry that is 'childish,' and who, having themselves perhaps never been *children*, never having possessed the tenderness and docility of that age, know not what the soul of a child is—how apprehensive! how imaginative! how religious!

We have touched upon some of the causes which we conceive to have been unfriendly to the author's former poems. We think they do not apply in the same force to the one before us. There is in it more of uniform elevation, a wider scope of subject, less of manner, and it contains none of those starts and imperfect shapings which in some of this author's smaller pieces offended the weak, and gave scandal to the perverse. It must indeed be approached with seriousness. It has in it much of that quality which 'draws the devout, deterring the profane.' Those who hate the Paradise Lost will not love this poem. The steps of the great master are discernible in it; not in direct imitation or injurious parody, but in the following of the spirit, in free homage and generous subjection.

One objection it is impossible not to foresee. It will be asked, why put such eloquent discourse in the mouth of a pedlar? It might be answered that Mr. Wordsworth's plan required a character in humble life to be the organ of his philosophy. It was in harmony with the system and scenery of his poem. We read Piers Plowman's Creed, and the lowness of the teacher seems to add a simple dignity to the doctrine. Besides, the poet has bestowed an unusual share of education upon him. Is it too much to suppose that the author, at some early period of his life, may himself have known such a person, a man endowed with sentiments above his situation, another Burns; and that the dignified strains which he has attributed to the Wanderer may be no more than recollections of his conversation, heightened only by the amplification natural to poetry, or the lustre which imagination flings back upon the objects and companions of our youth? After all, if there should be found readers willing to admire the poem, who yet feel scandalized at a *name*, we would advise them, wherever it occurs, to substitute silently the word *Palmer* or *Pilgrim*, or any less offensive designation, which shall connect the notion of sobriety in heart and manners with the experience and privileges which a wayfaring life confers.

Reviews of Wordsworth's 'White Doe of Rylstone'

Champion

June 25, 1815, pp. 205–06. The author was John Scott, a minor writer and editor of the Champion *from 1815 to 1817 and of the* London Magazine *from 1820 to 1821. The review was signed 'S*'; for the consequent attribution to Scott, see W. M. Parker and D. Hudson, 'Thomas Barnes and the Champion',* TLS, *Jan. 1 and 15, 1944.*

Mr. Wordsworth has lately published a second edition of his smaller poems, and with them he has given a dissertation, which, as it is an explanation of his principles, is of course a defence of his practice. His large work, the *Excursion*, a noble poem in blank verse, has been some time out; and the other day he presented us with the *White Doe of Rylstone*, a poem founded on a legendary historical tale. We do not think the last his best. The narrative part will be most attentively perused by readers, and it does not seem to be most successfully accomplished: the *White Doe* is the inspiration of the poem, and the most beautiful passages are connected with this fair and gentle mysterious creature.

[The story of the *White Doe* is briefly summarized, and the opening of Canto First is sketched, with lines 35–38 and 47–48 quoted.]

These preliminary circumstances are sketched with much feeling for their natural beauty; and by their gentle and pure influence, throw the reader into a happy mood for the introduction of the most interesting living agent in the poem. From under the arch, bound with ivy, that gives entrance into the churchyard. . . .

[Lines 55–66, 79–92, 100–05, and 142–47 are quoted.]

62

The rest of the poem we leave unnoticed, as a reward to the curiosity of the reader.

It has been boldly said of Mr. Wordsworth,—'his diction has no where any pretensions to elegance or dignity; and he has scarcely ever condescended to give the grace of correctness or melody to his versification.'[1] The reader, if he have never perused any of Mr. W.'s poetry before,[2] will judge whether the writer of the above pieces of touching harmony, which his ear will tell him are admirably tuned in soft beauty of expression to the delicious moral music of the strain of feeling, is likely to have sent out to the world four volumes of poetry, the diction of which should *no where* have *any pretensions* to elegance or dignity! We must maintain, on the contrary, that the great attracting body of these four volumes of Mr. Wordsworth's early poetry,—that which alone rivets the attention of candid and discriminating judges, and fixes the writer's place among the lights of fame, is of this unimpugnable kind,—legitimate in its kindred to the works of the long-standing and revered 'dynasties of genius,'—sanctioned by established precept, by the general sense of excellence, and even by the very prejudices which are wedded to the 'old oracles of poetical wisdom;'—therefore not to be decried without incurring the guilt and shame of treason against the acknowledged and rightful heirs of immortality. We may affirm this without disputing about the quality of those peculiar passages, which have been seized upon and dragged forward to a prominency which their number does not entitle them to receive, for the purpose of depreciating the sterling value of Mr. Wordsworth's talent, by inducing the bulk of persons to estimate him in the whole according to a few suspicious specimens. Of these we shall say, that some of them have been objected to, as in former times certain sublime doctrines were to the Jews stumbling blocks, and to the Greeks foolishness; and that others of them, as they gallantly encounter the arbitrary associations, the despotic dogmas, the standard etiquettes and fashions, of a highly artificial social state,—which is surely liable to at least the suspicion of being in some measure diseased,—may very possibly be less in the wrong than their critics. It is a sound maxim in politics, that, at certain intervals, the established institutions of government should be returned to their elements, in order that the wanderings of practice

[1] [This sweeping stigma was uttered as part of a review of two volumes, that contained, among many, many other specimens of exquisite language, clothing an exquisite fancy in 'fit sound'—the following sonnet, which for mellifluous flow of words, and deep solemn tenderness of sentiment, is not to be put in the second rank by any production, of a similar kind, of any place or at any time:— ('Composed upon Westminster Bridge' is quoted)—Reviewer's note.]

[2] [This is but too probable a supposition.—Reviewer's note.]

from original principles, and (what are more insidious) those violations of spirit which *creep* in under the guise of observances of the letter, may be corrected, and the forms and style of measures be brought back to the significancy of real purpose. In the same way Literature, in a country that has been long pursuing, amidst the pamperings and profusions of high civilization, a course of encreasing refinement of artifice, extending to every exertion of the hand, the temper, and the intellect, is apt to lose its native qualities in those adornments which were at first intended only to set them off, and to get away from all its true objects through pursuing them too far, or to miss them entirely in consequence of the first care being that the steps by which it is sought to arrive at them may be nice, delicate, clever, and shewy. To prevent this evil, or hinder it from arriving at its last stage, it is highly useful that men of vigorous talent, whose feelings are quickly excited, and when excited are powerful in their effects, should refer poetry back to its elements, which consist of what Wordsworth calls *'the plain humanities of nature.'* It is quite clear, however, that in doing this they must come in contact with the artificial frame of public taste, formed as has been described, and that they must lay themselves open to the critics of a day, when ladies' routs are quite as literary as their favorite quarto poems, when reviews are more substantial than books,—when poets dine with princes, and have leisure besides to do jobs for the booksellers, bringing them five or six thousand pounds a year. It is quite clear that this is a day for *'smooth-rubbed'* souls to flourish and have fame;—the art will then be held in more esteem than the essence; the shew of sharpened wit will bear away the palm from earnest feeling; and a lucky parodist, or a ballad-monger whose publisher fleeces the 'clean-shirted rabble,' his customers,—the studious readers on rosewood tables,—under pretence of procuring for their impatience *'A Mail Coach Copy,'* will be carried triumphantly through six or eight editions,—when the true poet, as described in the following fine verses, will scarcely drag through one:—

> 'The outward shews of sky and earth,
> Of hill and valley he has viewed;
> And in pulses of deeper birth
> Have come to him in solitude.
>
> In common things that round us lie,
> Some random truths he can impart,
> —The harvest of a quiet eye,
> That broods and sleeps on his own heart.'
> WORDSWORTH'S *Poems*, vol. 2, p. 100.

These are Wordsworth's verses,—and have they 'no pretension to elegance or dignity of diction?' We doubt not that many of our readers will be startled to find that eight lines so simply beautiful, so chastely sublime, can be taken from the works of an author whose writings they have never read, but have seen quoted in broken lines to be ridiculed for their quaintness and vulgarity. But the truth is, that the sneer of professional criticism, got up for drawing-rooms, to supply comments for fashionable coteries, will ever find most of its natural prey in the finest works of those

> 'Who give us noble loves, and nobler cares,—
> The Poets who on earth have made us heirs
> Of truth and pure delight by Heavenly Lays.'
> WORDSWORTH'S *Poems*, Vol. 2, p. 141.

In one of Shakespeare's best Sonnets we find the following line,

> 'And art made *tongue-ty'd* by authority?'

Modern criticism would pounce ferociously on the phrase 'tongue-ty'd', which it would represent as consigning the author to eternal ridicule,— there being no redemption for him in the exquisite conclusion—

> 'Tir'd with all these, from these I would be gone,
> *Save that to die, I leave my love alone.'*
> SHAKSPEARE'S *Sonnet*, 66.

The next Sonnet but one, seems to be levelled against the sin of wig-making:—it begins with these lines—

> 'Thus is his cheek the map of days outworn,
> *When beauty liv'd and died as flowers do now.'*

But what of these, or of their companions? The subject is enough to render it execrable in the estimation of persons who scoff at one of the deepest pieces of poetical pathos in the English Language, because the sufferer is described to be the wife of a weaver! We allude to a story in Wordsworth's *Excursion*, of which he says—

> '———'Tis a common tale,
> An ordinary sorrow of man's life,
> A tale of silent suffering.'
> *Excursion*, p. 34.

We do not, however, mean to conceal our opinion, that Mr. Wordsworth often most unguardedly and unnecessarily exposes himself to the enemy. A stricter principle of selection than this author chooses to exercise, seems to us essential to Poetry. We would suggest that a Poet should discriminate between all that he feels, and what he can successfully convey; and, with deference, we would say, that Mr. Wordsworth often neglects to do this. He has told us that to him

> —'the meanest flower that blows can give
> Thoughts, that do often lie too deep for tears;'—

but if there are narrower limits to language than to his thoughts, he should, in his publications, stop within the former,—for otherwise what takes place? That which is rich and dignified in its original existence, is rendered mean and poor in the process by which it is brought forward to challenge admiration. There are, no doubt, intense faculties, to which the seeming degrees and varieties of the earth are much lessened by the penetration of their possessor into the general scheme and system of things. There is one

> 'Who sees with equal eye, as God of all,
> A Hero perish, or a Sparrow fall,'

but it is neither pleasing nor useful to have all objects and events placed on an equality before mankind,—for the level must, with the generality, be brought about by reducing what is high,—and not by raising what is low.

But Mr. Wordsworth is a Poet of the first class: his mind is, what he has described,—'a mansion for all lovely forms;'—his memory is

> ———'a dwelling place
> For all sweet sounds and harmonies.'

He is now before the public in a variety of works,—of unequal merit certainly,—but in their collective testimony proclaiming him the greatest poetical genius of the age. It may be a question how far he is right and how far he is wrong; critics may employ themselves and amuse their readers in picking out what they think objectionable passages,— but his heavenly faculty raises him above the application of their rules, and even (which is the privilege only of the few first rates) places him out of the reach of being substantially injured by his own defects. It is said that the Booksellers do not find by the sale that his poetry is popular: the fact is no otherwise of importance than as illustrative of what we have been long ago told—that *the children of the world are wiser*, (that is to say more lucky) *than the generation of light.*

As for the effect of this on Mr. Wordsworth himself, it is sufficient to say that he is Nature's votary, and . . . .

[Lines 122–34 of 'Lines Composed a Few Miles above Tintern Abbey' are quoted.]

New British Lady's Magazine

II (July 1815), 33–37. The reviewer is unknown.

At a time when a just and general taste, which prevails for the best productions of our ancient masters of poetry, has led to a fervour of pursuit that has ransacked all the hidden literary stores, it seems strange that the works of the author now before us should have met with such unmerited obloquy. The name of no living poet is perhaps better known than that of Mr. Wordsworth, but there is no man whose works, if read, are less understood, or as to whose merits or defects so many persons, capable of forming a judgment of their own, have taken their opinions upon trust. The censure which has been applied to his productions, as undeserved as it has been indiscriminate, would almost lead us to doubt the existence of that admiration of the works of our older bards, and to fear, at least, that it was established on a foundation as superficial and unstable as the vagaries of fashion, with no hold upon the heart and understanding.

For the system of Mr. Wordsworth, called peculiar, is only so as compared with the writers claiming the same title of the present day. He does not set up in this latter age, while before him are all the glorious examples of his forefathers (those more than kindred ancestors of poetry, even to remotest times), to establish new rules and new laws of his divine pursuit; and there is no notion so mistaken as to suppose that his principles are other than those by which great poets in all ages have been governed. He treads in a path once familiarly beaten, though long forsaken; and, if he have not the merit of discovering it, he does claim the praise of being the first to retrace it by the almost obliterated prints of the hallowed footsteps of his predecessors. This additional applause may also be his, that, walking in their spirit, he has carried it even further than many of the greatest names that hitherto guided him, and has struck the shell of poetry in scenes that had seldom, if ever, been wakened by its melody.

To a certain extent this proceeding has been a novelty, but assuredly not an innovation; it may be new to modern readers, but the foundations of the system of his poetry are as ancient and as venerable as the foundations of the system of the world.

With regard to the result of the perseverance in that system—the productions which Mr. Wordsworth has laid before the world,—if we are not prepared at all times to enter fully into the enjoyment of them, we have only ourselves to blame, and our own insensibility to regret. If, through the eye of a poet, this author receives faint and delicate impressions upon his mind, afterwards transferred upon his paper, in the pleasure of which we are not prepared to participate, it ought to be a subject of lamentation as regards ourselves, and of admiration with regard to him. But, if we are not able to follow all the wanderings of his fancy, if he draws honey from flowers in which we can perceive, with our duller sense, neither fragrance nor flavour, if he, among the inferior and more trifling objects of the creations, discovers subjects that impress some important truth, some moral lesson, or afford some pleasing contemplation, some excitement to soothe sorrow or augment joy, so far we are losers, and so far Nature has endowed him with superior means of enjoyment and happiness. Of this kind are many of his smaller poems; but those who are not capable of entering into their spirit, even those who have most decidedly expressed their aversion to them, have not denied the merits of many of his longer performances, and some have candidly acknowledged the delight they received.

It is not, however, necessary, in speaking of the work now under review, 'the White Doe of Rylstone,' to enter further into this subject, or to dwell upon the justification of what may be deemed the peculiarities of Mr. Wordsworth, because this poem is almost entirely free from them, and we think will be perused by all classes, by all poetical sects, with a pleasure that experiences no drawback by the insertion of passages for which the reader's mind is not prepared. It was written, as the author informs us, in the year 1807, soon after he had made an excursion to the principal scene of action, and is founded upon an event that took place in the twelfth year of the reign of Queen Elizabeth, called *the rising in the North.*

[The historical background of the poem is given.]

In Dr. Percy's 'Collection of Reliques of Poetry' an ancient ballad is given upon this subject, which, to the facts already stated, adds an interesting and natural incident, probably founded in fact. It is this— that Richard Norton, having nine sons, eight of them only consented to take up arms with the father for the Catholic cause; while that the eldest, named Francis, being a Protestant, refused to fight: but, unwilling that his father and brothers should incur danger which he did not share, accompanied them unarmed in their perilous expedition. Mr. Wordsworth has confessedly employed and made most admirable use of this incident.

This addition is a great improvement to the story; and Mr. Wordsworth has included others that much heighten its interest and augment its beauty, particularly that which gives the first title to the poem 'the White Doe of Rylstone.' The foundation for this insertion is contained in Dr. Whitaker's 'History of Craven;' which, after referring to the desolate state of Rylstone and Bolton Priory, not far distant, states that it was a tradition among the aged people of the neighbourhood, that, not long after the dissolution of the monasteries, a white doe continued to make a weekly pilgrimage from Rylstone over the fells of Bolton, and was constantly found in the abbey churchyard during divine service; after the close of which she returned home as regularly as the rest of the congregation. Mr. Wordsworth is a strong and able advocate in favour of the more than half-reasoning affection and sympathy of dumb animals, particularly those of this graceful and poetical species, as may be seen by the poem of 'Hart-leap-well' among his lyrical ballads; and the mode in which he connects this tradition, related by Dr. Whitaker, with the story of the fate of the family of the Nortons, is as follows:—

[The story of the poem is summarized briefly.]

The first canto (there being seven in all) is employed in several very beautiful pieces of descriptive poetry, and in the reflections of various classes of persons on perceiving the white doe as they leave the church.

The second canto goes back to the time when the events occurred, and details the message received by Richard Norton, from the Earls of Northumberland and Westmorland, requiring his aid. The appeal of his eldest son, Francis, is very pathetic.

[Lines 381–97 are quoted.]

He pleads in vain; and, after foretelling the destruction of his race, Francis, unarmed, follows his father, his brothers, and the collected tenantry. In the next canto Norton joins his forces to those of the Earls. A part of the subsequent description of the sire and sons is, perhaps, not to be equalled:

> With feet that firmly pressed the ground
> They stood and girt their father round;

Such was their choice,—no steed will he
Henceforth bestride; triumphantly
He stood upon the verdant sod,
Trusting himself to earth and God.
Rare sight, to embolden and inspire!
Proud was the field of sons and sire,
Of him the most; and sooth to say,
No shape of man in all the array
So graced the sunshine of that day:
The monumental pomp of age
Was with this goodly personage;
A stature undepressed in size,
Unbent, which rather seemed to rise,
In open victory, o'er the weight
Of seventy years to higher height;
Magnific limbs of wither'd state,—
A face to fear and venerate,
Eyes dark and strong, and on his head
Rich locks of silver hair, thick spread,
Which a brown morion half concealed,
Light as a hunter's of the field;
And thus, with girdle round his waist,
Whereon the banner-staff might rest
At need, he stood, advancing high
The glittering floating pageantry.

[The remainder of the poem is summarized briefly, and lines 1188–91, 1294–95, 1331–39, 1470–1502, and 1898–1910 are quoted in the process.]

Thus concludes 'the White Doe of Rylstone,' of which we can scarcely pretend to have given even an imperfect sketch, partly from want of room, and partly (with unfeigned diffidence we say it) from incapacity to estimate worthily a man of Mr. Wordsworth's mind. This feeling is, we are happy to say, becoming more general; and, although perhaps the poem now before us will not contribute to raise him in the admiration of his friends, we doubt whether it will not render him more popular. Some persons may be apt to draw comparisons, but they will be no less injurious to the work than to the man.

Review of Wordsworth's 'The White Doe of Rylstone' and Collected 'Poems' of 1815

Quarterly Review

XIV (Oct. 1815), 201–25. The author was W. R. Lyall, a churchman: see Hill Shine and Helen C. Shine, The Quarterly Review under Gifford *(Chapel Hill, N.C., 1949), p. 49. The issue in which the review appeared was published in March 1816 (ibid., p. 48).*

Of the two publications selected for this article, the latter only can be said to come regularly under our cognizance; the contents of the former having been, for the most part, many years before the public: our attention, therefore, must be principally devoted to the prefatory and post-prefatory essays. The topics which these embrace are in themselves of some importance, and such as our author, from the nature of his pursuits, would seem to be professionally qualified to illustrate. We must, therefore, bespeak the patience of our readers for a few remarks upon some of his opinions; premising that we offer them, not so much in the hope of being able to throw any new light upon the subject, as from a wish to obviate an idea which we suspect has gone abroad, that because we admire the poetical talents of Mr. Wordsworth, we are therefore to be numbered as implicitly entertaining all the tenets of his poetical system.

Among those who are really qualified to judge for themselves in matters of taste, we think that one opinion only is entertained respecting the productions of Mr. Wordsworth,—that they exhibit a mind richly stored with all the materials from which poetry is formed;—elevation of sentiment—tenderness of heart—the truest sensibility for the beauties of nature—combined with extraordinary fervour of imagination, and a most praiseworthy love of simplicity both in thought and language. It would appear, however, upon a first view of the fact, that he has by no means turned these valuable endowments to their greatest advantage. If the business of the poet be to please, Mr. Wordsworth's endeavours have hitherto not met with the most flattering success. He professes, indeed, to be well content;— *neque te ut miretur turba, labores*,[1] is his motto; but even among those with whose applause he declares himself so satisfied, we doubt whether he can number the whole of that class whom Horace was so proud to reckon among his admirers.

It is indeed true, that the productions of our author furnish no very striking proofs of that large and vigorous understanding with which all the writings of the poet just mentioned, as of every other *great* poet, are so strongly impregnated: but neither are the productions of his competitors particularly imposing in this respect: and since they have managed to gain, notwithstanding, such a high place in the public estimation, compared with his own, it seems natural enough that he should be desirous of explaining the reasons for what would appear to be, at first sight, a very mortifying distinction.

Accordingly, in the essay subjoined to the volumes before us, Mr. Wordsworth professes to shew, that a fate similar to his, has in all ages been that of poets greatly endowed with originality of genius; and that the want of contemporary popularity affords a just criterion of a poet's demerits, only in the case of writers whose compositions have evidently been designed to meet the popular taste prevailing at the time. This essay may be considered as forming a supplement to the preface (now re-published) with which a former edition of his poems was accompanied, and in which the general principles upon which he professes to compose, are explained and enforced at considerable length.

With regard to the style in which Mr. Wordsworth writes, we doubt whether it can be greatly praised. There is indeed a raciness about his language, and an occasional eloquence in his manner, which serve to keep the reader's attention alive. But these advantages are more than counteracted by that same ineffectual straining after something beyond plain good sense, which is so unpleasant in much of his poetry. In other respects the comparison is in favour of the latter. Instead of that graceful softness of manner which forms so principal a charm in his poetic effusions, his prose is distinguished by a tone which, in any other

---

[1] 'You must not care for the admiration of the many'. Horace *Satires* i.10.73, trans. E. C. Wickham, *Horace for English Readers* (Oxford, 1903).

person, we should feel ourselves called upon to treat with some little severity. For a writer to protest that he *prides* himself upon the disapprobation of his contemporaries, and considers it as an evidence of the originality of his genius, and an earnest of the esteem in which he will be held by succeeding generations, is whimsical enough, to say the least of it; but Mr. Wordsworth ought, at all events, to be consistent with himself; and since he derives so many auspicious assurances from the opposition which his opinions have met with, he should speak with a little more moderation of those by whom they happen to be opposed. He should remember, moreover, that the public, and those who profess to be the organs of the public voice in these matters, have at least as much right to dislike *his* poetical taste, as he has to dislike *theirs*. If he voluntarily steps forward to make an attack upon the latter, the burthen of proof rests clearly upon him: to be in an ill temper merely because his opponents will not at once surrender at discretion, is surely most unreasonable.

It appears to us, that whatever difference of opinion may be entertained respecting the peculiarities of Mr. Wordsworth's poetical compositions, we might admit, in nearly all their extent, the poetical doctrines which he wishes to introduce, without materially touching upon the questions about which the public are really at issue with him. For example, it is a prominent tenet with him that the *language and incidents of low and rustic life* are better fitted for the purposes of his art, than the language and incidents which we have hitherto been accustomed to meet with in poetry; his reasons are:—

'Because in that condition of life the essential passions of the heart find a better soil in which they can attain maturity, are less under restraint, and speak a plainer and more emphatic language: because in that condition of life our elementary feelings co-exist in a state of greater simplicity, and consequently may be more accurately contemplated, and more forcibly communicated: because the manners of rural life germinate from those elementary feelings, and form the necessary character of rural occupations, are more easily comprehended, and are more durable: and lastly, because in that condition the passions of men are incorporated with the beautiful and permanent forms of nature.'—vol. ii. p. 366.

Now all this may be true, for aught that we know to the contrary; it may be very wrong, in a metaphysical point of view, for a person to have a predilection for other subjects; but the fact obviously is, that people do not resort to poetry for metaphysical instruction; and the question about which Mr. Wordsworth's readers are interested is, whether other subjects do not afford equal or superior pleasure, not whether they throw greater or less light upon the 'elementary feel-ings,' and 'essential passions,' and 'primary laws of our nature.' Let us suppose a person were to express a distaste for the subject of the poem, at vol. i. p. 328, upon a bed of daffodils; it would probably not at all alter his opinion to say that 'the subject is an elementary feeling and simple impression (approaching to the nature of an ocular spectrum) upon the imaginative faculty;' nor will the pleasure which most readers will probably receive from the lines at vol. i. p. 297, with which the 'Poems of the Imagination' are introduced, be at all augmented, by being told—what few would otherwise have guessed—that the poet was describing 'a commutation, or transfer of internal feelings, cooper-ating with internal accidents, to plant for immortality images of sound and sight in the celestial soil of the imagination.'[1] How far poetry, upon the principles of Mr. Wordsworth, is capable of being made subservient to a metaphysical analysis of the human mind, is an inquiry which we apprehend to be quite foreign to our present purpose; the question about which the public are at issue with him is, whether the doctrines which he wishes to establish are likely to open purer or more copious sources of poetical delight than those at which his readers hitherto have drunk.

With respect, then, to the 'primary laws of our nature,' 'elementary feelings,' 'essential passions,' and so forth:—if we are to understand by these words the passions of anger and jealousy, and love and ambition and all the modifications of moral pleasure and pain which it is the appropriate business of poetry to delineate, we are not aware of any good reason which would lead us to suppose that these feelings are not just as frequently and as powerfully excited in such scenes as Homer, Virgil and Milton have chosen, as in those to which Mr. Wordsworth professes to devote his muse. But we are told that in the scenes of 'low and rustic life,' they *co-exist in a state of more simplicity*, may be *more easily comprehended, more accurately contemplated*, and so on. No doubt, in pro-portion as we advance in years, or in station, or in knowledge, our feelings and passions embrace a greater variety of objects, and become more and more complicated and mixed. But although this may be a very sufficient reason why Mr. Wordsworth should prefer subjects taken from low life, it is plainly no reason whatever why his readers should. As in every other production of human intellect, so in poetry; the superior pleasure which one subject affords rather than another, is mainly ascribable to the comparative degree of mental power which

---

[1] The first quotation is from Wordsworth's note to line 21 of 'I wandered lonely as a Cloud' and the second is from the Preface to the *Poems* of 1815.

they may require; and this, it is plain, must be proportioned to the difficulties that are to be overcome, and not, as in the case of our author's favourite subjects, to the facilities which they afford.

These last, unquestionably, are susceptible, in a high degree, of poetical embellishment; and though Mr. Wordsworth is, we think, occasionally somewhat unlucky in the topics which he selects, yet we know not any writer who, upon the whole, has painted them with more pathos and fidelity. In themselves, however, they would not appear to be of the most difficult nature; it requires no extraordinary degree of judgment and penetration to discriminate the broad rough lines by which the characters of people in low life are commonly chalked out; nor can it require, considering the few and simple objects about which their thoughts must necessarily be conversant, any extraordinary force of imagination to enter into their feelings; natural sensibility, acquaintance with their manners, and a love of the scenes in which they pass their lives, are of course indispensable; other auxiliary qualities may be called in to advantage; but for those higher and rarer qualifications, which have their foundations in the understanding, and not in the mere liveliness of a susceptible imagination, we imagine the poet would seldom find occasion.

But Mr. Wordsworth is an advocate, not only for the 'incidents' of 'low and rustic life,' as better suited than any other for poetry, but also for its 'language,' which, on several accounts, he considers as being 'a far more philosophical language than that which is frequently substituted for it by poets.' Now, to talk of one language as being more *philosophical* than another, is, perhaps, not a very philosophical way of speaking; but be it as he supposes; still, we think, he will not deny, that the most convenient language, either for a poet or any other man to make use of, is that by which he can with most precision make himself understood by those to whom he addresses himself. Does our author then write for people in low and rustic life, or for people in high and educated life? If for the former, good; but if for the latter, surely to select a language in which, as he himself partly confesses, vol. ii. p. 390, he necessarily exposes himself to the danger of raising opposite ideas to those which he intended to convey, is paying to mere sounds (be they ever so philosophical) an homage which we can never be brought to believe that they deserve.

It is possible, no doubt, while describing such subjects as Mr. Wordsworth chiefly delights in, to pitch the language in too high a key; and this, perhaps, is a fault which pastoral writers have been too much in the habit of committing. But although we admit that there are some phrases and a sort of diction which a poet cannot, without in some sense violating costume, put into the mouths of characters belonging to a *low and rustic condition of life*, yet to avoid this fault is very different from putting into their mouths, phrases which persons of education have actually banished from their vocabulary. We are told indeed, that the language of 'low and rustic life' should be adopted, 'purified from its real defects,' and 'from all lasting and rational causes of dislike and disgust.' But the truth is, if the language of low life be purified from what *we* should call its *real defects*, it will differ only in copiousness from the language of high life; as to *rational and lasting causes of dislike and disgust*, it is plain that on the subject of language no such causes can, in any instance, be assigned. We suspect that in criticism Mr. Wordsworth feels no great reverence for constituted authorities, or he would, perhaps, have called to mind the lines, beginning

> Multa renascentur quae jam cecidere, cadentque
> Quae nunc sunt in honore vocabula, si volet *Usus*;
> Quem penes arbitrium est, et jus, et norma loquendi.[1]

Language, as every body knows, consists merely of arbitrary signs which stand for whatever it may have pleased custom to enact; and whatever changes may happen among them, are occasioned not by 'rational causes' but by accidental associations of one sort and another, of which, in general, we defy the most profound metaphysician to give any philosophical account. If a poet has the humour of despising them, he has clearly a right to consult his own pleasure upon the subject; but the chances are that he will draw down such a flight of small critics upon his head—and perhaps deservedly—as will, in all probability, soon teach him the greatness of his mistake.

But although we cannot bring ourselves to approve of Mr. Wordsworth's project for substituting the language of 'low and rustic life' in place of that which we are accustomed to meet with in poetry; yet, in many respects, we feel pretty much disposed to coincide with him in disapproving of the latter. We think, with him, that the language of poetry ought to be language really used by men, and constructed upon the same principles as the language of prose. That this cannot be affirmed of that peculiar sort of diction technically called *poetical*, a slight inspection of the poetry which has prevailed in this country since the Restora-

---

[1] 'Many a word long disused will revive, and many now high in esteem will fade, if custom wills it, in whose power lie the arbitrament, the rule and the standard of language.' Horace *Ars Poetica* 70, 72, trans. E. H. Blakeney, *Horace on the Art of Poetry* (London, 1928).

tion will, we think, sufficiently prove. How far Mr. Wordsworth's account of the origin and distinctive character of this artificial phraseology is just and satisfactory, we are, perhaps, not competent to decide; as far, however, as we were able to enter into his meaning, his observations upon the subject seemed in general well-grounded. To us it appears, that this diction does not essentially consist in any particular choice or arrangement of the words; for, to take the instance quoted by our author, Gray's sonnet to West, with the exception of the 6th, 7th, 8th, 13th and 14th lines, consists, as he justly observes, 'almost entirely of this diction, though not of the worst kind.' If, however, Mr. Wordsworth will refer to the remaining lines, he will immediately perceive that they do not consist 'of the language of passion wrested from its proper use;' perhaps the contrary is the fault which may be found with them; neither are the words inverted from their natural order, or such as, taken separately, would seem to belong to any particular condition of life; but the sun is 'the golden fire of reddening Phoebus;' the song of the birds is their 'amorous descant;' the grass of the fields is their 'green attire;' the produce of the earth is its 'wonted tribute;' and so forth.—Now, as addressed to our *reason*, all these expressions are perfectly intelligible; and supposing poetry to be nothing more than the art of paraphrasing our ideas, this sort of diction may furnish room for the display of much fancy and ingenuity. It is, however, manifest, that this indirect way of signifying things, is not the language of present feeling; and that the effect of it is to fix the imagination rather upon the real or fanciful analogies which objects may seem to possess among one another than upon the particular relations in which they actually stand to us. In those subjects in which Pope and Dryden chiefly excelled, where the poet addresses himself to the fancy and understanding rather than to the heart, we know not but that the method of versification to which we are alluding, may produce a good effect; indeed, in one point of view, it would seem to be that which nature points out. But when the business of the poet is to present us with an image of the scenes and objects among which we are placed, not in abstract description, but as they relate immediately to our feelings, his expressions cannot, as we conceive, be too free from rhetorical ornament. That the exclusion, or at least a more moderate use of this, need not interfere with the utmost degree of strength, nor the most refined harmony and elegance of language, is fully proved by many passages in the writings of our old and excellent dramatists; and indeed it is doing Mr. Wordsworth himself nothing more than justice to say, that in his happier hours of inspiration, when his theories and eccentricities happen to be laid aside, no writer of the day seems to understand

D

better the exact key in which the language of this last kind of poetry should be pitched. Unfortunately these hours are not so frequent with Mr. Wordsworth, as the lovers of poetry could wish; and upon the causes of this we shall now trouble our readers with a few remarks, which will, perhaps, assist us to explain the reasons why his popularity is less—we will not say than he deserves, for this would be to pre-judge the question—but less than such talents as he possesses have commonly conferred.

It is impossible to take up the works of Mr. Wordsworth without remarking that, instead of employing his pen upon subjects of durable and general interest, he devotes himself almost exclusively to the de-lineation of himself and his own peculiar feelings, as called forth by objects incidental to the particular kind of life he leads. Now, although this be a plan apparently contrived to gratify the pleasure which poets, as our author tells us, take in their 'own passions and volitions,' rather than any curiosity which the reader, generally speaking, can be supposed to feel upon the subject, yet, in common cases, it is productive of no very *positive* inconvenience. Poets, as well as other people, feel, for the most part, pretty much alike; so that what is true with respect to any individual, will commonly be' true with respect to mankind at large, under the same circumstances. As long as the feelings of the poet are founded on such occasions as ordinarily give rise to them, although the subjects of his effusions may be par-ticular, yet the interest and the application of them will be, to a great degree, general. But the fact is, that the habits of Mr. Wordsworth's life are not more different from those of people in general, than are the habits of his mind; so that not only the incidents which form the sub-jects of his poetry, are such as the greater part of his readers take much less interest in, than he imagines, but the feelings, moreover, with which he usually contemplates them are often such as hardly any per-son whatever can participate.

For example: a sensibility for the beauties of nature is, no doubt, a highly commendable quality, and to illustrate it is, we admit, the great business of descriptive poetry; nevertheless, however warmly we may sympathize with Mr. Wordsworth in his rapturous admiration of the great and striking features of nature;—though we cannot but think that even on this subject, his feelings are tuned much too high for the sobriety of truth;—yet when we are called upon to feel *emotions which lie too deep for tears even with respect to the meanest flower that blows, to cry for nothing, like Diana in the fountain,* over every ordinary object and every common-place occurrence that may happen to cross our way, all communion of feeling between the poet and those who know no more of poetry than their own experience and an acquaintance with the best models will bestow, is necessarily broken off. But it would be difficult to convey a just idea of the extent to which the peculiar habits of Mr. Wordsworth's mind have affected the character of his writings by citing particular examples. Our readers, however, will probably be able to judge for themselves, when they learn that, instead of looking upon this sort of exuberant sensibility to which we allude as a disadvantage, he regards it as a qualification of singular value; and formally places it, under the technical name of *poetic*, which he always distinguishes from merely *human* sensibility, among what he considers as being the characteristical attributes of the poetical character.

Our author justly observes, that 'poets do not write for poets alone, but for men. Unless, therefore, we are advocates for that admiration which depends upon ignorance, and that pleasure which arises from hearing what we do not understand, the poet must descend from his supposed height, and in order to excite rational sympathy, he must express himself as other men express themselves.' vol. i. p. 384. Nothing can be more true; but surely Mr. Wordsworth cannot but perceive, that if a poet, in order to excite rational sympathy, must *express* himself as other men express themselves; by a still stronger reason it would seem to follow that *he must descend from his supposed height*, and *feel* as other men feel.

Nothing is more easy to conceive than a sense of vision infinitely more acute than that with which it has been thought necessary to endow the human race. Nevertheless, however advantageous the gift of such a superiority might be considered, in a general point of view, yet it would really be inconvenient to a person desirous of turning painter; because, admitting that his pictures might be ever so admirable upon a supposition that other people's organs of sight were constructed upon the same principles as his own, yet they would clearly be of no value whatever except to himself, if we suppose the contrary to be the fact. It is precisely the same in the case of poetry; the merit of a poet does not essentially consist, as is sometimes supposed, in the possession of sensibilities different from or more intense than those of other people, but in the talent of awakening in their minds the particular feelings and emotions with which the various objects of his art are naturally associated. For this purpose he must, of course, consult his own feelings; it is, however, only so far as he knows them to be in unison with those of mankind at large, that he can safely trust himself to their direction; because, if they preserve not the same relative subordination and the same proportions among each other that they possess in the minds of people in general, it is plain that his composition must appear to the greater part of his readers like pictures constructed upon false principles of perspective, and whatever resemblance they may bear to objects as they appeared to his own mind, may bear no more resemblance to objects as they appear in nature than the fantastical devices of an Indian screen.

We are far from meaning to assert, by way of a general proposition, that the merit of a poem is to be measured by the number of its admirers; different classes of composition, no doubt, are adapted to different classes of readers: whatever it requires extraordinary powers of mind to produce, it must require some corresponding superiority of mind to understand; and we think Mr. Wordsworth intimates somewhere that this is partly the predicament in which his poetry stands. We shall not dispute upon this point; nevertheless we may remark that, although the above consideration will afford a satisfactory explanation of Quintilian's observation, that the Iliad is projected upon so vast a scale, as to require considerable greatness of mind even to comprehend its merits; yet this way of evading the dilemma to which Mr. Wordsworth's indifferent success has reduced him, will hardly apply to his case, upon a supposition at least, that his poetry really is what it professes to be: because, when a poet's avowed object is merely to trace in the plain and intelligible language of every-day life, those 'great and simple affections,' those 'elementary feelings' and 'essential passions' which are assumed, by definition, to be common to all men alike,—it would seem but reasonable to expect that it would find readers in every class of society. But then the poet must be supposed truly to perform what he promises; his poetry must not contain a mere portraiture of his own mind in those points in which he differs from other people, and with respect to which none but his particular friends can be supposed to feel an interest; but an image of human nature in general.

Our familiar matter-of-fact way of talking about an art which Mr. Wordsworth seems to think belongs rather to the divine than to human nature, will not, we fear, tend to impress him with a very favourable opinion of our profoundness;—mais la vérité est comme il peut; truth is as it happens, and not always exactly as men of fine imaginations wish it to be.—Accordingly, although we would not choose to be classed among those to whom our author alludes, 'who converse as gravely about a *taste* for poetry, as they express it, as if it were a thing as indifferent as a taste for rope-dancing,' yet we candidly confess, that we see nothing at all wonderful or mysterious about the art; nor, if we may judge from experience, any reason to suppose that it requires greater or more uncommon talents than any other among the higher productions of human intellect. In reply to this, Mr. Wordsworth will probably place us in that unhappy sub-division of critics, in which, he says, 'are found those who are too petulant to be passive to a genuine poet, and too feeble to grapple with him: men, who take upon them to report of the course *he* holds, whom they are utterly unable to accompany—confounded if he turn quickly upon the wing, dismayed if he soar steadily into "the region;" men of palsied imaginations and indurated hearts.'—vol. i. p. 348. All we can say is, that whenever Mr. Wordsworth's own flights are through 'the region' of truth and nature, and sober sense, we accompany him with pleasure; but when he penetrates into the *terra Australis* beyond, then, indeed, our inclination to continue of the party, as well as our ability, leaves us.

Having thus stated our opinions at length, upon the critical dissertations, we shall proceed to give our readers some idea of the poem.

The 'White Doe of Rylstone' is so out-of-the-way a production, in many respects, that we are not sure but it would be wiser in us gravely to 'shake the head' at such a ballad sort of poem, than to risk our authority with the public by recommending it to them as a beautiful performance. It is not, indeed, free from the singularities which arise from the particular point of view in which Mr. Wordsworth likes to look at things; but in the present instance, they fall in not unhappily with the whimsical nature of the subject, and give a tone of colouring to the poem, which, however peculiar, is far from being unpleasing. As a mere narrative, it does not possess much interest; the story is told, as it were, in scraps; a few prominent scenes are selected, and the circumstances which connect them left pretty much to the reader's imagination; and after all, instead of a denouement, we have merely the explanation of a certain strange phenomenon which had puzzled rather than interested our curiosity.

That the poem contains many beauties—exquisite tenderness of feeling, and often great happiness combined with the utmost simplicity of expression, will abundantly appear from the extracts which we shall make; but then, in other parts, it is just as much distinguished for obscurity and flatness; and throughout there is a something, not only about the rhythm and the language, but also about the turn of the thoughts and sentiments, which often left us at a loss to determine whether the hesitation which we felt, even as to being pleased, proceeded from mere fastidiousness on our part, or from a mistaken taste in Mr. Wordsworth. The poem, we admit, is written with simplicity; and so far as this is the indigenous growth of his own mind, it has our warmest praises. But Mr. Wordsworth's love of this first quality of all good poetry has made him resort to artificial means for producing it;

so that instead of the polished simplicity which belongs to an age of so much refinement as the present, he affects that rude kind which the writings of our forefathers exhibit, and which expressed the genuine character of the times. Now, be the merits of this last what it may when met with in our old ballads, it is plain, that in the present advanced stage of society, it can never be *natural* to a man like Mr. Wordsworth; in *his* writings, the manner which he studies is necessarily an affectation; and be the imitation ever so successful, a discriminating taste still perceives a something which is different from the native flavour of original simplicity. *Sic enim est faciendum*, says Cicero, in a section of his book De Officiis, which we recommend to Mr. Wordsworth's perusal, *ut contra universum naturam nihil contendamus; ea tamen conservata, propriam naturam sequamur; ut etiam si sint alia graviora atque meliora, tamen nos studia nostrae naturae regula metiamur.—Nec tam enitendum est, ut bona quae nobis non data sunt sequamur, quam ut vitia fugiamus.*[1]

At Bolton Priory, in Yorkshire, it seems, there is a tradition about a White Doe, who on every Sabbath-day, during the time of divine service, used to pay a visit to the church-yard; the problem which the poem proposes to solve, is, why the White Doe should do this? Mr. Wordsworth satisfactorily explains it, by means of an old ballad, in Percy's Reliques, called the 'Rising of the North;' and containing a succinct account of the total destruction which fell upon the Nortons, an ancient family of Yorkshire, in consequence of their share in that fatal act of rebellion.

The first Canto opens with the introduction of the 'White Doe;' and she is ushered in with some very pleasing lines.

[The first two Cantos are briefly summarized and lines 1–30, 49–62, 73–74, 126–47, 381–97, 527–33, and 542–93 are quoted.]

These lines (with which the second Canto closes) in spite of some expressions which made our critical nerves *wince* a little, afford no unfavourable specimen of that peculiar tenderness of manner for which we think the poem is chiefly remarkable.

The third Canto opens with spirit.

[Lines 594–620 and 715–52 are quoted with interlocking details.

---

[1] 'For we must so act as not to oppose the universal laws of human nature, but, while safeguarding those, to follow the bent of our own particular nature; and even if other careers should be better and nobler, we may still regulate our own pursuits by the standard of our own nature. . . . And we need not strive so hard to attain to points of excellence that have not been vouchsafed to us as to correct the faults we have.' Cicero *De Officiis* i.31, trans. Walter Miller, *Cicero: De Officiis* (Cambridge, Mass., 1913).

The description of the Nortons in lines 715–52 is said to have 'much merit'.]

The fourth Canto brings the reader back to Rylstone Hall. The description, with which it opens, of the old mansion by moonlight, is among the most successful passages of the poem. The sober tone of the language is well suited to the repose which belongs to the subject.

[Lines 938–57, 962–72, 981–1019, 1302–11 and 1501–23 are quoted, and Cantos Four through Six are summarized briefly. Emily's musings and prayer in Canto Four are 'told with considerable pathos'. The execution scene in Canto Five 'is described with considerable effect'.]

The above description [lines 1501–23] is not without poetry. We have, however, quoted it, chiefly because it relates an important circumstance in the story; in other respects, we fear, the language is too quaint to be generally pleasing.

Previously to the commencement of the seventh and last Canto, the story makes a pause.

[Canto Seven is summarized briefly, and lines 1629–64, 1743–50, 1811–25, and 1879–1900 are quoted. The description of the attachment of Emily and the doe in lines 1743–50 is said to be 'very pleasing'.]

Our readers now know why the 'White Doe' came from Rylstone to Bolton Priory every Sabbath day during the time of divine service. Whether the explanation will not, upon the whole, disappoint the curiosity which its mysterious appearance excited, we shall not attempt to determine: more particularly as the decision of the question will not very greatly affect the merits of the work, considered as a poem, however it may affect its popularity, considered merely as a story. In the former point of view, we think that our extracts will fully justify the praises which we have bestowed upon it; but we have also said, that it possesses great blemishes, and it now becomes the unpleasant part of our duty to instance a few particular examples.

Mr. Wordsworth, as our readers must have perceived, aims at great simplicity of language; but even supposing no objections to exist against the particular sort of which he is ambitious, still we must be permitted to observe, that mere simplicity of language is no merit at all, if it be purchased at the expense of perspicuity; and this is a price which our author is continually paying for it. We dislike minute criticism, not only for Horace's reason, of *non ego paucis*, &c.[1] but

---

[1] *Non ego paucis* [*offendar maculis*]: 'I will not be offended by a few slight faults. Horace *Ars Poetica* 351.

because we know that in the hands of unfair critics it is an engine by which a writer may be made to appear any thing they please; nevertheless as an example of what we mean, take the following passage: Mr. Wordsworth means to say, that Emily sate upon a primrose bank, neglecting outward ornaments, and having in her countenance a melancholy which seemed not to belong to the sweetness and gentleness of its natural expression; which is thus laboriously signified:—

> 'Upon a primrose bank—
> ——————————————————————
> Behold her like a Virgin Queen
> Neglecting in imperial state
> These outward images of fate,
> And carrying inward a serene
> And perfect sway, through many a thought
> Of chance and change, that hath been brought
> To the subjection of a holy
> But stern and rigorous melancholy!
> The like authority, with grace
> Of awfulness, is in her face—
> There hath she fixed it; yet it seems
> To o'er-shadow by no native right
> That face which cannot lose the gleams,
> Lose utterly the tender gleams,
> Of gentleness and meek delight
> And loving-kindness ever bright.'—p. 113.

Surely Mr. Wordsworth cannot need to be told, that such an unaccountable way of expressing himself as this, notwithstanding the humbleness of the style, is directly the reverse of simple. This, perhaps, is an extreme instance; but the fault is of perpetual recurrence. Again, with respect to his words themselves; we will not say that they are often too familiar, because we suspect Mr. Wordsworth does not regard that as a fault: but the truth is, that in the senses to which he applies them, they are often absolutely devoid of meaning—The following lines really would seem to have been written by a 'Lady of Quality.'

> 'The day is placid in its going
> To a lingering motion bound;
> Like a river in its flowing;
> Can there be a softer sound?'—p. 11.

Speaking of the Doe, wandering through sun and shade,

> 'What *harmonious pensive changes*
> Wait upon her as she ranges
> Round and through the hall of state!'

In this last quotation, we perceive the kind of impression which Mr. Wordsworth meant to convey; but in the following, we are equally at a loss to understand either the sense in which he uses his words, or the propriety of the sentiment which he intends them to express.

> 'For *deepest sorrows* that *aspire*
> Go *high*, no *transport* ever higher.'

But it is unnecessary to accumulate instances of the extraordinary want of precision with which Mr. Wordsworth is in the habit of expressing himself; he seems to think that if words only have a good character, and mean something pleasant when by themselves, whether they have any relation to one another in a sentence is a matter of no great importance. Hence it is, for we can no otherwise account for it, that Emily is always called the 'consecrated Emily,' and that every pleasant thought is a 'dream,' a 'vision,' or a 'phantom,' just as it happens. But it is irksome to expatiate upon particular faults; a task which we the more willingly abridge, because they are more than redeemed by that true feeling of poetry with which the poem is per-vaded. In this, as in any other line of poetry to which he may dedicate himself, Mr. Wordsworth has something to learn and a good deal to unlearn; whether he will endeavour to do either at our suggestion, is, perhaps, more than doubtful; he seems to be *monitoribus asper*,[1] in a degree which is really unreasonable; however, this is his business; all we can say is, that if he is not now or should not be hereafter, a favourite with the public, he can have nobody to blame but himself.

---

[1] 'Impatient of reproof.' Horace *Ars Poetica* 163.

Reviews of Wordsworth's 'Peter Bell'

European Magazine

LXXV (May 1819), 445–48. The reviewer is unknown, but his initials are given at the end of the review as 'J.B.'

The present period is rich in the master-spirits of poetry—perhaps at no time have more brilliant names adorned the poetical annals of our country than in our day—Even the age of Elizabeth, the Augustan era of our poetry in point of number and excellence, cannot be said to have surpassed our latter times.

In the first rank of the bards of our own day, Mr. Wordsworth may justly be classed. With that boldness which is the characteristic of genius, he has chosen a path rarely trodden by poets, and has shed over his uninviting and apparently sterile subjects an elegance and brilliancy which nothing but the energetic influence of such talents as he possesses could have communicated.

In his choice of these subjects, he seems rather to have been actuated by the discriminating influence of his own judgment, than the desire of gaining popularity; for with his high poetical feelings, it cannot be doubted, that had he chosen the more common subjects on which verse is employed, he would have succeeded better in obtaining the applause of the less reflecting part of his readers:—but an enthusiastic admirer of *Nature* in all her forms, he appears to be so completely devoted to his passion, that he despises the common machinery of poetry, and trusting to the inspiration of "the Goddess of his idolatry," floats gently down the current of his imaginations, and supplies by the naked beauty of his Muse the absence of all ornament,

'Nuda si, ma contenta.'[1]

---

[1] 'Naked, yes, but happy.'

His is the poetry of solitude, the very eloquence of the inanimate objects of Nature, and revives in our minds the impressions made by her beauties in those days of happy youth, when every breath of heaven, every flower which bloomed beneath our feet, spoke to the soul in a tone which awoke a vibrating chord of feeling. It penetrates the callousness which an intercourse with the world, and all its intricacies and disappointments, have collected round the heart. It is like the breathing silence of a summer's evening, where all is distinct and invigorating, but solemn, still, and gentle.

He sees with microscopic eyes the numerous beautiful productions which present themselves too frequently unheeded to the cursory observer, and exhibits with minute discrimination the harmonies which have lost their influence from their frequent occurrence; like a stranger in the land, he points out excellencies and discovers combinations which the denizens had never beheld, or to which their frequent familiarity had deadened their admiration.

The tale is preceded by a prologue, in which the poet takes occasion, in a playful and ingenious manner, to point out the inclination of his genius, which is under the form of a flying boat. After a long excursive range into regions of air and fancy, the poet wishes to return to his dear earth.

[Lines 131–50 are quoted.]

The substance of the tale is the most simple in its organization that can be imagined; its intent is to paint the effect produced on the mind of a reprobate vagabond by the mute force of solitude and of natural objects. The gradual progress from the first softening impulse to reflection on his guilty courses, thence to remorse, and finally to repentance, is developed in the most pathetic and masterly manner.

[Lines 206–07, 241–80, 286–95, 311–15, 369–70, 384–85, 436–40, 496–500, 526–30, 561–65, 886–90, 901–30, 954–60, and 1051–55 are quoted, with connecting links given in prose. The effect on Peter of the discovery of the body (lines 526–30) is said to be 'admirably described', and the widow's distress is said to be 'painted in touching and powerful colours'.]

The most eloquent and pathetic description is reserved to the last part of the poem, and forms a climax to the whole no less admirable in the idea than felicitous in the execution—it is the return of the son of the dead man, who has been seeking him in vain.

> 'But he who deviously hath sought
> His father through the lonesome woods,

Hath sought proclaiming to the ear
Of night his inward grief and fear—
He comes—escap'd from fields and floods;

With weary pace is drawing nigh,
He sees the ass—and nothing living
Had ever such a fit of joy
As had this little orphan boy,
For he had no misgiving!

Towards the gentle ass he springs,
And up about his neck he climbs;
In loving words he talks to him,
He kisses, kisses face and limb,—
He kisses him a thousand times!

This Peter sees, while in the shade
He stood beside the cottage door:
And Peter Bell, the ruffian wild,
Sobs loud, he sobs even like a child,
"Oh! God, I can endure no more!" '

Let the frivolous scoff at and the hard-hearted despise such poems as this; but we do not envy that man his strength of mind who reads Peter Bell without being beguiled of tears, or who rises from the perusal without the finer and more amiable feelings of his nature being strongly excited. J.B.

Examiner

May 2, 1819, pp. 282–83. The author was Leigh Hunt: see Edmund Blunden, ed., Leigh Hunt's 'Examiner' Examined (*London, 1928*), *p. 92.*

This is another didactic little horror of Mr. Wordsworth's, founded on the bewitching principles of fear, bigotry, and diseased impulse. *Peter Bell* is a potter, who has rambled about the country, and been as wilful, after his fashion, as any Lake poet. His tastes indeed are different. He sees no beauty in mere solitariness, and is not alive to the abstract sentiment of a ditch; neither does he dance with daffodils. He is, in fact, a little over social, chusing rather to dance with gypsies, and having had no less than a dozen wives. He is like the Friar in *Chaucer*; he

————*Will* drinke the liquor of the vine,
And have a joly wenche in everie towne.

One day, however, losing himself in a wood, he meets with a stray jack-ass, who lies upon the ground by a river's side, and looks mysterious. *Peter* has a royal contempt for inferior animals (not that the Poet so words it, but such is the fact), and belabours the poor jack-ass in a dreadful manner, till it groans and then looks into the water, and then at *Peter*. He looks in his turn, and in the water what does he see? This is a question which the Poet himself asks his Readers, putting a number of samples of horrid sights, by way of help to their memories. Of course they cannot answer him; but it turns out, that one thing at least which *Peter* did see, was the corpse of a man newly drowned, the owner of the jack-ass. The animal's attachment makes the first impression on *Peter's* imagination; he sees him inclined to shew him the way to the deceased's house, and accordingly rides him thither, where he finds the widow and children bitterly lamenting. For the final impression resulting from this scene he is also prepared, as he rode along, by the sound of a Damnation Sermon, which a Methodist is vociferating from a chapel. The consequence is, that after a melancholy of eleven months, he is thoroughly reformed, and has a proper united sense of hare-bells and hell-fire.

Now all this, we conceive, is as weak and vulgar in philosophy as can be. It is the philosophy of violence and hopelessness. It is not teaching ignorance, but scourging it. If Mr. Wordsworth means to say that fear may occasionally do good, we grant it; but we say that nine times out of ten, it does harm, and is likely to make a man's after-thoughts desperate and resentful, and still oftener selfish and servile. The very hope of such things as Methodism is founded in hopelessness, and that too of the very worst sort,—namely, hopelessness of others, and salvation for itself. *Peter Bell* is an ill-taught blackguard. There is his whole history. The growth of such persons must be prevented by good and kind teaching. If they are suffered to grow up without it, and are then to be dosed with horrors proportioned to the strength of the disease inflicted on them, they have as much right to complain as any that suffer from them. It is no more incumbent on them to think themselves objects of God's anger (thus giving them a bad idea of God, as well as man) than it is on the most didactic of the Lake Poets to think himself wise and virtuous. The good old fable of the son who bit off his mother's ear at the gallows, is, and will ever remain, worth a thousand such stories.

We are really and most unaffectedly sorry to see an excellent poet like Mr. Wordsworth returning, in vulgar despair, to such half-witted prejudices; especially when we meet with such masterly descriptions as the following. It is a portrait as true in the colouring as any of Mr. Crabbe's, and deeper thoughted.

89

[Lines 291–320 are quoted.]

But what is to be said to the following Methodistical nightmare? It is part of the questions of which we spoke, when *Peter* sees the spectacle in the water.

> Is it a fiend that to a stake
> Of fire his desperate self is tethering?
> Or stubborn spirit doom'd to yell
> In solitary ward or cell,
> Ten thousand miles from all his brethren?
>
> Is it a party in a parlour?
> Cramm'd just as they on earth were cramm'd—
> Some sipping punch, some sipping tea,
> But, as you by their faces see,
> All silent and all damn'd!

What pretty little hopeful imaginations for a reforming philosopher! Is Mr. Wordsworth in earnest or is he not, in thinking that his fellow-creatures are to be damned? If he is, who is to be made really better or more comfortable in this world, by having such notions of another? If not, how wretched is this hypocrisy?

Mr. Wordsworth, in the course of his mystic musings on *Peter*, has the following passage on a jackass's grin:—

> Let them whose voice can stop the clouds—
> Whose cunning eye can see the wind—
> Tell to a curious world the cause
> Why, making here a sudden pause,
> The Ass turn'd round his head—and *grinn'd*.
>
> Appalling process!—I have mark'd
> The like on heath—in lonely wood,
> And, verily, have seldom met
> A spectacle more hideous—yet
> It suited Peter's present mood.

Pray admire the way in which the poet first begs the question about a meaning in the ass's grin, and then calls upon those who 'can see the wind' to disprove it. Surely the burden of the proof lies upon the ass's worthy spectator. We refer him however, if he still makes his call, to the *Learned Pig*.[1]

[1] A trained pig, the discussion about which amused Dr Johnson. See Boswell's *Life of Johnson*, ed. G. B. Hill and revised by L. F. Powell (Oxford, 1934), IV, 373–74.

Yet it is in this morbid spirit that Mr. Wordsworth writes, for the benefit of the world!

The poem is dedicated in an odd shy way, that has any thing but the look of sincerity, to 'Robert Southey, Esq. P.L.', that is to say, (for Mr. Wordsworth has left it unexplained) not *Precious Looby*, but *Poet Laureat*. It has a Proem also, which the author thinks it necessary to inform us was written some years back,—about an aerial living Boat which he can ride if he chuses about the upper regions, but declines so doing for the benefit of the lower. There are fine passages in it, but Mr. Wordsworth should never affect vivacity. It leads him to expose himself in such unwieldy levities as these—

> There's something in a flying horse,
> And something in a huge balloon;
> But through the clouds I'll never float
> Until I have a little boat,
> Whose shape is like the crescent-moon,
>
> And now I *have* a little boat,
> In shape a very crescent-moon, &c.

The pamphlet concludes with three sonnets on some of Mr. Westall's landscapes. The first is a fine one, though running off into the old vein. The conclusion of one of the others is very melancholy, and would let us into the secret of Mr. Wordsworth's philosophy, if nothing else did. He forsakes the real cause of the world, and then abuses what he has injured. And yet this is he who would make us in love with the visible creation!

> Vain earth!—false world! Foundations must be laid
> In Heav'n; for, mid the wreck of is and was,
> Things incomplete and *purposes betrayed*
> Make sadder transits o'er truth's mystic glass
> Than noblest objects utterly decayed.

Alas! Alas for the *ci-devant* patriots, and *soi-disant* philosophers!—We happen to write this article on the First of May; and thanks to greater poets than Mr. Wordsworth, and to the nature whom he so strangely recommends, can enjoy the beautiful season on earth, without thinking the less hopefully of heaven.

British Critic

2d ser. XI (June 1819), 584–603. The reviewer is unknown.

The sentiments with which we regard Mr. Wordsworth as a poet, have been long before the public, in one of our earliest numbers; and a fuller consideration of his writings leaves us still satisfied with the opinions we there expressed. We think that there is no one of the present day, and none but the few giants of preceding ages, who have excelled him in some of his productions; in these and in parts of others he has displayed a splendour and purity of diction, a force, and skilful harmony of measure, with a depth, a truth, a tenderness, and a solemn sublimity of sentiment, which in their union remind us forcibly of the happiest, and most golden moments of the immortal Petrarch. Competent judges will not complain of this praise as exaggerated; and they only, who are miserably ignorant of the capabilities of a simple style, or (to speak more correctly) of the meaning of the term simplicity in style, will be surprized to hear us make mention of a diction which they have been accustomed to hear characterised as fit only for the mouths of nurses and infants. But without entering into that argument, which is foreign to our present purpose, we will satisfy ourselves with opening a single volume as it lies before us, and recommending those who doubt *the fact*, to the perusal of Ruth, or an exquisite little poem, beginning, 'Three years she grew in sun and shower.'[1] If they have formed their notions of simplicity in style from the pages of modern criticism, we can promise them at least the pleasure of a surprise from the perusal of these poems.

Still in our considerations of what Mr. Wordsworth might have been from what he sometimes is, we confess, regretfully, that he seems to us to have failed; not merely failed in the acquisition of present popularity, which he justly values at a very low rate, (for to the poet, beyond all other writers, the favourable judgment of an artificial and fashion-mongering age, offers but a doubtful assurance of real and abiding fame,) but also in our opinion he has not laid grounds for his permanent and unambiguous rank as an English Classic so high, as his peculiar powers, and the meritorious study which he has bestowed in the cultivation of them would have led us to anticipate for him. In every age, so long as our language be intelligible, whether living or dead, Wordsworth will have enthusiastic admirers, and to go a step farther, there will always be among them such admirers as a poet may with reason be most proud of; but we are much in error if in any age the

[1] [Lyrical Ballads, vol. ii 101, 136. 4th Edit.—Reviewer's note.]

ablest of those admirers will be able satisfactorily to answer the objections urged against him by candid and feeling readers of a different persuasion. We say this, reasoning partly from our own feelings, but still more from those of the ablest and fairest judges whom we have been able to consult; we scarcely ever met with a single person, whose opinion on the subject we valued, and who was open to express it, that could say he had read any whole poem of Wordsworth's composition, longer than a mere sonnet, without being obliged to get over, and subdue, in some part of it, offensive and disturbing feelings; to forget something that shocked his taste, and checked that full current of admiration, which the remainder excited; the latter feeling perhaps after all predominated, yet the mind was left in a state of incomplete satisfaction.

We are ourselves warm, very warm admirers of Wordsworth; yet if our opinion be worth asking, we must give it nearly in the words which we have written above. This is a fact, of which those who 'care for such things,' will consider it worthy of inquiry to ascertain the causes; and as we have never, we believe, attempted to develope them, though perhaps they may be deduced from our former reasoning, we will take the opportunity which Peter Bell affords us, to say a few words upon it. We see no cause for departing from the account which we have before given of the principles, on which Mr. Wordsworth's poetical system is built; they seem to us to be two in number, with an important corollary deducible from them; we perfectly agree in the truth and importance of the two first, and we are precluded from denying the abstract truth, though we doubt of the practical expediency of the last. The principles are, first, that 'whatsoever material or temporary exists before our senses, is capable of being associated in our minds with something spiritual and eternal;' and, secondly, that it is the business of the poet to see all things with a view to this capability of association, and to familiarize the process to his own, and to his reader's mind; the corollary is, that if all things are equally capable of the process, and in the availing itself of that capability, the true and essential excellence of poetry consists, then the commonest external thing, the most every day occurrence of life, or the meanest appearance of nature is equally capable of being made the ground-work or subject of poetry with the noblest and most uncommon.

We have said that these principles are true; on such subjects there is always danger of writing in a way which may seem mystical to many readers; we would earnestly desire to avoid this except at the expence of truth. As surely then as every human body contains within it an intellectual soul, so surely, we hold, does every thing external, animate and inanimate, *bear reference* to things internal and immaterial, which reference becomes apparent, and is brought as it were into action by the powers of analogy and association, in feeling acute and imaginative, that is to say, in poetical minds. The simplest truth sometimes assumes a solemn air, when formally announced, and such we fear may be the case with the present; but our proposition less regularly put is merely this, that every external object is capable of exciting in a poetical mind some analogous internal idea, and as a beautiful and irresistible proof of the truth of this we would refer our readers to Boyle's Occasional Reflections, where they will find the noblest, and most poetical train of thoughts often deduced from what might otherwise have seemed the most unpromising and unproductive ground-work. Admitting the truth of this proposition, it is clear, beyond dispute, that the internal idea to which the external object gives rise, is by far the more important of the two, considered either as the subject of communication or reflection; to take up our former comparison it is as the soul to the body of that from which it springs, and the poet or the painter, whose representation of externals fails to excite in minds sufficiently sensible the proper internal association, fails precisely in the noblest, and most essential part of his duty, and neglects to draw from things without the more important meaning and lesson which they are capable of conveying from within.

These principles then are not only true, but so far as poetry itself may be considered as one among many engines bestowed upon man by God for the improvement of his moral nature, no less than the mere adornment of his earthly existence, they must undoubtedly be ranked among moral, and highly important truths. Nor if we look at poetry merely as a source of intellectual pleasure, can we doubt that these principles are in that point of view equally considerable. We will not affirm that no pleasure is derivable from a merely exact delineation of any scene of nature or art, but we are sure that it is lame and poor to that vivid, and, as it were, electric delight, which the mind receives from a description, acting, not so much by itself, and in finished details, as by rousing the creative power within, and enabling it to see in more perfect beauty that which is only sketched, and faintly traced by the describer. It is not indeed easy to ascertain comparative quantities of pleasure; we may safely, however, appeal to the lovers of poetry for the truth of our last assertion: they will find it illustrated and proved in every page of our greatest poets; it is hardly possible to read a single description of Milton's, which does not contain some one or more words, the key notes, as it were, of the association, giving life to the whole passage, and limiting, not indeed the precise train, but the general direction of the correspondent thoughts and images which arise in the reader's mind.

Simple and self-evident as these propositions now are to ourselves, they were certainly lost sight of by the majority of our intermediate poets from the restoration down to a late period; laborious and unimpassioned description clothed in a conventional set of terms, and a language artificial, and often grossly misapplied, were substituted for the natural and individual, though highly cultivated, and highly raised poetry, which had gone before. So far then as our author revived, enforced, and exemplified these principles, so far as he manfully protested against, and very ingeniously demonstrated, the abuses of modern poetic diction by the indiscriminate and conventional use of those terms, metaphors, and figures, which had their merit in ancient poetry, from the propriety and dramatic truth of their application, so far as he evinced that it was as absurd to make passion and imagination speak the language of poetical *convention* as it would be to confine them to the terms of the schools or the courts; thus far he is entitled to our highest praises, and our warmest thanks; he by so doing unfettered the tongue of the Muse, and replaced in her hand the sceptre of power.

But when we come to the practical consequences which he has always maintained, and too often exemplified, we must in honesty hold a more measured language, and admit, that we see in them the excesses, from which no manliness or strength of mind seems able to guard the reviver of an old, or the inventor of a new system. We have said that we cannot deny the abstract truth of his corollary; if it be true that all things are capable of the process, and that in pursuing the process lies the true business of the poet, then any thing, that which is low as well as that which is high, is capable of being the subject of poetry. We grant it, and we grant no more; Wordsworth, as it appears to us, has advanced one step farther, and in that step the fallacy lies; he has substituted the words 'more fit for' in the place of 'capable of,' and has therein committed the same error which a statuary would, who, because all stone was capable of the process, in the performance of which his art lay, should therefore choose to execute his groups in granite, rather than in Parian marble. Wordsworth might have been well content simply to have established the truth of his proposition; he must have well known that merely as abstract truth, it was not so unimportant, as ignorant men would have imagined. To know that all nature, low as well as high, was equally submitted to his jurisdiction and within his province, was sure, on many occasions, to give a poet's hand that freedom and spirit which are inconsistent with the fear of overstepping certain limits, and straying into a forbidden country. To know this also was, in another view, important, because it implied and flowed from the still more important knowledge of the true principle of all poetical capability; when he announced that all things were subjects of poetry, he did so from correctly reasoning how it was that any single thing might be. Thus learned in the principles of his art, and gifted by nature as he is with the main ingredients of poetic genius, there seem to us to have been no bounds to the excellence which he might have maintained, but those which he has unfortunately set to himself, and these may be described in a single sentence; he has not suffered his poetry to be the expression merely of his natural and unperverted feelings; but *he has devoted it to the development and maintenance of a system*. Because he has discovered and maintained successfully, that good poetry may be written on a celandine or a daisy, he seems to have acted as if better poetry could be written on them than on subjects of a higher degree; he has neglected to take into the account that poetry is a communicative art, that the state of the recipient is to be considered, as well as that of the communicant; that it is little to have mixed up all the essential ingredients of poetic pleasure if they are to be neutralized or overpowered by certain accompanying feelings of disgust or ridicule.

We are aware that the poet himself will deny the grounds of our conclusion; he will declare, perhaps, that though his writings are in faithful adherence to a certain system, yet he writes with unshackled freedom, that it is an unconscious adherence, and undeviating, only because the system itself is built upon the laws of our nature. Such an answer, it is evident, will apply with equal force to a false and a true system; it is making the inveteracy of the habit its justification; but, indeed, with all our old, our unfeigned, our respectful, and even affectionate deference for Wordsworth, we are bold to say that he is no competent judge in this matter. That he writes under the impulse of a glowing and real enthusiasm we do not intend to deny; on the contrary, we are very sure that he feels whatever he describes himself as feeling in the contemplation of a bird's nest, or the sudden gleaming of a bunch of daffodils; but we cannot therefore conclude either that the thoughts which they excite are so important, as that they should form the principal subject of a wise man's contemplations; or that it is proper for a poet to make such feelings the principal topic of his communications to the world.

After all, what is poetry, or when do a certain train of thoughts, images, and words become poetry? certainly they are so when they first rise in the poet's mind; and a man may be a poet, in the full and common sense of the word, who has never committed a poem to paper or even recited a line to his friend. A man may satisfy himself with the solitary pleasure of such creations, content with his own vivid perceptions, and exulting within himself in the consciousness of his uncommunicated strength; he may feel no desire to communicate what has delighted himself, he may seek for no applause beyond that of his own breast. When this is the case, the world has no right to question him upon the subject or the manner of his meditations; but the moment the poet communicates to others, it is evident that as he has now a new object, so there is also a new party to be consulted in the attainment of that object. The poet who recites, or writes, or publishes, has clearly, in so doing, an object beyond the pleasure of poetic composition; he seeks for praise, for immortal fame, or to suit a poet's delicacy, he seeks to communicate pleasures to others. The process by which he arrives at that object is the exciting feelings correspondent to those which he has himself experienced; and he attains his object more completely, the greater number of persons he succeeds in thrilling with these similar emotions. Poets may coquette it if they please, and disclaim a desire of applause or fame; but he who publishes, must, by all fair rules of interpretation, be held to desire something external, either glory to himself, or the communication of pleasure to others; in either case the number of those who applaud, or who are pleased, is an essential part of the complete attainment of the object. We are aware of the distinction between popularity and fame, we give Wordsworth full credit for despising the former and desiring only the latter; but in this he is only a better arithmetician than many of his contemporaries; it is only because he knows that the popularity of to-day is no assurance for the fame of to-morrow, and that he whose admirers are the most judicious, and whose fame lasts the longest, will in the end have the greater number of readers.

The question then with a poet must always be, how can I excite in the greatest number of my fellow-creatures emotions similar to those which I feel myself? and when this is the question, it is obvious that he must take into the account something more than merely his own sensibilities, and the causes of excitement *to them*; he is bound to examine into the same things as they belong, or refer to others. His own constitution may be one of peculiar delicacy; circumstances may have rendered it morbid, or at least cherished its sensibilities to excess; his habits of life may have directed them into an uncommon channel, or may have attached importance to that which the mass of the world has been accustomed to consider trifling. In all these cases, the medium of communication between the poet and his readers, is disturbed; to say the least, he comes among them and proffers his thoughts for their acceptance, just as one buried for many years in the interior of Africa, might appear in the market here, with a string of cowries for his medium of commerce; they may have been valuable where they were procured, and may have cost him many a day's labour under a burning sun; they may indeed be intrinsically as fit for the purpose as gold and silver, or more perishable paper; but he must not expect to purchase with them here the article of which he stands in need. When this too happens, the poet must not too hastily conclude, any more than the African, that all the world is wrong, and he alone right; if, indeed, he is conscious of powers which may constrain the age and fashion, hearts and habits to his own bent, it is all well, at least for him, and his object will be attained in his own way. But since the poet has no controul over circumstances; since there will be always in the world bustle, and contention, and wars, and commerce, and litigation, it is perhaps greater wisdom to despair of altering that which flows from them, to renounce an attempt which the most vigorous son of the Muse has never made with success, and so far as may be done, without cramping the free step of genius, to accommodate oneself to the feelings and reasonings of others. In saying this, we are not the advocates of an unworthy compliance; the 'diversity,' as a lawyer would say, is to be noted between that which is the sickly and short-lived fashion of the day, and that which, proceeding from permanent causes, may be fairly expected to be itself permanent; the slave of the former deliberately renounces the very object, which we have supposed to be honestly and properly in the poet's view.

It will scarcely be asked how we apply this to Wordsworth, or how it accounts for that want of success, which we lament in his poetry. All objects or appearances in nature are intrinsically capable of that speculation and association which are the basis of poetical pleasure; a large class of them, however, from other circumstances, apparently permanent in their nature, and from inveterate counter-associations, whether reasonable or not, are either esteemed by the mass of men as trifling, or felt to be disgusting; when these, therefore, are made the subjects of grave or delicate speculation, the poet's associations and the reader's are at direct variance; and even if the powers of the former, with the intrinsic justice of his thoughts, should prevail over the mere habits and feelings of the latter, it is evident that a victory obtained by a struggle does not and cannot impart that full and perfect pleasure which it is the business of poetry to bestow. This we take to be a just account of the dispute between Wordsworth and the mass of his readers; there was something more than playful and good-humoured satire in the critic, that talked of the 'consecration of chicken,'[1] and such other

[1] Francis Jeffrey in his review of the *Poems in Two Volumes* in the *Edinburgh*

disgusting subjects in a review of his poetry; but saving the malice of the remark, it is undoubtedly true, that according to Wordsworth's principles carried to their full extent, (carried, let it be remembered, much farther than even his Quixotism has ever ventured in practice,) there is nothing too trifling for grave, too disgusting for pleasant speculation; the greatness, the goodness, the wisdom of the Creator are as fairly deducible from the fly that feeds upon corruption, nay from the corruption itself on which it feeds, as from the purest lily, the brightest sun-rise, the most glorious canopy of stars, or the fairest woman, that were ever celebrated by poet.

Two remarks remain to be made, one addressed to readers, the other with great respect to the poet himself. To the former, we would say, that if they have formed their opinions of Wordsworth from public reputation, from illiberal and unjust criticism, from any thing but an attentive and impartial study of his writings, they impeach their own justice; have done the poet great wrong, and themselves yet greater. We have stated our objections to certain of his opinions, and we repeat that we think he has shewn a perverse preference for the maintenance and exemplification of a system to the yielding to the nobler and more genial current of his natural feelings. Still, if we reject from the list of his poems whatever are most open to these objections, those in which the inventor or the reviver of a system predominates over the natural poet, enough and more than enough will yet remain in the volumes of Wordsworth, to reward with the richest fruits that poetry can bestow, a candid and attentive reader. It is pitiable and maudlin folly to consider poetry as the mere recreation of idleness, in which it is a fault if the mind is called upon for a moment's exertion; it is prejudice to take up our opinions for granted, and without examination, upon the word of a single critic; it is injustice for a single fault of taste to reject all the writings of any poet; let our readers only stand clear of this folly, and avoid this prejudice and this injustice, and we promise them that they will find in Wordsworth, poems, which it is a misfortune at least, we will not venture to say a disgrace, to be incapable of feeling and admiring.

We have also to address a few words to the poet himself. His writings are devoted to the cause of religion and morality, and in that holy cause we scarcely know a more zealous, a more fearless, or more eloquent advocate; it is quite refreshing to turn from the tawdry voluptuousness of one contemporary poet, or the gloomy misanthropy of another; the vague aspirations of this man, the cold scepticism of that,

---

Review, XI (Oct. 1807), 225, mentions the possibility of 'the evisceration of chickens' as a possible subject. See above, p. 21.

or the shocking blasphemy of a third, to the pure, manly, singleminded morality of Wordsworth. We give him credit too for feeling as he writes, and we are sure, that to promote virtue and purity, is, with him, beyond all profit, all praise, all pleasure. Upon this ground we take our stand, and we beseech him to consider, that whatever prevents his general acceptation, diminishes his power of doing good; we think he must be satisfied by a trial of so many years, that while he writes as he writes now, projecting his system at every angle, and presenting so many sides obvious to the perversions of ridicule and malice, he may indeed have a few passionate admirers, whose zeal and weight may suffice to console wounded vanity, but he never can have that general influence, nor produce that powerful effect, which of all living poets he is by nature most capable of producing. We do not prescribe the manner or the measure of alteration to the poet, we appeal to the man and the moralist, whether some alteration, some yielding to prejudices, if they be permanent, some departure from the very *summum jus* of abstract truth, be not both possible and expedient.

It is high time for us to come to the poem itself, which has furnished us with an excuse for so long a preface. It is introduced by a prologue, in which the poet explains his preference of the earth, and subjects connected with the daily feelings, and occurrences of man over all that is supernatural and marvellous. This is attempted to be done in a playful fiction of a

> 'Little boat,
> In shape a very crescent moon.'

In which the poet describes himself as taking a voyage in the air, but soon becoming tired of stars and planets, and begging to be reconveyed to earth. The boat cries shame upon him for a poet of faint heart, but offers to convey him, since heaven is too high for him, and the music of the spheres troubles him, to see all the wonders of the earth, and of fairy land; the poet rejects even this offer, and persists in being set down in his own garden, where round the stone table, 'beneath the spreading Weymouth pine,' a party of friends are assembled to hear him tell the tale of 'Peter Bell the Potter.' Playfulness is not Wordsworth's forte, and we think that in all the lighter parts of this *jeu d'esprit* he has failed; in these parts too he has indulged himself in the use of those familiar forms of speech, to which nothing can reconcile us in poetry that is in other passages so serious and philosophical as this. But there is something very glowing and tender in the expression of his feelings when he hangs over 'the town where he was born,' and the following stanzas are no less beautiful and well expressed, than true in the positions which they lay down.

[Lines 121–50 are quoted.]

The poem itself opens with a stanza, which Wordsworth seems to have placed boldly *in limine*, as a note of defiance to his critics, and a test of the passive obedience of his disciples.

> 'All by the moonlight river side
> It gave three miserable groans,
> " 'Tis come then to a pretty pass,"
> Said Peter to the groaning Ass,
> "But I will bang your bones." ' P. 15.[1]

We are as far as the poet himself can be from thinking that Peter the potter ought to storm at a poor ass in down-right heroics; but we beg to observe, that the tale might, in this part at least, have been as well conducted without making him speak at all; the speech is merely inserted *ornamenti gratiâ*; and if it was incorrect to make him speak in any other than forms and phrases inseparably connected with low and ridiculous associations, we think there can be no doubt, that the poet should have sacrificed the dramatic effect for the sake of excluding such associations, and merely told us in his own person and *in his own language*, that Peter beat the ass very unmercifully. Not, however, to renew an argument on which we have already said so much, we will only say one word with reference to the few lines which we addressed in the last page to Wordsworth himself, and upon a point on which we are sure that we must be better judges than he himself can be. Of all the persons who take up Peter Bell, we will venture to say, that a very large proportion, (and among them persons who might have been delighted and instructed with the tale if they could have been got fairly into it without prejudice on their minds) will take the colouring of their opinion, and receive a fatal disgust from this very unfortunate stanza. The poet may smile at this, the critic may hold for nothing judgments so formed, but the zealous moralist cannot consider such a fact as unimportant.

The audience who are assembled to hear the tale, very naturally expostulate upon this abrupt beginning, and in the manner of their doing so, Wordsworth has fallen into an inconsistency with his own position, which as an *argumentum ad hominem*, we cannot pass over without noticing to him.

---

[1] The last three lines were revised in the 1820 edition.

> ' "Good sir," the vicar's voice exclaimed,
> "You rush at once into the middle;"
> And little Bess, with accents sweeter,
> Cried "O dear sir, but who is Peter?"
> Said Stephen "'tis a downright riddle." ' P. 15.

We have no fault to find with this, but

> 'The Squire said, "sure as Paradise
> Was lost to man by Adam's sinning
> This leap is for us all too bold, &c." ' P. 16.

Now there may be some propriety in the squire's talking of a bold leap, but upon the same principle that Peter was found to talk of 'pretty passes,' and 'banging bones,' we contend that the squire's simile should have been, 'sure as a gun,' or 'sure as Carlisle race was lost to me by Adam's bolting,' or any other such form of speech. The fall of man, and the loss of Paradise are evidently dramatically improper in the mouth of the village squire.

This interruption, however, recalls the poet, and he begins his tale regularly, by an account of the occupation, habits, and character, of Peter Bell. This is admirably done in the best style of narration, with the truest pencil of moral delineation.

[The summary of the story continues; lines 246–75 are quoted in the process; and then the following lines are given.]

> 'And behold
> A scene of soft and lovely hue!
> Where blue and grey, and tender green,
> Together made as sweet a scene
> As ever human eye did view.

> 'Beneath the clear blue sky he saw
> A little field of meadow ground,
> But field, or meadow, name it not;
> Call it of earth a small green plot
> With rocks encompass'd round.

> 'The Swale flow'd under the grey rocks, &c.' P. 28.

There is something very exquisite to our feelings in these few lines of description; the drawing, it will be observed, is very general, a blue sky, a little meadow, rocks around, and a stream flowing under them; it is, we believe, in the very generality of the drawing, and the fewness of the features, that the charm consists; scarcely any one can wander much in countries but of common beauty, and be a real lover of nature, who will not be able to associate this description with some secluded glade, some little island in the woods, which arrested his steps in passing, and which it is delightful to have brought again to his memory. We could name several favourite spots upon both shores of Devonshire, that instantly rose to our recollection upon reading the lines.

In this lonely spot Peter finds nothing but a solitary ass, which he instantly determines upon stealing, and the poet as usual makes him announce this determination and address the ass in language, the only recommendation of which in his eyes can be that he supposes it dramatically correct. But a moment's observation suffices to shew that it has not even that merit; it is not humorous enough to excite a smile, and the poet has no intention of making us laugh; but it is low enough, and ridiculous enough to disturb our feelings. Peter Bell himself would never have so spoken, and we cannot conceive the merit of a false and artificial lowness.

> 'With better speed I'll back again,
> And, lest the journey should prove vain,
> Will take yon Ass my lawful prize.'

To so much of the speech we have no objection; it is the language in which our best poets would have clothed the same ideas, remembering that they were not bound to give the potter's own words, not to speak precisely as he would have spoken, but with all their own cultivation of mind, and addressing themselves to cultivated minds to speak *for* him; just as a person narrates a dialogue in low life, without *mimicking* the accents, provincialisms, or vulgarities of the speakers. But to pursue.

> 'Off Peter hied—"A comely beast,
> Though not so plump as he might be:
> My honest friend, with such a platter
> You should have been a little fatter,
> But come, sir, come with me." ' P. 29.

This is no more the language of Peter Bell, than of Peter the Great; it is indeed, exactly the manner in which full grown school-boys, smart, and frolicksome, would have expressed themselves upon such an occasion; and if the speech has not the merit of *propriety*, we really do not see in such a poem as this, what merit it has of any kind.

[The discovery of the corpse by Peter is described.]

The whole of this, to which it is impossible to do justice in a mere analysis, is admirably done; its merit, indeed, lies principally in that of which it is impossible to convey any idea in an analysis, namely, in the gradual impression of circumstances upon the hard and insensible heart of the savage; time, place, solitude, his own wanton and unlawful purpose, the strangeness of the resistance, the sudden noise redoubled by the echo in the still night, all these conspiring to produce that feeling of something supernatural, to which the most brutal nature is, perhaps, the most susceptible, and which, in Peter's mind, is consummated by the shocking close of the adventure.

He awakes from his swoon, the first, perhaps, into which he had ever fallen; the gradual return of recollection, and sense, is very well described.

[The recovery of the corpse and Peter's setting off for the dead man's house are described.]

We have seldom read a journey so beautifully conceived, so well described as this, it is little to say that it is full of the exquisite painting of nature, and that the scenes selected for the pencil are admirably in harmony with the incidents, and with the changing feelings of Peter.

This part of the poem, by far the longest, is entitled to higher praise; Wordsworth has here put forth all his powers, both in the 'moving incident,' and in tracing the various changes in the mind of his principal personage, from wonder to a sort of desperate and unresisting conviction of guilt, with an anticipation of speedy and inevitable punishment; a wild remorse for his past evil courses, a natural relapse to thoughtless hard-heartedness, a renewed remorse softening down to the deepest, and most painful repentance, and then the awakening of all those kindly and human feelings, which the circumstances before his eyes might breathe into the gentlest heart. Our readers must not, however, suppose that it is *merely* a scientific analysis of the workings of the human heart under given circumstances; it is that certainly, but it is much more; we should be as little disposed to commend a mere lecture on moral anatomy, as they could be to enjoy it. But to the commonest readers we can give our assurance, that they will find this a most pathetic tale; for ourselves we will confess that we have seldom met with one, over which, when we read it aloud, we find it so difficult to restrain our feelings.

The issue of the tale may well be supposed, and we decline the task of analysing the incidents, for we would neither rob them of their beauty and interest, nor anticipate the pleasure of our readers. Peter Bell becomes a 'good and honest man,' after months of sober melancholy, and rational repentance, and the ass is for many years the laborious, and useful servant of the unfortunate widow and her family. Our extracts have been very numerous already, indeed we may seem to have devoted an unreasonable portion of our number to remarks on so short a poem; but we cannot refrain still from adding to both. We have two extracts to make for which we must still find room, as they serve to put beyond a doubt Wordsworth's power in two of the essentials of poetry, picturesque drawing, and pathetic narration. In the course of the journey homewards to the cottage of the dead man, both Peter and the ass are startled by a shrill and doleful cry; the ass knows it well, for it proceeds from his master's son, who had been now for four days seeking his unfortunate father. The boy is not yet introduced actually into the poem, but the poet turning to 'little Bess,' who was much affected by this part of the story, tells her that the cry 'comes from the entrance of a cave;' and then exclaims.

> 'I see a blooming wood boy there,
> And if I had the power to say
> How sorrowful the wanderer is,
> Your heart would be as sad as his
> Till you had kiss'd his tears away.

> 'Holding a hawthorn branch in hand,
> All bright with berries ripe and red,
> Into the cavern's mouth he peeps,
> Thence back into the moonlight creeps;
> What seeks the boy?—the silent dead—

> 'His father.' P. 48.

Confining ourselves to the five lines which we have printed in Italics, the only descriptive lines of the passage (unless indeed the epithet 'sorrowful,' in the third line may more correctly be so considered) we do not know that in all the compass of English poetry we can turn to a more *complete* picture. No pencil can set the scene more perfectly before the eye, and yet our readers will not fail to remark that two or three general features are all the materials with which this *completeness* of effect is produced. The hawthorn branch 'with berries ripe and red,' might to an inattentive observer of the reality have seemed an unimportant feature, not worthy of introduction, nor properly to be introduced in so general a sketch; yet no one can study the picture, without remarking what a life and individuality, what a determinate character it gives to the more considerable features. We may seem to attach too

much importance to such a trifle, and to discourse on it with dispropor-
tionate earnestness, but it is in fact intimately connected with, and a
strong illustration of the truth of those principles in poetry, which we
have uniformly laboured to enforce, and to which we are convinced
both readers and writers must return, if the former would either really
delight in, or the latter successfully imitate, Shakspeare, Spenser, or
Milton, the great triad of English poetry.

The other, and the last extract which we shall make, is of a kind in
which Wordsworth has, on several occasions, shewn himself eminently
successful, and the present, perhaps, may fearlessly stand in competition
with the best of his preceding efforts. Taken by itself, and apart from
the context, we think it must strike the reader as a beautiful specimen
of pure and simple pathos, but it loses somewhat by being read as an
extract, for it occurs in the original very naturally, and conduces much
to the reformation produced in Peter's mind. He passes a little ivied
chapel (a scene by the way most exquisitely described) and in the
ruminating self-accusing mood into which he has been thrown, he
remembers that in such a ruin, 'in the shire of Fife,' he had deceived a
poor girl, and married her his sixth wife. He passes on by an ale-house,
whence issues the noise of a carousing, and drunken party, but this
sound, once so pleasing to him, now affects him with other sensations,
and turns him more wildly and gloomily to the consideration of all his
past irregular and wicked life.

[Lines 886–930 are quoted.[1]]

We must not allow ourselves to extend these remarks any further, as
there are some subjects, and some books, upon which it takes some
'beating of the brain' to produce an article of the adequate size, so there
are others, and among them the present, upon which we find it hard
to check our pen, but upon consideration of the patience of our readers.
Our last extract speaks for itself, and we would decline talking upon
poetry with any one who was incapable of feeling its beauty; to such a
man poetry must be as colour to the blind, or music to the deaf. Neither
can it be necessary to sum up our formal opinion of the poet, or the
poem; we have treated both with freedom, but it is manifest, that profound admiration predominates in our minds over all other feelings of
an opposite nature. But we do fear, lest our expressions may seem exaggerated to many among our readers, whose bosoms glow with poetic
pleasure as warmly as our own, and whose judgments may be more

---

[1] [Does Mr. Wordsworth pronounce squirrel 'squirl'; this is not his only offence
against rhyme; the more remarkable, because haste and inattention are none of his
faults. *Rev.*—Reviewer's note to line 889.]

matured, and better disciplined. To such persons we feel anxious to justify ourselves for our own sakes, and we will venture to add, for their own. When we first read Peter Bell, it was in the midst of business, and with that impatient haste, which one feels with regard to the 'last new poem' of a favourite author; we laid it down, we confess, much disappointed, and should have been ready to condemn, as injudicious and exaggerated, such a critique as we are now closing. As, however, we were to render an account of the poem to the public, it was natural to recollect, that it was more fair to distrust ourselves, than to condemn another on so hasty a perusal. We accordingly again read it, with a good deal of attention, and with a total change of opinion; we found that Peter Bell was worthy of its author's fame, and that its unobtrusive beauties, fairly weighed, and properly brought to light, were more than a counterbalance to the staring defects, which had influenced our first judgment. What has happened to ourselves, we shall venture to think may happen to other, and even wiser men; and we hope we may without presumption, urge upon them the propriety also of doing as we did, the giving the poet a second and a more attentive consideration. The man who reads a poem, as a lady does a newspaper, for the births, deaths, murders, and marriages it contains, who takes it up without a thought in his head, and puts it down again with no accession, but what scantily suffices for his table talk the same day at dinner, will waste his time on Peter Bell, or indeed any production of its author. Wordsworth demands from his readers, not only the sacrifice of many prejudices, and the conquest of some reasonable dispositions to laughter or mortification, but also an open heart, and a patient exercise of his intellect. People may doubt, whether a poet has a right to demand all these, but of this we are certain, that he who can, and will grant them, will derive from Wordsworth nearly as high gratification as any poet is capable of bestowing.

Review of Wordsworth's 'The Waggoner'

Monthly Review

XC (Sept. 1819), 36–40. The reviewer is unknown.

'The Waggoner,' and 'Sonnets,' in the same little drab-coloured pamphlet! Well! Our ancestors would have stared at these things: but we receive them with a good-humoured smile, and our taste is proportionably improved.

Mr. Wordsworth appears determined to try how far he can trample on the degraded poetry of his country. 'Keep it down,' seems to be his prevailing principle; and well may he add, 'now it is down.' He asks us, in his motto,

> 'What's in a name?
> 'Brutus will start a spirit as soon as Caesar!'

and, therefore, 'the Waggoner' will do as well as Brutus. Beautiful reasoning! and beautifully illustrated in the poem itself.

This tale is dedicated to Charles Lamb, Esq., to whose own poetical performances we hope soon to call the attention of the favoured few, who rejoice in the productions of the modern antique school: but Mr. Wordsworth apologizes for not adding *the Waggoner* to 'Peter Bell,'[1] (as Mr. Lamb, it seems, had wished; and the whole communication is *very* interesting to the public!) on account of 'the higher tone of imagination, and the deeper touches of passion,' attempted in 'Peter Bell!'—*Risum teneatis, amici?*[2]

---

[1] [See our last Review.—Reviewer's note.]
[2] 'Can you keep from laughing, friends?' Horace *Ars Poetica* 5.

For ourselves, we confess honestly that we consider 'the Waggoner' to be one of the best and most ingenious of *all* Mr. Wordsworth's poems. It manifests, occasionally, a classical style of language and versification which is wholly superior to his native manner; and, were it not for the internal evidence of several instances of extreme folly, we should really be disposed to suspect that some lighter and more joyous hand had here been at work. Throughout the piece, or at all events very frequently, we perceive a sly covert sort of irony, an *under-tone* of playfulness, smiling at the mock heroics of the author; and preserving that difficult but exact spirit of bombast, which betrays a consciousness of misapplied sublimity, without rendering it quite gross and ridiculous. Let our readers judge. Mr. Wordsworth's 'Waggoner,' who was wont, for many years, to carry the heavy goods (Mr. W.'s own works included) from the lakes to London, after most exemplary habits of sobriety, was tempted to stay too long at an ale-house with a drunken sailor, carrying a ship about as an exhibition, and is obliged to make unusual exertions up a northern hill to recover lost time. At this juncture, the *Pickwood* of those parts 'pricks forth from Keswick' to look after his waggon; when the exultation of inebriety (a state which Mr. Wordsworth has described with a degree of feeling that we should scarcely have expected) has passed away from the waggoner and his marine companion.

[Lines 83–115 of Canto Four are quoted.]

'Alas, what boots it?'—

This concluding question intimates the catastrophe of the story. Benjamin, with all his itinerary and vehicular virtues, is dismissed by his inexorable master; and the waggon droops, decays, and ceases to travel, in consequence. 'Eight sorry carts' supply its place; and, passing by Mr. Wordsworth's interesting windows, they will probably produce no more than 'eight sorry poems,' in the course of the next season. We subjoin the passage in which the cheerful effects of intoxication are so livingly depictured.

> 'Now, heroes, for the true commotion,
> The triumph of your late devotion!
> Can aught on earth impede delight,
> Still mounting to a higher height;
> And higher still—a greedy flight!
> Can any low-born care pursue her,
> Can any mortal clog come to her?

No notion have they—not a thought,
That is from joyless regions brought!
And, while they coast the silent lake,
Their inspiration I partake;
Share their empyreal spirits—yea,
With their enraptured vision, see—
O fancy what a jubilee!
What shifting pictures—clad in gleams
Of colour bright as feverish dreams!
Earth, spangled sky, and lake serene,
Involved and restless all—a scene
Pregnant with mutual exaltation,
Rich change, and multiplied creation!
This sight to me the Muse imparts;
And then, what kindness in their hearts!
What tears of rapture, what vow-making,
Profound entreaties, and hand-shaking!
What solemn, vacant, interlacing,
As if they'd fall asleep embracing!
Then, in the turbulence of glee,
And in the excess of amity,
Says Benjamin, "That ass of thine,
He spoils thy sport, and hinders mine:
If he were tether'd to the waggon,
He'd drag as well what he is dragging;
And we, as brother should with brother,
Might trudge it alongside each other!" '

When our readers have paused a moment to digest this last and very elegant line, we beg to ask them whether these results of conviviality are not most naturally represented?

'He best can paint them who shall feel them most.'

We call on Mr. Southey, on Mr. Coleridge, on Mr. Lamb, and on the *arbiter elegantiarum ac bibendi*[1] himself, to join in our sincere admiration of that truly picturesque couplet,

'What *solemn, vacant*, interlacing,
As if they'd fall asleep embracing!'

Seriously, we can no longer endure to hear the poets of so festive a school called the '*Water* Poets of the Lakes;' and from the strong spirit

[1] 'The master on taste and drinking.'

of humour evidently displayed in this memorable passage, we more than suspect where Mr. Wordsworth's real *forte* lies: we exhort him to cultivate his talent for the ridiculous; and we earnestly request him no longer to *laugh in his sleeve* at his 'solemn, vacant' admirers, but to come forth in that character for which nature has plainly designed him, 'the Prince of Poetical Burlesque.'

We must not dismiss this little work without a word of compliment to the versatility of genius that is exhibited, on all occasions, by its author. 'The Waggoner' has driven a small load of 'Sonnets' with him to town, and some of them breathe the true *simplicity* of the writer; as, for instance, when he calls building an imaginary castle on a rock an '*innocent scheme!*' or tells us that good old Isaac Walton, in his plain love of nature, was guilty of the metaphysical quaintness of '*exhorting*' us

> 'To reverent watching of each *still report*
> That nature utters from her *rural shrine*.'

This '*still report*,' or φωνη ἀφωνος[1] of nature, is a very remarkable thing; and we call the attention of every patient listener to watch and wait for it; or, peradventure, it may escape a common hearkening. Is it not like the ὀδμη ἀφεγγης[2] of the Prometheus?

Most prominently and peculiarly does Mr. Wordsworth stand forth, *all himself*, in that unrivalled Sonnet, ycleped '*The Wild-duck's Nest:*' for, at the end of this *idiosyncratical* production, the poet exclaims

> 'I gaze—*and almost wish to lay aside
> Humanity*, weak slave of cumbrous pride.'

Gaze at what? At a wild-duck's nest! Oh, 'Goosy-goosy-Gander!' friend of our infancy, resign thine honours! and thou, 'Happy, happy, happy Fly,' acquaintance of our manhood, sink into deep forgetfulness, before an author who wishes (almost) to lay aside *humanity*, at the sight of a wild-duck's nest!

Is it, in sober seriousness, possible that these things should be uttered by a person capable of composing the following sonnet?

['Captivity.—Mary Queen of Scots' is quoted in full.]

[1] 'Soundless sound.'
[2] 'Lightless odor.' Aeschylus *Prometheus Bound* 114.

Review of Wordsworth's 'River Duddon'

Blackwood's Magazine

VII (May 1820), 206–13. This review was probably written by either John Wilson or John Gibson Lockhart: see Alan L. Strout, A Bibliography of Articles in Blackwood's Magazine 1817–25 *(Lubbock, Texas, 1959), p. 68.*

There is something exquisitely discouraging in the conclusions to which a calm review of the effects of contemporary criticism in England must lead every man of tolerably sound judgment; and in regard to no department of literary exertions are these necessary conclusions so discouraging as in that of the criticism of Poetry. This age has unquestionably produced a noble band of British Poets—each separated from all the rest by abundant peculiarities of style and manner—some far above others in skill to embrace and improve the appliances of popularity—but all of them successful in the best and noblest sense of that term, because all of them bound together, (however little some themselves may suspect it) by rich participation in the stirring and exalting spirit of the same eventful age—an age distinguished above almost all its predecessors by the splendour of external things, but still more distinguished by the power and energy which these have reflected upon the intellect and imagination of its children. That the poetical productions of Scott, and Byron, and Wordsworth, and Southey, and Coleridge—however differing from each other in shape and feature—are yet all kindred to each other by their part in the common Soul and Thought of the time that has witnessed their birth, cannot be doubted by any man capable of reading them as they ought to be read—now: and will certainly be doubted by no one whatever that reads them fifty years hence. Yet when a man asks of himself, for a moment, what has really been said—what *remarks* worthy of the name have really been uttered concerning any one of these Poets—how lamentably must we feel the worthlessness of all the criticism of the most critical age ever the world produced. The result to which we come, must of necessity be this, that in the history, not of one, but of all and of each of these great Poets, the independence of the march of Genius towards Fame has been most fully and entirely exemplified. Who can suppose for a moment that the applauses of our Reviewers have contributed a single iota to the splendour of the reputation of the highest? The utmost vanity of the vainest critic alive, can scarcely lead him to flatter himself that the fame of Byron, for example, would have been one whit less, had he never acknowledged, by one expression of admiration, that his spirit was capable of understanding the mastery of Byron.

It is an easier matter, however, to prevent Reputation from beginning to rise, than to lend her effectual aid after her ascent has once been triumphantly begun: and therefore it is, that we consider the total failure of all the attempts which have been made to check the fame of Wordsworth, as a still more convincing proof of the imbecility concerning which we speak, than any one circumstance besides in the literary history of our time. If the shafts of dishonest malice have at any moment wounded the high spirit of the Poet himself—and if the pertinacity of the wicked zeal with which he has been persecuted, has prevented his genius from going abroad so speedily and so widely in its workings as nature meant it to do—the fault of the critics has not been small;—and their repentance should not be the less, because it is mingled with a sense of their own essential, if not universal inferiority to the person who has thus been injured.

Nothing is more common than to talk about the unpopularity of Wordsworth;—but, after all, we are inclined to doubt very much, whether at any moment for many years past, he can, with any propriety, be said to have lain under the reproach of unpopularity. The true Acceptation of a Poet does not surely consist in the wideness to which his name is blown on the four winds of heaven. Ever since Wordsworth began to write, he has fixed the attention of every genuine lover and student of English Poetry; and all along he has received from these the tribute of honour due to the felt and received power of his genius. And—much as is our admiration of some of his contemporaries, whose excellencies have been more universally applauded—we rather think that they may have more reason to envy Wordsworth for the depth of meditation which his productions have called forth, than he can have to envy them for any of their more buoyant and resplendent symbols of successful art. Besides, if we be not greatly mistaken, Wordsworth has been read by just as many on account of his *Poetry*, as ever read, the most popular of his contemporaries for the sake of *Poetry*. Nay, more, we doubt, whether the writings of Spenser, or of Dryden, or even of Milton himself, be at this instant truly familiar to a larger portion of the Reading Public of England than those of Wordsworth.

The way in which the fame of this poet had been attacked by the Edinburgh Reviewers, has already frequently induced us to speak of the philosophical spirit in which the more peculiar productions of his genius are conceived: but in the present volume, while the native strength and originality of his genius are most perfectly preserved, not a few of his customary singularities of style and manner are unquestionably less prominent than in any of his former publications; and therefore, it is not necessary to preface our extracts from it by any thing like an elaborate portico of disquisition. If the passages which we quote do not suffice to make our readers loath for ever all the cant about 'Lakish Ditties,' 'Pond Poets,' &c. and acknowledge at once that this author is a genuine English classic, in the purest and highest sense of the term, we shall despair for ever of the effects of poetry—which is a very different matter from despairing of the effects of criticism.

The first part of this volume is occupied with a series of Sonnets, which may be considered as forming something not unlike one poem —The subject, the river Duddon; a stream which, flowing down one of the most beautiful valleys in the country of the Lakes, has, throughout the whole of his life, been familiar and dear to the eye and the imagination of the poet. The idea of forming a poem on such a subject, belongs originally, as Mr Wordsworth mentions, to his illustrious friend, Mr Coleridge; who, many years ago, used to talk of writing 'The Brook.' It has been the fortune of Coleridge to see not a few of his plans executed by other hands than his own; but we are much mistaken if the present near approach to 'The Brook,' will give him any thing but pleasure. It is impossible for us to enter upon any analysis; but we give the following six as specimens of the whole thirty-three Sonnets.

[Sonnets VIII, XIV, XV, XXI, XXII, XXIX are quoted in full.]

Our next extract shall be *Dion*, a magnificent strain of most classical and energetic poetry, imbued intensely with the spirit of ancient grandeur, and enriched with all the depth and gracefulness of Mr Wordsworth's own most poetical philosophy. It will remind those acquainted with his earlier works, of the *Laodamia*; and satisfy them that have never seen that production, how absurdly the charge of 'silly simplicity' has been brought against the general tenour either of the thought or the language of Mr Wordsworth. The truth is, that among all the English poets who have written since Milton, there is none, except Gray, who has ever caught the true inspiration of the Grecian Lyre with the same perfect dignity as the great poet of the Lakes. Talking of language merely—we remember nothing in the whole poetry of his contemporaries, to be compared with the uniform and unlaboured stateliness of his march in the Laodamia, the Sonnets to Liberty, and the following piece:

['Dion' is quoted in full.]

This we have quoted at full length. We wish it were in our power to follow the same course with the fine old British or Armorican legend of *Artegal and Elidure*. We must omit, however, the introduction to it, which is as full of splendour as the tale itself is of tender and graceful simplicity.

[Lines 66–225 are quoted.]

The deep breath of simple unconscious grace diffused over the whole of this poem will, if we may judge from ourselves, to the mind of every reader

> 'Call up him that left half told
> The story of Cambuscan bold.'

Indeed the effect of the whole of the extracts we have made, will, we nothing doubt, be quite sufficient to convince every one who has made the character of English poetry his study, that so far from deserving to be held up to derision as a fanciful and conceited innovator, Mr Wordsworth (judged by the genuine spirit of his writings) is entitled to be classed with the very highest names among his predecessors, as a pure and reverent worshipper of the true majesty of the English Muse. Had he never written some few pieces, which are indeed most dear and precious to us, but the conception as well as execution of which we can easily conceive to be of far more questionable excellence in the eyes of the greater part of those who read them for the first time, we are satisfied that the most malignant critics would never have dared to say one word in derogation from the sublimity or the elegance of his compositions. But we can imagine nothing less enviable than the feelings with which, at this time of day—after he has lived to throw into shade the errors (granting them to have been errors) of a few of his earlier pieces, by the solid and reposing grandeur of the main structure of his poetry—than the reflections which his pertinacious detractors must make in spite of themselves on the conduct which they for so long a period adopted in regard to him. The senseless and boyish clamours with which they pursued a few trivial singularities of one of the proudest of men, probably served no purpose whatever, except that of confirming him in the belief, that what such people took upon them to consider as wrong, must of necessity be right.—Had they been silent in regard to the Betty Foys and the Alice Fells, we should in all likelihood have had fewer of that class—while, had they given the praise that was due to such poems as Ruth, Michael, and Laodamia, it is not impossible that these might, long ere now, have been followed up by many more productions equally free, as they must be allowed to be, from any of the real or supposed faults of the others.

Of the genius of Mr Wordsworth, in short, it is now in the hands of every man to judge freely and fully, and for himself. Our own opinion, ever since this journal commenced, has been clearly and entirely before them;[1] and if there be any one person, on whose mind what we have quoted now, is not enough to make an impression similar to that which our own judgment had long before received—we have nothing more to say to that person in regard to the subject of poetry. We conclude with a few specimens of the more miscellaneous part of this volume —which will be sufficient to shew, that that is nothing inferior to the other parts. To those who have long been familiar with Wordsworth, and sensible to his merits, the 'Pass of Kirkstone' will be additionally acceptable, on account of its connexion with the train of thought in one of the grandest of his early pieces, the Ode, 'Intimations of Immortality.'

['The Pass of Kirkstone' is quoted in full.]

The two following pieces require no comment to those that are acquainted with the sonnets on political subjects, in Mr Wordsworth's earlier volumes.

['On the Death of His Majesty' and 'Hint from the Mountains' are quoted in full.]

The volume is concluded with a very singular and striking prose description of the County of the Lakes; but of this we must defer our notice till some future opportunity—contenting ourselves, in the meantime, with assuring our readers, that it is by far the best specimen of the prose style of Wordsworth which has ever been given to the world.

[1] The opinion of *Blackwood's* was not altogether favorable as is here implied: see Alan L. Strout, 'John Wilson, "Champion" of Wordsworth', *Modern Philology*, XXXI (1934), 383–94.

II
Coleridge

Review of
Coleridge's 'The Friend'
(in Periodical Form)

Eclectic Review

VII (Oct. 1811), 912–31. The author was the essayist John Foster. Authority for the attribution is the list of Foster's contributions in J. E. Ryland, The Life and Correspondence of John Foster *(London, 1846),* II, 580–86. The review is reprinted in John Foster, Contributions, Biographical, Literary, and Philosophical to the Eclectic Review *(London, 1844). Page numbers of omitted passages refer to Volume II of B. E. Rooke's edition of* The Friend *(Princeton, N.J., and London, 1969).*

It was with no small pleasure we saw any thing announced of the nature of a proof or pledge that the author of this paper was in good faith employing himself, or about to employ himself, in the intellectual public service. His contributions to that service have, hitherto, borne but a small proportion to the reputation he has long enjoyed of being qualified for it in an extraordinary degree. This reputation is less founded on a small volume of juvenile poems, and some occasional essays in periodical publications, than on the estimate formed and avowed by all the intelligent persons that have ever had the gratification of falling into his society.

After his return, several years since, from a residence of considerable duration in the South East of Europe, in the highest maturity of a mind, which had, previously to that residence, been enriched with large acquisitions of the most diversified literature and scientific knowledge, and by various views of society both in England and on the continent; his friends promised themselves, that the action of so much genius, so long a time, on such ample materials, would at length result in some production, or train of productions, that should pay off some portion of the debt, due to the literary republic, from one of the most opulent of its citizens. A rather long period, however, had elapsed, and several projects had been reported in the usual vehicles of literary intelligence, before this paper was undertaken. An idea of the mental habits and acquirements brought to its execution, will be conveyed by an extract from the prospectus, which was written in the form of a letter to a friend.

[The first paragraph of the Prospectus is quoted (see p. 16).]

Being printed on stamped paper, these essays were conveyed by the post, free of expense, to any part of the country. In the mode of publication, therefore, and what may be called the exterior character of the project 'The Friend' was an imitation of those sets of essays which, from the Tatler down to the Rambler, and several much later works, had first supplied entertainment and instruction in small successive portions, during several months or years, and then taken their rank among books of permanent popularity. Mr. Coleridge has correctly distinguished, in a brief and general manner, the objects to which these works were mainly directed, and rendered a tribute of animated applause to their writers; at the same time bespeaking the candour of his readers to a series of essays, which should attempt to instruct after a very different method. It was avowed, that they would aim much more at the development of general principles; it would be inferred, of course, that they would be of a much more abstract and metaphysical character. Mr. C. fairly warned those whom he invited to become his readers, that, though he should hope not unfrequently to interest the affections, and captivate the imagination, yet a large proportion of the essays were intended to be of a nature, which might require a somewhat resolute exercise of intellect.—It was not proposed to terminate the series at any assigned point; it might be expected to proceed as long as the writer's industry and resources should command the public approbation. With one or two considerable interruptions, it reached as far as twenty-eight numbers, and there ended so abruptly that a memoir of Sir Alexander Ball was left unfinished. At several points in the progress of the work, the writer confessed that the public patronage was not such as to make it probable he could carry it forward to any great length: but no explanation was given of the suddenness of its discontinuance.

Perhaps it may be questioned, now after a portion of the intended work has been given, whether the project did not involve some degree of miscalculation. Even the consideration of a rather excessive price was likely to affect the success of work which, though coming with some of the exterior marks of a newspaper, was yet to derive nearly as little aid from the stimulant facts and questions of the day, as if it had been a commentary on Aristotle or Plato. A still more unfavourable augury might, perhaps, have been drawn from the character of Mr. Coleridge's composition, as taken in connection with the haste inseparable from a weekly publication. The cast of his diction is so unusual, his trains of thought so habitually forsake the ordinary tracts, and therefore the whole composition is so liable to appear strange and obscure, that it was evident the most elaborate care, and a repeated revisal, would be indispensable in order to render so original a mode of writing sufficiently perspicuous to be in any degree popular. And it is equally evident that the necessity of finishing a sheet within each week, against a particular day and hour, must be totally incompatible with such patient and matured workmanship. A considerable portion of the short allotment of time might, in spite of every better resolution, be beguiled away in comparative indolence; or it might be consumed by casual and unforeseen avocations; or rendered fruitless by those lapses into languor and melancholy, to which genius, especially of the refined and poetic order, is extremely subject; or even wasted in the ineffectual endeavour to fix exclusively on some one of many equally eligible subjects. It was to be foreseen that the natural consequences would be sometimes such a degree of haste as to leave no possibility of disposing the subject in the simplest clearest order, and giving the desirable compression, and lucidness, and general finishing to the composition, sometimes, from despair of doing this, a recourse to shifts and expedients to make up the number, in a slighter way than had been intended, and perhaps promised; and often a painful feeling of working at an ungracious task, especially if, in addition, the public approbation should be found to be less liberally awarded than had been expected. Such compulsory dispatch would have been a far less inconvenience in the conducting of a paper intended merely for amusement, or for the lightest kind of instruction, or as a weekly commentary on the contemporary measures and men—a department in which the facility and attractiveness of the topics, and the voracity of the public, exempt the writer from any severity of intellectual toil, or solicitude for literary perfection: but it was almost necessarily fatal in a work to be often occupied with deep disquisitions, and under the added disadvantage that the author had been previously much less accustomed to write than to think. When, besides, the work aspired to a very high rank in our permanent literature, there was perhaps an obvious impolicy in subjecting it to such circumstances of publication, as should preclude the minute improvements of even a tenth revision. It should seem probable, on the whole, that a mode better adapted to the effective exertion of Mr. Coleridge's great talents might have been devised, in the form of a periodical publication to appear in larger portions, at much longer intervals.

Some of the consequences thus to be anticipated from the plan of the undertaking, are actually perceptible in the course of the work. The writer manifests great indecision as to the choice and succession of his subjects. After he appears to have determined on those to be treated in the immediately ensuing numbers, those numbers, when they come, may be employed on totally different subjects,—introduced by accidental suggestion—or from their being such as would be more easily worked, in the brief allowance of time, into the required length and breadth of composition. Questions avowedly intended to be argued very early, as involving great fundamental principles, are deferred till the reader forgets what the author has said of their importance. Various subjects are adverted to, here and there in the course of the work, as to be hereafter investigated, and are never mentioned again. In some instances, the number to which the commencement or the conclusion of an important inquiry has stood over, will be found made up perhaps, for the greater part, of letters, or short fragments, with translations from a minor Italian poet. Several of the numbers, towards the latter end of the series, are employed on the character of the late Sir Alexander Ball, which, however meritorious, was not probably, in the opinion of the majority of the readers, of sufficient celebrity to claim so considerable a space in an expensive work; especially while several most interesting points of inquiry, of which they had been led to expect an early investigation were still, and indefinitely deferred. It is fair, however, to quote the author's apology or vindication, in which, toward the conclusion of the series, he attributes to his readers, the procrastination or relinquishment of the refined disquisitions, which he should himself have been happy to prosecute.

[One paragraph from p. 282 is quoted: from 'the remainder . . .' to ' "satis est" '.]

It may easily be believed that Mr. C. had cause to complain of the impatience of some of his readers, under those demands of a strong mental exertion which some of his essays have made on them; but the degree of this required exertion is greatly under-rated, we think, in the following observations in the same number.

'Themes like these, not even the genius of a Plato or a Bacon could render intelligible without demanding from the reader, *thought* sometimes, and *attention* generally. By *thought* I here mean the voluntary production in our own minds of those states of consciousness, to which, as to his fundamental facts, the writer has referred us: *while attention* has for its object, the order and connection of thoughts and images, each of which is in itself already and familiarly known. Thus the elements of geometry require attention only; but the analysis of our primary faculties, and the investigation of all the absolute grounds of religion and morals, are impossible without energies of thought in addition to the effort of attention. The Friend never attempted to disguise from his readers, that both attention and thought were efforts, and the latter a most difficult and labourious effort; nor for himself that to require it often, or for any continuance of time, was incompatible with the nature of a periodical publication, even were it less incongruous than it unfortunately is, with the present habits and pursuits of Englishmen. Accordingly, after a careful re-perusal of the preceding numbers, I can discover but *four* passages which supposed in the reader any energy of thought and voluntary abstraction. But attention I confess two thirds of the work hitherto have required. On whatever subject the mind feels a lively interest, attention, though always an effort, becomes a delightful effort; and I should be quite at ease, could I secure for the whole work, as much of it as a party of earnest whist-players often expend in a single evening, or a lady in the making up of a fashionable dress. But where no interest previously exists, attention, (as every schoolmaster knows) can be procured only by terror: which is the true reason why the majority of mankind learn nothing systematically, but as schoolboys or apprentices.'

Not to dwell on the arbitrary and rather tenebrious distinction between thought and attention, (which might be given as a fair specimen of the extent of the demand made on the reader's mind in a multitude of passages,) we cannot help saying, that this is a somewhat too reserved acknowledgment—that the 'Friend' has produced a volume, of which a considerable portion is hard to be understood, and some passages of which it may be doubted whether any one reader, after his very best efforts, has felt sure that he did so understand as to be able to put the meaning into other equivalent words of his own. We cannot but think that, in some still later re-perusal, the author himself will have perceived that not a few of his conceptions, taken as detached individual thoughts, are enounced with an obscurity of a somewhat different kind from that which may seem inevitably incident, in some degree, to the expression of thoughts of extreme abstraction. And sometimes the conjunctive principle among several thoughts that come in immediate succession is so unobvious, that the reader must repeatedly peruse, must analyze, we might almost say must excruciate, a considerable portion of the composition, before he can feel any confidence that he is master of the connexion;—and at last he is so little

123

sure of having a real hold of the whole combination, that he would not trust himself to state that particular part of the 'Friend's' opinions and sentiments to an intelligent inquirer. When he could perhaps give, in a very general form, the apparent result of a series of thoughts, he would be afraid to attempt assigning the steps by which his author had arrived at it.

There can be no doubt that, by such patient labour as the adopted mode of publication entirely forbade, the writer could have given, if we may so express it, more roundness and prominence to the logical fibres of his composition, and a more unequivocal substance to some of its more attenuated components; in short left nothing obscure but what was invincibly and necessarily so, from the profound abstraction and exquisite refinement of thought, in which Mr. C. would have extremely few equals in whatever age he had lived.

Our contracted limits will not allow more than a very brief notice of the several subjects on which the author's intellect and imagination have thrown their light and colours, in a more fixed or in a momentary manner, in the course of this desultory performance. It would be fully as interesting, though a more difficult task, to discriminate some of the qualities which distinguish his manner of thinking and writing: and we shall make a short attempt at this, though with no small degree of diffidence in our ability to render the more subtle characteristics palpable in description. Some of them are almost as undefinable, as the varied modifications of the air by which very susceptible organs can perceive the different state of that element as subsisting in one district and in another; almost as undefinable, as the tinge by which the light of the rising and setting sun in spring or autumn, is recognized as of a quite different character from its morning and evening radiance in the other seasons.

And while we are making this reference to the elements and phenomena of nature, we will confess that this author, beyond any other, (Mr. Wordsworth is next,) gives us the impression, or call it the fancy, of a mind constructed to bear a certain indescribable analogy to nature —that is to the physical world, with its wide extent, its elements, its mysterious laws, its animated forms, and its variety and vicissitude of appearances. His mind lives almost habitually in a state of profound sympathy with nature, maintained through the medium of a refined illusion of genius, which informs all nature with a kind of soul and sentiment, that bring all its forms and entities, animate and inanimate, visible and invisible, into a mystical communion with his feelings. This sympathy is, or involves, an exceedingly different feeling from that with which a strictly philosophic mind perceives and admires in nature the more definable attributes of variety, order, beauty, and grandeur. These are acknowledged with a vivid perception; but, in our author's powerful imagination, they become a kind of moral attributes of a half-intelligential principle, which dimly, but with mysterious attraction, discloses itself from within all matter and form. This sympathy has retained him much more effectually in what may be called the school of nature, than is usual to men of genius who enter so much into artificial society, and so extensively study the works of men: And the influences of this school have given that form to his habits of thinking which bears so many marks of analogy to the state of surrounding physical nature. To illustrate this we may observe, that he perpetually falls on analogies between moral truth and facts in nature: in his figurative language he draws his similies and metaphors from the scenes of nature in preference to the departments of art—though these latter are also very much at his command: his ideas have much of the unlimited variety of nature; they have much also of its irregularity, being but little constrained into formal artificial method: there is in his train of thinking a great deal of what may be called colour and efflorescence, and but little of absolutely plain bare intellectual material: like nature as to her productions, he seems as willing to bestow labour and completeness on little thoughts as on great ones: we may add, he does not shew any concern about mixing the little and great together, —sublime and remote ideas, and humble and familiar ones, being readily admitted, if they happen to come in immediate succession.

The above description of our author's sympathy with nature, and his mystical perception of something like soul and sentiment residing in all material elements and forms, will not be misunderstood to impute to him any thing like a serious adoption of the atheistical principle of Spinoza, or of the Stoic or Platonic dogmas about the Soul of the World. This converse with all surrounding existence is, in the perfect consciousness of our author's mind, no more than the emancipation of that mind itself; imparting, in its meditative enthusiasm, a character of imaginary moral being and deep significance to all objects, but leaving his understanding in the full and solemn belief of a Supreme Intelligence, perfectly distinct from the whole universe. But there is strong reason to suspect, that certain of his poetical contemporaries renounce the idea of such a Divine Intelligence, in their fancy of the all-pervading, inexplicable something, which privileged and profoundly thoughtful spirits may perceive, and without illusion, in the light of the sun, in clouds, in silent groves, and in the sound of winds and mountain torrents.

But we ought to have remarked, first, on some of the more easily definable of the distinguishing properties of the 'Friend's' intellectual and literary character. Among the foremost may be mentioned the independence and the wide reach with which he thinks. He has given attendance in all the schools of moral and metaphysical philosophy, ancient and modern, but evidently has attended there rather to debate the matter with the professors, than with submissive homage to receive their dictates. He would have been a most factious and troublesome pupil in the academy of Pythagoras. He regards all subjects and doctrines as within the rightful sphere of free examination: and the work affords evidence, that a very large number of them have actually been examined by him with extraordinary severity. Yet this freedom of thinking, supported as it is by the conscious possession of great power and exceedingly ample and diversified knowledge, does not degenerate into arrogance; a high and sincere respect being uniformly shewn for the great intellectual aristocracy of both the past and present times, but especially of the past. Of the eminent writers of our own country, he evinces a higher veneration of those of the seventeenth, than those of the subsequent century, and of the present time; and professes to have been of late years more familiar with them, and to have involuntarily acquired some degree of conformity to their manner of thinking and to their style.

Another instantly apparent distinction of our author's manner of thinking, is its extreme abstractedness. Considering that many of his subjects are not of that class which, by the necessity of their nature, *can* be discussed in no other than a metaphysical manner, he has avoided, in a wonderful and unequalled degree, all the superficial and obvious forms of thought which they might suggest. He always carries on his investigation at a depth, and sometimes a most profound depth, below the uppermost and most accessible stratum; and is philosophically mining among its most recondite principles of the subject, while ordinary intellectual and literary workmen, many of them barely informed of the very existence of this Spirit of the Deep, are pleasing themselves and those they draw around them, with forming to pretty shapes, or commodious uses, the materials of the surface. It may be added, with some little departure from the consistency of the metaphor, that if he endeavours to make his voice heard from this region beneath, it is apt to be listened to as a sound of dubious import, like that which fails to bring articulate words from the remote recess of a cavern, or the bottom of the deep shaft of a mine. However familiar the truths and facts to which his mind is directed, it constantly, and as if involuntarily strikes, if we may so speak, into the invisible and the unknown of the subject; he is seeking the most retired and abstracted form in which any being can be acknowledged and realized as having an existence, or any truth can be put in a proposition. He turns all things into their ghosts, and summons us to walk with him in this region of shades—this strange world of disembodied truths and entities.

He repeatedly avows, that it is less his object to teach truth in its most special and practical form, and in its detailed application, than to bring up into view and certainty a number of grand general principles, to become the lights of judgement, on an endless variety of particular subjects. At least this was the proposed object of the earlier part, the first twenty or thirty numbers, of the intended series. These principles were to be brought into clearness and authority, partly by statement and argument in an abstract form, and partly by shewing them advantageously in operation, as applied to the trial and decision of several interesting questions. But the abstruseness often unavoidable in the pure intellectual enunciation of a principle, prevails also in an uncommon degree, in the present work, through the practical illustrations—even when the matter of those illustrations consists of very familiar facts. The ideas employed to explain the mode of the relation between the facts and the principle, are sometimes of such extreme tenuity as to make a reader who is anxious to comprehend, but unaccustomed to abstraction, feel as if he were deficient by nearly one whole faculty, some power of intellectual sight or tact with which he perceives the author to be endowed,—for there is something that every where compels him to give the author credit for thinking with great acuteness, even when he is labouring in vain to refine his own conceptions into any state that can place him in real communication with the author's mind. The surpassing subtlety of that mind is constantly describing the most unobvious relations, and detecting the most veiled aspects of things, and pervading their substance in quest of whatever is most latent in their nature. This extreme subtlety is the cause of more than one kind of difficulty to the reader. Its *necessary* consequence is that refinement of observation on which we have so prolixly remarked; but it has another consequence, the less or greater degree of which depended on the author's choice. He has suffered it continually to retard him in, or divert him from, the straight forward line of thought to his object. He enters on a train of argumentative observations to determine a given question. He advances one acute thought, and another, and another: but by this time he perceives among these which we may call the primary thoughts, so many secondaries—so many bearings, distinctions, and analogies—so many ideas starting sideways from the main line of thought—so many pointings towards subjects infinitely remote—that, in the attempt to seize and fix in words these secondary thoughts, he will often suspend for a good while the progress toward the intended point. Thus each thought that was to have been only *one* thought, and to have transmitted the reader's mind immediately forward to the next in order and in advance, becomes an exceedingly complex combination of thoughts, almost a dissertation in miniature: and thus our journey to the assigned point (if indeed we are carried so far, which is not always the case) becomes nothing less than a visit of curious inspection to every garden, manufactory, museum, and antiquity, situated near the road, throughout its whole length. Hence too it often happens, that the transitions are not a little perplexing. The transition directly from one primary thought, as we venture to call it, in the train to the next, might be very easy: we might see most perfectly how, in natural logic, the one was connected with the other, or led to it; but when we have to pass to this next principal thought in the train, from some divergent and remote accessory of the former principal idea, we feel that we have lost the due bearing of the preceding part of the train, by being brought in such an indirect way to the resumption of it.

The same kind of observation is applicable to the comparisons and metaphors with which our author illustrates and adorns his speculations. In this component of good writing, we believe he has no superior in this or any other age. His figures are original, and various, and often *complexly* opposite, to a degree of which we do not at present recollect any example. They are taken indifferently from any part of a prodigious sphere of knowledge, and presented with every possible advantage of rich and definite expression. In the choice of them he very justly scorns, what has been noticed as a leading point of contradistinction of the French orators and poets from ours, the fastidiousness which declines similies taken from things of so humble a quality as to give to the figure a character of meanness. While he can easily reach, if he pleases, as far into remoteness and magnificence as the aphelion of a comet, for an object of illustrative comparison, he is not afraid to turn to literary account in the next paragraph, even a thing of so little dignity as those fastenings of garments called *hooks and eyes*. But the fault we venture to charge is, analogously to what we have said of the more austerely intellectual parts of the composition, the frequent extension of a figure into a multiformity which beguiles both the author and the reader from the direct and pressing pursuit of the main object. When the object is grave and important truth, the beauties of imagery, when introduced with a copiousness greatly beyond the strictest necessities of explanation, should be so managed as to be like flowery borders of a road: the way may have on each side every variety of beauty, every charm of shape, and hue and scent, to regale the traveller: but, it should still be absolutely a *road*—going right on—with defined and near limits—and not widening out into a spacious and intricate wilderness of these beauties, where the man that was to travel is seduced to wander. When an apt figure occurs to our author, his imagination (which has received with wonderful accuracy, and retained with wonderful fidelity, *all* the ascertainable points of appearance and quality of almost all objects,) instantaneously expands and finishes this figure, within his own mind, into a complete object or scene, with all its absolute and relative distinctions and circumstances; and his intellectual subtlety suddenly perceives, besides its principal and most obvious analogy with the abstract truth he is stating, various other more refined and minute analogies and appositenesses, which are more gratifying to his own mind than the leading analogy, partly from the consideration that only a very acute perception would have discerned them, and partly because a double intellectual luckiness is more unusual than a single one. Now, we have mentioned the *complexity* of appositeness, the several-fold relation between the figure and the truth to which it is brought as correspondent, as one of the *excellencies*, of our author's figures: and we have done so, because none but a writer of great genius will very frequently fall on such figures—and because a very specific rather than a merely general relation, an interior and essential rather than a superficial and circumstantial analogy, between the subject and the corresponding figure, *is* a great excellence as exhibiting the laws of reason prevalent through the operations of imagination; and it would often be found that the specific and pointed appropriateness of the comparison consists in its containing a double analogy. But when a subtle intelligence, perceiving something much beyond this duplicity of relation, introduces a number of perhaps real and exquisite, but extremely recondite correspondences, the reader, though pleased with the sagacious perception, so long as not confused by the complexity, is, at the same time, certainly diverted from the leading purpose of the discourse.

It is not alone in the detection of refined analogies that our author too much amplifies his figurative illustrations. He does it sometimes in the way of merely perfecting, for the sake of its own completeness, the representation of the thing which furnishes the figure, which is often done equally with philosophical accuracy and poetic beauty. But thus extended into particularity, the illustration exhibits a number of colours, and combinations, and branchings of imagery, neither needful nor useful to the main intellectual purpose. Our author is therefore sometimes like a man, who, in a work that requires the use of wood, but requires it only in the plain bare form of straight-shaped poles and stakes, should insist that it shall be *living* wood, retaining all its twigs, leaves and blossoms. Or, if we might compare the series of ideas in a composition to a military line, we should say that many of our author's images, and of even his more abstracted conceptions, are supernumerarily attended by so many related, but secondary and subordinate ideas, that the array of thought bears some resemblance to what that military line would be, if many of the men, veritable and brave soldiers all the while, stood in the ranks surrounded with their wives and children.

Of the properties which we have attempted, we sincerely acknowledge very inadequately, to discriminate and describe as characteristic of our author's mode of writing, the result is—that readers of ordinary, though tolerably cultivated faculties, feel a certain deficiency of the effective force which they believe such an extraordinary course of thinking ought to have on their minds. They feel, decisively, that they are under the tuition of a most uncommonly powerful and far-seeing spirit, that penetrates into the essences of things, and can also strongly define their forms and even their shadows—and that is quite in earnest to communicate, while they are equally in earnest to obtain, the most important principles which such a mind has deduced from a severe examination of a vast variety of facts and books. And yet there is some kind of haze in the medium through which this spirit transmits its light, or there is some vexatious dimness in the mental faculty of seeing so that looking back from the end of an essay, or of the volume, they really do not feel themselves in possession of any thing like the full value of as much ingenious, and sagacious, and richly illustrated thinking as ever, probably, was contained in the same proportion of writing.

We would not set down much of the difficulty of comprehending, so much complained of, to the *language*, so far as it is distinguishable from the thought; with the exception of here and there a scholastic phrase, and a certain degree of peculiarity in the use of one or two terms—especially *reason*, which he uses in a sense in which he endeavours to explain and prove, that all men are in equally full possession of the faculty which it denominates. Excepting so far as a slight tinge of antiqueness indicates the influence of our older writers, especially Milton and Bacon, on the complexion of our author's language, it is of a construction original in the greatest possible degree. That it could not well be otherwise may easily be supposed, when, premising, as we have done, the originality of the author's manner of thinking, we observe that the diction is in a most extraordinary degree conformed to the thought. It lies, if we may so speak, close to the mental surface, with all its irregularities, throughout. It is therefore perpetually varying, in perfect flexibility and obsequiousness to the ideas; and, without any rhetorical regulation of its changes, or apparent design, or consciousness in the writer, is in succession popular and scientific, familiar and magnificent, secular and theological, plain and poetical. It has none of the phrases or combinations of oratorical common-place: it has no settled and favourite appropriations of certain adjectives to certain substantives: its manner of expressing an idea once, gives the reader no guess how the same idea will be expressed when it comes modified by a different combination. The writer considers the whole congregation of words, constituting our language, as something so perfectly and independently his own, that he may make any kind of use of any part of it that his thinking requires. Almost every page therefore, presents unusual combinations of words, that appear not so much made *for* the thought as made *by* it, and often give, if we may so express it, the very colour, as well as the substantial form, of the idea. There is no settled construction or cadence of the sentences; no two, perhaps, of about the same length being constructed in the same manner. From the complexity and extended combination of the thought, they are generally long, which the author something less than half-apologizes for, and therefore something more than half defends. We will quote what he says on this point.

'Doubtless, too, I have in some measure injured my style, in respect to its facility and popularity, from having almost confined my reading, of late years, to the works of the ancients and those of the elder writers in the modern languages. We insensibly admire what we habitually imitate; and an aversion to the epigrammatic unconnected periods of the fashionable *Anglo-Gallican* taste, has too often made me willing to forget, that the stately march and difficult evolutions, which characterize the eloquence of Hooker, Bacon, Milton, and Jeremy Taylor, are, notwithstanding their intrinsic excellence, still less suited to a periodical essay. This fault I am now endeavouring to correct, though I can never so far sacrifice my judgement to the desire of being immediately popular, as to cast my sentences in the French moulds; or affect a style which an ancient critic would have deemed purposely invented for persons troubled with asthma to read, and for those to comprehend who labour under the more pitiable asthma of a short-witted intellect. It cannot but be injurious to the human mind never to be called into effort; and the habit of receiving pleasure without any exercise of thought, by the mere excitement of curiosity and sensibility, may be justly ranked among the worst effects of novel-reading. It is true, that these short and unconnected sentences are easily and instantly understood: but it is equally true, that, wanting all the cement of thought as well as of style, all the connections, and (if you will forgive so trivial a metaphor) all the *hooks-and-eyes* of the memory, they are as easily forgotten; or rather, it is scarcely possible they should be remembered. Nor is it less true that those who confine their reading to such books, dwarf their own faculties, and finally reduce their understandings to a deplorable imbecility.' p. 166.

He might, in contradiction to the vulgar notion that long sentences *necessarily* shew the author guilty of what is termed diffuseness, have added, that length of sentences furnishes a capital mean of being concise; that, in fact, whoever is determined on the greatest possible parsimony of words, *must* write in long sentences, if there is any thing like combination in his thoughts. For, in a long sentence, several indispensable conditionalities, collateral notices, and qualifying or connecting circumstances, may be expressed by short members of the sentence, which must else be put in so many separate sentences; thus making two pages of short sentences to express, and in a much less connected manner, what one well-constructed long sentence would have expressed in half a page:—and yet an unthinking reader might very possibly cite these two pages as a specimen of concise writing, and such a half page as a sample of diffuseness.

We have intended to make a few remarks on the several essays in this volume, considered as to their subjects; and on the most prominent of the principles endeavoured to be illustrated and established. But we have dwelt so long on the more general qualities of its intellectual and literary character, that our readers will very willingly excuse us from prolonging a course of observations, in which we have by no means succeeded to our wish in the attempt to convey a general idea of the most extraordinary production that has, at any time, come under our official notice. We confess, too, that we should feel no small degree of diffidence in undertaking any thing like an analysis of disquisitions so abstruse, so little reduced to the formal arrangement of system, so interrupted and unfinished, and so often diverging to a great distance from the leading direction.

The subjects largely discussed are few. Among them are, the duty and laws of communicating truth, including the liberty of the press; the theories of the several most celebrated political philosophers, or schools of philosophers; errors of party spirit; vulgar errors respecting taxation; the law of nations; Paley's doctrine of general consequences as the foundation of the criterion of morality; sketches of Sir Alexander Ball; the proper discipline for rising, in point of intellectual freedom and vigour, above the general state of the age; and several other topics of less comprehensive denomination. But no adequate guess can be made, from these denominations, at the variety and latitude of the inquiries and observations. There is not a great deal expressly on the subject of religion; the intended statement of the author's general views of it having been delayed till the work prematurely closed; but there are many occasional references in a spirit of great seriousness. He asserts the radical depravity, to a very great extent, of human nature, though in forms of language most widely different, to be sure, from that of orthodox sermons and bodies of divinity. As the basis, however, of some of his principles of moral philosophy, he claims a certain profound and half mystical reverence for the mental and moral essence and organization of man, which we find it somewhat difficult to render. He is a most zealous assertor of free-agency. In one place the word Methodism is used exactly in the way in which it is employed by those whom the author knows to be fools, profligates, or bigots. He is perfectly apprized, how much of intelligent belief and ardent piety is comprehended within the tenets and the state of the affections, to which this term of opprobrium is generally applied; and we were astonished therefore to see him so far consenting to adopt what he knew to be the lingo of irreligion.

A portion of his political reasonings and reflections, is retrospective to the times of the French revolution; and distinguishes and censures, with very great judgment and eloquence, the respective errors of our aristocratic and democratic parties at that time. Some interesting references are made to the author's own views, and hopes, and projects at that period. As those views and projects had nothing to do with revolutions in England, we wish that some passages expressed in the tone of self-exculpation had been spared. It was no great harm, if a young man of speculative and ardent genius saw nothing in the political state of any country in Christendom to prevent him wishing, that a new constitution of society could be tried somewhere in the wildernesses of America. In his professing to have very long since renounced the visionary ideas and wishes which, under various modifications of the notion and the love of liberty, elated so many superior minds in that eventful season, we were anxious to see him preserve the dignity of keeping completely clear of the opposite extreme of approving all things as they are—to see him preserve, in short, the lofty spirit in which he wrote, many years since, his sublime 'Ode to France.' And there is in the work less to displease on that head, than in many instances of the 'impetuous recoil' of men of talents from the principles of violent democracy. But we confess we have perceived a more favourable aspect than we should deem compatible with the spirit of a perfect moralist, philanthropist, and patriot, towards the present state of political institutions and practices. We should think that at least these are not times to extenuate the evil of enormous taxation;

to make light of the suggestion of the superior benefit of employing a given number of men rather in making canals and building bridges than in destructive military expeditions; to celebrate the happiness of having the much greater part of a thousand millions of a national debt, and the attendant benefit of a paper-currency; or to join in reprobating any party who are zealous for a reform of the legislature and political corruptions.—There is, however, in the work, much acute speculation on political systems that has no direct reference to the practical politics of the day. It should be observed too, that, beyond all other political speculators, our author mingles important moral and philosophical principles with his reasonings.

The most of what may be called entertainment, may perhaps, be found in a number of letters written from Germany by a young Englishman, who passed among his college companions by the name of Satyrane, and whom, if there were not so much said or implied in his praise, accompanied too by some slight expression as if he were not now surviving, we should mightily suspect to be no other than the author himself.

A whole number (the 13th) is occupied with the story of a tragical event that happened at Nuremberg, a little before Mr. C. first saw that place. The principal personages were a baker's orphan and outcast daughter, and a washerwoman. He is very particular in asserting the truth of the account; but if he had not, we should have believed it nevertheless; for the plain reason, that we think it surpasses the powers of fiction, the powers of invention of even Mr. C. No abstract can be given to make it at all intelligible; but it is so strange, so horrible, and so sublime, that we should think meanly of the feelings of any person, who, after reading it, would not turn with indifference from the comparative insipidity of any thing to be found in tragedy or romance.

We ought to have given a few extracts from the work; but we did not know where to select them, amidst such a wilderness of uncommon ideas. Many other passages may be more interesting than the following representation of one of Luther's skirmishes with Satan, in the Warteburg, a castle near Eisenach, in which he was confined many months, by a friendly and provident force, and where our author was shewn the black mark on the wall, produced as every visitant is told, by the intrepid reformer's throwing his ink-stand at the enemy.

[Two paragraphs from pp. 119–20 are quoted: from 'If this Christian . . .' to '. . . actually taken place'.]

We cannot conclude without expressing an earnest wish, that this original thinker and eloquent writer may be persuaded to put the literary public speedily in possession, by successive volumes of essays, of an ample portion of those refined speculations, the argument and the strongest illustrations of which he is well known to have in an almost complete state in his mind—and many of which will never be in any other mind, otherwise than as communicated from him. The chief alteration desirable, for his readers' sake, to be made in his mode of writing, is a resolute restriction on that mighty profusion and excursiveness of thought, in which he is tempted to suspend the pursuit and retard the attainment of the one distinct object which should be clearly kept in view; and, added to this, a more patient and prolonged effort to reduce the abstruser part of his ideas, as much as their subtle quality will possibly admit, to a substantial and definable form.

Review of Coleridge's 'Remorse'

Critical Review

4th ser. III (April 1813), 402–05. The reviewer is unknown.

The representation of a new tragedy, written by an author of established poetical fame, is, alas! so great a novelty in our theatrical annals, that it was hailed by the few surviving amateurs of the drama as the commencement of a new aera in dramatic history. Remembering the failure of De Montfort,[1] we were not quite so sanguine in our prognostications as some of those 'whose wish,' we fear, 'was father to their thought;' and, on the contrary, had our opinion been asked after the second performance of the piece (which we witnessed in person) we should probably have predicted a less degree of success than that which it has actually since experienced. To say the truth, then, it is our firm persuasion that no important revolution can be effected in the present degraded state of the stage, so long as the monopoly of the theatres continues.[2] Whenever a new theatre shall be established, of the old moderate dimensions, and devoted exclusively to the representation of such works as do honour to the national taste and genius, abandoning to the present magnificent houses those departments for which they are alone calculated, of broad farce and splendid spectacle, then, and not till then, we may hope to see a new aera of the drama which shall rival that of Elizabeth in warmth and vigour, without sacrificing the more correct attainments of a refined and critical age of poetry.

From this Utopia, we must now turn to the tragedy of Mr. Coleridge;

1 *De Montfort* was a play by Joanna Baillie produced with great splendor in 1800; it lasted eleven nights.

2 Only Covent Garden and Drury Lane, both of huge proportions, were licensed.

and, while we admit with pleasure that this work would have appeared to much greater advantage under circumstances such as we have been imagining than it has done, exhibited on the immense canvas, and with the gorgeous and overpowering frame of the new Drury Lane stage, we cannot, however, ascribe to it so much intrinsic merit as would entitle it to a very high rank among the productions of true dramatic genius. It announces, indeed, a poetical mind, such as its author is known already, upon other evidence, undoubtedly to possess; and we think it gives sufficient assurance that, with proper encouragement of his dramatic talent, his second, or third, or fourth essay in the art might have raised him far above his present level. With such an opinion, we can hardly repress our indignation at the treatment which this play experienced in a quarter from which, of all others, it might have been expected that that proper encouragement should have proceeded. The public is already pretty generally acquainted with the circumstances under which its representation was kept back ever since the year 1797, when it was first offered to, and received by, the then manager:[1] and all, who feel the least interest in the success and advancement of the dramatic art, have participated in our sentiments while they reflected that the time so unworthily lost to the author, might (with different treatment) have been employed by him in attaining an eminence at once honourable to himself and to his country. We are however glad that these circumstances are now publicly known. They may operate as an useful example to the future conductors of our stage—and we are convinced, (however remote we may be from the realization of our Utopian visions in other respects,) that a much more liberal, a more considerate, and a more humane spirit has prevailed since the period of those unfeeling and detrimental abuses.

It appears unnecessary to give any analysis of the fable of this tragedy, with which very few of our readers can now be supposed to be unacquainted. Our principal objection to it is its great moral improbability; a defect which, whenever it occurs, cannot fail to involve in it the absence of all strong dramatic interest. The disguise of Don Alvar has scarcely an adequate motive even in his misapprehension respecting the fidelity of his mistress; since that misapprehension is made (in his imagination), to amount even to certainty, and to leave little, if any, room for doubt and trial. But, after this misapprehension is removed, the continuance of the disguise is altogether inexplicable by any of the motives that influence ordinary humanity; and the exposure both of his own happiness and that of an innocent, afflicted, and beloved woman to the most imminent hazard for the romantic object of awakening

[1] See the Preface to *Remorse*.

remorse in the mind of his brother, may perhaps find some parallel in the extravagant and unnatural sentiment of a German theatre, but certainly none in the heart or head of any truly affectionate or reasonable being. After so serious a shock to the very foundation of the structure, no excellence of parts could in our apprehension have saved the vessel from a total wreck. But we can with difficulty find any such excellence as to warrant us in entertaining a very strong wish that it were possible to preserve it. The character of Ordonio is, we think, well sketched; but it is imperfectly finished. That of Naomi is less original, but is painted with some strength of colouring. The rest of the dramatis personae have little variety or discrimination to recommend them. Of the machinery, the scene of the murder of Isidore in the cavern, is gloomy and terrible, but nothing can be conceived more outré and ill-placed, nothing less calculated to produce any effect in point of interest or pathos, than the clumsy and unnecessary contrivance of the mock incantation. It tends to no end or purpose whatever; and Macbeth's three Witches have just as much to do with the progress and denouement of the plot, as this silly and puerile piece of spectacle. The author was aware of the nakedness of the plot he had chosen, but knew not how to remedy the radical evil.

After this, it is evident that in our opinion the whole reputation of the piece must hereafter rest upon its merits in respect of poetical sentiment and expression; and (in this point of view only) we think it will always maintain a respectable station on the shelves of a dramatic library, long after it shall have ceased to figure on the boards of a theatre.

[Lines 18–50 of Act I, scene ii, are quoted.]

This is extremely tender, and beautifully reminds us of the similar picture drawn by Miss Baillie, in her exquisite little opera of the Beacon. The following 'Prison Thoughts' of Don Alvar will more forcibly call to our recollection the peculiar and distinguishing traits of Mr. Coleridge's own poetical character.

[Lines 1–30 of Act V, scene i, are quoted.]

Reviews of Coleridge's
'Christabel' Volume

Critical Review

5th ser. III (May 1816), 504–10. The reviewer is unknown.

There is no quality of the mind more despicable than that love of censure and ridicule which has its origin in our own weakness, and which hunts for faults or singularities, not for the purpose of amending them, but for the sake of gratifying an imaginary superiority: those who thus flatter their vanity by reducing genius to the degraded level of their own understandings, who 'damn the worth they cannot imitate,' may find in the fragment before us some food to satisfy their diseased appetite; while those on the other hand who are hopeful yet humble, emulous yet not envious, who triumph in every fresh display of talent and genius as a fresh incentive to exertion, will read with generous enthusiasm the pages upon our table. If we had no other reason for so thinking, than the rapid sale of this poem, we should judge that the latter are a very numerous class: to the former Ben Jonson alludes in his Discoveries where he says that 'Critics are a sort of Tinkers, who ordinarily make more faults than they mend.' As it is a maxim of the criminal law of England, that it is better to find one man innocent than to convict ten men as guilty, so it ought to be [a] maxim of the critical law of literature, that it is more advantageous to point out one beauty than to discover ten deformities.

We apprehend that the most fastidious would find much more to praise than to blame in this newly published effort; but reading it in the wholesome spirit to which we have above referred, the defects will appear to bear a most insignificant proportion to the perfections: we could, it is true, point out expressions that might have been better turned, and lines that perhaps might have been better omitted; but deviations are not necessarily defects, and peculiarities may either be those of excellence or of error.

'Christabel' is a romantic fragment; the first part, as the author informs us, having been written in 1797, and the second in 1800, during which interval Mr. Coleridge visited Germany, still retaining the fabric of the complete story in his mind 'with the wholeness no less than with the liveliness of a vision,' and as the vivid impression continues to the present day, he undertakes 'to embody in verse the three parts yet to come, in the course of the present year.' We sincerely hope that this promise will be realized, but we fear that the task will be at least wearisome to a man of the listless habits of Mr. Coleridge. For ourselves we confess, that when we read the story in M.S. two or three years ago, it appeared to be one of those dream-like productions whose charm partly consisted in the undefined obscurity of the conclusion—what that conclusion may be, no person who reads the commencement will be at all able to anticipate. The reader, before he opens the poem, must be prepared to allow for the superstitions of necromancy and sorcery, and to expect something of the glorious and unbounded range which the belief in those mysteries permits; the absurd trammels of mere physical possibility are here thrown aside, like the absurd swaddling clothes of infants, which formerly obstructed the growth of the fair symmetry of nature.

[A brief summary of the poem is given, interspersed with the following lines: 43–52, 118–28, 141–42, 154–61, 239–54, 408–26, 584–87, 597–612, and 640–55. The following critical comments were also made of the images of the curl and leaf (in lines 43–52): 'It was impossible to select two circumstances that more perfectly shewed the dead calmness of the night.' The contrast between the two ladies passing through the gate and the army in battle array (in lines 125–28) is described as 'beautiful'. The disclosure of Geraldine's real nature is said to be 'gradual and beautiful'. The disclosure of what it is that Christabel sees when Geraldine disrobes is kept back 'by a poetical and most judicious abruption'. Lines 408–26, which contain a description of the friendship of Sir Leoline and Sir Roland, are said to be 'finer than any in the language upon the same subject, with which we are acquainted, more especially the noble image at the end'.]

We lament that our limits will not allow us to give more of this very graceful and fanciful poem, which we may say, without fear of contradiction, is enriched with more beautiful passages than have ever been before included in so small a compass. Nothing can be better contrasted than Christabel and Geraldine—both exquisite, but both different—the first all innocence, mildness, and grace; the last all dignity, grandeur, and majesty: the one with all those innate virtues, that working internally, mould the external shape to corresponding perfectness—the other possessing merely the charm of superficial excellence: the one the gentle soul-delighting Una—the other the seeming fair, but infamous Duessa.

Of the rich and luxuriant imagery with which this poem abounds, our imperfect sketch will afford but a faint idea, and we have been compelled to omit many descriptive passages of the first order. For these we must refer to the original, assured that, after reading our extracts, none will throw it aside because they meet with a passage or two in the threshold not exactly according with their pre-conceived notions of excellence.

Kubla Khan, a Vision, is one of those pieces that can only speak for itself, but from 'the Pains of Sleep' we cannot refrain from giving the following dreadful and powerful picture of a horrid dream.

[Lines 14–32 are quoted.]

Eclectic Review

2d ser. V (June 1816), 565–72. The author was Josiah Conder, a minor poet, bookseller, and editor of the Eclectic *from 1814 to 1836. Authority for this attribution is the marked staff copies of the* Eclectic *now in the London Library.*

We had frequently heard of Mr. Coleridge's manuscript of Christabel, as a singularly wild and romantic poem, the perusal of which had obviously suggested the idea of certain popular metrical romances of specious originality. Our curiosity to see this long-hoarded treasure, was proportioned to the pre-eminent abilities of which its Author is known by his friends, we cannot say to have the command, but to sustain the responsibility. A note in 'The Siege of Corinth,'[1] has recently attracted more general attention towards it; and at length, after sixteen years of concealment, it comes forth,—a fragment still. Two Cantos only out of five, are contained in the present publication: the remaining three exist only in the teeming chaos of the Author's brain. His poetic powers have, it seems, been, 'till very lately, in a state of suspended animation.' We should rejoice indeed to find, that the spell

[1] In a note to *The Siege of Corinth*, Byron calls 'Christabel' a 'wild and singularly original and beautiful poem' and expresses a wish that Coleridge should publish it.

which has so long locked up Mr. Coleridge's powers, not only is dissolved, but has left them unimpaired, in all the freshness of youth, as,
according to romantic fable, the enchanted virgin wakes from her age-
long slumber, untouched by time. Mr. Coleridge *trusts* that he 'shall be
able to embody in verse the three parts yet to come, in the course of
the present year!' We shall be glad to find that this trust is better
founded than were the hopes which his friends so long indulged in
vain.

In the mean time, we cannot conceal that the effect of the present
publication upon readers in general, will be that of disappointment. It
may be compared to a mutilated statue, the beauty of which can only
be appreciated by those who have knowledge or imagination sufficient
to complete the idea of the whole composition. The reader is obliged
to guess at the half-developed meaning of the mysterious incidents, and
is at last, at the end of the second canto, left in the dark, in the most
abrupt and unceremonious manner imaginable. Yet we are much mistaken if this fragment, such as it is, will not be found to take faster
hold of the mind than many a poem six cantos long. Its merit, in point
of originality, will be lost on most readers, in consequence of the
prior appearance of so great a quantity of verse in the same style and
measure.[1] But the kind of interest which the tale is calculated to
awaken, is quite different from that of the description of poems alluded
to. Horror is the prevailing sentiment excited by Christabel: not that
mixture of terror and disgust with which we listen to details of crime
and bloodshed, but the purely imaginative feeling, the breathless thrill
of indefinite emotion of which we are conscious when in the supposed
presence of an unknown being, or acted upon by some influence
mysteriously transcending the notice of the senses—that passion which
Collins has so beautifully apostrophized under the name of Fear, in
the Ode beginning

> 'Thou to whom the world unknown
> 'With all its shadowy shapes is shewn;
> 'Who seest appall'd the unreal scene,
> 'When Fancy lifts the veil between.'

Christabel opens with the following lines:

[Lines 1–70 of Part I are quoted. A brief summary of the story
follows, in which the following lines are quoted: 73–74, 154–63,
175–83, 245–54, 261–78, and 326–31 of Part I.]

---

[1] Among others, Scott's *The Lay of the Last Minstrel.*

With these lines the first part of the Poem concludes.

In the second, we are made imperfectly acquainted with the effect of the hideous spell worked by this false Geraldine. It appears to consist in the strange and terrible power of so working on the sympathy, as to make its victim passively conform itself to the impression made on the external senses, and by this means the framer of the spell is represented as exchanging both feeling and expression with the unhappy subject of her perfidious and refined sorcery. If this be the invention of the Poet's brain, and it partakes of his wildly metaphysical cast of thought, it must be conceded that he deserves a patent for its ingenuity. One cannot conceive of a more terrible engine of supernatural malice. But are not the spells of vicious example in real life almost a counterpart to this fiction?

Sir Leoline is fascinated by the false loveliness of Geraldine. Christabel shudders at the sight, but has no power to disclose what she has seen. The bard Bracy informs the Baron of a dream, in which he saw a dove within the coil of a bright green snake. Sir Leoline misapplies the dream to Geraldine, and vows to crush the snake. The scene which ensues, is finely conceived.

[Lines 572–620 of Part II are quoted.]

Here we may close our account of this singular production. The Conclusion to Part the Second, is, we suppose, an enigma. It is certainly unintelligible as it stands. We suspect that Mr. Coleridge's poetical powers began to yield to their sixteen years' nap just at this moment, and that he dreamed the few last lines.

As to 'Kubla Khan,' and the 'Pains of Sleep,' we can only regret the publication of them, as affording a proof that the Author over-rates the importance of his name. With regard to the former, which is professedly published as a psychological curiosity, it having been composed during sleep, there appears to us nothing in the quality of the lines to render this circumstance extraordinary. We could have informed Mr. Coleridge of a reverend friend of ours, who actually wrote down two sermons on a passage in the Apocalypse, from the recollection of the spontaneous exercise of his faculties in sleep. To persons who are in the habit of poetical composition, a similar phenomenon would not be a stranger occurrence, than the spirited dialogues in prose which take place in the dreams of persons of duller invention than our poet, and which not unfrequently leave behind a very vivid impression.

We closed the present publication with sentiments of melancholy and regret, not unmixed with pity. In what an humbling attitude does such a man as Coleridge present himself to the public, in laying before them these specimens of the rich promise of excellence, with which sixteen years ago he raised the expectations of his friends,—pledges of future greatness which after sixteen years he has failed to redeem! He is now once more loudly called upon to break off his desultory and luxurious habits, and to brace his mind to intellectual exertion. Samson could never have despaired of recovering his strength, till the baldness of age should fall upon him. We cherish a hope that the principle of strength, though dormant, is still unimpaired in our poet's mind, and that he will yet awake in his strength.

Examiner

June 2, 1816, pp. 348–49. The author was William Hazlitt: see Herschel Baker, William Hazlitt (*Cambridge, Mass., 1962*), p. 202n. *The review is reprinted in P. P. Howe, ed.*, The Complete Works of William Hazlitt (*London, 1933*), *vol. XIX.*

The fault of Mr. Coleridge is, that he comes to no conclusion. He is a man of that universality of genius, that his mind hangs suspended between poetry and prose, truth and falsehood, and an infinity of other things, and from an excess of capacity, he does little or nothing. Here are two unfinished poems, and a fragment. *Christabel*, which has been much read and admired in manuscript, is now for the first time confided to the public. The *Vision of Kubla Khan* still remains a profound secret; for only a few lines of it ever were written.

The poem of *Christabel* sets out in the following manner.

> 'Tis the middle of night by the castle clock,
> And the owls have awaken'd the crowing cock;
> Tu—whit! Tu—whoo!
> And hark, again! the crowing cock,
> How drowsily it crew.
> Sir Leoline, the Baron rich,
> Hath a toothless mastiff bitch;
> From her kennel beneath the rock
> She makes answer to the clock,
> Four for the quarters and twelve for the hour;
> Ever and aye, moonshine or shower,
> Sixteen short howls, not over loud;
> Some say, she sees my lady's shroud'.

We wonder that Mr. Murray, who has an eye for things, should suffer this 'mastiff bitch' to come into his shop.[1] Is she a sort of Cerberus to fright away the critics? But—gentlemen, she is toothless.

There is a dishonesty as well as affectation in all this. The secret of this pretended contempt for the opinion of the public, is that it is a sorry subterfuge for our self-love. The poet, uncertain of the approbation of his readers, thinks he shews his superiority to it by shocking their feelings at the outset, as a clown, who is at a loss how to behave himself, begins by affronting the company. This is what is called *throwing a crust to the critics*. If the beauties of *Christabel* should not be sufficiently admired, Mr. Coleridge may lay it all to two lines which he had too much manliness to omit in complaisance to the bad taste of his contemporaries.

We rather wonder at this bold proceeding in the author, as his courage has cooled in the course of the publication, and he has omitted, from mere delicacy, a line which is absolutely necessary to the understanding the whole story. The *Lady Christabel*, wandering in the forest by moon-light, meets a lady in apparently great distress, to whom she offers her assistance and protection, and takes her home with her to her own chamber. This woman,

> ————'beautiful to see,
> Like a lady of a far countree,'

is a witch. Who she is else, what her business is with *Christabel*, upon what motives, to what end her sorceries are to work, does not appear at present; but this much we know that she is a witch, and that *Christabel's* dread of her arises from her discovering this circumstance, which is told in a single line, which line, from an exquisite refinement in efficiency, is here omitted. When the unknown lady gets to *Christabel's* chamber, and is going to undress, it is said—

> 'Then drawing in her breath aloud
> Like one that shuddered, she unbound
> The cincture from beneath her breast:
> Her silken robe and inner vest
> Dropt to her feet, and full in view
> *Behold! her bosom and half her side*—
> A sight to dream of, not to tell!
> And she is to sleep by Christabel!'

[1] John Murray was the publisher of the volume.

The manuscript runs thus, or nearly thus:—

> 'Behold her bosom and half her side—
> *Hideous, deformed, and pale of hue.*'

This line is necessary to make common sense of the first and second part. 'It is the keystone that makes up the arch.' For that reason Mr Coleridge left it out. Now this is a greater physiological curiosity than even the fragment of *Kubla Khan*.

In parts of *Christabel* there is a great deal of beauty, both of thought, imagery, and versification; but the effect of the general story is dim, obscure, and visionary. It is more like a dream than a reality. The mind, in reading it, is spell-bound. The sorceress seems to act without power—*Christabel* to yield without resistance. The faculties are thrown into a state of metaphysical suspense and theoretical imbecility. The poet, like the witch in *Spenser*, is evidently

> 'Busied about some wicked gin.'—

But we do not foresee what he will make of it. There is something disgusting at the bottom of his subject, which is but ill glossed over by a veil of Della Cruscan sentiment and fine writing[1]—like moon-beams playing on a charnel-house, or flowers strewed on a dead body. Mr. Coleridge's style is essentially superficial, pretty, ornamental, and he has forced it into the service of a story which is petrific. In the midst of moon-light, and fluttering ringlets, and flitting clouds, and enchanted echoes, and airy abstractions of all sorts, there is one genuine burst of humanity, worthy of the author, when no dream oppresses him, no spell binds him. We give the passage entire:—

[Lines 403–30 are quoted.]

Why does not Mr. Coleridge always write in this manner, that we might always read him? The description of the Dream of Bracy the bard, is also very beautiful and full of power.

The conclusion of the second part of *Christabel*, about 'the little limber elf,' is to us absolutely incomprehensible. *Kubla Khan*, we think, only shews that Mr. Coleridge can write better *nonsense* verses than any man in England. It is not a poem, but a musical composition.

> 'A damsel with a dulcimer
> In a vision once I saw;

---

[1] The Della Cruscans were a late eighteenth-century school of poets in England whose poetry was sentimental and pretentious.

> It was an Abyssinian maid,
> And on her dulcimer she play'd,
> Singing of Mount Abora.'

We could repeat these lines to ourselves not the less often for not knowing the meaning of them.

Literary Panorama

2d ser. IV (July 1816), 559–63. The reviewer is unknown.

The first of these Poems, or rather—the fragment of a poem which stands first in this collection, has had honourable testimony borne to its merits by Lord Byron, who lately acknowledged its beauties, in a note to his 'Siege of Corinth.' The Author states the first part of *Christabel* to have been written in 1797, at Stowey, in the county of Somerset, and the second in 1800, at Keswick, in Cumberland. Since the latter date, he says his poetic powers have been, till very lately, in a state of suspended animation, and he assigns his indolence as the cause of that long trance or syncope, which all who know his abilities will regret. Mr. Coleridge, however, raises hopes that he may so far rouse himself as to conclude the story of Christabel in the course of the present year; but we fear it is from some lurking distrust of his best resolutions, that he has been tempted to mar the strong interest which his wild romantic tale would otherwise have excited, by thus communicating it in piecemeal. In such a case we are effectually prevented from giving our readers any idea of the main incidents of the poem—

> 'Daughter, the Spanish Fleet thou can'st not see
> Because it is not yet in sight'—

To extract parts from such a *morçeau* is to reduce what remains to a mere nothing; yet to content ourselves with general observations on its style and character, is impossible.

The opening is in the very spirit of 'Betty Foy:'[1]

> ''Tis the middle of night by the castle clock,
> And the owls have awakened the crowing cock,
> Tu—whit!—Tu—whoo!
> And hark, again! the crowing cock
> How drowsily it crew.'

[1] A character in Wordsworth's 'The Idiot Boy'.

But the poet soon quits insignificant objects—and the reader enters the regions of romance, and of romance described in the vivid colouring, and with the energetic pencil of our early writers, whose witching strain could arrest alike the attention of the mail-clad warrior, the blushing maid, the thoughtful scholar, and the unlettered vassal.

[The story of Part I is given briefly. Lines 15–22 and 43–52 are quoted.]

The accumulation of ominous signs is well described, and the mysterious lady begins to excite a most powerful interest ere the first part closes.

The second opens with the introduction of Geraldine to Sir Leoline, the father of Christabel.

[Lines 403–26 are quoted.]

It would be injustice to the author to break the powerful spell in which he holds his readers, by any imperfect description of the thraldom of Christabel to the mysterious Geraldine. Never was the withering glance of an evil eye better described. The poet's mind has combined the wilder graces of fiction, with the most vigorous and speaking descriptions.

Kubla Khan is merely a few stanzas which owe their origin to a circumstance by no means uncommon to persons of a poetical imagination. Our author falling asleep, under the influence of an anodyne draught, over 'Purchas his Pilgrimage' was sensible of composing from two to three hundred lines of poetry—'if that indeed,' says he, 'can be called composition, in which all the images rose up before him as *things*, with a parallel production of the correspondent expressions, without any sensation, or consciousness of effort.'—On awaking he began to write down these effusions; but being called off, and detained above an hour, he found to his great mortification on his return, that his visions of the night had melted into thin air, and left only a vague recollection of their general form and tendency. It is well known that a ruling passion will predominate even in sleep. The Alderman 'eats in dreams the custards of the day,' and the scholar, 'chewing the cud of sweet and bitter fancy,' ruminates on an intellectual banquet.—Tartini, the celebrated musician, dreamed that the devil took his violin from him, and played in strains so delightful that he awoke in utter despair of rivalling so skilful a performer; he however wrote down what he remembered, or something like it, and the piece is known by the name of the Devil's Concerto. But Tartini always declared it to be utterly unworthy of comparison with the production of his sleeping moments.

It should however be recollected, that in sleep the judgment is the first faculty of the mind which ceases to act, therefore, the opinion of the sleeper respecting his performance is not to be trusted, even in his waking moments. Still if Mr. Coleridge's two hundred lines were all of equal merit with the following which he has preserved, we are ready to admit that he has reason to be grieved at their loss.

[Lines 91–100 of 'The Picture' are quoted.]

'The pains of sleep' shews the vividness of the author's conceptions, mingled with that peculiarity of thought and diction which the mountain scenery of our lakes seems to inspire in all who court its influence. That Mr. Coleridge possesses strong powers of thought, with a command of original and striking images, unite to those softer touches of nature which speak at once to the heart, our readers have not now to learn.

Monthly Review

LXXXII (Jan. 1817), 22–25. The reviewer is unknown.

In a very circumstantial though short preface, Mr. Coleridge informs us that Christabel was written long ago; that consequently all marks of plagiarism which may be discovered in it are only chance-coincidences; and also that the metre of Christabel, though irregular, still has a 'method in its madness,' and 'counts the accents, not the syllables, in each line.' This variation from every former rule of versification is called 'a new principle;' and the reader is to be reasoned into a belief that a line of ten syllables is no longer than one of five, if there be no more *emphatic* syllables (for this is all that the author means by accent) in the one than in the other.

We have long since condemned in Mr. Scott and in Miss Holford, and in fifty other males and females, the practice of arbitrary pronunciation, assumed as a principle for regulating the length or rhythm of a verse; and we hereby declare to all whom it may concern, that they are guilty of neither more nor less than bombastic *prose*, and not even conscious of *bombastic* verse, who rest their hopes on the acquiescence of their readers in their own 'arbitrary pronunciation.' Let those readers only weigh and measure a few of Mr. Coleridge's lines in this poem of Christabel, which unfortunately was so long delayed in its publication, and which really did *not* pilfer any thing from previous poems. Let them form their opinion; and then let them say whether

Mr. Coleridge originally conceived, or surreptitiously obtained, such superb ideas!

> "Tis the middle of night by the castle clock!
> And the owls have awaken'd the crowing cock;
> Tu—whit!—Tu—whoo!
> And hark, again! the crowing cock,
> How drowsily it crew.'

Are we to be told that this is *nature?* '*Avec permission, Monsieur,*' &c. &c. (as Voltaire said in Dr. Moore's Travels,) we do not allow the plea.[1] When Virgil describes the dead hour of night; when Homer in a still bolder manner strikes out the scene before us; when Shakespeare, boldest, truest, and yet gentlest of all, presents the same picture to our eyes; they all fill their canvas with living objects, and with actual sounds: but they are all equally above that imitative harmony, that affected adaptation of sound to sense, which nothing but German music and German poetry could ever have attempted. They would have started with horror and astonishment from such an effort, in any language, as that which Mr. Coleridge is constantly making; namely, to dignify meanness of conception, to versify the flattest prose, and to teach the human ear a new and discordant system of harmony.

We shall give the public one opportunity of judging of this extravagant but not ingenious production:

[Lines 319–31 are quoted.]

This precious production is not finished, but we are to have more and more of it in future! It would be truly astonishing that such rude unfashioned stuff should be tolerated, and still more that it should be praised by men of genius, (witness Lord Byron and some others,) were we not convinced that every principle of correct writing, as far as poetry is concerned, has been long *given up*; and that the observance, rather than the breach, of such rules is considered as an incontrovertible proof of rank stupidity. It is grand, in a word, it is sublime, to be lawless; and whoever writes the wildest nonsense in the quickest and newest manner is the popular poet of the day! Whether this sentence

---

[1] In Dr John Moore's *A View of Society and Manners in France, Switzerland, and Germany* (London, 1779), I, 275, occurs the following passage describing a discussion about Shakespeare: 'A Gentleman of the company, who is a great admirer of Shakespear, observed, by way of palliation, that though those characters [the vulgar characters in Shakespeare's tragedies] were low, yet they were natural (dans la nature, was his expression). Avec permission, Monsieur, replied Voltaire, mon cul est bien dans la nature, et cependant je porte de coulottes.'

be considered as a positive truth, or as a splenetic effusion, by the different parties who *now* divide the literary world, we think that the time is fast approaching when all minds will be agreed on it; and when any versifier, who widely differs from the established standard of our nobler authors, will be directly remanded into that Limbo of vanity from which he most certainly emerged.

The fragment of 'Kubla Khan' is declared to have been composed in a dream, and is published as the author wrote it. Allowing every possible accuracy to the statement of Mr. Coleridge, we would yet ask him whether this extraordinary fragment was not rather the effect of rapid and instant composition after he was awake, than of memory immediately recording that which he dreamt when asleep? By what process of consciousness could he distinguish between such composition and such reminiscence? Impressed as his mind was with his interesting dream, and habituated as he is (notwithstanding his accidental cessation from versifying) to the momentary production of verse, will he venture to assert that he did not *compose*, and that he did *remember*, the lines before us? Were they dreamt, or were they spontaneously poured forth instantly after the dream,

> 'Without stop or stay,
> Down the rocky way
> That leads,' &c. &c.?

His 'psychological curiosity,' as he terms it, depends in no slight degree on the establishment of the previous fact which we have mentioned: but the poem itself is below criticism.—We would dismiss it with some portentous words of Sir Kenelm Digby, in his observations on Browne's *Religio Medici*:—'I have much ado to believe what he speaketh confidently; that he is more beholding to Morpheus for learned and rational as well as pleasing dreams, than to Mercury for smart and facetious conceptions.'

'The Pains of Sleep,' a little poem at the end of the pamphlet, has some better verses in it than its predecessors. Without in the least approving the spirit, we admire the simplicity of the following lines:

[The first thirty-two lines are quoted.]

We close the slight publication before us with unmingled regret. The author of 'Remorse' may perhaps be able to explain our feeling better than ourselves: but that so much superior genius should be corrupted and debased by so much execrable taste must be a subject of sincere lamentation to every lover of the arts, and to every friend of poetry.

Review of Coleridge's 'Sibylline Leaves' and 'Biographia Literaria'

British Critic

2d ser. VIII (Nov. 1817), 460–81. The reviewer is unknown. Line and page numbers of omitted passages refer to John Shawcross's edition of the Biographia Literaria (*Oxford, 1958*).

When a writer sets down to record the history of his own life and opinions, it certainly affords a presumption that he conceives himself to be an object of greater curiosity with the public, than it is quite modest in any man to suppose; but for a writer, the whole of whose works would probably not form a fair sized octavo volume, to compose an account of how he was educated, in what manner he formed his taste, what he has been in the habit of thinking upon this or that subject, and so forth, sounds even somewhat ridiculous. It is, however, but just to say, with respect to the excellent author of the 'Biographical Sketches,' before us, that it would be unfair to estimate the interest which his readers may be supposed to take in his history and opinions, by the number or importance of the writings which he has published; for some reason or other his name is familiar to numbers who are altogether unacquainted with his compositions; and connected as it has been with the names of his two celebrated friends, Mr. Southey and Mr. Wordsworth, it has certainly been mentioned both in conversation and in print, more frequently than it is perhaps quite easy to account for. In Mr. Coleridge's poetical compositions we own that we see but little on which it would be prudent to bestow unqualified commendation. They exhibit few traces of deep or fine feeling, and still fewer of correct and polished taste; wildness of imagination is the predominant quality of his genius, but it is so apt to degenerate into extravagance, that if we except his 'Ancient Mariner,' the verses called 'Love,' and perhaps a few, and but a few others, which might be mentioned, we think the character of his poetry is far from being pleasing. To follow his flights requires very commonly a painful effort of attention, and when we have gained the heights to which he carries us, instead of any objects opening upon our view to repay us for our labour, we commonly find ourselves enveloped in mistiness and clouds. But still his writings bear the impression of a mind of considerable powers; in whatever he composes, the workings of thought are almost always perceptible; and his failures are rather the result of an understanding that has been misguided than of any deficiency in respect of the requisite quantity of talent.

Mr. Coleridge tells us that the question 'What is poetry?' is so nearly the same thing as to ask 'What is a poet?' that in order to define the former he will give a description of the latter.

[Lines 9–29 of p. 12, Vol. II, are quoted.]

With such very intelligible ideas of the office of a poet, our readers need not be surprized if our author's conception of poetry is not always such as people, who think and feel in a common way, will easily enter into; but however his practice is not quite what his theory would lead us to anticipate; his verses are, indeed, often not intelligible, but they are not always so; in poetry as in prose, he is ever aiming at something that is transcendental, and in both cases his error (and an inexpiable error it is) is deliberate, and of fore-thought; but still he is not always in the clouds; he sometimes walks upon the earth like other men; and when he does, both his prose and his poetry evince an amiable, cultivated, and original mind.

We have said thus much respecting the character of our author's poetical genius, principally because it is with his poetry chiefly, that the public are acquainted; but partly because it appears to be his wish, that the two publications prefixed to this article, should be considered as belonging to each other; nevertheless, as all the poems (with two inconsiderable exceptions) included in the former, have been long before the public in an authentic shape, we do not think it necessary to enter into any detailed criticism of their separate merits. In fact, it is not our wish to review Mr. Coleridge's literary Life itself; our intention is to confine our attention to these 'Sketches' of it, which Mr. Coleridge has presented us with; and this with a view to give our readers some idea of the book itself, considered simply as a literary performance, rather than as a record of facts connected with the life of its author.

In naming the volumes, to which we propose confining our remarks,

'Biographical Sketches of his literary Life and Opinions,' Mr. Coleridge has signified very accurately the real nature of his publication; for it is with circumstances that have a relation to his literary life only, that he makes his reader acquainted; with respect to his birth, parentage, and personal history, he says almost nothing; these he tells us may afford materials for a separate work which he seems to contemplate; in the present he tells us little more of himself, than that he was educated at Christ's Hospital, was a member of Jesus College, Cambridge, was, at the beginning of the French revolution, editor of a paper called the Watchman; and subsequently, at the time of the peace of Amiens, conducted the Morning Post. These circumstances are only mentioned incidentally; the volumes are exclusively filled with abstracts of the literary opinions which he entertains; some of them upon subjects interesting enough, but a very large proportion upon subjects, which we fear our author will find some difficulty, in persuading his readers to feel quite so much respect for, as he seems to think them entitled to. The three prominent topics, upon which it would appear that our author has chiefly reflected, are, in the first place, philosophy; by which our readers must not suppose us to mean the writings of Locke or Newton, or Bacon or Aristotle, but of Jacob Behmen, Gemisthius Pletho, de Thoyras, Plotinus, and above all, the inscrutable Kant. The subject which seems to hold the second place in our author's esteem, is poetry; and to which, (in subordination to a critical review of Mr. Wordsworth's productions,) a very considerable portion of the two volumes is devoted. The third object of his attention, are anonymous critics in general, but more particularly the Edinburgh Review. This last topic, indeed forms a sort of *running accompaniment* to the second; for they seem so intimately connected in his thoughts, that he is seldom able to speak of poetry, or poets, or poetical criticism, but what we perceive (to use a very favourite expression of our author) an *under-current* to all his observations of hatred and contempt against our fellow-labourers (though we trust not in the same vineyard) of the north.

With respect to the general character of the work, it is certainly an able, and, notwithstanding our author's endless and bottomless discussion on metaphysical matters, upon the whole, an entertaining performance. Our author's incidental remarks upon criticism, politics, religion, and such other subjects as fall within the reach of an ordinary man's comprehension, are often just and striking, and invariably display a tone of mind that is both scholar-like and amiable. As to his style, we hardly know what to say of it; it is certainly expressive, but it does not seem to be constructed upon any settled principles of composition, farther than are implied in an apparent preference of our early writers, not only over those upon whose style the taste of the present day seems to be chiefly modelled, but over Addison and Dryden, and the writers of what we cannot but think the Augustan age of our prose literature.

Now, if our author is resolved to see no medium between the involved constructions and cumbrous phraseology of Milton and Jeremy Taylor, and the cheap finery of the *stylum pene cantiam*[1] of our fashionable historians and philosophers, we undoubtedly approve of the taste by which his preference has been guided. The faults of Clarendon and Hooker proceeded merely from a want of skill in composition, whereas the faults of those writers whom Mr. Coleridge seems so studious of not imitating, proceed from affectation and pretension. To say that our author has succeeded in reminding us of the models whom he appears desirous of emulating, is not saying much in his praise. It is just as easy to put into one sentence what ought properly to form three, as to put into three, what ought properly to form only one; nor is it a matter of much greater difficulty to sprinkle our manner of speaking with learned phrases and obsolete forms of expression. For example, when our author tells us that he 'had undertaken the new business of an author, *yea*, of an author trading on his own account.' Vol. I. p. 169. This, in fact, is only a peculiar species of coxcombry, and is better than the coxcombry of one of our modern *beau* writers, only as the gravity of a broad-brimmed hat, may be preferred to the levity of the *chapeau-bras*. It would, however, be unjust to our author, were we to describe the merits of his style, as consisting in a mere clumsy imitation of our early prose writers; on the contrary, he writes in general with an air of truth and simplicity, which is plainly natural to him; and his language, though sometimes pedantic, and often by no means free from that philosophical jargon which is almost the characteristical affectation of the present race of writers, is nevertheless, that of a scholar; to which we may add, that although a little innocent vanity is every now and then making its appearance, yet in general it merely gives an air of naivete and quaintness to his expressions, and never assumes the form of arrogance and self-conceit. But we have said enough respecting the style of the volumes before us; it is time to let our readers know some thing of their contents.

Of course, a work, which professes to give an account of opinions, that are linked to each other by no other connection, than that which arises from their having belonged to the same individual, cannot be supposed to be arranged upon any method founded on the nature of

[1] 'Almost singing style'? The Latin is ungrammatical.

things; and consequently to give a systematic criticism of them, would be altogether impracticable. We shall, therefore, not trouble ourselves by attempting to give our author's thoughts any better arrangement than he has himself thought necessary; but content ourselves with following his steps, merely stopping now and then to intersperse our abstracts and citations with such incidental remarks, as may happen at the moment to suggest themselves.

Our author's first chapter contains rather an interesting account of the discipline which his poetical taste received, while at Christ's Hospital, under the direction of the Rev. J. Bowyer, at that time the head master. In this age of systematic education, perhaps a plan of instruction which has the sanction of Mr. Coleridge's approbation, and of the benefits of which he considers his own taste a practical exemplification, may not be unacceptable to our readers.

[Line 9, p. 4 (of Vol. I), to line 28, p. 5, is quoted.]

We cannot say that we see any thing to object against, in any of the particulars related in this account of Mr. Bowyer's plan; yet we are very doubtful how far we should be desirous of seeing it generally practised; as it appears to us it may have answered very well with respect to particular boys, and perhaps under the superintendance of a particular schoolmaster; but we own, that in general, we would rather entrust the education of a boy's *taste* to nature and his own turn of mind, working upon the models that must in the regular course of instruction be placed before him, than subject it to the censorship of any ordinary schoolmaster: many reasons might be given for this; but it is sufficient to say, that the proper business of the master, (of a large school, more especially,) is to put into the hands of his scholars, the means and instruments of taste and learning; but taste and learning themselves are the growth of age and after-reflection.

The subject of his early education leads our author to notice the effect made upon his mind, when at the age of seventeen, by a perusal of Bowles's Sonnets: we shall not stop to examine the grounds of the very warm admiration, which Mr. Coleridge seems still to entertain, for what gave him so much pleasure, and inspired him with so much emulation when young; only we may be permitted to remark, that he seems to attach much more importance to the history of his poetical taste, than his readers will probably be made to feel. At whatever age Mr. Coleridge may have become first sensible of the inferiority of Pope's system of poetical diction to that of Milton, and of one or two of our early Poets, we confess we see nothing so remarkable in the discovery, as to require a detailed account of the grounds and process of it; we shall therefore not follow him through all the discussions into which this part of his subject leads him, but passing over the remainder of this first chapter, and all the second, (in which he attempts to disprove the imputation of peculiar irritability, under which men of poetical genius are supposed to labour,) we shall proceed to chapter the third. The subject of this is very high matter, being no less than that of a discussion concerning the usefulness, rights, and prerogatives of us, 'synodical individuals,' who call ourselves reviewers; nor does our author think it necessary to treat us hypothetically, and with reference to the principles of Plato's republic; but he denounces us by name, as nuisances to the republic of letters. Now we are not sure whether it quite comports with our dignity, to sanction any thing like an argument as to the competency of our tribunal; nevertheless, as we cannot but allow that our author has no particular reason to congratulate himself upon having been born in this age of critical illumination, we shall overlook the indiscreetness with which he speaks of reviews generally, in consideration of his particular case, and permit him to utter, what we should be very sorry our readers should believe. Our author tells us,

[Line 18, p. 29 (of Vol. I), to line 12, p. 30, is quoted.]

There is in the work before us, a good deal of reasoning like this, which we apprehend to be not very original, however plausible it may appear; and to say that it is even plausible, is perhaps saying quite as much as it deserves. For even taking our author's own illustration; if individuals retail adulterated wines or any other commodity of inferior quality, the public surely are benefited by being made acquainted with the fact, nor is it reasonable to accuse those of injustice, from whom the information is obtained. But the truth is, the illustration is by no means in point, except it be with reference merely to the comparatively harmless quality of an author's dullness; a writer, however, without being dull, may display bad taste or mischievous principles; he may distort facts from ignorance, or pervert them from prejudice; in short, his writings may in innumerable ways do a much more lasting injury to his readers, than merely sending them to sleep. To expose faults like these, has no doubt a tendency to diminish the sale of the work, in which they are contained; but an author has no better right to complain in such a case of the injury done to his private interests, by anonymous criticism, than a statesman to complain of being turned out of office, in consequence of his measures being proved to be prejudicial to the public. Authors are just as much public characters as secretaries of state are; if they voluntarily come forward upon the stage of public life, under pretence of being able to enlighten, or in any other way to benefit the community at large, of course they must expect that their pretensions will be canvassed; that their opinions and principles will become a subject of discussion; misrepresentation and misconception, unreasonable censure and blind admiration—these are matters of course —the penalty paid in all cases for publicity; but it would be about as wise to complain of the daily papers, on account of the abuse, which they mutually pour forth against the opponents of their respective parties, as to complain of anonymous critics, for the bitterness, with which they sometimes review the works of those, who profess principles and opinions, of which the former disapprove; and about as much for the interests of the community, to repress or discountenance them.

If the writers in either case, not content with combating principles and opinions, and public acts, trespass upon the sanctity of private life, and endeavour to prepossess the minds of their readers, by slander and calumny and personal invective; this no doubt is highly disgraceful to the individual, who so misuses his privilege of discussion; but his virulence is of little importance to the public, and nine times in ten, of not much more to him, who is the object of it. If one party condemn in excess, another will generally be found to praise in an equal excess; and after the first fermentation of contending opinions has a little subsided, the real truth gradually separates itself from the errors, with which it had been mixed, and becomes perhaps better and more certainly distinguishable, than by almost any other process, to which it could have been subjected. As in our courts of justice, one advocate is paid, to say all that can be said in favour of one side of the question; another, to urge in like manner all that can be said against it, the decision in the meanwhile resting with the jury: so it is with us critics; one review is set up by men strongly biassed in favour of one system of principles; another starts in opposition to it by men as warmly favourable to the opposite; both of them, indeed, affect to speak with the authority, that belongs to the judicial office; but they are listened to as judges, only by those of their own party; the public knows well, that they are mere advocates, hired by their prejudices to plead the cause of a particular sect; and by listening to both sides, is much more likely to be put in possession of all the arguments in favour of each, than if it implicitly trusted to the impartiality, with which any single review could state them. So far then, with respect to our author's sentiments concerning the merits of reviews generally; but the fact is, that his indictment, though worded somewhat sweepingly, is really intended to be preferred against one particular journal, which both in taste, morals, politics, religion, and even in manners, happens to have embraced a set of opinions directly counter to those which Mr.

Coleridge approves of. Now, in bringing forward what our author has to urge, in reprobation of the abusive spirit, in which the above-mentioned critics have reviewed his writings and the writings of his friends, we shall not enter into the critical merits of the case. Our opinions upon most of the subjects, upon which our author and his anonymous, though well known reviewer have split, are already before the public. That much childishness is mixed up with Mr. Wordsworth's poetry, and some extravagance in the poetry, and some want of moderation in the prose, of Mr. Southey, are, we apprehend, truths not to be denied; and if there are some, professing to be judges in these points, who are able to see in the writings of neither, any qualities besides, we really know not how the matter is to be mended by mere discussion. On this subject our author tells us a story, which will illustrate the real nature of the case before us, as well as the grounds of a great many other differences of opinion upon questions of taste.

[Line 27, p. 92 (of Vol. II), to line 26, p. 94, is quoted.]

This is a pleasant apologue and significantly applied; it is however plain, that if our author had no other grounds of complaint against his critics, than the above passage affords, he certainly would not be justified in using the epithets, made use of in the last sentence; for a critic cannot with any more propriety be called a 'quack' because he happens to be wanting in taste (even assuming the fact), than a poet could be, who should happen to be wanting in imagination. To speak passionately about questions of opinion, or contemptuously of whatever else we have not ourselves a taste for, are not to be sure the most unequivocal marks of a superior understanding; but men cannot obtain sense by merely wishing for it; and critics, like others, can only speak as they feel; all that authors or the public, can reasonably expect, is, that critics should *really* speak as they think, and not give decisions which they know to be partial, merely for the purpose of gratifying feelings of a personal nature. Now this is the charge which Mr. Coleridge explicitly and formally presses against the reviewer of himself and friends; and supposing, that the facts, which he asserts, are correctly stated, we think, that the public (supposing them to interest themselves about the matter) will not feel disposed to blame our author, for the strong language in which he sometimes expresses his sense of the unjustifiable persecution of which he, but in a more particular manner Mr. Southey and Mr. Wordsworth, have been for many years the constant objects. We shall not quote the passages, (that are scattered through almost every part of his work,) in which our author gives vent to the feelings, excited in his mind by the conduct of which he complains; but state the facts by which he conceives the resentment expressed by him to be warranted; and this we shall do, partly from regard to justice, and partly because reviews and reviewers seem to have been uppermost in our author's mind, when he projected the work before us, as they are scarcely ever lost sight of by him in the progress of it. There are few of our readers, probably, but are aware of the unmeasured contempt and unmitigated ridicule, with which the writings of Mr. Wordsworth have been treated in the journal, of which our author complains; few persons would, we think, imagine that the writer of the article, in which the offensive criticism was conveyed, could ever have expressed himself in private conversation in the manner in which Mr. Coleridge in the following passage states himself to have heard.

[Lines 17-27, p. 129 (of Vol. II), are quoted.]

In another part of the work Mr. Coleridge informs us that some years ago, upon occasion of the reviewer in question paying a visit to Cumberland, he was at his own request introduced to Mr. Southey, drank tea at his house, and was in all respects hospitably treated; but so far was he from permitting the recollection of the courtesies which he had received, to soften the asperity of his criticism, that his very first employment upon returning to Edinburgh, was to write a lampoon upon his host, in language still more offensive than upon any former occasion; designating him and the friends whom he met at his house, as 'whining and hypochondriacal poets,' and saying many other things, which a critic perhaps had a right to say, but which it was just as easy to have said in civil as in disrespectful language. The note, in which the charge is made, contains many other particulars, and is somewhat long; but as the contents of it have been thought so weighty, as to induce the reviewer to come forward in his own person and under his own name, in order to rebut it, perhaps it may gratify our readers to have the whole passage before them.

[The footnote to pp. 36-37 (of Vol. I) is quoted in full.]

Now, in the answer which our reviewer has put forth to the above charges,[1] he takes no notice of the warm admiration, which he is said to have expressed for the poetry of Mr. Wordsworth; we have therefore a right to conclude, that the article in which that gentleman's writings have been reviewed, were intended to convey into the mind of the reader, a different opinion from that which the reviewer himself

[1] Francis Jeffrey answered Coleridge's charges in a footnote to the review of the *Biographia Literaria* in the *Edinburgh Review*, XXVIII (August 1817), 507-12.

conscientiously entertained. As to the high-flown compliments with which he gratified Mr. Coleridge's vanity, we are told, that the reviewer paid them, because he thought he could perceive that they were as agreeable to our author, as they are to most people; by which we are left to infer, that what our honest reviewer *says*, is no better criterion of his real sentiments, than what he *writes*; and since he certainly cannot be accused of having flattered our author in the *latter* way, we suppose it is his opinion, that any injury done to truth by praising a man more than he deserves by word of mouth, and before his face, is wiped away, by abusing him in an equal degree beyond what truth will warrant, in writing, and behind his back. With respect to the other charge, which he pleads guilty to, it is to be sure rather of a ridiculous nature; he admits that he was received at Mr. Southey's house, and 'believes that coffee was handed to him;' but as he was not given to understand that this was offered to him, under any implied condition of praising on all future occasions, the poetry of his host, and that of his friends, he contends that he had a right to speak of them and their writings on his return to Edinburgh, in the same discourteous and abusive language as before. This is not to be disputed; the circumstance of having been received into his house, and treated with respect and civility, by a person to whom we were personally strangers, would weigh with some minds, to a certain extent at least; it might not, and perhaps ought not, to disarm justice, but it would, at all events, be an additional argument against passing sentence in the language of contempt and insult; it might not call forth any strong expressions of civility, nor make us express a degree of admiration, which we did not feel; but still one should suppose, that it would not produce an opposite effect; it would not excite an unfavourable prejudice, nor induce us to keep down our real feelings, and give utterance to none except such as were harsh and disrespectful. A man is not called upon to flatter another, merely because he has been in his house and received no unfriendly treatment; yet it would surely be still more strange to give this as a reason for abusing him.

It is true, indeed, if Mr. Southey and Mr. Wordsworth and Mr. Coleridge, whom he distinguishes as 'anti-jacobin poets,' are really and truly the sort of persons whom he describes them to be, our astonishment will cease; and we shall be forced to admire the moderation, with which he has expressed himself, when speaking of them and their works.

'Their inordinate vanity runs them into all sorts of extravagances, and their habitual effeminacy gets them out of them at any price. Always pampering their own appetite for excitement and wishing to astonish others, their whole aim is to produce a dramatic effect one way or other, to shock or delight their observers; and they are as perfectly indifferent as to the consequence of what they write, as if the world were merely a stage for them to play their fantastic tricks on. As romantic in their servility as in their independance, and equally importunate candidates for fame or infamy, they require only to be distinguished and are not scrupulous as to the means of distinction. Jacobins or anti-jacobins—outrageous advocates for anarchy and licentiousness, or flaming apostles of persecution—always violent and vulgar in their opinions, they oscillate with a giddy and sickening motion from one absurdity to another, and expiate the follies of their youth, by the heartless vices of their declining age. None so ready as they to carry every paradox to its most revolting and nonsensical excess,—none so sure to caricature in their own persons every feature of an audacious and insane philosophy. In their days of innovation, indeed, the philosophers crept at their heels like hounds, while they darted on their distant quarry like hawks; stooping always to the lowest game; eagerly snuffing up the most tainted and rankest scents—'

But we really can proceed no further with this delicately touched, nicely discriminated and altogether striking portrait; we have informed our readers, that the original from which it is drawn, are the author of Don Roderic, and his friends Mr. Wordsworth and Mr. Coleridge. Upon what feature of their characters or writings, the resemblance is founded, is not stated; but assuredly, if there be any truth whatever in the picture, we need not be surprized, if a reviewer should think it a matter of conscience, to allow no feelings either of admiration or of common courtesy, to interfere with the duty of discountenancing altogether writers of such a portentous, though somewhat non-descript kind of poetry. We shall not offend the pride of Mr. Southey, against whom the above sober piece of criticism was more particularly discharged, by taking up his defence against an adversary, whose weapons consist, in the use of such language as that which we have just quoted; for a critic to apply the epithets of 'audacious,' and 'insane,' and 'nonsensical,' to a writer; to talk of his being 'an apostle of persecution,' and a 'snuffer up of the rankest scents;' and then ingeniously to add, with an affected air of superior gentility, that he is, moreover, *vulgar and violent*,' is a stroke of character worth recording. But enough of reviews and reviewers; we have been led to say much more upon the subject than its importance deserved; to go on speaking of Mr. Southey may perhaps be considered as a sort of continuation of the discussion; but as his name has been introduced so often, we cannot resist a temptation to gratify our own feelings by presenting our readers with a character of this terrible 'anti-jacobin poet,' drawn indeed by a friend who has known him intimately for years, but who is not on that account the less able to speak of him as he really is. We are not sorry for an opportunity of contributing, by any means in our power, to the weight and reputation of a writer, who has written almost upon every subject, and exercised his talents in almost every species of composition, and in each displayed powers which would have ensured his name an honourable place in the annals of literature, even had he never attempted any other. The clearness, purity, and eloquent simplicity of his style, the richness of his fancy, and facility of his versification, form only one of his titles to our esteem; voluminous as his works are, we are not aware that he has ever published a line, at which the chastest delicacy, or the most severe morality could justly take offence. Whatever fame Mr. Southey possesses, is of that sort which will continue to increase; he has addressed himself, on no occasion, to the base and malignant feelings of mankind; and if his zeal, and the natural warmth of an ardent imagination, have sometimes carried him beyond the bounds of moderation, his indiscretion has arisen from the overflow of good-feelings, and such as are only blameable in their excess.

[Line 2 of p. 47 (of Vol. I) to line 2 of p. 49 is quoted.]

From the eloquent and well-deserved panegyric upon Mr. Southey, of which the above forms only an extract, our author proceeds, without any apparent plan in the selection, to discuss a variety of topics; Mr. Burke, the Spanish Revolution, the principles upon which our author conducted the Morning Post, during the time in which he was the editor of it, a vindication of himself from the charge of indolence which has so frequently been brought against him; these and similar discussions, alternately engage his attention, until we arrive within about one hundred pages from the end of the first volume: at this place our author takes a sudden plunge into a bottomless discussion respecting the esemplastic (from εἰς ἐν πλαττω) power of man and the phenomena of mind, that 'lie on the other side of the natural consciousness;' he continues out of sight of every human eye, groping in darkness for imaginary wealth, until the opening of the second volume, when he again rises upon our view, preparing to enter into a discussion of the merits and defects of Mr. Wordsworth's writings. This is a subject which our author discusses at so much length, that it is altogether out of our power to follow him through the progressive steps of his criticism: as we coincide with our author for the most part, in the substance of the opinions which he expresses upon this controverted subject, we shall merely extract a specimen of his critical judgment, and content ourselves with recommending this part of the volume to the attention of our readers, as containing one of the fairest and most able reviews of the peculiarities of Mr. Wordsworth's poetry, that we have met with. Mr. Coleridge's observations upon the diction of Mr. Wordsworth, contain many just and striking thoughts; and the analytical criticisms which occur in various parts of the discussion, upon one or two of the poems contained in the 'Lyrical Ballads,' impressed us with a very favourable opinion of his good taste and discrimination. As a specimen of his impartiality, and of the reasonable conditions under which he approves of the critical opinions of Mr. Wordsworth, concerning the proper objects and philosophical language of poetry, we shall select what our author says respecting the propriety of putting sentiments of a high and elevated tone into the mouths of persons taken from the lower ranks of life.

[Line 16 of p. 106 (of Vol. II) to line 2 of p. 109 is quoted.]

The above observations, and indeed the whole tenor of our author's criticisms upon poets and poetry, are for the most part so reasonable, that we own we have frequently found it difficult to understand, how the same author should have written them, and the 'Ode to the Rain,' and one or two other of the poems contained in the 'Sibylline Leaves;' poems which might perhaps have been *written* by a man of sense, but how a man like Mr. Coleridge should have thought them of so much value as to be worth *publishing*, is above our power to explain.

We should not be sorry, were we here to take leave of our author: for we are apprehensive that what we may add farther, will rather injure than improve the favorable impression which the greater part of what we have hitherto said, is calculated to convey of his talents. But in justice to our readers it is necessary to state, that a very large proportion of the two volumes which we have recommended to their perusal, is filled up with matter, which our author calls Philosophy; but it is philosophy of so very heteroclite a description, that we really hardly know how to allude to the subject, without using words that would convey an impression of our thinking much more slightingly of Mr. Coleridge's understanding, than the good sense displayed in other parts of the work would justify. Had we met with the metaphysical disquisitions to which we now allude, in an anonymous publication, we should unquestionably have laid them aside, as the production of a very ordinary writer indeed, with respect to talents; and supposing we had given ourselves the trouble of thinking farther about them, should probably have concluded that some doubts might be entertained respecting the perfect sanity of the mind in which they were engendered. 'The foolishness of fools, is folly;' but 'the foolishness' of a man like Mr. Coleridge, must, we take for granted, be impregnated with some portion of sense and reason. Impressed with a conviction of this, we were at the pains of reading faithfully, and as far as we were able, impartially, all our author's ten theses; his refutation of materialism; his discussions relative to the priority of 'subject' and 'object,' 'mind' and 'nature;' together with his other incidental criticisms upon Behmen, and Schilling, and Fichte, and Kant, and other inscrutable thinkers. What we think on all these subjects, and what we think of Mr. Coleridge's remarks upon them, we shall not venture to express; but we know so much of the present state of feeling in this country, upon the subjects into which, Mr. Coleridge wishes to embark philosophy, as emboldens us to prophesy, that if he persists in his present resolution of imparting to the world his intended commentary upon the Gospel of St. John, in the form of a dissertation upon the 'Productive Logos,' he will draw down upon his head such a tempest of ridicule and derision, as he may probably live long enough to repent of.

Review of Coleridge's 'Biographia Literaria'

Monthly Review

LXXXVIII (Feb. 1819), 124–38. The reviewer is unknown. Line and page numbers of omitted passages refer to John Shawcross's edition of the Biographia Literaria (*Oxford, 1958*).

We have so recently offered to the public an examination of the poetical pretensions of Mr. Coleridge, and have taken so much collateral notice of the powers and accomplishments of this peculiar writer, that our present task is necessarily much lightened. His collection of 'Sibylline Leaves,' or Poems, has served us for an Introduction to his 'Literary Life;' and thus we have reversed the order intended by the author himself: but, we hope, with no inconvenience to our readers. We have presented them with the fruits, or, at all events, with the '*Leaves*' of this original tree, before we displayed its roots, or pursued its ramifications; and perhaps, on the whole, the method which we have adopted may afford Mr. Coleridge the fairest chance of being duly appreciated. However this may be, we must now proceed to a comparatively brief analysis of the work before us; and, following the writer's own divisions, animadvert on the defects or lay open the fairer parts of the performance.

The most interesting portion of the first chapter is that in which the author narrates his early school-instruction, and offers a tribute of (we doubt not) deserved respect to the memory of his master, the Reverend James Bowyer, of Christ's Hospital. From this account of the first formation of Mr. Coleridge's taste, we shall make a selection:

[Line 9, p. 4 (of Vol. I), to line 3, p. 6, is quoted.[1]]

[1] [For 'Hipocrene' in the above extract, read *Hippocrene*. We take this opportunity

166

We should like to see those *'grounds of plain sense and universal logic'* on which 'the superiority of Lucretius and Catullus' in the extracts read by Mr. Coleridge at Christ's Hospital, and of Terence throughout, is to be established, in their comparison with the writers of the Augustan aera! The art of extracting sun-beams from cucumbers, as recorded in the Voyage to Laputa, we should conceive to be *nothing*, compared to the above-mentioned most wonderful process. Waiving, however, the positive nonsense of the opinion here so cavalierly asserted by Mr. Coleridge, we detect in it the germ of that false taste which, as we observed in our report of his 'Sibylline Leaves,' has obstructed his own progress towards a sound and permanent reputation; while, we fear, it has largely contributed, in his lectures and other temporary endeavours, to confirm the false estimate entertained by many of our countrymen respecting our own older writers. Here is the origin of that spirit which has been so idly at work for many years, and especially among the scribblers of the Lake-school, to depreciate the writings of the aeras of William, Anne, and the Georges; and to extol far beyond their due degree (with all their faults and all their follies included in the gross panegyric) the productions of the reigns of Elizabeth and the Stuarts. No opportunity is lost, in the pursuit of this unwise and invidious object. The 'stale, flat, and unprofitable' objections to the celebrated passage at the conclusion of the eighth book of Pope's version of the Iliad are here repeated; and they form indeed the sort of *single text* of the critical preachers of the day. It is all that they can discover as the basis of their censure of the great bard of Twickenham: it is a revival of the monotonous, confined, and obstinate *Zoilism* of the dunces of his own period. Why will no modern admirer of this great English genius attempt to *tack on* a fifth book to the Dunciad?— prophetic, if he pleases; and therefore, of course, inoffensive to his contemporaries.

'Ye unborn heroes, crowd not on my soul!'

would rush into the mind of such a writer.

The couplet which Mr. Coleridge has selected for reprobation, from the passage in Pope's version, is this:

'Around her throne the vivid planets roll,
And stars unnumber'd gild the glowing pole:'

to observe that the volumes are much disfigured by verbal errors—Reviewer's note to the passage quoted.]

of which he says that it is difficult to determine 'whether the sense or the diction be more absurd.' He has given *no* reasons for this opinion; —and we must wait till the publication of his celebrated lectures, recently delivered, (with which he positively threatens us,) for an opportunity to canvass his arguments, here so pompously and triumphantly announced. Meanwhile, when it is considered that the whole of this passage, in Pope's Homer, is obviously a paraphrase and not a translation of the original, it surely will follow that the proper subject for discussion is this; whether the English author has presented a great and glowing picture to the reader, sufficiently similar to the Greek for the purposes of general resemblance? With regard to his judgment, in chusing to paraphrase instead of translating Homer on this occasion, the unsuccessful attempts of Mr. Cowper, and of some others, to make a closer copy, will perhaps be deemed sufficient to decide the question.

In the same objectionable note in which the above heterodoxical paragraph occurs, is also an attack on Gray's Elegy; which Mr. Wordsworth (forsooth) has manifested to Mr. Coleridge, by the aid of his microscopic spectacles, to contain sundry blemishes!

> ''Twas *I*, says the Fly,
> With my LITTLE eye!'

These two *illuminati* have therefore been holding their conjoint 'farthing candle to the sun:' but the only spots, which Mr. Coleridge has told us they have detected in his bright countenance, are the subjoined. In the stanza in 'the Bard' (for in the 'Elegy' they are not kind enough to communicate their notable discoveries) which begins, 'Fair laughs the morn,' &c. Mr. Coleridge objects to the words 'realm' and 'sway;' which, he says, 'are rhymes dearly purchased.' What he means by this, we are at a loss to imagine. 'The azure realm' and 'the whirlwind's sway' appear to us as unobjectionable combinations as could be put together; and we plainly defy Mr. Coleridge to point out any intelligible or tenable objections to them. Does he deem it right to cast these reflections even *on the epithets* of the most fastidious of poets, without specifying their faults? He can venerate, even to idolatry, the loosest and most careless phrases of Shakspeare; and when he talks of the *imitation* in 'the Bard,' and then *contrasts* the noted simile in Shakspeare with the foregoing passage in Gray, he should have the candour to acknowledge that the '*sweeping whirlwind*' is at least as good and as poetical an image as the '*strumpet wind*;' although the said 'strumpet' is twice introduced, and, no doubt, with appropriate effect in a dramatic and sarcastic passage;—as unlike, by the way, in the character of the feelings which it wishes to impress on the hearer, as it is in its tone of expression; to the calm, dignified, and more soothingly pathetic description in Gray. We are not fond of *pitting* such great poets against each other; particularly where the points of similarity are so general and so faint as in the present passages: but Mr. Coleridge must answer for this offence;—and he has been guilty, we fear, of many offences, indeed, of a like nature, for which he owes a severe atonement to insulted taste and discrimination. We must add that Mr. C.'s preference of the *original*, as he calls it, to the *imitation* in the preceding instances, rests 'on the ground, that in the imitation it depended wholly in (on) the compositor's putting or not putting a *small capital* both in this, and *in many other passages* of the same poet,[1] whether the words should be personifications or mere abstracts.' May not this be said of almost any personification?—and

'Youth at the Prow, and Pleasure at the helm,'

are to be degraded by this contemptible species of *hyper*, or, rather, *hypo-criticism*. We cannot follow Mr. C. at present into his assertions as to the supposed corruption of English poetry, either by an imitation of the Iliad of Pope or by the practice of composing in Latin verse. With respect to the last of these intimations, we would ask him one question; —does he think that the exercise of writing Latin hexameters and pentameters impeded the poetic genius of Milton? We will also venture to subjoin a positive refutation, from our own knowledge and experience, of his opinion that 'it is not to be supposed in the present day that a youth can *think* in Latin.' Every upper form in our public schools could afford many examples to the contrary; and when we compared this opinion with the previous *assurance* that the master of Christ's Hospital 'sent *us* to the University *excellent* Latin and Greek scholars, and tolerable Hebraïsts,' we could not help considering it as an *assurance* indeed; nor could we, with our best endeavours, refrain from something very like a smile. It is modestly added; '*our* classical knowledge was the *least* of the good gifts which *we* derived from his zealous and conscientious tutorage.'

It is not allowable for us, however, to dwell longer on this portion of the biography; though, with the exception, perhaps, of that to which we shall next call the attention of our readers, we regard it as the most

[1] [*This* is the manner in which we have brought ourselves to talk of Gray!— 'Exoriare aliquis,' &c. &c.—Reviewer's note.] *Exoriare aliquis (nostris ex ossibus ultor)*: 'May some avenger arise from our bones.' Virgil *Aeneid* iv.625.

amusing in the whole publication. With the metaphysics, indeed,[1] and the rest of the '*omne scibile*' of the work, saving the extraordinary criticisms on Mr. Wordsworth, we shall not interfere; and our readers are now about to contemplate Mr. Coleridge in his early and most striking designation of an itinerant philosopher. Attend, then,

'Thelwall, and ye that lecture *as ye go*;'—

stationary as ye may now have become, the reminiscences of one of your most distinguished erratic brethren, of the very prince of the British Peripatetics, may be serviceable to you, and must be interesting, even in your most dignified retirements.

After having related an admirable story or two of unsuccessful authorship, whether in his own case or that of others, (stories which we seriously recommend to the careful perusal of those who are concerned,) Mr. Coleridge thus opens the narrative of his political and theological pilgrimage:

[Line 11, p. 114 (of Vol. I), to line 2, p. 117, is quoted. The passage describes Coleridge's campaign to obtain subscribers for the *Watchman*.]

Much more occurs, of the same amusing cast: but our limits forbid us to extract it, and we must proceed to another class of anecdotes; namely, the instances of most ludicrous as well as detestable *espionage* which Mr. C. has mentioned as having been exercised over him and a philosophical friend, during the reign of terror in England. Some of these incidents, indeed, wear *a little* the appearance of having been *heightened* for the purposes of entertaining narration; that, for example, in which a spy with a large nose, sent down to *watch* the author at his residence in the country, overhears him talking of *Spy Nosy*, (Spinoza,) and considers it as a personal allusion to himself!! In any case, however, the present division of the 'Literary Life' is very lively and laughable; and we offer our thanks to Mr. Coleridge for much good-humoured and rational exposure of his own follies, and those of the government (if *they* can be designated by so lenient a name) which descended to such unmeaning persecution.

Mr. Coleridge concludes the chapter in which these matters are detailed, with a brief retrospect of time mis-spent and talents mis-employed; with a simple and touching appeal to the sympathies of his readers, both in English and Latin verse: but the section which follows presents a peculiar claim to the attention of that numerous race of

---

[1] [When the author's great production on the *Logos* appears, there will be ample time to discuss his Germanized Platonics—Reviewer's note.]

well-educated young men in England, who are, or are aspiring to become, authors. The end of this chapter, we think, deserves quotation; and then (passing over the metaphysics) we must advance to the second volume, or rather to that division of it which relates to Mr. Wordsworth.

[Lines 11–29, p. 159 (of Vol. I), and the translation of the extract from Herder are quoted.]

The criticisms on Mr. Wordsworth, with which Mr. Coleridge commences his second volume, we have justly denominated *extraordinary*; for, though we may have perfect faith in his professed admiration of his friend, Mr. C. has nevertheless pointed out so many errors of design and execution in this very moderate writer, (as we must ever consider him,) and has furnished a clue to the exposure of so many more absurdities, that we cannot but here rank Mr. C. among the unintentional defenders of good taste and good sense in poetry. He *confines his opposition* to Mr. Wordsworth's *system* (if we must so call it) to the following points: first, to what Mr. W. intitles 'a selection of the *real* language of men;' secondly, to his 'imitation,' and his 'adoption, *as far as possible*, of the very language of men in low and rustic life;' and, thirdly, to his assertion that 'between the language of prose and that of metrical composition, there neither is, nor can be, any essential difference.' When it is recollected that these points form the very groundwork, and much of the superstructure, of Mr. Wordsworth's plan for vulgarizing poetry, it seems strange that Mr. Coleridge should talk of *confining his opposition* to them alone; and, by a few extracts from the second volume of this 'Literary Life,' we think that we shall be able to expose the manifest flaws in Mr. W.'s title to *any* estate or heritage in the manors of Parnassus, Helicon, and the lands lying thereabout. Mr. Coleridge saves his consistency, indeed, by an asseveration that the faults of Mr. W.'s theory are *rarely* exemplified in his practice: but, as the force of this remark lies entirely in the adverb *rarely*, an arithmetical process, instituted on the cases in question in the 'Lyrical Ballads,' will be the only method of settling the dispute between our brother-critic and ourselves. The result of our sum is very different from his: but we are perfectly agreed in our principles of calculation.

Mr. C. thus marshals his objections to his friend's absurd fancies on the foregoing topics:

[Line 15, p. 41 (of Vol. II), to line 18, p. 42, is quoted.]

These remarks we regard as very sensible, and urged with much conciseness and force of reasoning. Combined with what follows, they are obviously and utterly destructive of the very foundations of Mr. Wordsworth's *system.*—We subjoin another extract, with a quotation from the 'Lyrical Ballads;' to which we shall add several others, and then close this brief but we trust convincing exposure of the greatest piece of folly and arrogance, (the pretensions, we mean, of Mr. W.'s poetry to any thing either meritorious or original,[1]) which has disgraced the present *prodigious* aera of our poetical literature.

[The first forty-four lines of Chap. XVIII are quoted.]

We shall merely, *en passant*, observe on a criticism by Mr. Wordsworth, applied to Gray's Sonnet on the Death of West, and here quoted by Mr. Coleridge, that, when Mr. W. asserts that the only good lines in the Sonnet are those which he has marked with italics, he has betrayed his usual caprice. For example; one of his *italic* lines is the following:

'A different object *do* these eyes require;'

and one of his *roman* lines (not supposed to have the same merit) is this:

'These ears, alas! for other notes repine.'

If such capricious nonsense were allowed to pass for *criticism*, we should be inclined to resign our office in shame and confusion. We find ourselves unable to abridge, with any clearness, Mr. Coleridge's train of argument which establishes, in opposition to his whimsical friend, the *essential* difference between the language of prose and that of poetry. We must therefore be satisfied with quoting his final appeal to an undeniable fact; leaving the inference with our readers, who perhaps may consider so *self-evident* a matter as scarcely worth a dispute in the 19th century.

'Lastly, I appeal to the practice of the best poets of all countries and in all ages, as *authorizing* the opinion, (*deduced* from all the foregoing) that in every import of the word ESSENTIAL, which would not here involve a mere truism, there may be, is, and ought to be, an *essential* difference between the language of prose and of metrical composition.'

Let us now quote the promised examples of the happy results of Mr. W.'s theory. Will that mistaken gentleman ever be persuaded that,

[1] [We deny the originality of this author, on the ground of those numerous nursery-poems which existed before his own weak attempt to palm such productions on mature understandings.—Reviewer's note.]

if thought be the soul of poetry, expression is its body; and that both body and soul are of a peculiar and plainly distinguished cast and character? With the 'Lyrical Ballads' before us, we could add, *usque ad nauseam*, to the subjoined list of childish trifles: but, in a review of Mr. Coleridge's life, we are bound to confine ourselves to *his* criticisms on passages in Mr. Wordsworth.

[The last three stanzas of Wordsworth's 'The Sailor's Mother,' quoted by Coleridge on p. 54 of Vol. II, are quoted.]

How are we sure what a book-maker will vend next for poetry, who has already offered for sale such inconceivable trash as this?

We owe it to Mr. Coleridge to state that he labours very assiduously, by selections from his friend's few successful attempts, to counterbalance, nay to overwhelm, the effect of his own vituperative criticisms, on the remaining and (as we contend) much the larger portion of his poems. We are quite ready to allow that, when Mr. Wordsworth steps out of himself, when he no longer appears in the character of the *rustic egotistical metaphysician*, he writes very passably, and just like other poets on similar topics:—but, as we are of opinion that a great part of the bad taste of the day has arisen from that foolish good-nature which, for the sake of a few unobjectionable or even excellent passages, praises and gives popularity to whole poems, we hold it to be the duty of every classical scholar, or lover of genuine poetry, to discountenance either by a judicious silence, or by a well chosen opportunity of vigorous censure, the vain assumptions of our numerous poetical *charlatans*.

From the Blind Highland Boy.

' "And one, the rarest, was a shell,
Which he, poor child, had studied well:
The shell of a green turtle, thin
And hollow;—you might sit therein,
  It was so wide and deep."

' "Our Highland Boy oft visited
The house which held this prize, and led
By choice or chance did thither come
One day, when no one was at home,
  And found the door unbarred." '

In a succeeding extract, Mr. Coleridge applauds a couplet in which a lark is described, (a 'drunken lark!' by the way,)

' "*With a soul as strong as a mountain river
Pouring out praise to th' Almighty giver!*" '

De gustibus, &c.

Again;—Mr. C. quotes, but not with applause,

> ' "Close by a pond, upon the further side
> He stood alone; a minute's space I guess,
> I watch'd him, he continuing motionless;
> To the pool's further margin then I drew;
> He being all the while before me full in view." '

Which of the numerous happy parodists of Mr. Wordsworth has attributed to him a heaviness and an absurdity greater than the preceding?—Again;—extracted from a general panegyric, by Mr. Coleridge himself:

> 'He with a smile did then his tale repeat;
> And said, that, gathering leeches far and wide
> He travelled; stirring thus about his feet
> The waters of the ponds where they abide.
> "Once I could meet with them on every side,
> But they have dwindled long by slow decay;
> Yet still I persevere, and find them where I may." '

We beg our readers to pardon us for so long detaining them on such perfectly ludicrous matters: but we hope that we may be spared, in future, the necessity of troubling them or ourselves with any exposure of the hollowness of Mr. W.'s poetical reputation. If it be thought that we have already dwelt too much on his follies, be it remembered that he is the very founder and father of that modern school, which we have always wished to see held up to the general ridicule that it deserves; and if it be not thus overpowered, woe to the taste, judgment, and whole understanding of the rising generation!—It must also be considered that the space, which we have allotted to Mr. Coleridge's just but evidently reluctant criticisms on his friend, has enabled us to give our readers so much the less of Mr. C. himself as a biographer and metaphysician; and that we have had the charity to abstain altogether from any mention of Mr. Southey, who claims his portion in this volume of triple admiration: dedicated to that trio, whose mutual puffs have so often linked them in harmonies of applause, but at whose frequent union in literary censure Mr. Coleridge expresses the most innocent surprize!

We are sorry to be obliged to omit a large remaining portion of the

Biographia Literaria[1]; and especially the chapter of it in which Mr. Coleridge presents us with a masterly, spirited, and moral critique on that reproach to the tragic muse of England, the *tragedy* of 'Bertram.' *O si sic omnia!*

[1] [Among our omissions, we must reckon the discovery of a plagiarism in David Hume from Thomas Aquinas.—Reviewer's note.]

Review of Coleridge's 'Sibylline Leaves'

Edinburgh Magazine

2d ser. I (Oct. 1817), 245–50. The reviewer is unknown.

Every reader of modern poetry is acquainted of course with 'the Ancient Mariner' of this author. It is one of those compositions, indeed, which cannot be perused without a more than ordinary excitation of fancy at the time; and which, when once read, can never afterwards be entirely forgotten. What we mean, however, more particularly to say at present, is, that this production has always appeared to us in the light of a very good caricature of the genius of its author. It displays, in fact, all the strength and all the weakness,—all the extravagancies and eccentricities,—all the bold features, and peculiar grimace, if we may so express ourselves, of his intellectual physiognomy,—and in forming an opinion respecting the talents which he possesses, this composition may serve the very same purpose which an overcharged drawing of a countenance could answer to one who would form to himself some general idea of the kind of features by which an individual was distinguished. In order to adapt such a representation to the reality of the case, we must of course soften its prominences, and correct its extravagancies; we must raise some parts and depress others; and while we retain the general likeness and grouping of the individual features which compose the countenance, we must reduce the whole to that medium character, from which, amidst the infinite varieties that occur, it is the rarest of all things to meet with any great deviation.

Mr Coleridge, we understand, has sometimes expressed an unwillingness, in so far as the character of his poetry is concerned, to be classed with the other members of what has been called the Lake School; and it is impossible, we think, for any candid mind not to perceive, that, as in some respects the individuals of that association differ essentially from each other, there are also respects in which the compositions of this author are strikingly and most advantageously distinguished from those of all the rest. He displays, it is true, on many occasions, the same sickly sentimentality,—the same perverted disposition to invest trifling subjects with an air and expression of great importance and interest,—to treat subjects of real grandeur in a manner unsuited to their native majesty of character,—and to employ, occasionally, expressions which are merely vulgar or ridiculous, instead of that direct and simple diction which is the most natural language of intense feeling. Along with these peculiarities, however, it cannot be denied, that there are other qualities of Mr Coleridge's poetry which entitle it to a place among the finest productions of modern times. There is, in particular, a wildness of narrative, and a picturesque grouping of qualities and objects, which are in fine contrast to the tameness and placidity of ordinary poetry;—a freshness of colouring and a delicacy of shading, which mark the hand of a great master. Amidst some obscurity and occasional failures, there are also every where to be discovered those incidental touches of true grace which indicate the native riches and power of the artist; and along with all these qualities, there is a fine adaptation, frequently, of the style and manner of our older masters to the improved design of modern times, which sheds a venerable air over the whole composition, and seems to embalm it with all the flowers and odours of the 'olden time.' These better qualities, it ought also to be recollected, are the more prevailing characteristics of our author's manner, and though there are occasional passages, and even entire pieces, in this collection, which none but a poet of the Lake school could have written, and which, without any intimation of the name of the author, would at once, in the opinion of any ordinary judge, determine his place of residence and habits of fellowship, there is no doubt that there is a still greater number of passages which remind us of an era of far better things.

Nothing, we apprehend, is more difficult than to characterize correctly the genius of an author whose productions possess so many opposite qualities, and whose excellencies and extravagancies are so curiously blended; especially as the work in which these combinations occur is not one uniform picture of any landscape in nature, or one unbroken narrative of some moral tale; not a regular and didactic poem, nor even a series of poems, marked by one prevailing character, and intended for the production of one common effect; but a great assemblage of unconnected pieces, which differ in subject, in character,

177

and in style,—sibylline leaves, which have long been tossed by all the winds of heaven, and are now collected into one precious fasciculus, —some inscribed with interesting lessons of domestic love and family affection,—some dedicated to enthusiastic celebration of the grand or the beautiful in natural scenery,—not a few devoted to inspired wailings over the fates and hopes of national enterprise,—and a very considerable number merely employed by the poet, for the purpose of being inscribed, as might suit his humour, with the incoherent ravings of his indolence or gaiety. Taking them altogether, however, we shall endeavour, though with a very general and rapid glance, to mark the prevailing qualities of the group, and to enable our readers also, by the specimens we shall select, to form for themselves an estimate of the merits of our author, independent of any judgment we may happen to express.

We have already hinted, that the prevailing characteristic of the compositions of this author is a certain air of wildness and irregularity, which equally belongs to his narrations of events, and to the pictures he has offered of the aspects of Nature. It would require, we believe, a greater expenditure, both of time and of space, than we can at present afford, to say exactly wherein this quality consists. We think, indeed, that an examination of its nature presents a subject of very interesting study to those who delight to speculate on the wonderful varieties of human character, or to mark, with the eye of philosophical discernment, the predilections which determine the excursions of fancy throughout the unbounded range of ideal combinations. Every person, however, may form to himself some analogical representation of this attribute of mind, who can contrast, in the imagination of external nature, the scenery of a rugged and finely wooded landscape, with the drowsy stillness of a champaign country, of which riches and uniformity are the prevailing characteristics,—or the progress of a torrent amidst rocks and forests, with the course of a stream which flows full and unbroken through the placid abundance of a cultivated region,—or the music of the winds as it is modulated and aided in its progress through a landscape or woods and of mountains, with those harmonious adaptations of kindred sounds which science and taste are capable of forming. We cannot pretend, however, to give instances of this quality, which is, indeed, the characteristic attribute of our author's genius, and which, of course, displays itself in some degree in all his productions;—we must, therefore, content ourselves at present with referring such of our readers as think they should, above all things, be delighted with a genius of this order, to the actual productions of the author before us, as the greatest master in this style with whom we are acquainted; and, in the meantime, we shall proceed to notice some other qualities of his works which can more readily be illustrated by quotations and references.

Mr. Coleridge, like Mr. Southey, possesses, in no ordinary perfection, the power of presenting to the imagination of his readers a correct idea of natural scenery. There is a remarkable difference, however, as it appears to us, in the character assumed by this faculty in the case of these two writers. The delineations of Mr. Southey are true to the reality, as if his single object in description had been to represent every hue and variation of the object before him; his descriptions, accordingly, are admirably adapted for affording subjects to a painter; and, indeed, we know not any author by whose writings so many admirable facilities of this nature are afforded. His descriptions, at the same time, are frequently destitute of that far higher character which they might have assumed, if employed only as the ground-work for the production of emotion. We do not see wandering round his tablet those countless forms of moral excellence which almost bedim, by the brilliancy of their superior nature, whatever of beautiful belongs to mere form or colours; nor do we so often feel, as in the writings of Mr Coleridge, that his chief object in presenting to us a picture of woods, or waters, or lofty mountains, was to aid him in communicating, with more perfect success, the vivid emotion which was present to his mind; and which, while it adds prodigiously to the effect of his scenes, throws often around them an aërial dimness, that seems to take something away from their merely material nature. This, we apprehend, is one of the chief excellencies of the author before us, and though we might refer in proof of it to almost any page of the present volume, we shall select as a specimen the opening of the 'Hymn, before sun-rise, in the vale of Chamouny,' in which this peculiarity is at once exemplified and explained:

[The first thirty-eight lines are quoted.]

And so on, in a strain of most exquisite poetry, of which we regret that we cannot continue our extract.

A second characteristic of our author's power of description, and one which is intimately connected with that we have already noticed, is the delightful freshness which nature seems to assume whenever the light and sun-shine of his genius fall on it. It is never nature merely as invested with form and colour which he paints, but nature breathing all pleasant odours, and glittering with all brilliant lights,—nature as she appears when moistened and sparkling with the rain of heaven, and when all her finest contrasts are exhibited beneath the cloudless radiance of a summer sky. As an instance, we may quote the following lines from the beginning of the poem entitled 'Fears in Solitude:'

[The first twenty-one lines are quoted.]

The conclusion of this poem will awaken, we are persuaded, many kindly feelings in the bosoms of those who, like ourselves, have often gained, after a day of solitary wandering among the hills, the summit of the highest mountain in the group, and have felt the sight of the open landscape operate like a sudden restoration to life itself, upon the mind wearied and depressed with intense meditation.

[The last twenty-nine lines are quoted.]

With respect to Mr Coleridge's powers of description, we have still further to remark, that we do not know any author who possesses a finer talent for relieving his pictures by judicious contrast. As an evidence of which, the reader may take the following passage, the admirable picture in which is merely produced by way of contrast to the dark and barren character of the desart stream that is intended to be described:

[Lines 72–101 of 'The Picture' are quoted.]

And so on, with some more beautiful painting; after which the author thus proceeds:

[Lines 111–15 are quoted.]

The pages of Mr Coleridge are not characterized by those fine touches of genuine pathos, which, amidst all the ravings of his mystical poetry, give often so inexpressible a charm to the compositions of Mr Wordsworth. Yet is there a pathos of another kind which is very frequent with our author; a gentle and subdued tone of sympathy with human happiness or human suffering; an exquisite feeling of the charities and joys of domestic life; and a just appreciation of the necessity and value of religious consolations to the agitated and wayward heart of man—which communicate to his poetry not the least delightful of its attractions, and which never fail to make us love, while we respect, the author. We may assert, indeed, that the whole tone of our author's poetry is favourable to virtue and to all the charities of life,—and we could quote several beautiful passages of this nature, did not the very copious extracts we have already given preclude us from this pleasure.

We must confess, at the same time, that, along with these excellencies, there are several great and very obvious defects in the poetry of Mr Coleridge. His manner of describing natural objects is too apt to degenerate, as we have already hinted, into that morbid sentimentality which of late has become so general a characteristic of the poetry of this country—he is fond of expressing and illustrating the notion, that

> 'Outward forms, the loftiest, still receive
> Their finer influence from the life within.'

And that mystical interpretation of the expressions of Nature, which has become the favourite occupation of Mr Wordsworth's muse, and which has infected the taste of Lord Byron himself, has frequently exerted a seductive power over the fancy and feelings of this still more congenial spirit. We might mention also among the faults of his poetry, a degree of obscurity which sometimes occurs, not to such a pitch, perhaps, as in any instance to render his writings absolutely unintelligible, but sufficiently often to make the reader uneasy lest he should at every step encounter some such mystical passage—and to lead him onward, not with the gaiety and confidence which the song of the poet ought always to inspire, but with that sort of watchful jealousy which is natural to a person who is in the company of one that is disposed to puzzle him. We may mention, in the last place, that there is a good deal of affectation occasionally in the style of our author; he sometimes uses expressions which are altogether unsuitable to the dignity of poetry; and curious inversions of phrase are every now and then occurring, which, to our ears at least, give neither grace nor vivacity to his works. There is one form of expression, in particular, of which our author is so fond, as to have rendered his frequent use of it quite ridiculous,—it occurs in such lines as the following:

> '*Nor* such thoughts
> Dim and unhallowed dost thou *not* reject.'
> '*Nor* dost *not* thou sometimes recal those hours.'

To this enumeration of faults we may add, that there are some pieces in this collection which to us appear to be quite silly and vapid. The following 'Verses,' for instance, 'to a Young Lady on her recovery from a Fever:'

> 'Why need I say, Louisa, dear!
> How glad I am to see you here,
>   A lovely convalescent;
> Risen from the bed of pain and fear,
>   And feverish heat incessant.

'The sunny Showers, the dappled Sky,
The little Birds that warble high
    Their vernal loves commencing,
Will better welcome you than I,
    With their sweet *influencing*.

[The two remaining stanzas are also quoted.]

We shall not, however, quote any thing more of this kind. From what we have said, the reader will perceive, that we entertain a very high idea of Mr Coleridge's poetical merits. He has intimated, however, in his preface, that he intends for the future to devote himself chiefly to studies of a different nature. We do not, it is true, give much credit to such a promise—because we have something of the same idea respecting the writing of poems, which Goldsmith had respecting slander, that it is like the propensity of a tyger which has once tasted of human blood,—not easily divested of the appetite it has indulged. Taking the promise of the poet, however, as seriously given, we should be disposed to say, that if he is conscious of no desire to produce poems more free from faults than most of those in the volume before us, we do not think that the reputation of the artist would be much injured by his relinquishing the study; because, what is now attributed to mere negligence and apathy, would soon come to be considered as an inherent defect in his genius. We cannot help adding, however, that if Mr Coleridge would give his mind more exclusively to what appears to us to be his true vocation, and would carefully avoid those extravagancies of sentiment and singularities of expression to which we have slightly alluded, we have no doubt that he might yet produce a work which would place him in the first rank of British poets,—which would entirely justify the high opinion very generally entertained of the capabilities of his genius,—and be fully adequate to all the compliments, whether sincere or adulatory, he has ever received.

III
Byron

Review of Byron's
'Hours of Idleness'

Edinburgh Review

XI (Jan. 1808), 285–89. The author was Henry Brougham, a lawyer and Whig M.P., who became Lord Chancellor in 1830. The authority for this attribution is Walter E. Houghton (ed.), The Wellesley Index to Victorian Periodicals *(Toronto, 1966), p. 442. This was the review which was instrumental in calling forth Byron's* English Bards and Scotch Reviewers.

The poesy of this young lord belongs to the class which neither gods nor men are said to permit. Indeed, we do not recollect to have seen a quantity of verse with so few deviations in either direction from that exact standard. His effusions are spread over a dead flat, and can no more get above or below the level, than if they were so much stagnant water. As an extenuation of this offence, the noble author is peculiarly forward in pleading minority. We have it in the title-page, and on the very back of the volume; it follows his name like a favourite part of his *style*. Much stress is laid upon it in the preface, and the poems are connected with this general statement of his case, by particular dates, substantiating the age at which each was written. Now, the law upon the point of minority, we hold to be perfectly clear. It is a plea available only to the defendant; no plaintiff can offer it as a supplementary ground of action. Thus, if any suit could be brought against Lord Byron, for the purpose of compelling him to put into court a certain quantity of poetry; and if judgement were given against him; it is highly probable that an exception would be taken, were he to deliver *for poetry*, the contents of this volume. To this he might plead *minority*; but as he now makes voluntary tender of the article, he hath no right to sue, on that ground, for the price in good current praise, should the goods be unmarketable. This is our view of the law on the point, and we dare to say, so will it be ruled. Perhaps however, in reality, all that he tells us about his youth, is rather with a view to increase our wonder, than to soften our censures. He possibly means to say, 'See how a minor can write! This poem was actually composed by a young man of eighteen, and this by one of only sixteen!'—But, alas, we all remember the poetry of Cowley at ten, and Pope at twelve; and so far from hearing, with any degree of surprise, that very poor verses were written by a youth from his leaving school to his leaving college, inclusive, we really believe this to be the most common of all occurrences; that it happens in the life of nine men in ten who are educated in England; and that the tenth man writes better verse than Lord Byron.

His other plea of privilege, our author rather brings forward in order to wave it. He certainly, however, does allude frequently to his family and ancestors—sometimes in poetry, sometimes in notes; and while giving up his claim on the score of rank, he takes care to remember us of Dr Johnson's saying, that when a nobleman appears as an author, his merit should be handsomely acknowledged. In truth, it is this consideration only, that induces us to give Lord Byron's poems a place in our review, beside our desire to counsel him, that he do forthwith abandon poetry, and turn his talents, which are considerable, and his opportunities, which are great, to better account.

With this view, we must beg leave seriously to assure him, that the mere rhyming of the final syllable, even when accompanied by the presence of a certain number of feet; nay, although (which does not always happen) those feet should scan regularly, and have been all counted accurately upon the fingers,—is not the whole art of poetry. We would entreat him to believe, that a certain portion of liveliness, somewhat of fancy, is necessary to constitute a poem; and that a poem in the present day, to be read, must contain at least one thought, either in a little degree different from the ideas of former writers, or differently expressed. We put it to his candour, whether there is any thing so deserving the name of poetry in verses like the following, written in 1806, and whether, if a youth of eighteen could say any thing so uninteresting to his ancestors, a youth of nineteen should publish it.

> 'Shades of heroes, farewell! your descendant, departing
>   From the feat of his ancestors, bids you, adieu!
> Abroad, or at home, your remembrance imparting
>   New courage, he'll think upon glory, and you.
>
> Though a tear dim his eye, at this sad separation,
>   'Tis nature, not fear, that excites his regret:

Far distant he goes, with the same emulation;
  The fame of his fathers he ne'er can forget.

That fame, and that memory, still will he cherish,
  He vows, that he ne'er will disgrace your renown;
Like you will he live, or like you will he perish;
  When decay'd, may he mingle his dust with your own.' p. 3.

Now we positively do assert, that there is nothing better than these stanzas in the whole compass of the noble minor's volume.

Lord Byron should also have a care of attempting what the greatest poets have done before him, for comparisons (as he must have had occasion to see at his writing master's) are odious.—Gray's Ode on Eton College, should really have kept out the ten hobbling stanzas 'on a distant view of the village and school of Harrow.'

'Where fancy, yet, joys to retrace the resemblance,
  Of comrades, in friendship and mischief allied;
How welcome to me, your ne'er fading remembrance,
  Which rests in the bosom, though hope is deny'd.'—p. 4.

In like manner, the exquisite lines of Mr Rogers, '*On a Tear*,' might have warned the noble author off those premises, and spared us a whole dozen such stanzas as the following.

'Mild Charity's glow,
  To us mortals below,
Shows the soul from barbarity clear;
  Compassion will melt,
  Where this virtue is felt,
And its dew is diffus'd in a Tear.

The man doom'd to fail,
  With the blast of the gale,
Through billows Atlantic to steer,
  As he bends o'er the wave,
  Which may soon be his grave,
The green sparkles bright with a Tear.'—p. 11.

And so of instances in which former poets had failed. Thus, we do not think Lord Byron was made for translating, during his non-age, Adrian's Address to his Soul, when Pope succeeded so indifferently in the attempt. If our readers, however, are of another opinion, they may look at it.

'Ah! gentle, fleeting, wav'ring sprite,
Friend and associate of this clay!
  To what unknown region borne,
Wilt thou, now, wing thy distant flight?
No more, with wonted humour gay,
  But pallid, cheerless, and forlorn.'—page 72.

However, be this as it may, we fear his translations and imitations are great favourites with Lord Byron. We have them of all kinds, from Anacreon to Ossian; and, viewing them as school exercises, they may pass. Only, why print them after they have had their day and served their turn? And why call the thing in p. 79 a translation, where *two* words (θελω λεγειν) of the original are expanded into four lines, and the other thing in p. 81, where μεσουμχτιοις ποθ' ὡραις, is rendered by means of six hobbling verses?—As to his Ossianic poesy, we are not very good judges, being, in truth, so moderately skilled in that species of composition, that we should, in all probability, be criticizing some bit of the genuine Macpherson itself, were we to express our opinion of Lord Byron's rhapsodies. *If,* then, the following beginning of a 'Song of bards,' is by his Lordship, we venture to object to it, as far as we can comprehend it. 'What form rises on the roar of clouds, whose dark ghost gleams on the red stream of tempests?' His voice rolls on the thunder; 'tis Orla, the brown chief of Otihona. He was,' &c. After detaining this 'brown chief' some time, the bards conclude by giving him their advice to 'raise his fair locks;' then to 'spread them on the arch of the rainbow;' and 'to smile through the tears of the storm.' Of this kind of thing there are no less than *nine* pages; and we can so far venture an opinion in their favour, that they look very like Macpherson; and we are positive they are pretty nearly as stupid and tiresome.

It is a sort of privilege of poets to be egotists; but they should 'use it as not abusing it;' and particularly one who piques himself (though indeed at the ripe age of nineteen), of being 'an infant bard,'—('The artless Helicon I boast is youth;')—should either not know, or should seem not to know, so much about his own ancestry. Besides a poem above cited on the family seat of the Byrons, we have another of eleven pages, on the self-same subject, introduced with an apology, 'he certainly had no intention of inserting it;' but really, 'the particular request of some friends,' &c. &c. It concludes with five stanzas on himself, 'the last and youngest of a noble line.' There is a good deal also about his maternal ancestors, in a poem on Lachin-y-gair, a mountain where the spent part of his youth, and might have learnt that *pibroch* is not a bagpipe, any more than duet means a fiddle.

As the author has dedicated so large a part of his volume to immortalize his employments at school and college, we cannot possibly dismiss it without presenting the reader with a specimen of these ingenious effusions. In an ode with a Greek motto, called Granta, we have the following magnificent stanzas.

'There, in apartments small and damp,
   The candidate for college prizes,
Sits poring by the midnight lamp,
   Goes late to bed, yet early rises.

Who reads false quantities in Sele,
   Or puzzles o'er the deep triangle;
Depriv'd of many a wholesome meal,
   In barbarous Latin, doom'd to wrangle.

Renouncing every pleasing page,
   From authors of historic use;
Preferring to the lettered sage,
   The square of the hypothenuse.

Still harmless are these occupations,
   That hurt none but the hapless student,
Compar'd with other recreations,
   Which bring together the imprudent.' p. 123, 124, 125.

We are sorry to hear so bad an account of the college psalmody as is contained in the following Attic stanzas.

'Our choir would scarcely be excus'd,
   Even as a band of raw beginners;
All mercy, now, must be refus'd
   To such a set of croaking sinners.

If David, when his toils were ended,
   Had heard these blockheads sing before him,
To us, his psalms had ne'er descended;
   In furious mood, he would have tore 'em.'—p. 126, 127.

But whatever judgment may be passed on the poems of this noble minor, it seems we must take them as we find them, and be content; for they are the last we shall ever have from him. He is at best, he says, but an intruder into the groves of Parnassus; he never lived in a garret, like thorough-bred poets; and 'though he once roved a careless mountaineer in the Highlands of Scotland,' he has not of late enjoyed this advantage. Moreover, he expects no profit from his publication; and whether it succeeds or not, 'it is highly improbable, from his situation and pursuits hereafter,' that he should again condescend to become an author.[1] Therefore, let us take what we get and be thankful. What right have we poor devils to be nice? We are well off to have got so much from a man of this Lord's station, who does not live in a garret, but 'has the sway' of Newstead Abbey. Again, we say, let us be thankful; and, with honest Sancho, bid God bless the giver, nor look the gift horse in the mouth.

[1] Byron's Preface, with its ingenuous air of the poetical *amateur*, who wrote 'to divert the dull moments of indisposition, or the monotony of a vacant hour' and published 'at the request and for the perusal of . . . friends', could be considered a partial excuse for this sarcasm.

Review of Byron's 'English Bards and Scotch Reviewers'

Critical Review

3d ser. XVII (May 1809), 78–85. The reviewer is unknown.

It would be much for the advantage of literature, that every ten or twenty years should produce a new Dunciad to expose the ravings of folly, the coxcombry of learning, and the aberrations of genius. It will hardly be disputed that the present age presents a most fertile field for such an enterprize. 'The pursuits of Literature,'[1] notwithstanding the many admirable strokes of satire which it contained, was a work in which virulence, malevolence, and party spirit so predominated, as entirely to defeat the grand purposes of correction and amendment, which can alone justify the indulgence of a satirical temper. Besides, its most just and cutting irony was so concealed under an ostentatious display of learning, and (what is worse) was so exclusively confined to that part of the work which bore the appearance of a simple appendage, that the reader required some portion of the author's malevolence to enable him to wade through the insipid text, and its pompous accompaniments for the purpose of arriving at what is really worth the labour of seeking it.

But 'farewell, a long farewell,' to this once celebrated satire. Its day is gone by—the very objects of its spleen and virulence are (for the most part) rolled into oblivion.

The 'Baviad,' and 'Maeviad,'[2] were as superior in merit, as distinguished in effect, above the 'Pursuits of Literature.' Their satire was

[1] *The Pursuits of Literature* (1794) was a satire by Thomas J. Mathias on contemporary literature.

[2] The *Baviad* (1794) and *Maeviad* (1795) were verse satires written against the Della Cruscan school of poets by William Gifford, later editor of the *Quarterly*

principally levelled against a particular class of writers who had made rapid advances towards establishing the empire of consummate nonsense. It completely answered the end proposed, and dissolved in an instant the air-built fabric of the Della-Crusca school. But here again more than half the force and humour of the satire has evaporated together with the objects which gave birth to it; and new generations of dunces have risen since the days of Rosa-Matilda, which call most powerfully for the scythe and pruning-hook of reform.

If we say that the satire now before us does not prove its author to be as yet sufficiently qualified for so Herculean a task, it is not for want of evidence that he is gifted with all the talents requisite for the undertaking, if more matured by reflection, and polished and refined by use. The first and most striking objection to the present essay is that it opens upon a field much too enlarged for the present extent of the author's observation. In its object, it appears to embrace the whole circle of modern poetry and criticism, and it required a regular and systematic plan of operations to cover so vast a space with judgment and effect. This is by no means the case, however, with the present performance, which is a sort of skirmishing attack upon a number of individual writers, unconnected in its pursuit and undefined in its end. Many notorious offenders escape unnoticed; some are acquitted or marked with applause, whom a more correct judgment would have condemned; and some are censured with acrimony whom a more refined and comprehensive taste might acknowledge to have deserved a far different fate at the tribunal of just criticism. But in spite of these defects and errors enough appears to convince us that the principles which regulate the author's judgment are in general sound, though experience has not yet taught him the art of modifying them with just discrimination and applying them to every particular instance as it may occur. In the other qualifications of satire he is more uniformly successful. His verse is flowing and energetic, his imagination active, and his powers of expression fully equal to the true spirit of his theme.

We shall lose no more time in these general observations, but proceed to find some extracts from the work, which must either justify or condemn our opinion.

After an introduction *in form*, extolling the bards and critics of the 'olden time,' at the expense of these 'degenerate days,' the Bard begins to particularize the objects of his censure. He points one of his earliest arrows at no ignoble quarry.

Review. Anna (not Rosa) Matilda was a pseudonym for Mrs Hannah Cowley, a member of the school.

[Lines 143–84 (on Scott) are quoted.]

We have transcribed the foregoing passage, not as a favourable specimen of the writer's talent, but as the most striking instance, through the work, of the defects of judgment, which we have before noticed in him. We must beg Mr. Scott's pardon for so often bringing his name forward, and canvassing the merits of his poems on occasions where they do not immediately fall under our notice; but we cannot resist the inclination to oppose ourselves to a very unjust outcry, which has been set up to his prejudice by critics who style themselves his friends, and which has been followed by many who have wanted either taste or leisure to examine into its propriety. As for ourselves we have not the honour of being known in the slightest degree to the gentleman in question; and he may perhaps think that in criticising some of his publications we have used the privilege of utter strangers somewhat rudely. But, whatever may be our sentiments respecting certain points in his poetical character, our general opinions are much less at variance with those which he professes than with those inculcated by the northern directors of the taste of Britain.[1] His choice of subjects presents at least one advantage of no inconsiderable weight,—the charm of novelty. That it is deficient in interest we cannot readily admit; since it exhibits the strong and faithful representation of character and manners at a period of society with which till of late years we were comparatively very little acquainted, but which has since engrossed the attention of a large class of literary adventurers, and amply rewarded the labours of investigation. We confess but little obligation to those severe or supercilious critics, who would drag us back to the 'thrice-told tales' of classical fable from a pursuit of most interesting variety, which at every turn presents us with 'something new and strange,' and in which, with every step that we advance,

> 'our views expand,
> And all the scenes of fairy-land
> Come swelling on the sight.'

Were the substitution of new and romantic machinery the only advantages gained to the cause of poetry by this new pursuit, we should think the gain considerable, and can see no possible objection on this score to the introduction of 'Messieurs the spirits of Flood and Fell,' or even of little 'Gilpin Horner,'[2] supposing them to be 'discreetly

[1] The *Edinburgh Review*.

[2] The 'spirits of Flood and Fell' are the River and Mountain spirits who converse in stanzas XV–XVII of Scott's *The Lay of the Last Minstrel*. Gilpin Horner was an elf said by Scott in a note to be the prototype of the dwarf in the same poem.

and reverently' brought into notice. They suit the character of the age described; and, however 'Messieurs the critics of Bond-street or the Canon-gate,'[1] may rail at us, we vastly prefer a *modern* poem in which the supernatural agency is assigned to such monkish sprites, than one which formally presents us to the Jupiter and Juno, the Vulcan and Momus of antiquity; nor can we anywise comprehend why the former should be less dignified or more ridiculous than the latter.

But it is on the ground of faithful adherence to the just and original *costume* of character, that Mr. Scott may rest his claims to pre-eminence with the greatest security. It is in this strong-hold that 'Messieurs his *friends*' have thought proper to attack him with the greatest vehemence; and we are really sorry to see that the writer of this satire (otherwise very far from *complaisant* to the critics above mentioned) has blindly followed their authority on the very point in which their authority is the worst that can be relied upon. The character of *Deloraine*[2] cannot but be acknowledged for as true and spirited a delineation from human nature as ever was attempted by the most consummate master of the art. On what grounds then our author directs his satire against this portion of Mr. Scott's first and best romances we cannot even form a guess. But in saying that 'Marmion is exactly what Deloraine would have been, &c. &c. &c.' we must affirm that he only betrays his ignorance of human nature, or his gross want of discrimination. The charge is copied, (not indeed in word, but in spirit) from a review of the work in question,[3] to which we have often before alluded; and if any of our readers are not satisfied with the observations which we found occasion to make in our article of 'Partenopex de Blois' (vol. XIV) on the same subject, we will refer him for his further assurance (that Marmion is a picture from the life) to the lives of the abbots of St. Albans at the end of Watts's edition of Matthew Paris, p. 104, where they may read a long story how Robert Fitzwalter, one of the richest and most powerful barons of England, (cui vix aliquis comes potuit aequiparari; erat enim in armis strenuus, animosus, et superbus, multis abundans possessionibus, *generosus*, et potentum consanguineorum numerositate et affinium septus multitudine ac roboratus,)[4] bribed William Pigun, a monk of St. Albans, to steal the abbey-seal, with

[1] Fashionable readers in London and Edinburgh.

[2] Sir William of Deloraine is a character in Scott's *The Lay of the Last Minstrel*.

[3] Jeffrey in the *Edinburgh Review*, XII (April 1808), 11, had criticized the character of Marmion as sordid and unnatural.

[4] 'To whom scarcely anyone could be compared, for he was vigorous in arms, courageous, and haughty, abounding in many possessions, *noble*, and surrounded and strengthened by a large number of powerful people, relatives, and a multitude of in-laws.'

which he made a false deed and took possession, under colour of it, of the wood of *Northawe* rightfully belonging to the monastery.

But we are ashamed of ourselves for quoting a single instance in support of a fact respecting the character of the *chivalrous* ages, which is much too notorious to all men who have read enough to entitle them to give any opinion on the subject.

We return with pleasure to less exceptionable parts of the poem before us.

The poetical fraternity of the lakes are noticed, and their peculiar and well-known vices pointed out, with a great deal of real humour in several succeeding verses. The wonder-working Lewis,[1]

> 'Who fain would make Parnassus a church-yard,'

is then *complimented* with about twenty lines of *panegyric*, concluding thus,

> ———'if tales like thine may please,
> St. Luke's alone can vanquish the disease;
> Even Satan's self with thee might dread to dwell,
> And in thy skull discern a deeper hell.'

Anacreon Moore,[2] 'the young Catullus of his day,' is next subjected to the lash; and, coupled with him (but surely with great injustice) the translator of the sonnets of Camoens.[3]

'Hayley, in vain attempting something new,' 'the Sabbath Bard, Sepulchral Grahame,' and 'Harmonious Bowles, the first, great oracle of tender souls,' form the next illustrious trio.[4]

Montgomery,[5] the bard of '*classic* Sheffield,' who, whatever may have been his faults, certainly discovered a genius which no true friend to English literature would have attempted to stifle in its birth, is

[1] Matthew Gregory 'Monk' Lewis (1775–1818), now remembered mainly for his gothic novel, *The Monk*.

[2] Thomas Moore, nicknamed Anacreon for his translation (1800) of that poet's odes.

[3] Percy Clinton Sydney Smythe, Sixth Viscount Strangford (1780–1855), published his translation of Camoëns in 1803.

[4] William Hayley (1745–1820), a poet now known mainly for the illustrations done for him by Blake; William Lisle Bowles (1762–1850), a divine and poet, whose sonnets were admired by Coleridge; James Grahame (1765–1811), a divine and morbidly religious poet.

[5] James Montgomery (1771–1854), a minor poet and reviewer for the *Eclectic Review*. His review of Wordsworth's *Poems in Two Volumes* is reprinted in this edition.

afterwards noticed, chiefly for the purpose of introducing the assault on the strong-hold of northern criticism.

> 'Though fair they rose, and might have bloom'd at least,
> His hopes have perished by the northern blast:
> Nipp'd in the bud by Caledonian *gales*,[1]
> His blossoms *wither*, as the *blast* prevails!'

We shall, perhaps, be accused of illiberality for noticing with praise, or even with complacency, the ensuing attack upon one who is generally considered as president of the northern board of criticism;[2] but in justice to our author, we cannot pass over what is perhaps the most spirited portion of his satire, and that which affords the strongest evidence of those talents for which we have given him ample credit. We are perfectly silent as to the *justice* of the case, and only hope (for the honour of all parties concerned) that it will lead to no such *fatal* catastrophe as that deplored in the following verses:

[Lines 438–43 and 460–97 are quoted. Lines 440–43, 470–73, 481–83, and 497 are italicized by the reviewer. The '*fatal* catastrophe' mentioned above is a facetious reference to the duel (described in the passage) between Jeffrey and Thomas Moore, which was stopped at the last moment.]

We must now put an end to this article without taking notice of the remaining topics which the poem embraces. Our readers must judge for themselves whether our general commendation and censure has been such as the occasion demanded. We are not ignorant that the name of a very young man has been whispered about as that of the author—but even should the report be correct, we are unwilling to contribute to the circulation of what, for his sake, we wish had been kept a close secret.[3] The wit and force of the satire will only render its personality more offensive to the number who are either its immediate victims or in some measure involved in the effects of it. It is not desirable even in a just cause to volunteer a service which must create many enemies and comparatively few friends; but in the present instance we are confident that the author has too often suffered his satirical vein to attain an ascendancy over his better judgment, and

---

[1] [We should object to the word *gales* as very unsuitable to the subject, and merely used for the sake of the rhyme, unless it be meant to imply that the very *zephyrs* of Scotland are rude enough to nip the fairest buds of a more genial climate.—Reviewer's note.]

[2] Francis Jeffrey, editor of the *Edinburgh Review*.

[3] *The English Bards and Scotch Reviewers* was published anonymously.

fear that he may repent too late in his maturer years of having inflicted some wounds where they were not deserved, and driven into the ranks of his foes, some persons whom he might have been proud to embrace as his friends. It may be required of us, especially after stating the prevalent report as to the youth of the author, to point out some of the less important defects of style and method, which are easily discoverable in the work; but we are persuaded that his own taste and judgment will be more serviceable to him as he advances in life than any observation of ours in the correction of trifling errors, and besides it may be unjust not to leave them, as the means of revenge, untouched in the hands of the northern critics.

Review of Byron's 'Childe Harold's Pilgrimage', Cantos I–II

Monthly Review

LXVIII (*May 1812*), *74–83*. *The author was Thomas Denman, a lawyer who became Lord Chief Justice in 1832: see B. C. Nangle*, The Monthly Review, Second Series (*London, 1955*), *p. 98.*

The high popularity, which this singular production has so rapidly attained, will materially abridge our critical labors; since few of our poetical readers, or of those readers who peruse poetical articles in a Review, will by this time stand in need of our information on the subject. We may therefore spare ourselves the task of tracing the desultory windings of Lord Byron's plan with any degree of accuracy, and might be almost contented with adding our humble praise to those general applauses which we have witnessed with the more pleasure, because they are the accomplishment of the favourable predictions which we confidently hazarded,[1] on his Lordship's first appearance before the public. We shall, however, do something more than this: we shall enrich our own pages with a few of the best stanzas in the poem; and we shall flatter ourselves that any observations, which may be excited in the course of a re-perusal, will contribute to give a permanency to the noble author's reputation, that may not be inferior to the splendor of his present success.

Childe Harold, sick of the voluptuous dissipation of an unrestrained youth, resolved to change the scene, to shake off *ennui*, and to give a new stimulus to an exhausted mind, by foreign travel:

[Stanza XI of Canto I is quoted.]

[1] [See M. R. for November, 1807.—Reviewer's note.]

198

Who Childe Harold was, we are wholly at a loss to inform the inquirer. We only know that his satiated appetite is said to have made him selfish, gloomy, discontented, and suspicious; and we are warned against supposing that any real personage is represented by him. In some trivial and local particulars, it is indeed admitted that grounds might exist for such a notion; and certainly those tourists, who have visited Newstead Abbey,[1] will easily recognize its likeness in several parts of the poem:

> 'It was a vast and venerable pile;
> So old it seemed only not to fall,
> Yet strength was pillar'd in each massy aisle.
> Monastic dome! condemned to uses vile!
> Where Superstition once had made her den,'—&c. P. 6.

Again, the Childe is told by his staunch yeoman;

> 'My spouse and boys dwell near *thy hall*,
> *Along the bordering lake.*'—

Not to mention several minor points of resemblance:—but, as Lord B. expresses his hope that, in the main points, no similarity can be supposed to exist, we must conclude that his choice of a hero was directed not by sympathy of character, but by coincidence of circumstances, which may be justly deemed very remarkable.

With this matter, however, the reader and the reviewer have little concern; except that some disappointment, perhaps, results from the promise of a story which is never told, and that the interest is too much divided between the poet and his imaginary traveller. Why did the title page raise such magnificent expectations? *The Pilgrimage of Childe Harold* teems with images of chivalrous antiquity, heroic adventure, and affecting superstition; with visions of our Lady of Loretto, or of the Pillar; with votive offerings at the shrine of St. Jago of Compostella; with barefoot-marches to the Holy Sepulchre; and with all the varieties of self-imposed penance, by which knights-errant could hope to subdue, rather than win, the affections of unrelenting beauties.—Why also is the term *Romaunt* applied to a series of the most elegant and correct descriptions, interwoven with reflections which are full of good sense and shrewdness, but which may as well be styled religious as romantic? No effect is produced, no incident created, by this imaginary *Childe*; who in the whole poem does nothing but go over the ground which Lord

[1] [Lord B.'s seat in Nottinghamshire.—Reviewer's note.]

Byron traversed, write verses very much in the style of the detached pieces at the end of the volume, and make remarks and observations which might with equal probability have occurred to his Lordship's own mind. Indeed, when we read of him, we involuntarily think of the author; and when we have accompanied the author in fifteen stanzas of very impressive meditation, we are somewhat angry at finding our *tête-à-tête* interrupted by the needless inquiry,—'*But where is Harold?*'

Possibly, these strictures may be deemed premature, since the poem is not yet completed; and its hero may hereafter be led over other regions, and do something more than think and feel. He may be impelled to useful and vigorous exertion, and destined to redeem the follies of his wild boyhood by pursuing that honorable course which shall enroll his name among the worthies of his country. If he cannot entirely subdue the long indulged propensity to satire, he may at least point it against the deserving heads of meanness, perfidy, and folly; and if he be induced to lift up his voice in that senate in which his birth shall place him, he will boldly assert the eternal principles of liberty: distinguishing between the momentary heat of faction, and the lasting importance of those great truths which have not only conferred the highest benefits on mankind, but have reflected the purest honor on their disinterested advocates.—We must not, however, drop the veil of a romance of the older times; though it seems to have been rather loosely worn by an author who makes *Childe Harold* give vent to certain political disgusts, on viewing 'Mariava's dome,'—'Oh dome unpleasing unto British eye!' where the convention of Cintra was negotiated, and 'Policy regained what arms had lost.'

One advantage is obtained by the semblance of antiquity; that of licensing the introduction of old words, and producing a variety of style which is peculiarly necessary to give ease and animation to the Spenserian stanza. To this purpose, it has here been judiciously made subservient, without unnecessary affectation of *ekes* and *algates*; and we are disposed to think that no writer in our language has been so successful as Lord Byron in the management of this structure of verse, —perhaps not even Spenser himself. The fault most commonly imputed, viz. languor and tardiness, from which that great poet is seldom long exempt, and which most of his imitators seem to have deemed sufficient to constitute a resemblance to him, is not to be found in the pages before us. Thomson was perhaps right in considering it as no blemish in his delightful allegory, 'the Castle of Indolence;' and Shenstone certainly felt the tone of lengthened garrulity to be most in unison with the subject of his singularly happy sketch, 'the Schoolmistress.' The respectable gentlemen, contributors to Dodsley's miscellany,[1] who adopted this measure, seem to have built their preference on its absolute freedom from the necessity of compressing language or concentrating thought. Beattie's 'Minstrel,' with some passages of considerable force, and many of great majesty, is notwithstanding very frequently rendered feeble and indistinct by the untowardness of the metre: but of the late short continuation of his poem, the principal fault is that of being left unfinished.[2] Against the present work, no charge of weakness or wearisomeness can fairly be made; and though bad lines do occur, and we can remark an occasional incorrectness of expression, the whole effect is powerful and elastic: the concluding line of the stanza in particular being no 'wounded snake,' but a vigorous serpent, which takes a keen aim, and darts at its object with its full collected strength.

This desultory hero quits his native country, and, visiting Spain and Portugal, makes such observations as the present state of those regions naturally suggests; delineating the most prominent features on which the eye of a traveller would rest. We transcribe a short and very spirited passage, descriptive of the array of the hostile armies on the eve of battle:

[Stanzas XXXVII–XLI of Canto I are quoted.]

The tribute of praise and admiration to the maid of Saragoza is warmly and feelingly paid:

[Stanzas LIV–LVI of Canto I are quoted.]

Here the poet digresses into a description of the Andalusian ladies, which he pens, singularly enough, at the foot of Parnassus; challenging the hoary giant to surpass them with all the beauties who danced around him in the prosperous days of Greece.

The Spanish character is then touched with uncommon spirit; as well as the mixture of gallantry and devotion, and the strange growth of patriotism out of a despotic government, and loyalty to princes whose conduct neither consulted the happiness nor flattered the pride of their subjects. We have also a brilliant panorama of Cadiz, a bird's eye view of the country in general, and a particular but rather a long description of a bull-fight.

Canto II. opens at Athens, which seems to have inspired the deep and solemn feelings which belong to that 'swelling scene.' The author is here led by a train of thought not unlike that which occurs in Sulpicius's fine letter to Cicero, to indulge in some melancholy

---

[1] *A Collection of Poems by Several Hands* (1748), edited by Robert Dodsley.
[2] [See Rev. Vol. lix. N.S. p. 214.—Reviewer's note.]

forebodings of futurity: but, as he views only one side of the question, we may hope that his deliberate opinions are not consonant to these chilling speculations, which are expressed with much power. We have then a few beautiful stanzas alluding to the voyage, and some insinuations about a lady living at Calypso's island, who vainly strove to win the new Telemachus, Childe Harold, and was not a little amazed at the coldness of one who was so famous for sensibility.—We pass to Albania.

[Stanzas XXXVIII, XXXIX, XLII, XLV, and XLVI of Canto II are quoted.]

Our extracts would be wholly out of proportion, if we were to cite all the striking and beautiful descriptions which ensue: but it would be injustice to withhold the following picture of a night-scene among the Suliotes, who appear to have hospitably received the hero, when driven on their coast by adverse winds:

[Stanzas LXXI–LXXII of Canto II and 'Tambourgi! Tambourgi! thy 'larum afar' are quoted.]

This wild chant is composed of several scraps of Albanese poetry, which Lord Byron heard in the familiar ballads of that people. His notes give an interesting account of their manners, habits, and appearance, in all of which he observed a strong resemblance to the Scotch highlanders; and several very striking traits of character are collected.

Some papers are subjoined on the general state of Greece. The following observations have a tone of practical good sense, which pleases us much:

[The first four paragraphs of Byron's note (to stanza LXXIII of Canto II) entitled 'Franciscan Convent, Athens, January 23, 1811', are quoted.]

Lord B. then speculates on the probable deliverers of this once glorious region of the earth: but perhaps he rather under-rates the value of the co-operation of the natives, which would certainly be essential on such an occasion, and most undoubtedly would not be obtained without more awakened and more romantic hopes than political calculators may deem strictly rational. We see no harm in those hopes being excited, by any power that may undertake their emancipation; and it is difficult to assign limits to the exertions which might thus be stimulated, or the effects which those exertions might produce.

These papers are followed by some poems of uncommon beauty, others that are whimsical, and a few that may perhaps be termed affected. We have no room for any more extracts.—An appendix gives a list of Romaic authors, and several passages in modern Greek. Though we lately expressed our hopes[1] of soon receiving some information on this curious subject, we rather grudge the space which it occupies in the present volume; and we shall probably meet with little difference of opinion, in expressing our wish that in its stead a third canto of the poem had made its appearance, though it cannot be denied that the traveller in Greece will find these collections useful. Among other things, Réga's patriotic song,—Δεμτε παιδες των 'Ελληνων—is preserved; and a translation of it is given, which is injured by the attempt to follow the original metre too closely.

We need scarcely add, in general terms, to what we have already said, that we think very highly of Lord Byron's genius: but we hope that he will in future endeavour to excite a more powerful interest than his present plan allowed,—or rather than his want of plan permitted,—by unity of story, connection of incidents, and distinctness (not to say attractiveness and variety) of character. The judicious employment of these valuable materials has often given no slight advantage to very inferior poetical powers, and has not been disdained by the two greatest of all poets, Homer and Shakspeare; while the want of sufficient attention to the grand point of *interest* has contributed to keep him who approaches them the nearest, our immortal Milton, in a state of comparative neglect among general readers.

On Lord Byron's style we shall offer one remark;—it is rather too full of classical allusions. Hades, Eros, Lethe, &c. may be considered as exploded; and his great command of graceful and unaffected diction renders needless all resort to allegory or mythology.

[1] [In our Review of Mr. Gell's Itinerary, M. R. for August, 1811.—Reviewer's note.]

Review of Byron's 'Giaour'

Christian Observer

XII (Nov. *1813*), *731–37*. The reviewer is unknown.

If any edict were issued to incarcerate this particular poem, something after the manner of the unfortunate female whose history it records, we should be well content to have it in its prison, instead of blazoning it upon the page of criticism. But the state of things is widely different. The 'Childe Harold' was sure to secure a pretty general reading for any poetical production of Lord Byron's. That poem was recommended to multitudes by its genius; to some, by its irreligion; to others, by its accurate delineation of the feelings and passions of a class of characters always abounding in a luxurious country; to some, by its insolent contempt of established opinions and institutions; to the bad, by its occasional sensualism; to the good, by its exemplification of the misery of vice, and by certain passages in which lofty truths were conveyed in masculine and elevated language. It was a robe of many colours, and had a patch for almost every eye. Thus constituted for popularity, it was abundantly read, criticised, applauded, and condemned; and naturally left all parties in a posture of mind, to read, criticise, condemn, or applaud any other gift the noble author might be pleased to lay upon the altar of literature. Accordingly, the Giaour was no sooner issued than bought up. Edition trod upon the heels of edition; and before we had time to determine whether we ought to review it, the fifth with large *additions* (we wish we could add *subtractions*) is laid upon our table. Though several motives, therefore, would have induced us not to notice the work, we can no longer be silent under the perpetually reiterated question, 'How do you like the Giaour?' We wish the answer could be made as brief as the query; but as it cannot, our readers will bear with us in a reply, which we promise to make as little prolix as possible.—We shall first add a few observations to those we before offered, on the excellences and defects of his Lordship's muse and mind, and then proceed to illustrate them by some extracts from the poem before us.

One great attraction in Lord Byron, is the strength and nature of his colouring. We conceive that few poets ever put their readers in more complete possession of a country they have never seen, than his Lordship of the coasts, country, and population of Greece. And this end he accomplishes not by a laboured and minute exposition of particulars, but by a few simple touches, which at once seize and display the characteristic features of the landscape. The poem before us exhibits a striking proof of this peculiar power in the description of modern Greece, part of which we shall hereafter present to our readers.

Another feature of attraction in his Lordship's composition, is the habit of associating moral sentiments with the scenery before him. Lord Byron is by no means a mere spectator or artist, as he treads amidst the wonders of nature or the relics of genius. He pauses at every spot calculated to awaken the stronger affections of the mind. Studying the dumb language of the landscape, he extracts, not indeed the best lesson which it is calculated to teach, but one which at least produces considerable excitement: he thus allies matter to mind—and finds 'tongues in the trees, books in the running brooks;' though he fails, as a happier constitution of mind would have enabled him, to find 'sermons in stones, and good in every thing.'—There is the sort of difference between Lord Byron and Thomson, for instance, that there is between Tacitus and Livy. Though he sometimes, we venture to say, makes the landscape talk nonsense, and sometimes a species of sense to which nonsense would be preferable, still it is generally eloquent in his hands. In this busy and thinking age, such a quality as this cannot fail to constitute a title to popularity. Many who have no time merely to look, rejoice to look and think in the same glance.

A third attraction of Lord Byron's poetry, is the extraordinary vigour of his language. This quality also adapts the author for a busy age. Poetry is designed to teach by pleasing; and nothing is likely to please which occupies more time than the reader can safely or comfortably give. Now the noble Lord will very rarely try his patience, or detain him long from worthier pursuits. In the present instance, indeed, he has so extravagantly accommodated himself to the perpetual hurry of the days we live in, as utterly to omit all those parts of the poem which he conceives would be least interesting; to build a fabric of picturesque fragments; to present us, in imitation we suppose of one of the Roman epicures, with a dish exclusively of singing birds. Now, on this score we cannot defend either his judgment or taste. We cannot bring ourselves to think the shattered skeleton of a regiment quite as fine a spectacle as a complete regiment. Nor should we, independently of the associations which ruins may bring along with them, be disposed to lavish the same praise upon the fragments of the Pantheon as upon the Pantheon itself. The fact is, that it is these very associations which bestow at least one half of the picturesque effect upon the relics of antiquity. It is not simply the 'marble waste' of ancient Athens we admire; but no sooner does the eye survey its dilapidated grandeur, than a procession of lofty and affecting visions pass before us. We seem to see the heroes who fought and died beside the altar of Liberty. Amidst the groves and porches, the scattered memorials and relics of Grecian wisdom, we seem again to hear the voice of Socrates and Plato. It is not the dumb ruins which charm us; it is the spirits which appear to walk among them; it is the mighty scenes and images which they conjure up; it is the train of magnificent ideas they suggest to the mind; it is the admiration they awaken in us of men shut out from the glorious light of revelation, who struggled in many instances so hard and so successfully to discover truth amidst the falsehoods and absurdities of their monstrous superstition. But, if this be true, that the beauty of ruins is to be sought in the associations which they create, then the man who *erects* a ruin wholly mistakes the real source of the gratification they afford. It suggests no train of feelings; awakens neither admiration nor melancholy; excites no wish, either to imitate the good, or to escape the crimes and calamities of the bad. And such, we contend, is precisely the case with artificial fragments in poetry. They suggest to us no feeling but those of suspicion and inquiry, whether a want of skill in the artist to produce an entire edifice did not compel him to erect a half-one. Imperfection is no part of the sublime or beautiful. If a wise man stutters, it is because he cannot speak plain: if he limps, it is because he has not the free use of his limbs. And ruins, deprived of their associations, are defective just to the amount in which they fall short of a whole. Symmetry, harmony, completeness, have their associations also; but, with these, ruins can have nothing to do.—But we have insensibly wandered from general praise of Lord Byron's poetry, to the condemnation of a particular example of it; and have thus forestalled one of our future objections. The praise of vigour and condensation of expression, which we had begun to bestow upon him, he undoubtedly deserves. It must be owned, indeed, that he roams far and wide for his masculine words; that he is frequently coarse in aiming to be strong, and sometimes obscure in labouring to be magnificent. But still he has succeeded in conveying strong ideas in Herculean language. It is somewhat singular that it should be possible to express sentiments more briefly and strongly in verse, artificially constructed, than in prose: and yet such is the fact. Pope states it as one of his reasons for putting the Essay on Man into verse, that he could not otherwise attain to the same condensation and brevity. And it certainly is a chosen office of poetry to compress weighty sentiments into a small space; to absorb the current coin, which like the Spartan money, has much bulk and little value; and to issue its own notes, by which a man may carry his fortune in his waistcoat pocket. Lord Byron is in this sense a better poet, perhaps, than any of his contemporaries. We heartily wish, that the sentiments he has thus enshrined in his vigorous language, were not often more worthy of forgetfulness than preservation; to be kept as cinders in the urn, rather than as mummies in their cases. But here the opinions of the author are evidently more in fault than his skill.

We have now pretty much exhausted our topics of commendation: our Review of Childe Harold will shorten the catalogue of his faults. Something, however, justice, morality, and good taste require of us.

When we say that *justice* requires some notice of his poetical misdemeanours, it is partly from the exaggerated commendations which it has pleased certain critics to bestow upon him. In the infancy of his poetical career, his Lordship had felt the fangs of that critical monster, whose brightness, fierceness, and locality entitle it to be called the Ursa Major of modern criticism. Having, however, handled it pretty roughly by an instrument designed for the purpose, he seems to have secured to himself a full indemnity against all future offences. He has let his rash assailants off, we conceive, only on the pledge, that like hired clappers, they shall in future praise whatever he may choose to write; reserving the loudest applause for the most manifest faults. Nothing but this can explain their laborious defence of 'fragments.' Nothing but this can, we think, account for their unbounded eulogy of a poem which more unrestrained critics will be apt to deem a somewhat opaque mass of images and sentiments, streaked here and there by the lights of genuine poetry.

The offences against '*morality*' in the poem are almost innumerable. It is rather peculiar to Lord Byron, among poets, as we have already had occasion to observe, to excite all the interest of his readers for thoroughly unworthy objects. We know not who is the most shameless offender against all the laws and better feelings and rights of man; the Childe Harold, or the Giaour. If the latter personage was not mad, it is devoutly to be lamented: apology there is none for offences such as his. Lord Byron is, we conceive, a man of considerable powers. He has at all events sufficient largeness of view to discover that morality is essential to the welfare of states. By his rank, he is a constituted guardian of the state; nay, a privileged adviser of the crown itself. Let him, then, reflect upon the manner in which he is discharging his solemn function. His present distinction among his countrymen, the star of his nobility, is this; that he has endeavoured to ally lofty with vicious qualities; to kindle our admiration for persons whom every honest man ought to loath; to present to our idolatry wretches at whose approach good men must tremble. We do not simply appeal to his love of fame, which we confidently believe would instruct him to aim at permanent celebrity, by appealing to the better feelings of the mind— by winning the esteem of those whose admiration he seeks;—but we appeal to his honour; to his humanity; to that 'love of the people' of which he is not slow to boast; to his public spirit; to his experience of the indissoluble connection between morals and prosperity, gained amidst the prostrate cities of Greece: and we beseech him not to add himself to the infamous catalogue of those who have endeavoured to make vice reputable, who have ruined their country by overthrowing its altars and expelling its gods. In some countries and ages, the names of poet and prophet have been identified. In others, poetry has been the ally of religion and morality. The two great poems of Homer were written, one to display the crime and the consequences of adultery, the other, the reward of conjugal love, and both to uphold the popular mythology. The Æneid records his triumphs who bore, as the chosen relics of his ruined fortunes, an aged father and his household gods. The strains of Tasso chaunt the obsequies of Crusaders, and the deliverance of the City of God. Of Milton, and Racine, and Cowper, we need not speak. All felt the policy, and most of them the desire, of calling out those feelings and passions which are the best relics of the fall; of enlisting the conscience on the side of their verses, and securing our love while they invited our admiration. Surely Lord Byron has no such love of innovation as to fancy that he can lay a new basis for fame, or strike out a perfectly novel system of national happiness. If not, let him be contented with the precedents of all ages. Let him not covet a celebrity, like that of him who fired the temple of Ephesus, conferred by the singularity of our vices; but those amaranthine honours which God gives, and which the world can neither give nor take away.

But the present poem offends also considerably against the canons of *taste*. Passing over the flippancy, the puerility, and the licentiousness of some of the notes; all which qualities are so many violations of pure taste; we shall notice the faults of this kind in the poem itself. That to which we chiefly allude is the laboured similes or rather parallelisms with which the poem abounds. It is an old rule, not 'to make similes run upon all fours.' The mischief of the practice is, that as no two things are alike in all points, for then they would be the same thing, he who leads us very curiously to search for points of resemblance, forces us also to notice the points of dissimilarity. Lord Byron is a capital offender upon this score; and it is the greater offence because evidently not the consequence of forgetfulness, but of labour; not of accident, but premeditation.

Another defect in the present poem is, its occasional inaccuracy of language. If some parts of the work did not convince us of the ease and fluency with which the author writes, we should be tempted to attribute his inaccuracies to a want of skill; but we rather imagine that his industry is more in fault than his powers of composition.

Having thus noted a few of the excellences and faults of the poetry of Lord Byron, we shall proceed to give a slight sketch of the Giaour, and to make some extracts from it confirmatory of our preceding observations.

Giaour is the Turkish word for an infidel, be he a real Christian, or a profligate ruffian, like this particular Giaour. In the serai of an emir of the name of Hassan, is a female of the name of Leila, whom the Giaour, to show his abhorrence we apprehend of Mohammedanism, and his zeal for the true religion, proceeds to seduce. Hassan discovers the attachment, and, in a paroxysm of jealous rage, wraps her in a sheet, rows her out to sea, and plunges her into the devouring waters. Having thus satiated his revenge, he proceeds to console himself under his loss by wooing another lady. But little knows he what is to be anticipated from the fury of a Christian of Lord Byron's creation. On his journey, he is beset and assassinated by the Giaour. The murderer, for such in plain prose he appears to us to be, sick of the world and himself, lacerated by his passions, haunted by the visions of former joys, friendless and unprincipled, retires to a monastery—not indeed to lay to his wounded bosom the balm of religion, not to master his passions or propitiate his God, but to rave amidst its shades and cells on the charms of Leila, on the crime of Hassan, and on the extreme purity and propriety of his own conduct. In his dying moments, he discloses to a venerable friar the history of his stormy life, and makes the confession, which, perhaps, the friar would have done as well, in conformity with the obligations of his order, to have kept from the world.—Such is the tale, for a brief statement of which we beg our readers to remember their obligations to ourselves; as the readers of Lord Byron by no means make themselves masters of it in the same space of time or with the same degree of labour. The story itself is such as evidently admits of a good deal of poetical ornament; and though a bad poet could make nothing of it, a good one might, Lord Byron does, make a great deal. There are parts of the poem, which, if our admiration were not disturbed by the constant extravagance of the sentiments, and the want of nature and keeping in the characters, we should be tempted to rank high amidst the best specimens of poetic skill.

The first quotation we shall give is illustrative alike of the genius and the incorrect taste of the author.

[Lines 68–102 are quoted.]

This fine passage is followed by a lofty address to the prostrate cities of Greece; cities prostrated (let his Lordship remember) chiefly by the licentious indulgences of the people. Indeed, he himself proclaims this source of their ruin:

> 'Enough; no foreign foe could quell
> Thy soul, till from itself it fell,
> And self-abasement paved the way
> To villain bonds, and despot sway.'

Turning, however, from the melancholy ruins of Grecian grandeur, the bard soon enters upon his tale.

'*Who* thundering comes on blackest steed?' It is the Giaour: and then follows an awful and powerful portrait of him, as he first hesitates, and then rushes on to the murder of Hassan. After a spendid picture by anticipation of the palace of Hassan, before and after his death, the story suddenly goes back to the procession, conveying the sheeted Leila to her watery grave. The immersion of the body is well described, p. 20.

[Lines 374–87 are quoted.]

This is followed by a well-executed simile, comparing, or rather identifying, a captive butterfly with a ruined maid. The parallel is of the protracted kind of which we have complained. The comparison also wants tenderness and majesty; and, though pretty as a song, or as mere *vers de societé*, is, we think, out of place where it is.

Then comes another simile also overlaboured, and somewhat obscure, but indicating the hand of a master, p. 22.

[Lines 422–38 are quoted.]

The strength of his Lordship's pencil will be discovered in the following description of one of his heroes mourning his calamities in a state of solitude. p. 47

'Even bliss 'twere wo alone to bear;
The heart once left thus desolate,
Must fly at last for ease—to hate.
It is as if the dead could feel
The icy worm around them steal,
And shudder, as the reptiles creep
To revel o'er their rotting sleep,
Without the power to scare away
The cold consumers of their clay!'

Nor is the picture which follows this inferior to it, p. 48.

[Lines 957-70 are quoted.]

From the concluding part of the poem, in which the Giaour makes his dying confession, we have neither space nor much disposition to quote. Parts of it are indeed exceedingly powerful; but the great mass savours too much of Newgate and Bedlam for our expurgated pages. We do not, of course, mean to fasten any of the Giaour's sentiments upon the author. But we heartily wish that his Lordship had not endeavoured to create any spark of interest for such a wretch; and had painted his own abhorrence of these desperate and abandoned lovers in as strong language as that in which the Giaour proclaims his love.

We cannot conclude without acknowledging one obligation which society owes to Lord Byron. He never attempts to deceive the world by representing the profligate as happy. It is difficult to say which is the more hopeless and agonized culprit—the surly 'Childe,' or the stormy 'Giaour.' We thank him for the honesty with which he thus traces causes to their consequences, in a matter of such paramount importance to human kind. None will be allured, we conceive, by his pictures to seek their comforts in the field of unlicensed pleasures, or unbridled passions. And his testimony is of the more value, as his situation in life must have permitted him to see the experiment tried under the most favourable circumstances. He has probably seen more than one example of young men of high birth, talents, and expectancies, on whom the eye of an anxious country rested, and for whom the loftiest niche of distinction and the richest rewards of virtue and piety were prepared, sink under the burden of unsubdued tempers, licentious alliances, and enervating indulgence. He has seen these high pretenders to this world's good become objects of contempt to the world, of pity to the thoughtful, of sorrow to the pious. He has *seen* a wish devoutly felt, that his usefulness may be commensurate with all this; nay, perhaps—But we check our pen—and will conclude with his talents; and that he, who has *thus* taught us to dread vice, may go on to display the dignity and the happiness of virtue.

Review of Byron's 'Corsair'

Theatrical Inquisitor

IV (Feb. 1814), 105–08. The review was signed 'H.', but the reviewer is unknown.

It is with a pleasure commensurate with our admiration of Lord Byron's genius, that we learn from the Dedication of 'The Corsair,' to Mr. Moore, his determination 'to attempt no farther, for some years, the awards of Gods, men, nor (*or*) columns.' Possessing the most brilliant fancy, and the most exquisite powers of sentiment and description, it is evident that his lordship's taste is unformed, and that his talents are yet susceptible of laborious cultivation. The great imperfections of his *Corsair*, like those of the 'Giaour and Bride of Abydos,' are occasional obscurity of narration, abruptness and inaccuracy of construction; a diction too fluent to admit of skilful selection, or felicitous adaptation; and the employment of forms of speech and artifices of metre neither authorized by the example of our standard poets, nor consistent with the idiom or analogy of the English language. An assiduous study of the best models; the selection of some important theme, adapted to awaken and expand to perfection those powers that are now exhausted in hasty and desultory effort; and a determination to leave no blemish untouched, no error uncorrected, will yet be necessary to the full attainment of that rank among his contemporaries, or that claim on the gratitude and reverence of posterity, of which we hope, and have reason to believe, that he is ambitious.

If any justification of these remarks were required, the following casual and unselected examples of affectation, negligence, and bad taste, would plead our apology:

> 'Select the arms, to each his blade assign,
> And careless eye the blood that dims its *shine*.'

213

The employment of the word *shine* in this couplet cannot be justified, we believe, by a single appeal to any classical authority; nor, if one or two instances of such an anomaly can be produced, will they form an excuse for its introduction into so short a poem.

> 'She walks the waters like a thing of life,
> And seems to dare the elemental strife.'

We beg leave to doubt whether the first of these lines presents any distinct idea of a ship in full and triumphant sail.

> 'And other gifts shew'd mean beside his word.'

i.e. *Compared with his word.*

> 'The wish is wrong, nay, worse for female, vain.'

This mode of introducing the word *female* is seldom found but in the writings of the lowest poetasters. If the term *woman* cannot be substituted, the passage should be entirely recomposed.

Even when no positive fault can be found with any single word, and it is impossible to pronounce his sentence ungrammatical, there is an awkwardness of idiom which evinces his destitution of taste or industry.

> 'His wounds too slight, though *taken with that will*,
> Which would have kissed the hand *that then could kill.*'

But the most striking and the most ludicrous of his improvements in the art of *writing with ease*, is the repetition, *ad libitum*, wherever he is at a loss for an additional foot, of some useful little monosyllable.

> 'And to itself—all—all that self reveals.'
> 'My *love* stern Seyd's, oh *No! no! not* my love.'
> 'I feel, I feel, love dwells *with—with* the free.'

If this artifice be once admitted, except in cases where the repetition is decidedly emphatic and poetical, farewell to the difficulties of metre, and the restraints of prosody! To make a line of any determinate length and cadence, will be as easy as the—

> '*Mos, flos, ros, et Tros, mus, dens, mons, pons, simul et fons.*'

Or,

'*Bifons, custos, bos, fur, sus, atque saecerdos:*'

of the compilers of *Propria quae maribus*.[1]

His lordship condescending to inform us, that the sight of the *Corsair* would have deprived *Medora*, by the shock, of life and sense, thus expresses the idea—

'His very sight had *shock'd* from *light and sense.*'

The rhymes of 'The Corsair' are too frequently supplied by superfluous and mean, or unemphatic words.

'And those sustain'd he—boots it well or ill,
Since not to sink beneath is something *still.*'

The subjoined lines will puzzle the sagacity of the most careful and curious reader:

'By those that deepest feel, are ill exprest,
The indistinctness of the suffering breast;
Where thousand thoughts begin to end in one,
Which seeks from all the refuge found in none.'

That is, (unless *which* refers to *breast*) one thought, compounded of a thousand other thoughts, seeks from those thousand thoughts of which it is compounded, refuge to be found in no thoughts at all. If *which* do [*sic*] refer to *breast*, the meaning is not much improved, and the construction is inaccurate.

We shall not anticipate the story, because it is better calculated to stimulate curiosity, and excite the feelings in its progress, than to satisfy reasonable expectation by its denouement. The only personages in any degree marked or conspicuous, are Gulnare, Medora, and the Corsair, and of these alone the latter is distinguished by originality of character. Lord Byron's portraiture of his hero, is delineated with the highest powers of imagination and intellectual discernment; the vigor, promptitude, and self-confidence, of the pirate's mind; his brooding, gloomy, and determined hatred to mankind; and even the selfish malignity of his love, which gluts his pride rather than soothes his malignity, are described with a vigor, distinctness, and knowledge of human nature, that testify of themselves the exalted rank to which

---

[1] The quotations are lists of nouns given as illustration (and for ease of retention) of, respectively, masculine nouns of one syllable and nouns of mixed gender.

Lord Byron may attain among our national poets, when his exuberance is chastened by reflection, his taste corrected by assiduous study, and his rich and varied powers matured and expanded by regular and fastidious devotion to some great and noble object of poetical ambition.

A series of attacks upon Lord Byron have lately issued from the press, in which he is assailed with all the vehemence of scurrility, because, in his 'English Bards, and Scotch Reviewers,' he ridiculed the very individuals to whom he has dedicated his late productions. Is it so criminal, then, in a young man to retract his erroneous opinion, and correct his errors? or is there any more striking and convincing proof of an exalted mind, than his very willingness to confess his youthful misconceptions? For our own parts, selected personally as we have been, on a former occasion, as the object of his lordship's mistaken resentment, we are happy to witness these indications of his frankness and high mindedness; and are confident, that, when the opportunity presents itself, he will be as proud to do justice to the writer of this article, comparatively humble as he is, as to the wits, the orators, and the statesman, with whom both fortune and merit enable him to associate.[1]

[1] [See our poetical article.—Reviewer's note.]

Review of Byron's 'The Siege of Corinth' and 'Parisina'

Champion

Feb. 11, 1816, pp. 45-46. The reviewer is unknown.

These two poems, included in one small pamphlet, of a now well-known external appearance, are stated, in Mr. Murray's announcements, to be from the pen of Lord BYRON. His Lordship's name is not to be found on the title-page, but, in the notes to *Parisina*, he very plainly acknowledges himself. So long as an author's faithfulness to his vows 'to write no more,'[1] leads to what are called, in the common phrase, *agreeable disappointments*, he will not be harshly treated for breaking his word;—although a frequent quarrelling with one's bread and butter, —quickly and constantly succeeded by an eager taking to it again, may be an amusing, but is by no means a dignified exhibition. *She would and She would not*, is a pleasing comedy, when performed by a lovely woman; but a change of gender converts it into a farce. Allowances are due to the caprices of genius,—but is it worthy of a man of genius to be perpetually claiming them? Besides, let it be considered what a dangerous responsibility is thus incurred: a freak to be excusable must be delightful,—the moment dullness is perceptible it becomes a piece of impertinence. It is a device of theatrical management to announce last performances that are followed by more that are last; but the trick has never been thought respectable. We entirely acquit Lord Byron of intending a trick;—but we do not acquit him of a self-estimation inordinately great, and a self-knowledge inordinately small, leading him to trifle with the public and to treat them indecorously.

[1] In the Dedication to *The Corsair*, Byron claimed that it was the last he would publish 'for some years'.

He will and he won't: he regrets having written at all, and anon he writes again: he will not write for some years, and he cannot hold for a few weeks. Poetry is no toy of the moment, to be lightly taken up, and scornfully laid down. It is to be permitted to those who publish poisonous calumnies in the glow of youthful enthusiasm, to retract them, and promise to publish no more:—what a man does in haste and ignorance he must be suffered to repent at leisure, and in conviction;— but it may at last become the duty of criticism to declare to even a noble author, that he who engages in the highest labours of Literature, makes a serious engagement: that, after a certain time, it is demanded of him that what he submits to the public taste and understanding, which must help to adjust the public reputation of the period, should at least bear his own serious reflection,—and not be like the effusions of the evening's intoxication, which are repented of in the morning's fit of nausea. It is very certain, that, if popularity long attends these instances of wilfulness, it must be by the force of a seduction hurtful to good taste, and probably to virtue.

We speak thus severely, because we see that the moment has arrived when Lord Byron must either lose part of his popularity, or it must continue at the expense of public discernment. The pamphlet before us,—which is another breach of an engagement to abstain from writing for some years,—is neither more nor less than another of those brief, mannered, indistinct sketches, which deserved and received the highest praise as the first exercises of a masterly spirit, supposed to be preparing itself for productions of sound meaning and fine and finished arrangement. It was in this light that we contemplated and admired the *Giaour*, the *Bryde of Abydos*, the *Corsair*, and *Lara*—all of them better poems than the present. The *Childe Harold* was justly deemed a work of great power and beauty but it took its character from a bias of feeling, which was only to be tolerated as a temporary paroxysm, incidental to a certain period and certain circumstances, and hopeful as it manifested an energy of constitution, which, when health was restored, might be expected to achieve wonders. The *Ode to Napoleon Buonaparte* was a piece of stormy precipitation, corresponding with the event it celebrated; and the *Hebrew Melodies* were—bad.

We have, on former occasions, expressed ourselves of a contrary opinion to those who have severely blamed Lord Byron's poetry as of a vicious moral tendency, and indicative of bad moral feelings:— but we certainly did not expect, that the public were never to receive any thing from his hand, to amuse and instruct them, but the half-filled apparitions of ruffian adventurers, all wearing the same fierce but un-intellectual features,—all displayed, like the figures of the modern French painters, in violent attitudes and false lights,—and, like these, producing a strong effect to captivate and deprave the common taste, by an elaborate working-up of the inferior parts which should be kept subordinate, while gross neglects and deficiencies are found in what ought to be made principal,—together with a total want of refined sentiment.—It is not that we would now lay any accusation against his Lordship's morality; it is not for us to inquire who sits for his portraits—no human being we should suspect:—we do not pry into the frame-work of his heart,—and we are prepared to maintain, that the delineation of the bad passions, and of their effects, as subjects of human interest, fall honestly within the province of Art. Nor do we hold it necessary to couple every sin with its proper caution in poetical description. Our charge against Lord Byron is, that, in a temper of restless and indecent disdain, he presumes on his popularity to become a downright scribbler,—trying the public to what extent they will receive what he does not think it worth his while to prepare. He does not even affect the slightest respect for the public taste, or care for its quality;—he rubs in a few heads, all as exactly alike to each other as those that first appear on a painter's canvas, when he is arranging his composition;—they are all staringly violent in action and expression, but without variety or real meaning:—he then very elaborately works-up some bits of the back-ground,—takes great trouble with some of the draperies,—and throws in a few strong but coarse and scattered lights, which glare upon stark and stiff horrors, like the rosin lightning of the stage when it flashes upon Mr. Conway, in a melodrama of midnight murder. We repeat, that, for a time, it was presumable, that these were but the youthful exercises of a masterly hand; but now that we find Lord Byron running riot on the strength of his neglects, waxing more and more insolent because of indulgence, and forcing upon us, as food of the mind, what, if report be true, turns his own stomach,—criticism can scarcely be accused of captiousness, if it protests strongly against this perversion of poetical talent, this corruption of feeling, and arrogant disregard of what is due to consciousness and obligation. The great mischief is, that these fiery applications destroy the healthy tone of the public's sensibility: they lead it to cherish that fatal fondness for quick and forced excitement, which utterly kills in the mind the capacity of serious enjoyment of natural sentiment;—the niceties of genuine character and situation are deemed feeble and tedious after these seductions of exaggeration and artifice. Lord Byron's readers are led to mistake hurry-skurry for noble rapidity,—and there is a proneness in the common taste to this mistake, which renders him who administers to it, very reprehensible.—His exhibitions are those of a magic lanthorn,—shadowy, coarse, and confused,—producing their effects through trick rather than skill; very wonderful and striking in the opinion of the multitude,—interesting, at first, to better judges, but felt to be tiresome, tawdry, and poor, when too often repeated.

The *Siege of Corinth* and *Parisina*, are his two worst poems,—and the unfortunate word, worst, conveys all that they have of novelty. They are mere repetitions in style, and personages, of what he has done before.—The hero of the *Siege of Corinth* is *Alp*;—and *Alp*, under a new name, is an old acquaintance,—as for example—

> 'He stood alone—a renegade
> Against the country he betrayed;
> He stood alone amidst his band,
> Without a trusted *heart* or *hand*:
>
> *   *   *   *   *   *   *   *   *   *   *
>
> They did not know how pride can stoop
> When baffled feelings withering droop;
> They did not know how hate can burn
> In hearts *once changed from soft to stern.*'

[A brief summary of the story is given: lines 131–36, 177–84, 454–61, 605–19, 575–78, 643–54, and 663–66 are quoted. The fourth passage (lines 605–19) is said to be 'extremely beautiful'.]

To this poem, Lord Byron affixes the following motto:

> '*Guns, Trumpets, Blunderbusses, Drums, and Thunder.*'

This is to indicate his own appreciation of the work which he gives to the public; but nevertheless it contains several very exquisite passages. The fine idea of the cloud passing over the moon, he states, in the notes, has been taken from '*Vathek.*'

The poem of *Parisina* is shorter than the other:—we think it less striking, and not more sound. The following extract from Gibbon is prefixed as explaining the facts on which the story is founded.

[The first three sentences quoted from Gibbon by Byron in his Advertisement are given.]

In this poem (p. 70) there is a thought taken from Burke, which is embodied in much finer poetry in the political work, than in Lord Byron's version.

Review of Byron's 'Poems
[on his Domestic Circumstances]'
(John Murray, 1816)

Eclectic Review

2d ser. V (June 1816), 595–99. The author was Josiah Conder, a minor poet, bookseller, and editor of the Eclectic *from 1814 to 1836. Authority for this attribution is the marked staff copies of the* Eclectic *now in the London Library.*

We hesitated to notice on their first appearance, the poems ascribed to Lord Byron, professedly connected with 'certain domestic occurrences,' although it was generally understood that the publication of them originated with the Author, and there was therefore no room for doubting their authenticity, nor occasion for delicacy in speaking of them. But they hardly seemed to deserve attention from a literary Journal. It appeared to us, indeed, sufficiently obvious, that the poems alluded to, were written expressly for the public eye; since it would be difficult on any other supposition, to account for their having been written at all. Dr. Johnson, it is said, loved a good hater. The 'Sketch from Private Life' discovers sufficient energy of hatred, but it breathes still more of spleen and unmanly revenge, vented in the impotency of words on an individual defenceless, and possibly unoffending; or rather, it may be, affected for the purpose of diverting to that individual a portion of the indignant feeling which it might be apprehended the incidents alluded to, would excite in the public mind. For our own parts, we considered it as a disgusting display of prostituted talent. And indeed, as the poem is omitted in the present publication, it is but fair to conclude that even Lord Byron is heartily ashamed of having written it.

The 'Farewell' is a poem of a different description; but we find it equally difficult to believe that, had those verses originated in the feelings they described, the public eye would have been suffered to rest upon them. They are undeniably beautiful and touching: they fall short of nature only from not being *vraisemblable*. There have been actors, whose consummate accuracy in displaying the semblance of passion has been such, as not only powerfully to work upon the feelings of the audience, but to delude them into imagining that the tragedian himself felt, from strong sympathy, with the ideal personage he represented. The absence of all feeling on his part, was, however, proved by the perfection of the imitation. Garrick, in the most pathetic part of King Lear, had his mind sufficiently at leisure to observe the aspect of his audience, and to whisper, with a low oath, to a fellow actor, 'Tom, this will do.' Sterne, the licentious, the unfeeling Sterne, could excel in pathos. The voluptuous Moore has produced some touching little songs. Shaw wrote a monody on the wife who died heart-broken from his unkindness.[1] And Lord Lyttleton, a man far more estimable than any of the former, wrote a monody on the *irreparable* loss of his first wife, and married a second the following year.[2] What do we adduce these instances to prove? It is not necessary to refer all such cases either to hypocrisy, or to deliberate affectation. It was probably the sincere *sentiment* of grief that prompted the noble husband to frame so classically elegant and polished a tribute to the memory of his lady; and many a marble monument has been erected to testify equal sincerity of grief, although it is impossible to consider such an expression of feeling as intended solely in honour to the dead. What we mean to assert is this, that the sentiment of pathos, the sensibility of taste, may exist where there is little real feeling, and less moral principle; that a poet may as easily attain the pathetic without strong natural affection, as the sublime without native grandeur of character. With regard to many productions of the *affecting* kind, the harrowing tale of madness, or despairing love, or frantic grief, the very skill displayed in such moral dissections proves that the Author has more nerve than sensibility; or to change the figure, betrays the mind of an artist at leisure, coolly to attend to the costume of the passions he delineates. It is true that

> 'The Poet's lyre, to fix his fame,
> Should be the Poet's heart.'

[1] Cuthbert Shaw (1739–71) published his *Monody to the Memory of a Young Lady Who Died in Childbed* in 1768.

[2] Lord Lyttelton (1709–73) published a *Monody* to the memory of his wife in 1747.

The genuine language of poetry is the language of genuine feeling. But it is the *recollection* of passions and feelings by which at the time we were incapacitated for the measured utterance of art, rather than the *presence* of deep emotion, which constitutes the source of the inspiration.

> 'When the wounds of wo are healing,
> When the heart is all resigned,'

then is the season for cherishing the 'joy of grief,' and for giving permanence to sentiments which when fresh were simply painful, even to agony. Yet after all, the deepest, tenderest, holiest feelings are such as, perhaps, no man really conscious of them would think of dilating into poetry; or if he should succeed in giving them external shape, he would be little disposed to exhibit them to the cold proud eye of the world. He that bares his heart to strangers, has nothing left for a friend.

Our readers must make their own application of these remarks, which are we believe, at any rate, just in themselves. Certainly the ostensible purpose of Lord Byron's poems, was that of indirect self vindication; and it is needless to say, that this purpose they did not answer.

Little remains to be said of the contents of the present pamphlet. The Verses addressed to Madame Lavalette, The Farewell to Malta, and the very fine and spirited Ode beginning

> 'Oh, shame to thee, Land of the Gaul!'

which were given as Lord Byron's, in the different editions of 'The Seven Poems,' published by Messrs. E. Wilson, Edwards, Hone, Cox, &c. are omitted in this publication, we presume as spurious. The Star of the Legion of Honour, Waterloo, and Bonaparte's Farewell to France, are preserved. The two latter are designated 'From the French', as an apology for their being inserted among the acknowledged works of a man born an Englishman. His Lordship appears to be ambitious of the dignity of Poet-laureate to Napoleon Bonaparte, as his friend Mr. Hobhouse would seem to claim the post of historiographer to his Ex-Majesty.[1]

From the original pieces we select the following stanzas, addressed, we believe, to his Lordship's sister.

['To ———' ('Stanzas to Augusta' ['When all around grew drear and dark . . . .']) is quoted in full.]

---

[1] John Cam Hobhouse published *The Substance of Some Letters Written by an Englishman Resident at Paris during the Last Reign of the Emperor Napoleon* in 1816.

These are followed by a short poem of an elegiac nature, a Song, dated 1808, and two poems, entitled Stanzas for Music. The 'Fare thee well,' and four of the other poems already published, make up the contents.

Review of Byron's 'Childe Harold's Pilgrimage', Canto III, and 'The Prisoner of Chillon, and other Poems'

Eclectic Review

2d ser. VII (March 1817), 292–304. The author was Josiah Conder, a minor poet, bookseller, and editor of the Eclectic from 1814 to 1836. Authority for this attribution is the marked staff copies of the Eclectic now in the London Library.

There is a stanza in the third Canto of Childe Harold's Pilgrimage, referring to Rousseau, which so exquisitely expresses all that the most laboured critique could say of these productions, taken in connexion with the private circumstances to which they explicitly allude, that it were almost sufficient to transcribe them, and leave our readers to make the application.

> 'Here the self-torturing sophist, ...
> . . . . he who threw
> Enchantment over passion, and from woe
> Wrung overwhelming eloquence, first drew
> The breath which made him wretched: yet he knew
> *How to make madness beautiful, and cast*
> *O'er erring deeds and thoughts a heavenly hue*
> *Of words, like sunbeams, dazzling as they past*
> *The eyes, which o'er them shed tears feelingly and fast.*'

With whatsoever sentiments respecting the Author as a member of society, (in which character his Lordship has made the public his confidant,) a person may sit down to the perusal of these poems, it will be impossible, if he has a human heart, not to have his judgement disarmed by his feelings, and to be dazzled even to tears. The very first line strikes upon the heart with the thrilling effect of a sudden knell: the knell of an unhappy being self-exiled from the living interests of society, rung by his own returning spirit, as if to compel our sympathy.

> 'Is thy face like thy mother's, my fair child!
> Ada! sole daughter of my house and heart?
> When last I saw thy young blue eyes they smiled,
>   And then we parted,—not as now we part,
> But with a hope.—
>   Awaking with a start,
> The waters heave around me; and on high
> The winds lift up their voices: I depart
> Whither I know not; but the hour's gone by
> When Albion's lessening shores could grieve or glad mine eye'

Did it form any part of our duty to the public, to make these poems serve as an occasion for instituting an inquiry into Lord Byron's domestic conduct, we certainly could not accept his eloquence as a witness in the cause, or suffer our verdict to be influenced by the impression he succeeds in making on our feelings. We could not suffer ourselves to forget that Ada has another parent, and that that mother's silent wrongs might be such as to out-plead the most pathetic appeals of the father. But living, as happily we do, remote from the sphere of Lord Byron's

> 'self-sought foes
> 'Or friends by himself banished,'

we feel ourselves by no means called upon either to become his apologists, or to sit as his censors; not having had the privilege of personal intimacy which our fellow Journalists may have enjoyed, to warrant our assuming the office of the friend, and having no feelings to gratify by the execution of a sterner task.

Lord Byron has indeed, in these poems, invited the attention of the public to his own peculiar character and fortunes. He has the air of a man that at once courts and disdains the vote of the many, on which his fame depends. He seems willing to receive from the impersonal multitude that homage of sympathy, which perhaps he would be too proud to accept from an individual who could answer or gaze upon the speaker. The species of egotism, however, which pervades his Lordship's productions, appears less like the display of his own feelings, than the effect of their perpetually haunting him, intercepting and colouring his view of every other object, and rendering it impossible for him to forget

'the weary dream
'Of selfish grief or gladness.'

In the present Canto, Childe Harold is scarcely to be recognised as an ideal personage. We almost question, indeed, whether Lord Byron has not 'thought too long and darkly' on one real person, to be capable of giving birth to a purely imaginary being, the independent sportive creation of fancy. We question whether any of Lord Byron's characters are strictly fictitious; for whatever variation of costume is thrown over them, and whatever are the circumstances of the tale, it is still the same combination of morbid feelings and phrensied passions, aggravated into various degrees of guilt, which is personified in the successive *avatars* of his Lordship's genius; and all the subordinate personages of the drama have the same relation to that one, as the gaudy clouds of evening have to the sun which imparts to them their interesting hues: they are only shadowy outlines which serve to express, in the symbolic language of poetry, the objects of passionate emotion and of remembrances not unreal. Medora, the most lovely and interesting by far of these cloud-like phantoms, is not an individual, but an abstraction in the form of woman; her whole character consists in being that which Conrad loved. And Conrad himself, and Lara, and Alp, and Harold, are but the varied expression of one class of feelings condensed as it were into one vivid conception in the mind of the poet. On this one image, thus multiplied in the fantastic reflections of thought, it seems to be the highest intellectual solace for the Author to fix the intent gaze of his imagination; not like Narcissus, enamoured of the reflection of himself, but losing in the contemplation of that social shadow, the conscious wretchedness of the original.

'Tis to create, and in creating live
A being more intense, that we endow
With form our fancy, gaining as we give
The life we image.'

But that very passion for intensity of feeling, which is the unhappy characteristic of Lord Byron's mind, renders him incapable of taking pleasure in the creation of imaginary beings from the purer elements of fancy, and the ordinary materials of humanity. If any thing has power to banish for a moment the ever present thought of self, which like an external presence seems to haunt him, it must be of a nature too horrible, too agonizing to be simply pleasing, or else of that commanding sublimity which suspends, as by physical force, our individual recollections, 'lulling them to sleep amid the music of nobler thoughts.' Of the power of natural scenery to produce this adequate excitement, and to hold the faculties in a trance-like oblivion of the insignificant interests of this world, no one appears to be more deeply susceptible than the Author of these poems; and few have succeeded so well in breathing an intellectual soul into the inanimate forms of grandeur, power, and beauty he describes. The following stanza presents a striking instance.

'But these recede. Above me are the Alps,
The palaces of Nature, whose vast walls
Have pinnacled in clouds their snowy scalps,
And throned eternity in icy halls
Of cold sublimity, where forms and falls
The avalanche—the thunderbolt of snows!
All that expands the spirit, yet appals,
Gather around these summits, as to show
How earth may pierce to heaven, yet leave vain man below.'

The descriptive power displayed in the next specimen we shall transcribe, is of the very highest order of excellence. Wordsworth, whose strength lies in enduing materiality with intelligence, has nothing finer of the kind.

[Stanzas LXXXV–LXXXIX and XCII–XCIII are quoted.]

In these extracts there may still be recognised the peculiarity of talent by which Lord Byron is distinguished. The scenery is at once revealed to our inmost feelings, not through the medium of description, as a picture, but in its effect upon the imagination. We do not see, we feel, the living landscape, by sympathy with the intense feelings of the poet, who, unable to divest his mind of the individuality of self even amid the conflict of elements, and the infinity of solitude, claims to be 'a portion of the tempest' and of night, and makes Nature itself serve as the expression and voice of his own emotions.

'I live not in myself, but I become
Portion of that around me; and to me

> High mountains are a feeling.—'
> 'Are not the mountains, waves, and skies, a part
> Of me and of my soul, as I of them?'

Yet this perpetual egotism never sinks into monotony. The subject may sometimes pain, but it never wearies us, and wander where we will, Childe Harold cannot fail of being interesting.

Perhaps the living poet who, in respect of some of these peculiar traits, bears the nearest resemblance to Lord Byron, although his character presents so direct a contrast, is Montgomery.[1] He too, 'paints from the looking-glass,' and gives us his own portrait in his heroes. He not less than Lord Byron is truly and irrecoverably a poet by the necessity of his temperament, and an egotist from the morbid excess of feelings stimulated by imagination, and nourished in solitude. But his egotism, though less commanding than that which appears in Lord Byron to proceed from the stormy violence of engrossing passions, is of a far more amiable, and in itself more interesting cast. In point of intellectual power and range of thought, we do not mean to institute any comparison between the two, but Montgomery has a lyre of un-rivalled sweetness of tone. It is remarkable that Lord Byron, in his juvenile satire, 'English Bards and Scotch Reviewers,' bore testimony to the genuine character of Montgomery's genius; and in his ode to Napoleon Bonaparte, his Lordship has adopted the exact form of the stanzas in which the 'Cast away Ship,' is written, which is certainly one of the most exquisite ballads in the language. Between the stern and fierce misanthropy of Childe Harold, and the tender melancholy and pure affection which breathe through the compositions of the Sheffield bard, there might seem at first to be not the remotest analogy; but the poetry of both pleases from the same cause, and notwithstanding the very different emotions they excite, pleases us in the same way, as a tale of the human heart, an exhibition of individual character. This would not indeed be the effect, were a person of ordinary mind or under ordinary circumstances to attempt to interest us by the delinea-tions of his own feelings: were not the sufferings he disclosed evidently sincere, were they not founded upon reality, were not the circum-stances, in fact, such as called forth those emotions, whether of pity or of terror, which it is the very business of poetry to excite, the egotism of the poet would be repulsive. On this account, other writers have by a far more sparing and incidental reference to their individual circum-stances, drawn down upon themselves the imputation of vanity. Why? Because theirs were perhaps, the circumstances of peaceful domestic

[1] See p. 195, note 5 above.

life and prosperous fortune, and made no appeal to our pity. It is not with the happy that we sympathize.

We have expressed a doubt whether Lord Byron could give birth to a purely imaginary being, that is, whether he could for a sufficient period, abstract himself from his own feelings, to allow of his forming a distinct conception of a character altogether distinct from himself in its intellectual and moral lineaments, and of his giving it the bodily form of words. Nobody would think of finding any thing in common between Hamlet, or Falstaff, or Othello, and the individual character of their author. They are not copies, or expressions of certain thoughts and feelings, but pure combinations of creative fancy, that seem almost to have an existence external to the mind from which they emanated. Or to descend to our own times, we do not think of recognising Southey in his Madoc, or in his Roderick: they are distinct human characters, portions of our common nature individualized by a strong exercise of poetical conception. To an effort of this kind we do not conceive that Lord Byron is fully adequate; not perhaps owing to any natural inferiority, for the intellectual power which makes itself felt in his expressions, would lead us to suppose him originally capable of any poetical achievement; but from the settled habits of his mind. The range of his sympathies is contracted; human nature has no power to interest him; the purest sources of earthly enjoyment, the very Castalia of imagination, are closed to him: he is a sceptic as to those virtues in others which he has renounced in himself, and it would therefore be doubly difficult for him to surrender himself up to the illusions of romance, of which hope and love are the very elements.

We are disposed to consider 'the Prisoner of Chillon' as one of the highest efforts of Lord Byron's imagination. It may indeed be considered as forming in some degree an exception to these remarks. Still, the vigour of conception which it displays, has no reference to character, but is limited to peculiarity of situation, and is employed simply in realizing the gradual influence of imprisonment upon the human faculties. It is written throughout with exquisite delicacy and pathos, in a tone of feeling absolutely different from the former compositions of the Author, and more nearly resembling the best of Wordsworth's lyrical ballads, than any other poetry we have met with.

The Chateau de Chillon is situated between Charens and Villeneuve, on the lake of Geneva, which washes its walls, and has been fathomed below it to the depth of nearly a thousand feet. Within it are a range of dungeons, in which the early reformers, and, subsequently, prisoners of state, were confined. 'Across one of the vaults is a beam black with age, on which we are informed that the condemned were formerly executed. In the cells are seven pillars, in some of which are rings for the fetters and the fettered.' Here three brothers are immured for their religious sentiments, each chained to a column, 'together, yet apart.' The eldest brother alone survives to relate the sad story of his imprisonment.

The following is his account of the death of the youngest: one had already pined away.

[Sections VIII–X are quoted.]

We must be brief in adverting to the remaining poems. Lord Byron has presented to us in this collection two specimens of blank verse, which shew that he is as competent to master that difficult rhythm in all its varied harmony, as any form of metrical verse. The first is entitled 'Darkness,' and represents the effects which the poet imagines would be consequent on the extinction of the sun and the heavenly bodies. It is Fuseli *out-Fuselied*;[1] horror accumulated upon horror in naked hideousness, up to the highest point of exaggeration. It required indeed a very extraordinary power of conception, to make such a rabble of misshapen and ghastly ideas pass before the mind in any order, and submit to be defined into form, and cohere together for the purpose of the poet. But few persons, we think, will be inclined to read it twice: it is any thing but pleasing, and can answer no purpose but that of exhibiting the ingenuity of the Author in investing with a sort of spectral sublimity a subject which otherwise must have been purely absurd.

The other poem in blank verse is entitled 'The Dream.' It is obviously intended to convey in the language of allegory, some secret history, to which many of his Lordship's minor pieces have apparently an indistinct reference; and it would seem that it was designed to intimate just so much to the reader, as might disarm him of any indignant feelings which circumstances of public notoriety might have drawn forth towards the hero of this tale of pity and mystery. The Author betrays a consciousness of how much there exists which needs all the extenuation that this soul-harrowing record, if faithful, would involve. But this is a subject on which we have no desire to enter. Lord Byron has produced a very touching and beautiful poem: it tells us he is wretched, and if he be so, in whatever his unhappiness originates, he must command our sympathy; but this is all that poetry can do.

'The Incantation' is distinguished by great rhythmical beauty; and though the fire which gleams and sparkles in the verse, is stolen from

---

[1] Henry Fuseli (1741–1825) was an English painter known for his extravagant and gloomy paintings.

the cauldron, it charms us by its horrific lustre. Coleridge's Lady Geraldine might envy the inventive felicity of such a spell.

We transcribe a few stanzas.

['The Incantation' was incorporated into Act I, scene i, of *Manfred*. Stanzas one and three through five (as they stand in *Manfred*) are quoted.]

Two other poems are entitled 'Churchill's Grave,' and 'Prometheus:' but the most pleasing poem in the Collection, is that entitled 'Stanzas to ———': that is, pleasing, if dissociated from the circumstances to which they seem to allude.

[Lines 17-36, and 45-48 of 'Stanzas to [Augusta]' are quoted.]

We could easily have extended this article by extracts of beauty equal to any we have made. In the third Canto of Childe Harold especially, the reflections on the field of Waterloo, the apostrophe to General Howard, and the subsequent stanza, are of surpassing merit: but they are already familiarized to many of our readers.

We have also forborne to comment on the moral sentiments interspersed through these poems, because we do not think they are calculated to spread infection, and the radical taint of his Lordship's feelings it is not in the power of sage philosophy to medicate. Lord Byron says,

> 'I have not loved the world, nor the world me—
> But let us part fair foes; I do believe
> Though I have found them not, that there may be
> Words which are things,—hopes which will not deceive,
> And virtues which are merciful, nor weave
> Snares for the failing: I would also deem
> O'er others grief that some sincerely grieve,
> That two, or one, are almost what they seem,
> That goodness is no name, and happiness no dream.'

It is obvious that there must be some affectation, or much ingratitude in this misanthropy. Lord Byron has taken the trouble to inform the public even of the names of many friends whose intimacy he professes to prize and to enjoy, and we know that at any rate all these have not forsaken him. Lord Byron has had many friends, and it is his own fault if the world is not his friend, for to poets and to peers, especially to one like him, the world is in its disposition most friendly. It were easy to retort upon our English Timon, the demand—What has he done to make the world love him? Have his labours, his words, his poetry, been directed to make that world better, which he esteems so bad? Even a critic might be allowed to start these questions; but he would ask them in vain. Our business, however, is not with Lord Byron, but with his readers and ours, who, we doubt not, will be able to discriminate, at the very height of their admiration, between the brilliant coruscations of sentiment, which flash from his Lordship's genius, and the legitimate evidence of correct principle. How very far more elevated in sentiment, whatsoever inferiority of poetical merit they display to the lines we have just quoted, is the apostrophe of a contemporary writer to this same world, on which Lord Byron looks back with misanthropic pride!

> 'O for a soul magnanimous to know,
> 'Poor world, thy littleness, and let thee go!
> 'Not with a gloomy, proud, ascetic mind,
> 'That loves thee still, and only hates mankind;
> 'Reverse the line, and that my temper be,
> 'To love mankind, and pour contempt on thee.'
> *Essays in Rhyme by Jane Taylor*

Reviews of Byron's 'Manfred'

Literary Gazette

June 21, 1817, pp. 337–38. The reviewer is unknown.

The prolific pen of Lord Byron has presented us with another work, in the form of a Drama, but evidently not intended for representation. It is distinguished by all his Lordship's usual characteristics; by the same tone of deep feeling, the same carelessness of versification, the same contempt of life and life's concerns, the same secret canker preying upon the heart, and the same mystery spread around its hero. Indeed, the gloomy heroics of Manfred go a shade or two deeper than those of the Corsair, Lara, or Childe Harold; and we doubt whether any human being ever felt, or ever could feel, such hyperbolical despair, such magnificent misery, such inexorable, endless and terrific remorse as Manfred. In fact, between his conversations with witches, spirits, the destinies, Nemesis and Arimanes, (truly rather a heterogeneous assemblage of mythology,) his conjurations, and his mystical soliloquies, we lose sight, during three-fourths of the work, of his mortality, and neither sympathize with his sufferings, nor acquire respect for his unbending spirit. A great deal of genius is visible throughout the performance; perhaps, too, of a higher order than many former productions of the noble poet: but then, there is so little fable, (indeed, none whatever,) and the dramatis personae, with the exception of a drivelling Abbot, and a well-sketched Chamois hunter, are either so trite or so uncongenial with the poetry of this or any other country, that we confess, with pain, we felt ourselves stimulated onward to the last page, more by our knowledge that Lord Byron was the author, than by any interest the work itself excited in us. Besides, there is another deficiency which disappointed us not a little. The supernatural beings, who could not be made interesting, ought, at least, to have been made poetical.

234

But this is not the case. They are absolutely the most prosaic, namby-pamby personages, in the whole poem.

We shall now proceed to give a sketch of the plan, (for plot there is none,) and extracts which may the better enable our readers to judge of the work.

[A summary of the story is given, and, in the process, lines 28–49 and 188–93 (of Act I, scene i), 17–30 (of Act II, scene i), 97–139 (of Act II, scene ii), and 59–79 and 142–53 (of Act III, scene iv) are quoted. The conversation between Manfred and his menials in Act III, scene ii, is said to be 'trivial', and Manfred at the beginning of scene iv, Act III, is described as 'alone, and as usual in a long soliloquy'.]

We fancy we can perceive some symptoms of incipient orthodoxy in the religious doctrines of Lord Byron, and we should hail any appearances of that nature with unfeigned delight. Were we to identify him with Manfred in the same manner that our reviewing brethren have identified him with his other heroes, we should say, that he is at this moment investigating the truths of religion—*we hope*, with a sober and rational desire to benefit himself, and not to astonish the world with some new creed of poetical theology.

Some of the language in this Drama is accurate and polished. Other parts are rugged enough and even ungrammatical. We object to such expressions as 'Rise *boilingly* higher,' 'shoot *soaringly* forth,' and 'I hear ye *momently* above.' These adverbs are as ugly as they are new.

British Review

X (*Aug. 1817*), *82–90. The author was William Roberts, a lawyer and editor of the* British Review *from 1811 to 1822: see Arthur Roberts,* The Life, Letters, and Opinions of William Roberts (*London, 1850*), *p. 43.*

As we have long considered Lord Byron as our patient, every resource of our medical skill has been exerted upon his morbid intellect: every thing has been tried from a soothing syrup, to a blistering plaster; but since this poem of 'Manfred' has appeared, we doubt whether any thing less potent than hellebore will prove efficacious. Sometimes, indeed, we are induced to doubt whether a cure might be altogether desirable, since, if the complaint is habitual, and constitutional, the removal of it might give room to some worse disease, or let in a general languor upon the system. Perhaps, after all, Dr. Spurzheim could show that some incurable tendency resides in the organs, to which the creation of such a monotonous series of whimsical hypochondriacs is scientifically to be ascribed.[1]

It was a circumstance rather agreeable to us in opening this little poem, to find that the scene was in Switzerland. This, at least, gave us a hope that we were safe from our old enemies in turbans; from languishing pirates, gentlemen-thieves, and pensive cut-throats, with all the bloody delights of the divan, the kiosk, and the haram: but, alas! the Noble Poet knows only, understands only, feels only one solitary character, the prototype of which is for ever in his imagination. The constituent parts of this strange composition of a man are easily enumerated: save that he is violently in love, he is altogether a desperate villain, with just so much of palliation as a certain degree of craziness, produced by crime, may be said to afford. Without this demon to inspire him, it seems as if his Lordship were incapable of all effort; for whenever he attempts any thing independently of his assistance, absolute failure seems to be the penalty of his desertion. Now, if this be so, however we may morally regret the necessity, we scarcely know how to blame the poet. His case, indeed, is to be lamented as well as that of his readers, since all those glowing and picturesque descriptions of scenery, in which he so eminently excels, are thus under a law which compels them to pass through the mind of this conscience-smitten hero, who is sure to mix with them, in their passage, a portion of his own malignant ill-humour. From the Giaour, or perhaps from the Childe, with whom Lord Byron first started in his career of sentimental poetry, an unity of character has pervaded all the principal personages of this poet, with only that variety which the deepening shades of villainy has supplied, as his muse has proceeded. The renegade, who figured in the 'Siege of Corinth,' was certainly in considerable advance beyond his predecessors in crime. He had assumed the costume and religion of a Turk, to participate in the massacre of his own countrymen, the Venetians, in revenge for some imagined wrong received from some of them. Parasina, a tale of woeful debauchery, presents us with an improvement upon the turpitude of Lord Byron's former heroes; we had there the amour of a bastard son with his father's wife. This favourite character of Lord Byron seemed in this last display to have done his worst. It seemed impossible to carry him a stage further in depravity without bringing him very near his infernal home; and accordingly, in the poem now in our hands, we find our old companion in downright fellowship with familiar spirits.

Count Manfred has an insufferable load of crime upon his conscience;

[1] Dr Spurzheim was a popular phrenologist of the time. See note 1, p. 302 below.

—some black and atrocious deed or deeds, the nature of which is scarcely hinted in the course of the poem; and in virtue of his crime or crimes, he appears to have been invested with a magician's art, and to have received, or acquired, the knowledge of some spells too strong for the principalities and powers of darkness to resist, whenever it was his pleasure to summon them. He has also, by what charter it is impossible to say, a controul over very odd beings, of whom but little, if any thing, has been heard in romance,—ministering destinies, and talking elements, and young and florid witches. He is withal an astrologer, and no stranger to the visions of the Apocalypse. Arimanes is also one of the spiritual persons of this unintelligible drama, whose part is as short as it is significant, almost all he has to say being condensed in the solemn monosyllable 'yea.' The other spirits, however, make up for the taciturnity and reserve of their prince. When first summoned by Manfred, they appear to be officiously disposed to serve him, and to enter into a full communication with him. But it does not seem that the Count, when he has got them about him, knows exactly what to do with them. He has no commands for them. But it occurs to him at length to desire to see these spirits in their accustomed forms. They tell him they have no forms of their own, being mere mind and principle; but that they can assume any form, and they desire him to choose one. He declines making any choice, and one of them appears in the shape of a beautiful female: in this figure is involved the great mystery of the poem; he rushes forward to embrace it, but it vanishes. And now follows the incantation, which was printed some time ago among the poems of which the Prisoner of Chillon is the principal. As it stood in that publication without a bearing upon any events, it had more than its original vacancy of meaning, and served as a curious instance to show what liberties with the public the poet felt he could take upon the strength of his established reputation. The reader will be at once in full possession of Manfred's character, and sufficiently reminded of a personage with whom he has been well acquainted ever since he has known Lord Byron's muse, by the following soliloquy of the hero of this dramatic poem.

[Lines 65–81 of Act I, scene ii, are quoted.]

Manfred is on the point of throwing himself headlong from the brow of one of the Alpine crags, when a Chamois hunter comes just in time to save him. This Chamois hunter, who talks in the strain of a buskined hero, is the character next in importance to the Count himself; he comes and goes however, with this one scene, and contributes nothing to the development. One address, however, of Manfred to this honest villager puts his character in very pleasing contrast with his own, and shows the poet to have very accurate views of those unsophisticated joys, of which we heartily wish he had a more practical relish, and were more frequently employed in describing.

[Lines 63–71 of Act II, scene i, are quoted.]

Among the crimes of Manfred, one great and cardinal sin is constantly in his thoughts, frequently alluded to, but never distinctly divulged. It seems, however, to have partly consisted in breaking the heart of a young lady of great perfections by his ill-treatment; and we obscurely collect that the unhappy victim was so nearly related to him as to stamp an unholy character on the sentiment with which he had regarded her. When the Chamois hunter invites him to taste his wine, the following dialogue takes place:

[Lines 21–30 of Act II, scene i, are quoted, and a brief summary of the rest of the poem is given; lines 30–47 of Act III, scene iii, are quoted in the process.]

And thus ends this new deformed bantling of Lord Byron's muse, scarcely better than an abortion in moral form and structure, but nourished, and cradled, and rocked, as all this progeny have been, by the hand of a fostering genius, and the lullabies of melodious song.

The mischief that lurks in all Lord Byron's productions is this— they are lying representations of human nature; they bring qualities of a most contradictory kind into close alliance; and so shape them into seeming union as to confound sentiments, which, for the sake of sound morality and social security, should for ever be kept contrasted, and at polar extremities with respect to each other. Manfred is represented to have loved but one, and the heart of that one he cruelly broke; his very love, too, appears to have been of that sort which lies under a natural interdict. He also confesses himself to have been a man of crime and blood; and yet a certain air of native nobleness, a mysterious grandeur of character, an elevation far above ordinary humanity, all these qualities are made to throw a sort of brilliance around him, and to seem, like the sun-bow of the mountain cataract, the still and magnificent product of the conflict beneath it. These representations go beyond mere contradictoriness of character; they involve a confusion of principle, and operate very fatally and very diffusively in strengthening prejudices, which are at the bottom of our falsest estimations of men and things. In Lord Byron's own mind, we perceive this proneness to childishly erroneous impressions of human worth. The agents of a mild and regular government; those by whom the great machine of society is kept in repair, and peaceful limits imposed upon passion and ambition, or what may be called by some the privileges of genius, receive but little quarter from his muse, while the fate of a sanguinary tyrant, whose present restraint is the pledge of security and peace to the world, has been lamented in the third canto of the Childe Harold, with ludicrous sensibility.

It would be an idle parade of criticism to enter into the merits of this performance, as a specimen of dramatic composition. It has none of the properties of this kind of writing, but the division into scenes, and the conduct of the story by the means of dialogue. It affords, indeed, a pretty good ground for inferring the unfitness of the poet for this province of the art.

His peasant converses in the same language and sentiment as his nobleman; and to make up the complement of characters essential to the prosecution of the story, he throws in an old Abbot, whose province it is only to ask questions and offer advice: a couple of domestic servants, who talk together for the sake of the reader, and half a score of spirits and witches, distinguished only by their ordinal descriptions of first spirit and second spirit, first destiny and second destiny. One only character has absorbed the whole of Lord Byron's creative power. 'The steady aspect of one clear large star,' of demoniac influence, has fascinated his genius, and we perfectly despair of ever seeing the spell broken, and a natural, free, and wholesome exercise of those very superior talents which he unquestionably possesses. The present poem is certainly not without specimens of those talents, of which few have been greater admirers than ourselves, and none have more feelingly lamented the waste and abuse. The following address of Manfred to the 'Witch of the Alps,' rising beneath the arch of the sun-beam of the torrent, is full of Lord Byron's descriptive vigour.

[Lines 13–32 of Act II, scene ii, are quoted.]

The account which Manfred gives of himself, and his early addictions, it is impossible not to admire, notwithstanding it has so much of the mannerism of the poet.

[Lines 49–91 of Act II, scene ii, are quoted.]

The effect of the Coloseum and surrounding scene of storied ruins, in a starry night, is the passage most laboured, and perhaps most successfully so, in the poem, and it would be scarcely just towards Lord Byron not to give it a place.

[The first forty-one lines of Act III, scene iv, are quoted.]

We trust we have done justice to this little poem, which, as a drama, or as a whole, we cannot praise; as a repetition of the old story of one of Lord Byron's pleasant fellows, full of crime, and yet full of conscious superiority, we cannot but condemn; but which, for its particular passages of poetical excellence, we consider as worthy of the fame of the author.

Review of Byron's 'Beppo'

Edinburgh Review

XXIX (Feb. *1818*), *302–10*. *The author was Francis Jeffrey: see Walter E. Houghton (ed.)*, The Wellesley Index to Victorian Periodicals (*Toronto, 1966*), *p. 457*.

Though there is as little serious meaning or interest in this extraordinary performance, as can easily be imagined, we think it well entitled to a place in our fastidious Journal—and that, not merely because it is extremely clever and amusing, but because it affords a very curious and complete specimen of a kind of diction and composition of which our English literature has hitherto afforded very few examples. It is, in itself, absolutely a thing of nothing—without story, characters, sentiments, or intelligible object;—a mere piece of lively and loquacious prattling, in short, upon all kinds of frivolous subjects,—a sort of gay and desultory babbling about Italy and England, Turks, balls, literature and fish sauces. But still there is something very engaging in the uniform gayety, politeness, and good humour of the author—and something still more striking and admirable in the matchless facility which he has cast into regular, and even difficult versification, the unmingled, unconstrained, and unselected language of the most light, familiar, and ordinary conversation. The French have always had a great deal of this sort of poetry—though with a very severe regard to the purity of the diction—and the Italians also, in a looser and more extravagant tone; but, in England, it seems never to have been naturalized. The nearest approach to it is to be found in some of the tales and lighter pieces of Prior—a few stanzas here and there among the trash and burlesque of Peter Pindar—and in several passages of Mr Moore, and the author of the facetious miscellany, entitled, the Twopenny

Post Bag.[1] Chaucer and Shakespeare had ease and gayety enough for the style of which we are speaking—but it belongs intrinsically to the silver, and not to the golden age of poetry; and implies the existence of certain habits of dissipation, derision, and intelligence in general society, and of a sort of conventional language, for the expression of those things, which were still to be formed in the days of these great masters.—It is scarcely necessary to add, except for our duller readers, that this same familiar, lively, conversational poetry, is perfectly distinct both from the witty, epigrammatic and satirical vein, in which Pope will never be surpassed—or equalled; and from the burlesque, humorous and distorted style which attained its greatest height in Hudibras, and has been copied abundantly enough by humbler imitators. The style of which we are speaking is, no doubt, occasionally satirical and witty and humorous—but it is, on the whole, far more gay than poignant, and is characterized, exactly as good conversation is, rather by its constant ease and amenity, than by any traits either of extraordinary brilliancy, or of strong and ludicrous effect. There must be a certain allowance of sense and sagacity—and little flying traits of picturesque description—and small flights of imagination—and sallies of naïveté and humour—but nothing very powerful, and nothing very long. The great charm is in the simplicity and naturalness of the language—the free but guarded use of all polite idioms, and even of all phrases of temporary currency that have the stamp of good company upon them, —with the exclusion of all scholastic or ambitious eloquence, all profound views, and all deep emotions.

The unknown writer[2] before us has accomplished all these objects with great skill and felicity; and, in particular, has furnished us with an example, unique we rather think in our language, of about one hundred stanzas of good verse, entirely composed of common words, in their common places; never presenting us with one sprig of what is called poetical diction, or even making use of a single inversion, either to raise the style or assist the rhyme—but running on in an inexhaustible series of good easy colloquial phrases, and finding them fall into verse by some unaccountable and happy fatality. In this great and characteristic quality it is almost invariably excellent. In some other respects it is more unequal. About one half is as good as possible, in the style to which it belongs; the other half bears perhaps too many marks of that haste with which we take it for granted that such a work must necessarily be written. Some passages are rather too foolish, some too snappish,

---

[1] The *Intercepted Letters; or, The Two-penny Postbag* was published anonymously by Thomas Moore in 1813.

[2] *Beppo* was published anonymously.

and some run too much on the cheap and rather plebeian humour of out-of-the-way rhymes and strange sounding words and epithets. But the greater part is very pleasant, amiable, and gentlemanlike.

It is not perhaps worth while to give any account of the subject of a work which almost professes to have no subject. But as it has a name, and a sort of apology for a story, we shall proceed, according to our laudable custom, to teach our gentle readers all we know. . . .

[A brief summary of the story is given.]

This story, such as it is, occupies about twenty stanzas, we think, out of the ninety-five of which the poem consists. The rest is made up of digressions and dissertations at the author's discretion; and these form unquestionably by far the most lively and interesting part of the work, of which we must now give our readers a few specimens—to explain and make amends for our critical disquisitions. We may begin at the tenth stanza.

[Stanzas X–XI and XVII are quoted.]

It may be right now to give a small sample of the narrative part, to show how airily the author deals with his story. After Beppo's disappearance, the condition of his lady is thus represented.

[Stanza XXIX is quoted.]

The charms of the cavalier are then described—and the tale proceeds.

[Stanzas XXXV–XXXVII and the first four lines of stanza XL are quoted.]

At this point the author breaks off into one of those lively digressions which give its charm and its character to this curious little work. Nothing can possibly be better, in its way, than what follows.

[Stanzas XLI, XLIII, and XLIV are quoted.]

> 'I like the women too (forgive my folly),
>   From the rich peasant cheek of ruddy bronze,
> And large black eyes that flash on you a volley
>   Of rays that say a thousand things at once,
> To the high dama's brow, more melancholy,
>   But clear, and with a wild and liquid glance,
> Heart on her lips, and soul within her eyes,
> Soft as her clime, and sunny as her skies.' pp. 20–22.

In these last lines, it will be observed, that the author rises above the usual and appropriate pitch of his composition, and is betrayed into something too like enthusiasm and deep feeling for the light and fantastic strain of his poetry. Neither does the fit go off immediately; for he rises quite into rapture in the succeeding stanza—in which he seems to have caught a spark from the ardent genius of Byron.

> 'Eve of the land which still is paradise!
>   Italian beauty! didst thou not inspire
> Raphael, who died in thy embrace, and vies
>   With all we know of Heaven, or can desire,
> In what he hath bequeath'd us?—in what guise,
>   Though flashing from the fervour of the lyre,
> Would *words* describe thy past and present glow,
> While yet Canova can create below?' pp. 22, 23.

This, however, is the only slip of the kind in the whole work—the only passage in which the author betrays the secret—which might however have been suspected—of his own genius, and his affinity to a higher order of poets than those to whom he has here been pleased to hold out a model.

The following lines on England form a fair counterpart to the preceding on Italy—though the taste, we think, is less pure, and the style rather too smart and epigrammatical.

[Stanzas XLVII–XLIX are quoted.]

There are traits of Lord Byron, again, in the following whimsical verses.

[Stanzas LX–LXI are quoted.]

Nothing can be cleverer than this caustic little diatribe, introduced *à propos* of the life of Turkish ladies in their harams.

[Stanzas LXXII–LXXIII, LXXV–LXXVI, and the first two lines of stanza LXXVII are quoted.]

One little bit more, for the breaking up of the ball.

[Stanzas LXXXII–LXXXIV and the first four lines of stanza LXXXV are quoted.]

We must add the scene of the final *anagnorisis* of Beppo, and the pathetic discourse which the modern Penelope addresses to him on his return.

[Stanzas XCI–XCIII are quoted.]

We are not in the secret of this learned author's incognito; and, at our distance from the metropolis,[1] shall not expose ourselves by guessing. We cannot help thinking, however, that we have seen him before, and that 'we do know that fine Roman hand.' At all events, we hope we shall see him again; and if he is not one of our old favourites, we are afraid we may be tempted to commit an infidelity on his account,— and let him supplant some of the less assiduous of the number.

[1] The distance between Edinburgh and London, 'the metropolis'. More modern, swifter transportation was being developed, but in the early years of the century (when judged by the standards of the mid-century), 'the capitals of Scotland and of England were then about 2,400 miles asunder' (Henry, Lord Cockburn, *Life of Lord Jeffrey* [Edinburgh, 1852], I, 159).

Review of Byron's 'Childe Harold's Pilgrimage', Canto IV

Quarterly Review

XIX (*April 1818*), *215–32. The author was Walter Scott: see Hill Shine and Helen C. Shine,* The Quarterly Review under Gifford (*Chapel Hill, N.C., 1949), p. 62. The issue containing the review appeared in Sept. 1818 (ibid., p. 60).*

[Stanza CLXXXVI is quoted.]

This solemn valediction, the concluding stanza of Lord Byron's poem, forms at once a natural and an impressive motto to our essay. 'There are few things,' says the moralist, 'not purely evil, of which we can say, without some emotion of uneasiness, *this is the last*. Those who could never agree together shed tears when mutual discontent has determined them to final separation, and of a place that has been frequently visited, though without pleasure, the last look is taken with heaviness of heart.' When we resume, therefore, our task of criticism, and are aware that we are exerting it for the last time upon this extraordinary work, we feel no small share of reluctance to part with the Pilgrim, whose wanderings have so often beguiled our labours, and diversified our pages. We part from 'Childe Harold' as from the pleasant and gifted companion of an interesting tour, whose occasional waywardness, obstinacy and caprice are forgotten in the depth of thought with which he commented upon subjects of interest as they passed before us, and in the brilliancy with which he coloured such scenery as addressed itself to the imagination. His faults, if we at all remember them, are recollected only with pity, as affecting himself indeed, but no longer a concern of ours:—his merits acquire double value in our eyes when we call to mind that we may perhaps never more profit by them. The scallop-shell and staff are now laid aside, the pilgrimage is accomplished, and Lord Byron, in his assumed character, is no longer to delight us with the display of his wondrous talents, or provoke us by the use he sometimes condescends to make of them,—an use which at times has reminded us of his own powerful simile,

> 'It was as is a new-dug grave,
> Closing o'er one we sought to save.'

Before we part, however, we feel ourselves impelled to resume a consideration of his 'Pilgrimage,' not as consisting of detached accounts of foreign scenery and of the emotions suggested by them, but as a whole poem, written in the same general spirit, and pervaded by the same cast of poetry. In doing this, we are conscious we must repeat much which has perhaps been better said by others, and even be guilty of the yet more unpardonable crime of repeating ourselves. But if we are not new we will at least be brief, and the occasion seems to us peculiarly favourable for placing before our readers the circumstances which secured to the Pilgrimage of Childe Harold a reception so generally popular. The extrinsic circumstances, which refer rather to the state of the public taste than to the genius and talent of the author, claim precedence in order because, though they are not those on which the fame of the poet must ultimately rest, they are unquestionably the scaffolding by means of which the edifice was first raised which now stands independent of them.

Originality, as it is the highest and rarest property of genius, is also that which has most charms for the public. Not that originality is always necessary, for the world will be contented, in the poverty of its mental resources, with mere novelty or singularity, and must therefore be enchanted with a work that exhibits both qualities. The vulgar author is usually distinguished by his treading, or attempting to tread, in the steps of the reigning favourite of the day. He is didactic, sentimental, romantic, epic, pastoral, according to the taste of the moment, and his 'fancies and delights,' like those of Master Justice Shallow, are sure to be adapted to the tunes *which the carmen whistle*. The consequence is, not that the herd of imitators gain their object, but that the melody which they have profaned becomes degraded in the sated ears of the public—its original richness, wildness and novelty are forgotten when it is made manifest how easily the leading notes can be caught and parodied, and whatever its intrinsic merit may have been, it becomes, for the time, stale and fulsome. If the composition which has been thus hunted down possesses intrinsic merit, it may—indeed it will—eventually revive and claim its proper place amid the poetical galaxy; deprived, indeed, of the adventitious value which it may at first have acquired from its novelty, but at the same time no longer overshaded and incumbered by the croud of satellites now consigned to chaos and primaeval night. When the success of Burns, writing in his native dialect with unequalled vigour and sweetness, had called from their flails an hundred peasants to cudgel their brains for rhymes, we can well remember that even the bard of Coila was somewhat injured in the common estimation—as a masterpiece of painting is degraded by being placed amid the flaring colours and ill-drawn figures of imitative daubers. The true poet attempts the very reverse of the imitator. He plunges into the stream of public opinion even when its tide is running strongest, crosses its direction, and bears his crown of laurel as Caesar did his imperial mantle, triumphant above the waves. Such a phenomenon seldom fails at first to divide and at length to alter the reigning taste of the period, and if the bold adventurer has successfully buffeted the ebbing tide which bore up his competitor, he soon has the benefit of the flood in his own favour.

In applying these general remarks to Lord Byron's gravest and most serious performance, we must recal to the reader's recollection that since the time of Cowper he has been the first poet who, either in his own person, or covered by no very thick disguise, has directly appeared before the public, an actual living man expressing his own sentiments, thoughts, hopes and fears. Almost all the poets of our day, who have possessed a considerable portion of public attention, are personally little known to the reader, and can only be judged from the passions and feelings assigned by them to persons totally fictitious. Childe Harold appeared—we must not say in the character of *the author*—but certainly in that of a real existing person, with whose feelings as such the public were disposed to associate those of Lord Byron. Whether the reader acted right or otherwise in persisting to neglect the shades of distinction which the author endeavoured to point out betwixt his pilgrim and himself, it is certain that no little power over the public attention was gained from their being identified. Childe Harold may not be, nor do we believe he is, Lord Byron's very self, but he is Lord Byron's picture, sketched by Lord Byron himself, arrayed in a fancy dress, and disguised perhaps by some extrinsic attributes, but still bearing a sufficient resemblance to the original to warrant the conclusion that we have drawn. This identity is so far acknowledged in the preface to the Canto now before us, where Lord Byron thus expresses himself.

248

'The poem also, or the pilgrim, or both, have accompanied me from first to last; and perhaps it may be a pardonable vanity which induces me to reflect with complacency on a composition which in some degree connects me with the spot where it was produced, and the objects it would fain describe; and however unworthy it may be deemed of those magical and memorable abodes, however short it may fall of our distant conceptions and immediate impressions, yet as a mark of respect for what is venerable, and of feeling for what is glorious, it has been to me a source of pleasure in the production, and I part with it with a kind of regret, which I hardly suspected that events could have left me for imaginary objects.'—pp. vi, vii.

But besides the pleasing novelty of a traveller and a poet, throwing before the reader his reflections and opinions, his loves and his hates, his raptures and his sorrows; besides the novelty and pride which the public felt, upon being called as it were into familiarity with a mind so powerful, and invited to witness and partake of its deep emotions; the feelings themselves were of a character which struck with awe those to whom the noble pilgrim thus exposed the sanctuary of his bosom. They were introduced into no Teian paradise of lutes and maidens, were placed in no hall resounding with music and dazzling with many-coloured lights, and called upon to gaze on those gay forms that flutter in the muse's beam. The banquet had ceased, and it was the pleasure of its melancholy lord that his guests should witness that gloominess, which seems most dismal when it succeeds to exuberant and unrestrained gaiety. The emptied wine-cup lay on the ground, the withered garland was flung aside and trodden under foot, the instruments of music were silent, or waked but those few and emphatic chords which express sorrow; while, amid the ruins of what had once been the palace of pleasure, the stern pilgrim stalked from desolation to desolation, spurning from him the implements of former luxury, and repelling with equal scorn the more valuable substitutes which wisdom and philosophy offered to supply their place. The reader felt as it were in the presence of a superior being, when, instead of his judgment being consulted, his imagination excited or soothed, his taste flattered or conciliated in order to bespeak his applause, he was told, in strains of the most sublime poetry, that neither he, the courteous reader, nor aught the earth had to shew, was worthy the attention of the noble traveller.—All countries he traversed with a heart for entertaining the beauties of nature, and an eye for observing the crimes and follies of mankind; and from all he drew subjects of sorrow, of indignation, of contempt. From Dan to Beersheba all was barrenness. To despise the ordinary sources of happiness, to turn with scorn from the pleasures which captivate others, and to endure, as it were voluntarily, evils which others are most anxious to shun, is a path to ambition; for the monarch is scarcely more respected for possessing, than the anchoret for contemning the means of power and of pleasure. A mind like that of Harold, apparently indifferent to the usual enjoyments of life, and which entertains, or at least exhibits, such contempt for its usual pursuits, has the same ready road to the respect of the mass of mankind, who judge that to be superior to humanity which can look down upon its common habits, tastes, and pleasures.

This fashion of thinking and writing of course had its imitators, and those right many. But the humorous sadness which sat so gracefully on the original made but a poor and awkward appearance on those who

> ———wrapp'd themselves in Harold's inky cloak,
> To show the world how 'Byron' did *not* 'write.'

Their affected melancholy shewed like the cynicism of Apemantus contrasted with the real misanthropy of Timon. And, to say the truth, we are not sorry that the fashion has latterly lost ground. This species of general contempt of intellectual pleasures, and worldly employment, is more closely connected with the Epicurean philosophy than may be at first supposed. If philosophy be but a pursuit of words, and the revolutions of empires inevitable returns of the same cycle of fearful transitions; if our earliest and best affections 'run to waste, and water but the desert,' the want of worthier motives to action gives a tremendous and destructive impulse to the dangerous *Carpe diem* of the Garden—that most seductive argument of sensual pleasure. This doctrine of the nothingness of human pursuits, not as contrasted with those of religion and virtue, (to which they are indeed as nothing,) but absolutely and in themselves, is too apt to send its pupils in despair to those pleasures which promise a real gratification, however short and gross. Thus do thoughts and opinions, in themselves the most melancholy, become incitements to the pursuit of the most degrading pleasures; as the Egyptians placed skulls upon their banqueting tables, and as the fools of Holy Writ made the daring and fearful association of imminent fate and present revelling—*Let us eat and drink, for to-morrow we die.*

If we treat the humour less gravely, and consider it as a posture of the mind assumed for the nonce, still this enumeration of the vain pursuits, the indulged yet unsatiated passions of humanity, is apt to weary our spirits if not our patience, and the discourse terminates in a manner as edifying as the dialogue in Prior's Alma:—

' "Tired with these thoughts"—"Less tired than I,"
Quoth Dick, "with your philosophy—
That people live and die I knew,
An hour ago as well as you;
What need of books those truths to tell,
Which folks perceive who cannot spell;
And must we spectacles apply,
To view what hurts our naked eye?
If to be sad is to be wise,
I do most heartily despise
Whatever Socrates has said,
Or Tully wrote, or Wanley read."
   'Dear Drift! to set our matters right,
Remove these papers from my sight,
Burn Mat's Des-carte and Aristotle—
Here, Jonathan, your master's bottle.'

But it was not merely to the novelty of an author speaking in his own person, and in a tone which arrogated a contempt of all the ordinary pursuits of life, that 'Childe Harold' owed its extensive popularity: these formed but the point or sharp edge of the wedge by which the work was enabled to insinuate its way into that venerable block, the British public. The high claims inferred at once in the direct appeal to general attention, and scorn of general feeling, were supported by powers equal to such pretensions. He who despised the world intimated that he had the talents and genius necessary to win it if he had thought it worth while. There was a strain of poetry in which the sense predominated over the sound; there was the eye keen to behold nature, and the pen powerful to trace her varied graces of beauty or terror; there was the heart ardent at the call of freedom or of generous feeling, and belying every moment the frozen shrine in which false philosophy had incased it, glowing like the intense and concentrated alcohol, which remains one single but burning drop in the centre of the ice which its more watery particles have formed. In despite of the character which he had assumed, it was impossible not to see in the Pilgrim what nature designed him to be, and what, in spite of bad metaphysics and worse politics, he may yet be, a person whose high talents the wise and virtuous may enjoy without a qualifying sigh or frown. Should that day arrive, and if time be granted, it will arrive, we who have ventured upon the precarious task of prophecy—we who have been censured for not mingling the faults of genius with its talents—we shall claim our hour of heartfelt exultation. He himself, while deprecating censure on the ashes of another great but self-neglected genius, has well pleaded the common cause of those who, placed high above the croud, have their errors and their follies rendered more conspicuous by their elevation.

> 'Hard is his fate on whom the public gaze
> Is fix'd for ever to detract or praise;
> Repose denies her requiem to his name,
> And Folly loves the martyrdom of Fame:
> The secret enemy, whose sleepless eye
> Stands sentinel, accuser, judge, and spy;
> Her for the fool, the jealous, and the vain,
> The envious, who but breathe in others' pain:
> Behold the host delighting to deprave,
> Who track the steps of Glory to the grave.'

For ourselves, amid the various attendants on the triumph of genius, we would far rather be the soldier who, pacing by the side of his general, mixes, with military frankness, censure amid his songs of praise, than the slave in the chariot to flatter his vanity by low adulation, or exasperate his feelings by virulent invective. In entering our protest therefore against the justice and the moral tendency of that strain of dissatisfaction and despondency, that cold and sceptical philosophy which clouds our prospects on earth, and closes those beyond it, we willingly render to this extraordinary poem the full praise that genius in its happiest efforts can demand from us.

The plan, if it can be termed so, hovers between that of a descriptive and a philosophical poem. The Pilgrim passes from land to land, alternately describing, musing, meditating, exclaiming, and moralizing; and the reader, partaking of his enthusiasm, becomes almost the partner of his journey. The first and second Cantos were occupied by Spain and Greece—the former, the stage upon which those incidents were then passing which were to decide, in their consequence, the fate of existing Europe; the latter, the country whose sun, so long set, has yet left on the horizon of the world such a blaze of splendour. It is scarcely necessary to say, that in both countries, but especially in the last, the pilgrim found *room for meditation even to madness.* The third Canto saw Childe Harold once more upon the main, and traced him from Belgium to Switzerland, through scenes distinguished by natural graces, and rendered memorable by late events. Through this ample field we accompanied the Pilgrim, and the strains which describe the beauties of the Rhine and the magnificence of the Leman lake, are still glowing in our ears. The fourth Canto now appears, and recals us to the immediate object of the present article.

The poem opens in Venice, once the mart of the universe—

[Stanza I is quoted.]

The former greatness of this queen of commerce is discribed and mingled with the recollections associated with her name, from the immortal works of fiction of which she has formed the scene.

[Stanzas IV and V are quoted.]

That this is true in philosophy as well as beautiful in poetry; that fiction as well as reality can impress local associations of the most fascinating kind, that not alone the birth-place or tomb of the man of genius, but the scenes which he has chosen for the action of his story remain dear 'to our memories,' and have to our ears and eyes a fascinating charm, was repeatedly experienced during the Peninsular war. Spain, separated by the ocean and the Pyrenees from the rest of Europe, and seldom in collision with Britain, save when we have encountered her fleets upon the seas, lying also beyond the ordinary course of travellers and tourists, has little familiar to us as readers of history or as members of British society. But the authors of fiction had given associations to this country of the most interesting kind, to supply the deficiencies of the slender list afforded by history or conversation. The British officers rushed with the eagerness of enthusiasm to find in the tower of Segovia the apartment from which Gil Blas, in his captivity, looked over the wanderings of the Ebro:—even the French dealt mildly with the city of Toboso, because it had given name to the celebrated Dulcinea; and amid the romantic deserts of the Sierra Morena the weary step was rendered lighter to the readers of Cervantes, who at every turn of their march among the landscapes which he has described with such exquisite truth and felicity, expected to see the doughty knight-errant and his trusty squire, or the beautiful vision of Dorothea, when she was surprized in boy's attire washing her feet in the rivulet. Such is the prerogative of genius! and well may it be celebrated by one who has himself impressed associations upon so much scenery, which will never, while Britons speak their present language, be seen without recollecting the pilgrim and his musings.

The contrast of the former and present state of Venice calls forth naturally a train of moral reflections suitable to the occasion; but the noble pilgrim, standing on the Bridge of Sighs, and having beneath his feet the dungeons of the most jealous aristocracy that ever existed; in the vicinity also of the palace of the Council of Ten, and of those 'lions mouths' by means of which the most treacherous and base of anonymous informers possessed full power over the life and fortune of the noblest citizens, might have spared his regret for the loss of that freedom which

Venice never possessed. The distinction, in this and many other cases, betwixt a free and an independent nation, is not sufficiently observed. The Venetians were never a free people, though the state of Venice was not only independent, but wealthy and powerful, during the middle ages, by the extent of her commerce and the policy of her wise rulers. But commerce found a more convenient channel round the Cape of Good Hope for that trade which Venice had hitherto carried on. Her rulers over-rated her strength and engaged in a war against the confederated force of Italy, from the consequences of which, though gloriously sustained, the state never recovered. The proud republic, whose bride was the Adriatic, shared the fate of Tyre and Sidon—of all nations whose wealth and grandeur are founded exclusively on ships, colonies, and commerce. The 'crowning city, whose merchants were princes, and whose traffickers were the honourable of the earth,' had long passed into a state of the third class, existing merely because not demolished, and ready to give way to the first impulse of outward force. The art of the Venetian rulers in stooping to their circumstances, and bending where they must otherwise have broken, could only protract this semblance of independence until the storm of the French Revolution destroyed Venice, among many other governments which had been respected by other conquerors from a reverence to antiquity, or from a regard for existing institutions, the very reverse of the principle which actuated the republican generals. It is surely vain to mourn for a nation which, if restored to independence, could not defend or support itself; and it would be worse than vain, were it possible, to restore the Signoria with all its oligarchical terrors of denunciation, and secret imprisonment, and judicial murder. What is to be wished for Italy, is the amalgamation of its various petty states into one independent and well-governed kingdom, capable of asserting and maintaining her place among the nations of Europe. To this desirable order of things nothing can be a stronger obstacle than the reinstatement of the various petty divisions of that fair country, each incapable of defending itself, but ready to lend its aid to destroy its neighbours.

Of Italy, in its present state, it is impossible to think or speak without recognizing the truth as well as the beauty of the following lines.

[Stanza XXVI is quoted.]

Through these delightful regions the Pilgrim wanders, awakening by the flashes of his imagination that of the reader, as the face of the country suggests topics of moral interest, and reminds us alternately of the achievements of the great of former days, in arms and in literature, and as local description mingles itself with the most interesting topics of local history. Arqua, 'the mountain where he died,' suggests the name of Petrarch; the deserted Ferrara the fame and the fate of Tasso fitly classed with Dante and Ariosto, the bards of Hell and Chivalry. Florence and its statues, Thrasimene and Clitumnus start up before us with their scenery and their recollections. Perhaps there are no verses in our language of happier descriptive power than the two stanzas which characterize the latter river. In general, poets find it so difficult to leave an interesting subject, that they injure the distinctness of the description by loading it so as to embarrass rather than excite the fancy of the reader; or else, to avoid that fault, they confine themselves to cold and abstract generalities. The author has in the following stanzas admirably steered his course betwixt these extremes; while they present the outlines of a picture as pure and brilliant as those of Claude Lorraine, the task of filling up the more minute particulars is judiciously left to the imagination of the reader; and it must be dull indeed if it does not supply what the poet has left unsaid, or but generally and briefly intimated. While the eye glances over the lines, we seem to feel the refreshing coolness of the scene—we hear the bubbling tale of the more rapid streams, and see the slender proportions of the rural temple reflected in the crystal depth of the calm pool.

[Stanzas LXVI and LXVII are quoted.]

By mountain and cataract, through this land of existing beauty and heroic memory, the pilgrim at length reaches Rome:—Rome, first empress of the bodies, then of the souls, of all the civilized world, now owing its political and, perhaps, even its religious existence to the half contemptuous pity of those nations whom she formerly held in thraldom—Rome is the very ground on which we should have loved to cope with Childe Harold.

'———in those sullen fits,
For then he's full of matter.'

Nor have we been disappointed in our wishes and expectations; for the voice of Marius could not sound more deep and solemn among the ruined arches of Carthage than the strains of the Pilgrim amid the broken shrines and fallen statues of her subduer. We can but touch partially upon these awful themes. The Palatine is thus described:—

[Stanzas CVII and CXVI are quoted with connecting prose comment.]

The Coliseum is described in the midnight gloom of a cloudless Italian sky; its vast area recalls the bloody games of the Romans, and the poet has vied with the memorable sculptor who produced the dying Gladiator,—superior in this, that equalling the artist in his faculty of impressing on the fancy the agonies, he can extend his power into incorporeal realms, and body forth not only the convulsed features and stiffened limbs, but the mental feelings and throes of the expiring swordsman.

[Stanzas CXL and CXLI are quoted.]

The Pantheon, the Mole of Hadrian, St. Peter's, whose vastness expands and 'renders colossal' the mind of the gazer, the Vatican, with its treasures of ancient art, are all placed before us with the same picturesque, and rendered real by the same earnest and energetic force of Lord Byron's poetry, in which the numbers seem so little the work of art or study, that they rather appear the natural and unconstrained language in which the thoughts present themselves. The deep-toned melancholy of the poet's mind at length rests on a theme where it must long find a response in every British bosom—on the event which cut down the hope of our nation, sparing neither bush nor blossom, when we most expected to have seen it fulfilled. Liberal as we have been in quotation we cannot resist the opportunity of meeting Lord Byron on a public ground, in which his exquisite strains are an echo to our own thoughts, and where we can join without any of those mental protests which we are too often compelled to make against the correctness of his principles, even when admitting the power of his language and the beauty of his poetry.

[Stanzas CLXVII–CLXX are quoted.]

From the copious specimens which we have given, the reader will be enabled to judge how well the last part of this great poem has sustained Lord Byron's high reputation. Yet we think it possible to trace a marked difference, though none in the tone of thought and expression, betwixt this canto and the first three. There is less of passion, more of deep thought and sentiment, at once collected and general. The stream which in its earlier course bounds over cataracts and rages through narrow and rocky defiles, deepens, expands, and becomes less turbid as it rolls on, losing the aspect of terror and gaining that of sublimity. Eight years have passed between the appearance of the first volume and the present which concludes the work, a lapse of time which, joined with other circumstances, may have contributed somewhat to moderate the tone of Childe Harold's quarrel with the world, and, if not to reconcile him to his lot, to give him, at least, the firmness which endures it without loud complaint.—To return, however, to the proposition with which we opened our criticism, certain it is, that whether as Harold or as Lord Byron no author has ever fixed upon himself personally so intense a share of the public attention. His descriptions of present and existing scenes however striking and beautiful, his recurrence to past actions however important and however powerfully described, become interesting chiefly from the tincture which they receive from the mind of the author. The grot of Egeria, the ruins of the Palatine, are but a theme for his musings, always deep and powerful though sometimes gloomy even to sullenness. This cast of solemnity may not perhaps be justly attributed to the native disposition of the author, which is reported to be as lively as, judging from this single poem at least, we might pronounce it to be grave. But our ideas of happiness are chiefly caught by reflection from the minds of others, and hence it may be observed that those enjoy the most uniform train of good spirits who are thinking much of others and little of themselves. The contemplation of our minds, however salutary for the purposes of self-examination and humiliation, must always be a solemn task, since the best will find enough for remorse, the wisest for regret, the most fortunate for sorrow. And to this influence more than to any natural disposition to melancholy, to the pain which necessarily follows this anatomizing of his own thoughts and feelings which is so decidedly and peculiarly the characteristic of the Pilgrimage, we are disposed in a great measure to ascribe that sombre tint which pervades the poem. The poetry which treats of the actions and sentiments of others may be grave or gay according to the light in which the author chuses to view his subject, but he who shall mine long and deeply for materials in his own bosom will encounter abysses at the depth of which he must necessarily tremble. This moral truth appears to us to afford, in a great measure, a key to the peculiar tone of Lord Byron. How then, will the reader ask, is our proposition to be reconciled to that which preceded it? If the necessary result of an inquiry into our own thoughts be the conviction that all is vanity and vexation of spirit, why should we object to a style of writing, whatever its consequences may be, which involves in it truths as certain as they are melancholy? If the study of our own enjoyments leads us to doubt the reality of all except the indisputable pleasures of sense, and inclines us therefore towards the Epicurean system,—it is nature, it may be said, and not the poet which urges us upon the fatal conclusion. But this is not so. Nature, when she created man a social being, gave him the capacity of drawing that happiness from his relations with the rest of his race, which he is doomed to seek in vain in his own bosom. These relations cannot be the source of happiness to us if we despise or hate the kind with whom it is their office to unite us more closely. If the earth be a den of fools and knaves, from whom the man of genius differs by the more mercurial and exalted character of his intellect, it is natural that he should look down with pitiless scorn on creatures so inferior. But if, as we believe, each man, in his own degree, possesses a portion of the ethereal flame, however smothered by unfavourable circumstances, it is or should be enough to secure the most mean from the scorn of genius as well as from the oppression of power, and such being the case, the relations which we hold with society through all their gradations are channels through which the better affections of the loftiest may, without degradation, extend themselves to the lowest. Farther, it is not only our social connections which are assigned us in order to qualify that contempt of mankind, which too deeply indulged tends only to intense selfishness; we have other and higher motives for enduring the lot of humanity—sorrow, and pain, and trouble—with patience of our own griefs and commiseration for those of others. The wisest and the best of all ages have agreed that our present life is a state of trial not of enjoyment, and that we now suffer sorrow that we may hereafter be partakers of happiness. If this be true, and it has seldom been long, or at least ultimately, doubted by those who have turned their attention to so serious an investigation, other and worthier motives of action and endurance must necessarily occur to the mind than philosophy can teach or human pride supply. It is not our intention to do more than merely indicate so ample a topic for consideration. But we cannot forbear to add, that the vanishing of Lord Byron's Pilgrim strongly reminded us of the close of another work, the delight of our childhood. Childe Harold, a prominent character in the first volume of the Pilgrimage, fades gradually from the scene like the spectre associate who performed the first stages of his journey with a knight-errant, bearing all the appearance of a living man, but who lessened to the sight by degrees, and became at length totally invisible when they approached the cavern where his mortal remains were deposited.

CLXIV.

'But where is he, the Pilgrim of my song,
The being who upheld it through the past?
Methinks he cometh late and tarries long.
He is no more—these breathings are his last;
His wanderings done, his visions ebbing fast
And he himself as nothing:—if he was
Aught but a phantasy, and could be class'd
With forms which live and suffer—let that pass—
His shadow fades away into Destruction's mass.'—p. 85.

In the corresponding passage of the Tales of the Genii, Ridley, the amiable author or compiler of the collection, expresses himself to the following purport, for we have not the book at hand to do justice to his precise words,—'Reader, the Genii are no more, and Horam, but the phantom of my mind, fiction himself and fiction all that he seemed to write, speaks not again. But lament not their loss, since if desirous to see virtue guarded by miracles, Religion can display before you scenes tremendous, wonderful, and great, more worthy of your sight than aught that human fancy can conceive—the moral veil rent in twain and the Sun of Righteousness arising from the thick clouds of heathen darkness.' In the sincere spirit of admiration for Lord Byron's talents, and regard for his character which has dictated the rest of our criticism, we here close our analysis of Childe Harold.

Our task respecting Lord Byron's poetry is finished, when we have mentioned the subject, quoted passages of superior merit, or which their position renders most capable of being detached from the body of the poem. For the character of his style and versification once distinctly traced, (and we have had repeated occasion to consider it,) cannot again be dwelt on without repetition. The harmony of verse, and the power of numbers, nay, the selection and arrangement of expressions, are all so subordinate to the thought and sentiment, as to become comparatively light in the scale. His poetry is like the oratory which hurries the hearers along without permitting them to pause on its solecisms or singularities. Its general structure is bold, severe, and as it were Doric, admitting few ornaments but those immediately suggested by the glowing imagination of the author, rising and sinking with the tones of his enthusiasm, roughening into argument, or softening into the melody of feeling and sentiment, as if the language fit for either were alike at the command of the poet, and the numbers not only came uncalled, but arranged themselves with little care on his part into the varied modulation which the subject requires. Many of the stanzas, considered separately from the rest, might be objected to as involved, harsh, and overflowing into each other beyond the usual license of the Spenserian stanza. But considering the various matter of which the poet had to treat—considering the monotony of a long-continued smoothness of sound, and accurate division of the sense according to the stanzas—considering also that the effect of the general harmony is, as in music, improved by the judicious introduction of discords wherewith it is contrasted, we cannot join with those who state this occasional harshness as an objection to Lord Byron's poetry. If the line sometimes 'labours and the words move slow,' it is in passages where the sense is correspondent to these laborious movements. A highly finished strain of versification resembles a dressed pleasure ground, elegant—even beautiful—but tame and insipid compared to the majesty and interest of a woodland chase, where scenes of natural loveliness are rendered sweeter and more interesting by the contrast of irregularity and wildness.

We have done with the poem; we have, however, yet a few words to say before we finally close our strictures.

To this canto, as to the former, notes are added, illustrative of the contents; and these, we are informed, are written by Mr. Hobhouse, the author of that facetious account of Buonaparte's reign of an hundred days, which it was our office last year to review. They are distinct and classical illustrations of the text, but contain of course many political sentiments of a class which have ceased to excite anger, or any feeling stronger than pity, and a sense of the weakness of humanity which, in all ages, has inclined even men of talents and cultivation to disgrace themselves, by the adoption of sentiments of which it is impossible they can have examined either the grounds or the consequences—whence the doctrines come, or whither they are tending. The mob of a corrupt metropolis, who vindicate the freedom of election by knocking out the brains of the candidate of whom they disapprove, act upon obvious and tangible principles; so do the Spenceans, Spa-fieldians and Nottingham conspirators. That 'seven halfpenny loaves should be sold for a penny,' —that 'the three-hooped pot should have ten hoops,'—and that 'the realm should be all in common,'—have been the watch-words of insurrection among the vulgar, from Jack Straw's time to the present, and, if neither honest nor praiseworthy, are at least sufficiently plain and intelligible. But the frenzy which makes individuals of birth and education hold a language as if they could be willing to risk the destruction of their native country, and all the horrors of a civil war, is not so easily accounted for. To believe that these persons would accelerate a desolation in which they themselves directly, or through their nearest and dearest connections, must widely share, merely to remove an obnoxious minister, would be to form a hasty and perhaps a false judgment of them. The truth seems to be, that the English, even those from whom better things might be expected, are born to be the dupes of jugglers and mountebanks in all professions. It is not only in physic that the names of our nobility and gentry decorate occasionally the list of cures to which the empiric appeals as attesting the force of his remedy. Religion, in the last age, and politics in the present, have had their quacks, who substituted words for sense, and theoretical dogmata for the practice of every duty.—But whether in religion, or politics, or physic, one general mark distinguishes the empiric; the patient is to be cured without interruption of business or pleasure—the proselyte to be saved without reformation of the future, or repentance of the past—the country to be made happy by an alteration in its political system; and all the vice and misery which luxury and poor's rates, a crouded population, and decayed morality can introduce into the community, to be removed by extending farther political rights to those who daily show that they require to be taught the purpose for which those they already enjoy were entrusted to them. That any one above the rank of an interested demagogue should teach this is wonderful—that any should believe it except the lowest of the vulgar is more so—but vanity makes as many dupes as folly.

If, however, these gentlemen will needs identify their own cause with that of their country's enemies, we can forgive them as losers, who have proverbial leave to pout. And when, in bitterness of spirit, they term the great, the glorious victory of Waterloo the 'carnage of Saint Jean,' we can forgive that too, since, trained in the school of revolutionary France, they must necessarily abhor those

> ————whose art was of such power
> It could controul their dam's God Setebos,
> And make a vassal of him.

From the dismal denunciations which Lord Byron, acting more upon his feeling than his judgment, has made against our country, although

> Were ne'er prophetic sounds so full of woe,

we entertain no fears—none whatever.—

At home, the noble author may hear of better things than 'a permanent army and a suspended Habeas Corpus'—he may hear of an improving revenue and increasing public prosperity. And while he continues abroad he may haply call to mind, that the Pilgrim, whom, eight years since, the universal domination of France compelled to wander into distant and barbarous countries, is *now* at liberty to travel where he pleases, certain that there is not a corner of the civilized world where his title of Englishman will not ensure him a favourable and respectful reception.

Review of Byron's 'Mazeppa' and 'Don Juan', Cantos I–II

Monthly Review

LXXXIX (*July 1819*), *309–21. The reviewer is unknown.*

We shall, perhaps, be borne out by experience in the observation that, as real genius is of much rarer occurrence than superior talent, so, where it exists, it is far from being versatile in its nature, but is generally limited by the peculiar scope and bias with which it was at first developed. This principle is more particularly applicable to poetry, and hence the generic distinctions of pastoral, descriptive, lyric, or dramatic poets.

When, however, a genius arises which appears to unite in itself many of these opposite characteristics of the imitative powers, it must surely be drawn from the fountains of nature herself, must be highly original, and must become deservedly popular: yet, which may appear paradoxical, but is nevertheless true, it is frequently born possessed of faults almost as numerous as its beauties. The '*aliquando dormitat Homerus*'[1] was therefore well applied even to the most transcendant genius on earth. Moreover, this is by no means the only or the worst sin which is liable to be committed; the opposite extreme of exaggeration and profuseness being more to be feared from *exquisite* spirits than even the 'nodding with the muse.' These *Scylla* and *Charybdis* of the poets require all the wisdom and skill of Homer's Ulysses to be avoided; but is it not more glorious to fail here, than to seek for safety in the trite and dull track of mediocrity? As to the cause of the beauties of a finer genius being often accompanied by great defects, this is a question of

---

[1] 'Sometimes Homer slept.' Horace *Ars Poetica* 359 (adapted).

a different nature:—but we think that Shakspeare, Dryden, and we may add Lord Byron, will warrant us in stating the fact.

As a proof of this limitation of genius, and of such illustrious exceptions, if we examine from the age of Chaucer to our own, we shall find the poetical world apportioned to its respective masters, with as much arbitrary distinction as we perceive in the various professions and institutions of society; and it would appear as if nature dispensed with this impartial rule in favour only of those 'heaven-awakened few,' whose unbounded strength and restlessness of spirit overpower the common limits of mind; and whose language, like the thunder of the heavens, rebounding from the cloud to the mountain, and from the mountain to the valley, fills the surrounding echoes with its awful music. There *are* master-spirits in the strange history of mind, which, unsatisfied with any partial views, seem to compass in the keenness of their vision those prospects which are distributed among *numbers* of an inferior class; and they are the musicians of nature, who, confined to *no* key, run through the whole scale of harmony from the lowest to the highest note; exhibiting the sublime or the trifling, the witty or the impassioned, the elegant or the impetuous, as the Proteus-god prevails.

Although our opinion of the varied powers of the noble author, who has now given us an additional proof of them in Don Juan, though perhaps not in Mazeppa, has altered with his productions since his first appearance, which we hailed with gladness, to the epoch during which he has risen to his present eminence; yet we always regarded him as superior in versatility of thought and numbers to any single poet of our times. This characteristic becomes still more surprizing, if we consider the comparatively small period during which his numerous pieces have been produced. His early poems partake of that lavish and extravagant vein of thought which always ripens into strength, and to which we are indebted for a Romeo and Juliet, a Richard the Second and Third: the same that characterized the early writings of Dryden. Lord Byron's satirical productions were certainly astonishing at his age, though they did not possess the close strength and vigour of Pope; and in 'Childe Harold' he gave new language and meaning to the Spenserian stanza, while he exhibited as many faults as his hero. The progress of the traveller's steps was not greater or more variable than that of his mind: to impetuosity of feelings was added a strength of sentiment; and philosophical reflection completed what nature had begun. Yet, as we more particularly pointed out in a late Review, how many blemishes cast too deep a shade over the work! The display of terrific character in his various heroes is given in a style of drawing equally false and grand; and the poet here manifests himself the true brother of a Salvator Rosa. In his 'Corsair,' he approaches Pope, and even Dryden, but can never sustain the parallel; while his subsequent pieces yield a final test of his genius in the wit and ease which are found in the first only of our poets. With all these advantages, he is encumbered with too many failings. His strength often swells into turgidity; his descriptions and characters are rather exaggerated; he aims at expressing more than the subject will bear; and his feelings betray him into tautology and egotism.

While his sentiments are peculiar, and often false, his philosophical observations become obscure; and his restlessness of feeling often breaks through the connection of his thoughts, to surprize us with comparisons neither agreeable nor true. He is the real poet of passion: but he describes passion of an untamed nature, which recoils with increasing force from every weight that is laid on it. He is likewise too fond of anatomizing, and unfolding to our view, the inclinations rather than the duties or the finer action of our nature. This perversion of mind is busy with incongruous images, with which it may illustrate its subject; we must not therefore expect those pleasing pictures of melancholy truth which Shakspeare gives, and which are the offspring of pity, not of misanthropy.

The story of Mazeppa possesses the novelty of a lively vein introduced into the octo-syllabic measure, which was before sacred to the author's *dreadful* heroes: but it is certainly not one of his happiest efforts, although it contains some good description of Siberian scenery.

[The historical background of the poem is given briefly.]

As the basis of this narrative, viz. a love-intrigue, is in conformity with Lord Byron's favourite contemplations, so the horrors of the result are congenial to the general nature of his pictures. Something new, however, is certainly presented in this incident, together with the descriptions and feelings to which it gives rise; and in these particulars the poem has its chief and perhaps its only merit. We shall not dwell long on it, but offer to our readers two or three passages:

[Lines 668–708 and 763–95 are quoted with connecting prose links.]

This poem is followed by an ode on the present falling fortune of the once proud Venice, and a fragment of a prose tale, which seems to have been the commencement of a Vampyre story, connected with the circumstances which we have mentioned in our account of Dr. Polidori's tale on that subject, in our Number for May last. Neither of these productions needs longer to detain us from the more singular and very superior poem of Don Juan;—a poem, however, which has also such demerits, that neither his Lordship nor his usual publisher has chosen to acknowledge it: but which, if originality and variety be the surest test of genius, has certainly the highest title to it; and which, we think, would have puzzled Aristotle with all his strength of Poetics to explain, have animated Longinus with some of its passages, have delighted Aristophanes, and have choked Anacreon with joy instead of with a grape. We might almost imagine that the ambition had seized the author to please and to displease the world at the same time: but we can scarcely think that he deserves the fate of the old man and his son and the ass, in the fable, or that he will please nobody, how strongly soever we may condemn the more than poetic license of his muse. He has here exhibited that wonderful versatility of style and thought which appear almost incompatible within the scope of a single subject; and the familiar and the sentimental, the witty and the sublime, the sarcastic and the pathetic, the gloomy and the droll, are all touched with so happy an art, and mingled together with such a power of union, yet such a discrimination of style, that a perusal of the poem appears more like a pleasing and ludicrous dream, than the sober feeling of reality. It is certainly one of the strangest though not the best of dreams; and it is much to be wished that the author, before he lay down to sleep, had invoked, like Shakspeare's Lysander, some good angel to protect him against the *wicked* spirit of slumbers. We hope, however, that his readers have learnt to admire his genius without being in danger from its influence; and we must not be surprized if a poet *will* not always write to instruct as well as to please us. Still we must explicitly condemn and reprobate various passages and expressions in the poem, which we shall not insult the understanding, the taste, or the feeling of our readers by pointing out; endeavouring rather, like artful chemists, to extract an essence from the mass, which, resembling the honey from poisonous flowers, may yet be sweet and pure.

Love is here again the prime agent. Our Opera-house and our other theatres have made Don Juan, the libertine, perfectly familiar to the British public; and Lord Byron has chosen to select this votary of licentiousness for his hero, whose birth, education, and adventures, he undertakes to pourtray. Two cantos, now presented to us, give his early history; his first *amour* with a married lady; and his subsequent expatriation, shipwreck, and escape, to be *dis*covered and *re*covered by a beautiful young female, with whom in course 'the game of love again is played.' What but similar pictures of meretricious events, in themselves scarcely diversified, but relieved no doubt by new episodes, and supported by every varied charm of description, can be supposed to be destined to occupy the 'twelve, or twenty-four' cantos which are threatened to complete the poem? We trust, however, and we believe, that the noble author will pay sufficient deference to the public morals, and to that public voice which we doubt not will in this instance call on him, to abstain from pursuing a design which may indeed add to his poetic reputation, but can never procure for him any moral fame.

Don Juan's history being by no means *regular* and unbroken, we shall intrench on his life and adventures as arbitrarily as we please, and share his confidence only in those moments in which the true spirit of love and nature is manifested in him, strong and great. For a specimen of real grief and pathos, we give the lamentation of Donna Julia, the lady from whom he is torn away, which is worthy of Ariadne or of Dido:

[Stanzas CXCII–CXCVII of Canto I are quoted.]

The poet then proceeds to comment on this letter in an opposite tone of levity and cool indifference, and at the same time facetiously lets us into the design of his new Epic: ending with some brief 'poetic commandments,' in a style of parody which must disgust every good feeling of a pious mind. Ideas of another nature then come over the writer; and he appears as if he despised himself because he could be taught to 'smile at any thing.'

[Stanzas CCXIV–CCXXII of Canto I are quoted.]

Although these stanzas are not without palpable faults, they are bold, and sometimes extremely poetic. When the author gives way to his satirical humour in the delineation of character, as in that of Donna Inez, he is ridiculously happy: but we have no room to quote, as we intended, stanzas 22. to 32. In canto the second, when Don Juan is leaving his friends and country for a long voyage, we have a singular mixture of the sentimental and the ludicrous:

[Stanzas XVIII–XXII of Canto II are quoted.]

Still, whenever the poet chooses to confine himself to real energy and even sublimity of poetry, it is always at his command. His account of the shipwreck in the wide ocean, followed by the miseries of some survivors in a boat, who are reduced to the necessity of feeding on their own companions, is terrible even to the ear.

[Stanzas LII–LIII of Canto II are quoted.]

Lord Byron appears, however, to have worked up no part of his poem with so much beauty and life of description, as that which narrates the loves of Juan and Haidee. Whether it be an episode, or an integral portion of his epic, it is well worth all the rest. We quote as much as we dare, or can. On the beach, by moon-light, Juan has fallen asleep, with Haidee in his arms:

[Stanzas CXCVI–CCIII of Canto II are quoted.]

Lord Byron talks of his hair being grey at thirty: we have hair still whiter and years yet graver: but

'Old as we are, for ladies' love unfit,
The power of beauty we remember yet,
Which once inspired our love, and still inspires our wit.'

Voluptuous, then, as is his delineation of the delight which the sex confer on us in this world, and powerful as are the varied attractions of his pen, it requires some exertion to withdraw ourselves from his spell, and to bestow merited censure on all the abuses which he commits both as a painter and as a writer. We must, however, close his volume; and *again* we would remind him that these are not the deeds of which the recollection will enable him to say, on his deathbed, '*Nec me vixisse paenitet, quoniam ita vixi ut me non frustrà natum existimen.*'[1]

---

[1] 'I am not sorry to have lived, for I have lived in such a way that I do not consider my birth to have been in vain.'

Review of Byron's 'Don Juan', Cantos I–II

British Critic

2d ser. XII (*Aug. 1819*), *195–205. The reviewer is unknown.*

The cold reception of Mazeppa, must have given to Lord Byron rather a broad intimation of his decline in the public favour. Monotonous and mouthing mediocrity is but ill adapted to sustain a character which owes its advancement to a brilliant, wild, but meretricious irregularity. In Mazeppa, the noble Lord has travelled out of his usual latitude; his genius appears to have been chilled by the inclement air of the North, and even where it would rouse itself into exertion, it only the more betrays by a speedy relapse, the lethargy increasing upon it. If the poet be dull, the public will be indifferent; and Lord Byron has at last discovered that the occasional brilliancies of his former poems have not cast a protecting shield over the insignificance of his last. Some unusual exertion was necessary to recover the waning admiration of the public. A Satire was accordingly announced, in terms so happily mysterious, as to set the town on the very tiptoe of expectation. A thousand low and portentous murmurs preceded its birth. At one time it was declared to be so intolerably severe, that an alarming increase was to be apprehended in the catalogue of our national suicides—at another, it was stated to be of a complexion so blasphemous, as even in these days of liberality, to endanger the personal security of the bookseller.—The trade, it was whispered, had shrunk back, one by one, from all the splendid temptations which attended its publication.— Paternoster-row was paralysed.—As the time of its birth drew near, wonders multiplied; and, as at that of old Owen Glendower,

> '———At its nativity,
> The front of heaven (or *Morning Post*) was full of fiery shapes
> Of burning cressets.'

Fearful indeed was the prodigy—a book without a bookseller; an advertisement without an advertiser—'a deed without a name.' After all this portentous parturition, out creeps DON JUAN—and, doubtless, much to the general disappointment of the town, as innocent of satire, as any other Don in the Spanish dominions.

We confess that, notwithstanding all this mysterious machinery, we were rather incredulous as to the appearance of such a satire as was generally expected. We never doubted the rich store of poisoned arrows which lie ready for use in his Lordship's quiver, still less should we doubt his inclination to use them; but strange to say, we could hardly imagine an object against which they could be with safety discharged. The bad he knows that he dare not offend; the good he knows that he cannot hurt. Experience has furnished him with an ample store of anecdote and information, but experience has also taught him the value of his secret. The Noble Lord is now old enough to know the danger of offending his warmest admirers, and of quarrelling with his best friends. The Regent and his Ministers are game of a fairer and of a safer kind, inasmuch as the Satirist, is in their cases enabled to give full loose to those powers of invention, which might lead him into awkward consequences, if applied in the same sort of way to the characters of individuals. These, therefore, with two or three helpless poets, are the only objects upon which the Noble Lord could exercise his satirical propensities with security and effect.

If Don Juan then be not a satire—what is it? A more perplexing question could not be put to the critical squad. Of the four hundred and odd stanzas which the two Cantos contain, not a tittle could, even in the utmost latitude of interpretation, be dignified by the name of poetry. It has not wit enough to be comic; it has not spirit enough to make it lyric; nor is it didactic of any thing but mischief. The versification and morality are about upon a par; as far therefore as we are enabled to give it any character at all, we should pronounce it a narrative of degrading debauchery in doggrel rhyme.

But putting morality out of the question, the style which the Noble Lord has adopted is tedious and wearisome to a most insufferable degree. We are perfectly aware that it is not his own, but that it is borrowed from poets of high authority in ancient days. It is not, however, our intention to enter into any comparison of the imitation with the original, but simply to remark that no authority can justify what is radically tiresome and irrational. In the didactic, an easy flowing negligence of versification, is often peculiarly successful. But the hand of a master is even here especially required to check the licentiousness of indolence, and to prevent the familiar and the unnatural from degenerating into the vapid and the vulgar. The satires of Horace, and the Religio Laici of Dryden, cost them each as much or more trouble and care; than their more florid and elevated compositions; the former, indeed, appears anxious to repel the imputation either of carelessness or of haste, and the latter expressly declares, that the language of a poem designed for instruction 'ought to be plain and natural, and yet majestic.' The same characteristics should appear with but little variation in the satirical or the comic narration. The Absalom and Achithophel of Dryden, and the tales of Prior, though different in their subject and their style, are yet each in their way examples of the highest excellence in this department of poetry. We would not degrade them by drawing a comparison between them and the work before us.

Hudibras, indeed, is grossly familiar, but Hudibras is a burlesque; yet still, with all vigour of fancy and variety of learning, which adorn its inimitable author, Hudibras, as a whole, cannot be read without fatigue. Don Juan is no burlesque, nor mock heroic: it consists of the common adventures of a common man ill conceived, tediously told, and poorly illustrated. The Broad Grins of the facetious Colman, are tales somewhat in the style of our author: but amidst much vulgar ribaldry and licentious indecency, there is a broad and boisterous humour, both in his incidents and his character, which is quite irresistible: and in spite of our better sense, provokes a free and hearty laugh. Now certainly in the present thick and heavy quarto, containing upwards of four hundred doggrel stanzas, there are not a dozen places that even in the merriest mood could raise a smile. It is true that we may be very dull dogs, and as little able to comprehend the wit of his Lordship, as to construe his poetry.

Our account of the poem before us must necessarily be concise. Common decency will prevent us from following the hero of the Noble Lord through some of his adventures, and common sense through others. To give the reader, however, some notion of the style and manner of the whole, we shall present him with the birth and parentage of Don Juan.

[Stanzas VIII–XIV of Canto I are quoted.]

Now all this, we suppose, is very facetious. The Noble Lord is clearly desirous of displaying his wit, but we must confess that the joke is rather enigmatical. Where the point is to be found, and in what the humour consists, our dull brains are unable to discover. As in every block of stone there is a statue, so in every stanza there is doubt-less a joke, if we were initiated sufficiently in the art to find it out. But, alas, to our obtuse understandings the marble is marble still, and like the stanzas which we have cited, cold, rude, and heavy. Perhaps the Noble Lord considers the little touch of blasphemy, at the conclusion, as a sharp hit; to us it appears neither more nor less than a specimen of gross impiety, and flippant vulgarity.

We shall not conduct our readers through the shameless indecency, which characterizes the first canto. The apology of the Noble Lord at the conclusion is quite sufficient.

[Stanzas CCVII–CCVIII of Canto I are quoted.]

Surely this is trash—trash of the lowest order, and the dullest species; and as for the joke with which it is concluded, it is too stale for Joe Miller, too childish for Mr. Wewitzer, and too dull even for the moral *jocilegium* of Mr. Kett.[1] What the drift of the two following stanzas may be, we leave for others to discover.

CCIX.

'The public approbation I expect,
    And beg they'll take my word about the moral,
Which I with their amusement will connect,
    (So children cutting teeth receive a coral);
Meantime, they'll doubtless please to recollect
    My epical pretensions to the laurel:
For fear some prudish readers should grow skittish,
I've bribed my grandmother's review—the British.

CCX.

'I sent it in a letter to the editor,
    Who thank'd me duly by return of post—
I'm for a handsome article his creditor;
    Yet if my gentle Muse he please to roast,
And break a promise after having made it her,
    Denying the receipt of what it cost,
And smear his page with gall instead of honey,
All I can say is—that he had the money.' P. 107.

Whether it be the British Critic, or the British Review against which the Noble Lord prefers so grave, or rather so facetious an accusation,

[1] *Joe Miller's Jests* was a collection of jokes reputedly by Joe Miller, an actor and humorist, first published in 1739; similar collections were published by Henry Kett and Ralph Wewitzer in 1814 and 1815, respectively.

we are at a loss to determine. The latter, we understand, have thought it worth while, in a public paper, to make a serious reply.[1] As we are not so *seriously* inclined, we shall leave our share of the accusation to its fate—simply remarking, that authors who write for their bread, have too many calls for their money to waste it upon Editors, or their Reviews.

In the second canto, the Noble Lord has presented us with a ship-wreck. The vessel goes to the bottom, the crew are set adrift upon the ocean in an open boat, their provisions are exhausted, they draw lots who shall be immolated to satisfy the hunger of the remainder. These are circumstances which are drawn from the very depths of human woe. They are such as not only make the good and tender heart to melt, but even the most hardened to shudder. In these fearful narrations, pain and misery are not presented to our view merely in an embodied form; they are dissected and anatomized, as it were, before our eyes. There is a variety, there is a length, there is an endurance of evil which bows down our spirits while we read. In the scenes of confusion and agony attending a shipwreck, in the struggles for self-preservation, in the loss of so many souls, perhaps but too unprepared for their great account, in tracing the protracted sufferings of those whose lot is still to linger on in desperation drearier than death, in viewing a company of fellow-creatures on the wide ocean, devouring their last morsel, in witnessing hunger and thirst increasing upon them, the cannibal passions beginning to rise, the casting of lots for destruction, the self-immolation, the feast upon human blood, the frantic feeling of satiety—surely in bringing all these things home to our hearts, we can ill endure a full-born jest. Much less can we tolerate the mixing up these fearful events with low doggrel, and vapid absurdity. The poverty of a man's wit is never so conspicious, as when he is driven to a joke upon human misery.

[Stanzas XLIII–XLIV of Canto II are quoted.]

This specimen of the taste, the feeling, and the wit of the Noble Lord, will fully suffice. We will not, cannot follow him through the remainder of his disgusting melange. '*Sunt lacrymae rerum, et mentem mortalia tangunt*'[2] will ever be the honest, the tender feeling of the British nation.

---

[1] William Roberts, in the *British Review*, XIV (August 1819), 267–68, very solemnly denied the 'accusation', and this provoked Byron's 'Letter to My Grandmother's Review' in the first issue of the *Liberal*. Roberts, in his next review of *Don Juan* in the *British Review*, XVIII (December 1821), 263, claimed that he was aware of the ruse all along.

[2] 'There are tears for our affairs, and human mortality touches the soul.' Virgil *Aeneid* i. 461.

Notwithstanding his Lordship, and a few exotic dandies, who wear black stocks, and fancy that they look like his Lordship, may be of another notion, and another heart.

This is not

> 'Moody madness laughing wild
> Amid severest woe.'

In madness there is not a callous insensibility to human woe. In madness there is an excess of acute and irritable feeling. If in madness there is a quick perception of the ludicrous, there is a rapid, and almost electrical return to the serious. Even in the humour of a madman there is an acute apprehension of reality, which finds its way to the heart. But in the flippant doggrel of the Noble Lord, we can discover neither madness, nor its genius. All is calculating, vapid, and heartless. It is not mad, but bad—bad in expression, worse in taste, and worst of all in feeling and in heart.

Upon the indecency, and the blasphemy which this volume contains, a very few words will suffice. The adventures which it recounts are of such a nature, and described in such language, as to forbid its entrance within the doors of any modest woman, or decent man. Nor is it a history only, but a manual of profligacy. Its tendency is not only to excite the passions, but to point out the readiest means and method of their indulgence. Vice is here represented not merely in that grosser form which carries with it its own shame, and almost its own destruction, but in that alluring and sentimental shape, which at once captivates and corrupts. If without knowing the name of the poet, or the history of the work, our opinion had been required of the intention of the canto, we should have answered—that it was a calm and deliberate design to palliate and recommend the crime of adultery, to work up the passions of the young to its commission, and to afford them the most practical hints for its consummation. But it is not, we trust, by the maudlin and meritricious cant of the lascivious Little,[1] nor by the doggrel narrations of his friend and admirer, the author of the poem before us, that the British nation is to be tricked out of that main bulwark of its national strength, its sturdy and unbending morality.

Of the blasphemous sneers, so liberally scattered through the present volume, it is our intention to say but little. He that has no regard for the feelings of human misery, or for the claims of public morality, has not (and we should be sorry if he had) the slightest respect for public

[1] Little was a pseudonym used by Thomas Moore in his *Poetical Works of Thomas Little* (1801).

religion. The assaults of such a man are true Religion's best defence. Nor is it to be wondered, that the man who can so laboriously inculcate the breach of one commandment, should furnish a parody, *a la* Hone, of all the ten.[1] A parody indeed it is, but so miserable and poor, that it is really difficult to say whether the bad principle, or the bad poetry, most predominates. It certainly has not the sin of recommending itself by its wit.

The beauties of this strange production are very few. The best stanzas in the poem are the following:

[Stanzas CXXII–CXXIV of Canto I are quoted.]

The two first stanzas, though the ideas which they contain are common, have yet a sweetness, and an elegance in their expression, that gives them an air even of originality. In the third there is a lamentable falling off; we have seen many a better one upon the same subject, both in the work of Master George Dallas, aged only thirteen,[2] and of other school-boys equally precocious. In the second canto, there are stanzas descriptive of the sinking of the ship, in which the Noble Lord rises out of the circum-ambient doggrel.

[Stanzas LII–LIII of Canto II are quoted.]

We do not affect to say that we can construe, or understand every line of the preceding stanzas; but, in justice to the Noble Lord, we would not let any part of the poem which has the appearance even of beauty pass by, without paying it its due respect. We are the more anxious to present to the reader all that is worthy of his approbation, as we trust that the work itself will never be read, but in a Review. The good sense, and the good feeling of the English nation must, and will banish it from their houses. We should have the worst opinion indeed of any man, upon whose family table this volume were to lie exposed.

Reports from without, and evidence from within, fix this composition upon Lord Byron.[3] His name indeed is not upon the title-page; but this is not the first time that his Lordship has played off that piece of coquetry with the public. Should however his Lordship be tempted in reality to disavow it, we shall be among the first to hail the disavowal,

---

[1] William Hone was a Radical author whose satires on the government, published in 1817, were entitled *John Wilkes's Catechism, The Political Litany*, and the *Sinecurist's Creed*.

[2] Robert Charles Dallas, son of Sir George Dallas, in 1819 published the *Ode to the Duke of Wellington and other poems . . . written between the ages of eleven and thirteen.*

[3] *Don Juan* was published anonymously.

and to give it the publicity which it deserves, accompanying it with our sincere apology for having in common with the whole English nation, fixed upon his Lordship the stain of so flippant, dull and disgraceful a publication.

Review of Byron's 'Sardanapalus', 'The Two Foscari', and 'Cain'

Baldwin's *London Magazine*

V (Jan. 1822), 66–71. The author was probably Thomas Noon Talfourd, a lawyer, poet, and early editor of Lamb and Hazlitt. The authority for this tentative attribution is T. Rowland Hughes, 'The London Magazine' (Ph.D. dissertation, Oxford University, 1931).

'Once a jacobin, always a jacobin,' was formerly a paradox; 'but now the time gives it proof.' 'Once an aristocrat, always an aristocrat' might pass, with as little question, into a proverb. Lord Byron, who has sometimes sought to wrap himself in impenetrable mystery, who has worn the fantastic disguises of corsairs, giaours, and motley jesters, now comes out in all the dignity of his birth, arrayed in a court suit of the old French fashion, with the star glittering on his breast, and the coronet overtopping his laurels. The costume only has been changed, the man has been the same from the first. He has played off his most romantic vagaries from mere recklessness of will, in legitimate defiance of the world. When he sneered at human glory, at patriotism and virtue, put religion aside as an empty name, and scoffed at immortality as a 'tale that is told,' his rank gave him confidence and success. If he ranged over the mournful scenes of classic desolation, and called up the spirit of their old magnificence, he appealed almost exclusively to aristocratic sympathies. If he sought to represent the violence of passion as justifying its own excesses—to command admiration for the darkest spirits —or to bid a proud defiance to all established opinions and prejudices, he dared scarcely less as a lord than as a poet. In his very scorn of kings and rulers, there has been little regard for the common sorrows of the people; but a high feeling of injured dignity, a sort of careless ferocity, like that of Cataline amidst his hated foes and his despised supporters. On a lonely rock amidst the storm, in the moonlight shadows of the Colosseum, or pensively musing on the sad and silent shores of Greece, his nobility is ever with him. And now this Alcibiades of our literature, who has set all rules at defiance, who thought it sport to drag the critics 'panting after him in vain,' whose whole course has been one marvelous deviation from the beaten track of laureled bards, comes forth with his eulogies on Pope, and is pleased to patronize the unities![1] He who breathed about 'Manfred' its mighty mysticism, and there mingled in splendid confusion the spirits of various superstitions, now appears as the champion of dramatic coherence after the straitest sect in criticism. The 'chartered libertine,' who has made humanity a jest—who has scoffed not only at the forms and creeds of the pious, but at all which raises man above the dust on which he tramples—to whom the spirit of poetry even in himself has been a thing to mock at—now plays the rhetorician's part; discovers ethical poetry to be the finest thing in the world; and the author of that piece of shallowest philosophy, the Essay on Man, to be the first of ethic poets! This is the natural course of a man who has great powers, and great pride, with rank to sustain his excesses, and without that presiding and majestic faculty which would enable him to be master in his own heart, and to dispose into harmonious creations the vast elements within him. His present change, from the wild to the austere, is not the result of any principle harmonizing his faculties; but only a rash excursion into another style. Like a military adventurer drunk with glory, he rushes with half his forces into a strange country, trusting to his fortune and his name to defend him.

There are two of Lord Byron's characteristic excellencies which he never leaves behind in his most fantastic expeditions, and which he has accordingly brought into his new domain of classic tragedy. One of these is his intense feeling of the loveliness of woman—his power, not only of picturing individual forms, but of infusing into the very atmosphere which surrounds them the spirit of beauty and of love. A soft roseate light is spread over them, which seems to sink into the soul. The other faculty to which we allude is his comprehensive sympathy with the vastest objects in the material universe. There is scarcely any pure description of individual scenes in all his works; but the noblest allusions to the grandeurs of earth and heaven. He pays 'no allegiance but to the elements.' The moon, the stars, the ocean, the mountain desart, are endowed by him with new 'speech and language,'

---

[1] In his *A Letter to [John Murray] on the Rev. W. L. Bowles' Strictures on the Life and Writings of Pope* and in his Preface to *Sardanapalus*.

and send to the heart their mighty voices. He can interpret between us and the firmament, or give us all the sentiment of an everlasting solitude. His power in this respect differs essentially from that of Wordsworth who does not require an over-powering greatness in his theme, whom the 'meanest flower' can move to sweetest thoughts, to whom all earth is redolent with divinest associations, and in whose lowliest path beauty is ever present, 'a simple product of the common day.'

We believe that we may safely refer to one or other of these classes of beauty and grandeur almost every passage in the tragedies before us which deserves a place in the memory. Excepting where these occur, the plays appear to us 'coldly correct, and critically dull.' They abound in elaborate antitheses, frigid disputations, stately common places, and all the lofty trifling of those English tragedies which are badly modeled on the bad imitations of the Greeks by the French. There is little strongly marked character, little picturesque grouping, and scarcely any action. For pages together of laboured dialogue, the fable makes no progress—but the persons develope their own characters with the most edifying minuteness. We almost wish the rule of our law, that no man shall be a witness for or against himself, were rigidly applied to the drama. In the French courts of justice, and on the French stage, the rule is otherwise; but we need not desire to imitate the taste of our neighbours in criminal jurisprudence or in tragedy.

The poverty of the piece, on the striking history of *Sardanapalus*, has really surprised us. It afforded such room for towering luxury, such hints for the embodying in the person of the hero a mighty hunger and thirst after enjoyment, such fitting space for a great picture of Assyrian pomp, ennobled by the striking spectacle of the brave sensualist leaping from the dreamy deliciousness of his regal couch into a fiery grave, that we anticipated from the title a splendid wonder. How would some of our old poets have rioted in such a theme! How would their verses have breathed of the spicy east—how would they, with liberal hand, have showered on us 'barbaric pearl and gold'! But Lord Byron has been a very niggard of his Asiatic stores. His hero is a gentle epicurean philosopher, who is slothful on system, buries himself in his palace in mercy to his subjects, and is actually distinguished only from the class of sovereigns by his love for a lady to whom he is not married, and his neglect of his Queen. His tremulous abhorrence of even necessary bloodshed is utterly out of character in an oriental sensualist who can have no sense of the value of human existence, and is belied by the very carelessness with which he resigns his own. There is no feeling of luxury communicated to the mind of the reader; for the whole pomp hinted at in the course of the play, if faithfully copied, would hardly furnish one scene for a Covent Garden show. Even its catastrophe does not astonish or appal us; but happens almost as a thing of course. How little action it comprises, may be shortly known by a mere recapitulation of its scenes.

[A brief summary of Acts I–III is given. In Act II, a priest and a nobleman are said to 'hold long and leisurely conversations'.]

In the fourth act, Myrrha is discovered watching the troubled slumbers of the king, who, on waking, relates to her a frightful dream, which is the most ambitious piece of writing in the play; but it seems to us quite artificial and frigid.

Salemenes then begs his brother-in-law to grant his sister an interview, in which her patience and enduring love revive his old affection within him. This is the most beautiful and affecting scene in the play; but too long to be extracted. After another scene with Myrrha, beginning in coldness and ending in love, and a consultation with Salemenes on the posture of affairs, the monarch hastens again to battle. The fifth act opens with the following speech of Myrrha, who is gazing on the sun as it rises:—

[Lines 1–38 of Act V, scene i, are quoted.]

The greater part of this speech is very beautiful, though the description of the sun rolling back the vapours is apparently imitated from a magnificent scene in the second book of Wordsworth's Excursion which far surpasses it; and the closing lines are obscure. Salemenes is brought in to die; Sardanapalus enters defeated; news arrives that the Euphrates has swept down the bulwark; and the king, after providing for the safety of his friends, and ordering a funeral pyre to be heaped round the throne, dismisses all but Myrrha, who resolves to die with him. Nothing is then left them but to perish: Sardanapalus ascends the throne, and Myrrha fires the pile and prepares to rush into the flames, when the curtain falls. We will give the close of this scene, that the reader may decide on the justice of our opinion respecting its singular feebleness.

[Lines 467–98 of Act V, Scene i, are quoted.]

Can any thing be more ill-timed than the moralizing of the dying king about the Egyptian pyramids? The last thought in the speech, too, is taken from Fuller, the Church Historian, who quaintly observes, 'the pyramids, doting with age, have forgotten the names of their founders.' When we consider, that this play is nearly twice the length of any acted tragedy, we shall scarcely wonder that these incidents, expanded into such a length, are weakened by the plenitude of words. The following little dialogue, respecting the irruption of the river, may serve as a specimen of the expansive art of writing:—

> *Pania.*　　　　　With your sanction
> I will proceed to the spot, and take such measures
> For the assurance of the vacant space
> As time and means permit.
>
> *Sardanapalus.*　　　　About it straight,
> And bring me back as speedily as full
> And fair investigation may permit
> Report of the true state of this irruption
> Of waters.

The 'Two Foscari' is founded on the interesting story of the Son of a Venetian Doge, who was suspected of murder, and sentenced to exile; and who returned to his beloved home, only to be tortured and sent back into banishment, where he died broken hearted. Lord Byron has only taken the latter part of the tale: his piece opens with the sufferings of the young Foscari, after his return, and contains no incidents, except the repetition of his tortures, his second sentence of banishment, his death, and the deposition and death of his father. There is no character in it, except that of the old Doge, who is admirably depicted;—the quiet dignity, the deep, silent agony, scarcely perceived amidst the careful discharge of his great office, the noiseless attention to all forms and observances, while his aged heart is breaking; and the withering of the last support at the toll of the bell for the installation of his successor, form a fine Titian-like picture. But young Foscari, and his wife Marina, are merely the creatures of circumstance, excepting that he is a gentle, and she a vociferous sufferer. There are a few splendid speeches, and many choice felicities of expression in this piece; but, like Sardanapalus, it is far too much diluted. The reflections of poor Jacopo Foscari, on looking on the sea, while enjoying a short respite from torture, are very picturesque and intense. The guard opens a window in the prison, and addresses him:—

[Lines 92–127 of Act I, Scene i, are quoted.]

'Cain, a Mystery,' is altogether of a higher order than these classical tragedies. Lord Byron has not, indeed, fulfilled our expectations of a gigantic picture of the first murderer; for there is scarcely any passion, except the immediate agony of rage, which brings on the catastrophe; and Cain himself is little more than the subject of supernatural agency.

This piece is essentially nothing but a vehicle for striking allusions to the mighty abstractions of Death and Life, Eternity and Time, for vast but dim descriptions of the regions of space, and for daring disputations on that great problem, the origin of evil.

[A very brief summary of the story is given.]

The ground-work of the arguments, on the awful subjects handled, is very common place; but they are arrayed in great majesty of language, and conducted with a frightful audacity. The direct attacks on the goodness of God are such as we dare not utter or transcribe. They are not, perhaps, taken apart, bolder than some passages of Milton; but they inspire quite a different sensation, because, in thinking of Paradise Lost, we never regard the Deity, or Satan, as other than great adverse powers, created by the imagination of the poet. God is only the name for the King of Heaven, not for the Father of all. The personal identity which Milton has given to his spiritual intelligences,—the local habitations which he has assigned them,—the material beauty with which he has invested their forms,—all these remove the idea of impiety from their discourses. But we know nothing of Lord Byron's Lucifer, except his speeches; he is invented only that he may utter them; and the whole appears an abstract discussion, held for its own sake, not maintained in order to preserve the dramatic consistency of the persons. He has made no attempt to imitate Milton's plastic power;—that power by which our great poet has made his Heaven and Hell, and the very regions of space, sublime realities, palpable to the imagination, and has traced the lineaments of his angelic messengers with the precision of a sculptor. The Lucifer of 'Cain,' is a mere bodyless abstraction,—the shadow of a dogma; and all the scenery over which he presides is dim, vague, and seen only in faint outline. There is, no doubt, a very uncommon power displayed, even in this shadowing out of the ethereal journey of the spirit and his victim, and in the vast sketch of the world of phantasms at which they arrive; but they are utterly unlike the massive grandeurs of Milton's creation. This is one of the eloquent exclamations of Cain as he proceeds:

[Lines 98–117 of Act II, Scene i, are quoted.]

The region of the phantoms thus appears to Cain:—

[Lines 44–62 of Act II, Scene ii, are quoted.]

We are far from imputing intentional impiety to Lord Byron for this 'mystery;' nor, though its language sometimes shocks us, do we apprehend any danger will arise from its perusal. The difficulty on which it founds its 'obstinate questionings' has often recurred to every mind capable of meditating; it is equally felt in every system, except absolute Atheism; and, if it is reverently pursued, serves, while it baffles our scrutiny, to make us feel all the high capabilities, and intense yearnings, of our own immortal nature.

Review of Byron's 'Age of Bronze'

Blackwood's Magazine

XIII (April 1823), 457–60. The author was John Wilson, a minor poet and mainstay of Blackwood's: *see Alan L. Strout,* A Bibliography of Articles in Blackwood's Magazine 1817–1825 *(Lubbock, Texas, 1959), p. 107.*

This versifier has a slight and superficial knowledge of various matters of importance, gleaned from the Opposition newspapers, and the talk of inferior Whigs. He could write a leading article in the Morning Chronicle on the 'State of Europe,' or 'The Church;' and, no doubt, is reckoned eloquent by the gentlemen of the press over a board of oysters, or a trencher of tripe. But there is one thing which he does not know, although it is known to all his readers, *videlicet*, that he is an Ass. He vainly imagines that he neighs—a gross mistake;—it is a bray, we swear by all that is deep-drawn and long-winded. He supposes that his ears are pointed—not they indeed—they go flap-flapping over his forehead, a-la-donkey. He believes he *trots*—but it is all a shuffle. To be horse-whipped, is evidently the height of his ambition; but no—no— Peter Bell still lives, and with 'a sapling white as cream' he will 'bang thy bones.'[1]—So, come along, Jack-ass, and be cudgelled.

'The Age of Bronze' is not, by any means, a bad name for a Satirical poem, very far from it—and is evidently above the reach of the writer of the verses. It was probably a bright blunder of some one of his chums, to whom he had been braying a recital. Deady's heavy wet had inspired Pylades thus happily to designate the face of his Orestes. We can easily imagine that this felicitous discovery of a 'title,' must have led the two Arcadians into the most ruinous extravagance. A pot of porter would seem nothing in their exalted imaginations.—'Another Welch rabbit—Tommy—damn the expence;' and, on leaving the lush-crib,

---

[1] Phrases taken from the 1819 edition of Wordsworth's *Peter Bell.*

we can figure them giving fippence to the drawer. All down Chancery Lane chuckled the Cockneys, 'The Age of Bronze! The Age of Bronze!' while even their beloved washerwoman, now 'a maid that loves the moon,' wriggled before them unheeded under Temple-Bar.

This is not wholly a conjecture of ours—for something not unlike it was told us by a person of some veracity. He assured us that he was sitting close by the Cockneys and their cheese—with only a half-drawn curtain between; and that although he frequently coughed, and hemmed, and knocked the candlestick on his table, they were deaf to all entreaties, and let out

> 'Such tales as, told to any blade,
> By two such youths in the green shade,
> Were perilous to hear.'

Among other enormities, one of them, with a sort of Tims' face, proposed accusing Lord Byron of being the author.[1] That seemed at first a staggerer to the cove whose bunch of fives had actually committed the offence; but, after a few gulps of froth, he became courageous, and swore that 'it should be fathered upon Byron.' These, we are assured by a gentleman whose authority is far superior to that of Mr Nicholas Bull of Reading,[2] were without any exaggeration, the precise words. And accordingly, the 'Age of Bronze,' begotten by a Cockney, on the body of a muse, name unknown, is laid upon the steps before his Lordship's door. The noble Childe, careless about such matters, tells his valet to give the bantling to any woman in the house who chances to be nursing; and thus the ricketty wretch passes for the work of one whose real progeny always shew blood and bone, and glory in the sin of their sire.

In short, the author of the 'Age of Bronze'—the publisher thereof— and the paid puffers in the Radical newspapers, all know, that when they attribute the doggrel to Lord Byron—they are a pack of liars. The Cockneys have told the public, through their mouth-piece Hazlitt, that they have been damned by us, and that not a single Christian will look at any of their productions, lest suspicion might fall upon him of being acquainted with the author. The knaves, therefore, call themselves 'Byron!!' We remember once overtaking a person on foot near Lowood, on the banks of Windermere, who maintained that he was Mr Wordsworth. We had never seen the Great Laker at that time, yet well knew this was an imposter.—'I trow, sir,' quoth he, 'you never saw a more wonderful mountain than that there Langdale Peaks.' We gave

---

[1] *The Age of Bronze* was published anonymously.
[2] 'Mr Nicholas Bull' was probably an inside joke among the *Blackwood's* group.

him a slight kick, at which, we remember, he could scarcely conceal his irritation, and added, 'that the evening being calm, we should pursue our journey.' So we parted.

Now, the vagabond we kicked that evening, while the waters of Lowood Bay were murmuring near our foot, was not nearly so impertinent an imposter as the poor devil we have now put into the stocks. For, in the first place, he was sorely muddled with good Mr Ladyman's home-brewed; and, in the second place, he actually had written in a spunging-house (as we afterwards learned) some Sonnets for Baldwin's Magazine, in imitation of Wordsworth's Sonnets dedicated to Liberty. He therefore really had some sort of reason to believe himself a Lake poet, and we forgive him from the bottom of our souls, as we hope he forgives us from the bottom of his body. But the rogue in hand, although no doubt muddled also when he wrote his verses, may have been occasionally sober when they were going through the press, and we are afraid cannot be thought, even by the most charitable, to have been drunk every day on which his poem was sent to the newspapers for advertisement with Lord Byron's name. Paley, we think, considers drunkenness a palliation of guilt, and so does North; but the authority of these two great moral writers cannot exculpate this Cockney, unless he can prove to our satisfaction, that his knowledge-box was filled with the fumes of Daffy's elixir, from the first moment of conception, until the delivery of the foetus. He is plainly a scoundrel, who collects coin under false pretences; and his next heroic measures should be laid in the tread-mill.

But methinks we hear some gentle reader cry, 'This is not criticism—this is mere abuse.' We know it; it is not meant for criticism. If you catch a hand in your pocket, filching your purse, are you expected to criticise the shape of the fingers, or rather to wrench the wrist till the small bones crack? If a fellow, drest in his master's clothes, ring the bell at your front door, and leave his master's card, do you criticise or kick him? Let us therefore hear no more about our being abusive. This Cockney is a fool and a liar, in league with fools and liars; and neither he nor his fools and liars can take offence at being told so, except in as far as detection may prevent their future depredations on the public.

Let us see how this swindler personates Byron. Imagine that it is Byron who writes the following character of Pitt:—

'All is exploded—be it good or bad.
Reader! remember when thou wert a lad,
Then Pitt was all; or if not all, so much,
His very rival almost deem'd him such!!!'

What grandeur of thought and expression! Is not that at least equal to the Cockney's—whom we kicked—imitation of Wordsworth? Now for his character of Napoleon.

[Lines 131–40 are quoted.]

But hear—hear the swindler on Waterloo! Some one has told him that Byron hates Wellington, or pretends to do so; and the swindler makes a hit.

> 'Oh, bloody and most bootless Waterloo,
> Which proves how fools may have their fortune too
> Won, half by blunder, half by treachery.'

Various modes of punishing such a dishonest idiot as this must suggest themselves to the benevolent reader. Suppose him stripped naked to the very want of shirt, and tarred and feathered. Up Hampstead Hill he goes, with his downy posteriors, like one of Mr Moore's Angels,[1] to recover himself, to a crowing fit on his own dunghill. Flap flies the feathered fool past Mother Red-cap's on a Sunday evening, and haply takes refuge in an arbour of a tea-garden. Or suppose him ducked in a shallow, green-mantled, slimy, froggy pool, with a sludge bottom, and then rubbed down with a towel of nettles. Or suppose him condemned to a year's solitary confinement in the jakes, without the use of either pen, ink, or paper.

But let us hear his opinion of Congress:

[Lines 398–411 and 434–43 are quoted.]

Now here let us make, not a political, but a personal observation. We have seen the Czar—and he is a strapping fellow, upwards of six feet high—good looking—healthy—broad-shouldered—an excellent dancer —a tolerable musician—fences well—and altogether is a man likely to make his way through a crowd. Now, who the devil, Mister Bronze, are you, to talk so of a man who could swallow you any morning before breakfast? We sink the Emperor at present altogether—and we compare merely Calmuck or Cossack with Cockney. We shall suppose Alexander a beggar like yourself—with not one shilling to rub against another. Were you both to endeavour to gain your bread by honest industry as paviers—you know that Alexander would plant ten pebbles for your one. Were you both to rob on the highway, you know that he would knock down a man and his wife with ease, while Master Tommy would take you prisoner. Were you both to woo a rich widow

[1] Thomas Moore had published his *Loves of the Angels* in 1823.

286

—conscience must whisper that she would prefer 'the Calmuck beauty with the Cossack wit,' to the little impotent Cockney. Were you both to appear in the Row, or offer yourselves contributors to Colbourn, is there a publisher or editor in London city, who would not smile upon the Russ? In short, is there an occupation extant, except tailoring and polishing of silver tea-spoons, in which the Calmuck would not beat the Cockney to utter starvation?

Much light, we think, may be thrown on subjects of this kind, by such a simple treatment. Scribblers, who bite their nails in Great Britain, take it into their heads, that because they have been born in this island, (no matter whether spuriously or not) they are entitled to despise, be he who he may, the Emperor of all the Russias. But there are base Britons—and a base Briton is the basest of beings. No Russ can be so wretched as he—and the Cockney who writes as above, of the battle of Waterloo, is a more degraded culprit than any slit-nosed, knouted Muscovite, that ever journeyed across the steppes to Siberia.

[Lines 528-39 are quoted.]

Silence—slave! If you yourself—your abject most miserable self—were to go into a jeweller's shop, and purloin a number of gold brooches—were to be detected in the act, and brought back shrieking in the grasp of the shop-keeper's daughter—were to be committed to New-gate—and there to contrive, in fear of the gallows, to effect strangulation with your dirty worsted garters, or fetid leather braces—is there a single person in all London who would not turn away, almost with something like pity mingled with disgust, from the hole in the cross-ways, into which were flung the petty remains of the pilfering *felo de se*? Do you know that?—and yet—but silence—slave! Who would spit upon a toad crawling in its unwieldy and freckled putrefaction? It is enough to see the reptile drag itself in slime away into some common sewer—to be washed down by the mingled mud of kennels, along with every stinking thing, into a subterranean receptacle of filth, there to rot among the hidden abominations—

'The Age of Bronze' by Lord Byron!!!

Review of Byron's 'Don Juan', Cantos IX–XI

Blackwood's Magazine

XIV (Sept. 1823), 282–93. The author was John Gibson Lockhart, a writer, lawyer, and later editor of the Quarterly Review: *see Alan L. Strout,* A Bibliography of Articles in Blackwood's Magazine 1817–1825 *(Lubbock, Texas, 1959), p. 111. This review is in the form of a letter from Morgan ODoherty to Christopher North (usually John Wilson), both of them fictitious characters used by the magazine. Lockhart was also the author of the vicious attack on Keats in* Blackwood's.

DEAR NORTH,—I have a great respect both for old Tickler and yourself, but now and then you both disquiet me with little occasional bits of lapses into the crying sin of the age—*humbug!* What could possess him to write, and you to publish, that absurd critique—if indeed it be worthy of any such name—upon the penult batch of Don Juan?[1] The ancient scribe must have read those cantos when he was crop-sick, and had snapped his fiddle-string. You must never have read them at all.

Call things wicked, base, vile, obscene, blasphemous; run your tackle to its last inch upon these scores, but never say that they are stupid when they are not. I cannot suffer this sort of cant from YOU. Leave it to Wordsworth to call Voltaire 'a dull scoffer.' Leave it to the British Review to talk of 'the dotage' of Lord Byron. Depend upon it, your chief claim to merit as a critic has always been *your justice* to INTELLECT.

[1] 'Letters of Timothy Tickler. No. VII, *Blackwood's Magazine*, XIV (July 1823), 80–92. William Maginn and Lockhart himself collaborated on the section concerning *Don Juan*: see Alan L. Strout, *A Bibliography of Articles in Blackwood's Magazine 1817–1825* (Lubbock, Texas, 1959), p. 110.

I cannot bear to see you parting with a shred of this high reputation. It was you 'that first praised Shelley as he deserved to be praised.' Mr Tickler himself said so in his last admirable letter to you. It was in your pages that justice was first done to Lamb and to Coleridge—greatest of all, it was through and by you that the public opinion was first turned in regard to the poetry of Wordsworth himself.—These are things which never can be forgotten; these are your true and your most honourable triumphs. Do not, I beseech you, allow your claim to this noble distinction to be called in question. Do not let it be said, that even in one instance you have suffered any prejudices whatever, no matter on what proper feelings they may have been bottomed, to interfere with your candour as a judge of *intellectual* exertion.—Distinguish as you please: brand with the mark of your indignation whatever offends your feelings, moral, political, or religious—but 'nothing extenuate.' If you mention a book at all, say what it really is. Blame Don Juan; blame Faublas; blame Candide; but blame them for what really is deserving of blame. Stick to your own good old rule—abuse Wickedness, but acknowledge Wit.

In regard to such a man as Byron, this, it must be evident, is absolutely necessary—that is, if you really wish, which you have always said you do, to be of any use to him. Good heavens! Do you imagine that people will believe three cantos of DON JUAN to be unredeemedly and uniformly DULL, merely upon your saying so, without proving what you say by quotation? No such things need be expected by you, North, far less by any of your coadjutors.

I maintain, and have always maintained, that Don Juan is, without exception, the first of Lord Byron's works. It is by far the most original in point of *conception*. It is decidedly original in point of *tone*, (for to talk of the tone of Berni, &c. being in the least like this, is pitiable stuff: Any old Italian of the 15th or 16th century write in the same tone with Lord Byron! Stuff! stuff!)—It contains the finest specimens of serious poetry he has ever written; and it contains the finest specimens of ludicrous poetry that our age has witnessed. Frere may have written the stanza earlier;[1] he may have written it more carefully, more musically if you will; but what is he to Byron? Where is the sweep, the pith, the soaring pinion, the lavish luxury, of genius revelling in strength? No, sir; Don Juan, say the canting world what it will, is destined to hold a permanent rank in the literature of our country. It will always be referred to as furnishing the most powerful picture of that vein of thought, (no matter how false and bad,) which distinguishes *a great*

[1] John Hookham Frere had used the ottava rima in his *Prospectus and Specimen of an Intended National Work, by William and Robert Whistlecraft* (1817–18).

portion of the thinking people of our time. You and I disagree with them—we do not think so; we apprehend that to think so, is to think greenly, rashly, and wickedly; but who can deny, that many, many thousands, do think so? Who can deny, that that is valuable in a certain way which paints the prevailing sentiment of a large proportion of the people of any given age in the world? Or, who, that admits these things, can honestly hesitate to admit that Don Juan is a great work—a work that must last? I cannot.

And, after all, say the worst of Don Juan, that can with fairness be said of it, what does the thing amount to? Is it *more* obscene than Tom Jones?—Is it *more* blasphemous than Voltaire's novels? In point of fact, it is not within fifty miles of either of them: and as to obscenity, there is more of that in the pious Richardson's pious Pamela, than in all the novels and poems that have been written since.

The whole that can with justice be said of Byron, *as to these two great charges*, is, that he has practised in this age something of the licence of the age of our grandfathers. In doing so, he has acted egregiously amiss. The things were bad, nobody can doubt that, and we had got rid of them; and it did not become a man of Byron's genius to try to make his age retrograde in anything, least of all in such things as these. He also has acted most unwisely and imprudently in regard to himself. By offending the feelings of his age, in regard to points of this nature, he has undone himself as a popular writer.—I don't mean to say that he has done so for ever—Mercy and Repentance forbid! but he has done so most effectually for the present. People make excuses for Fielding and Voltaire, because they don't know in how far these men may have been acted upon by circumstances: but people will not make *such* excuses for Lord Byron, because they know, we all know, that he was educated among the same sort of people as ourselves, that he must know and feel the same things to be wrong which his neighbours know and feel to be so. He, therefore, is no longer a popular author. But,—and here I come back to my question—Is he no longer a great author? Has his genius deserted him along with his prudence? Is his Hippocrene lazy as well as impure? Has he ceased, in other words, to be Byron, or is he only Byron playing mad tricks?

The latter is my opinion, and I propose to convince you, in case you are not already of the same mind, by quoting a few passages from the other three cantos that have just appeared—and which I humbly conceive to be the very best, in so far as talent is concerned, of all that have as yet come forth. I desire you to match me, if you can, the things I shall extract from this *dull* work. I should be glad to know where you can shew me anything better than this. Read it as I send it to you. I have scored out abundantly, but I have added nothing; and I defy you to say the description is not admirable, or to mention anybody, except Byron, who could have penned it.[1]

[The last two lines of stanza XLII–XLVII, LI–LIV, the last four lines of stanza LVII–LXI, and LXVII–LXVIII of Canto IX are quoted. A note by Christopher North to line 342 reads: 'We do not believe anything about Leigh Hunt's having interpolated Don Juan; yet candour must admit, that the mention of the yellow breeches here is startling.

'Our own opinion is, that Byron put them in as a quizz upon the Cockney, just to see what he would swallow.']

The following is part of an apostrophe to Mr Francisculus Jeffrey, whose prosing Review of April was a year [a year ago?][2] his Lordship really seems to have been a little touched by.

[Stanzas XIV–XV of Canto X are quoted. The last two lines read:

—not so *you*, I own;
As Caesar wore his robe you wear your gown.]

What is the meaning of the compliment in the two last of these lines? Jeffrey wears his *gown* as Julius did his *robe*! The only particular mention that I remember of Caesar's robe is, that he used it to cover his fall. In the language of old Plutarch, 'they surrounded him in such a manner, that whatever way he turned he saw nothing but steel gleaming in his face, and *met nothing but wounds*. Like some savage beast, attacked by the hunters, he found every hand lifted against him. *Some say he opposed the rest, and continued struggling and crying out, till he perceived the sword of Brutus; but that then he* DREW HIS ROBE OVER HIS FACE, AND YIELDED TO HIS FATE.'—(LANGHORNE's *Plutarch*, vol. v. p. 362.) What, then, is the meaning of Byron? Is it that so long as Jeffrey was attacked by 'the rest of the critical hunters,' he continued struggling, but that when he saw the sword of the god-like Brutus North, Esq., he yielded to his fate, and drew his gown over his face—that is, gave up Blue and Yellow,[3] and slunk into the mere Advocate! This, certainly, is the natural construction of the passage, and most true it certainly is, that, comparing

---

[1] [We mention Mr. O'Doherty for one.—C. N.—Note by Christopher North, pseudonym of John Wilson.]

[2] The review probably meant was Francis Jeffrey's critique of Byron's *Sardanapalus* volume in Vol. XXXVI, dated February 1822.

[3] Buff and blue, the colors of the Foxite Whigs, adorned the covers of the *Edinburgh Review*.

very great things to very small ones,—'as Julius wore his robe, Jeff wears his gown.'

The following account of Juan's life at Petersburgh, is, I think extremely good:—

[Stanzas XXIII–XXXIV of Canto X are quoted.]

What can be better, again, than the rapid sketch of the hero's journey from Russia to England?—Take this specimen.

[Stanzas LX–LXV and LXXI of Canto X are quoted.]

Take this one stanza on the first glimpse of LONDON! How many hundred times has the thing been *tried* before?

[Stanza LXXXII of Canto X is quoted.]

My excellent friend, John Bull,[1] quotes the following incident on Shooter's Hill as *bad*:—I, Morgan ODoherty, quote it as exquisitely good. Judge between us! I conceive it to be almost, if not altogether, as fine as a certain passage in the life of Ferdinand Count Fathom—of which it is indeed (in so far) a manifest imitation. I think the slang very commendable; and I think, in short, that the little bits I have put in Italics are superb.

[Stanzas VIII–XXIV of Canto XI are quoted. Lines 124–28 and all of stanza XXIV are italicized by the reviewer.]

What think you of the ensuing *morceau* on Life in London?

[Stanzas LXV–LXIX of Canto XI are quoted.]

Or what thinks any one that has more NOUS than Dr Tornhippson,[2] of this verse on 'the Young Noble?'

[Stanza LXXV of Canto XI is quoted.]

Or of this noble burst?

[Stanzas LXXVI–LXXVII and LXXIX–LXXXII are quoted.]

Now, my dear North, I sincerely hope you will gratify me so far, as to put these verses in without curtailment, and that for three good and sufficient reasons, viz.—

1st, They occur in the original work in the midst of so much beastliness, gross filth, outrageous filth, abominable filth, that it is quite impossible they should have been seen by far the greater proportion of

---

[1] *John Bull* was a violently reactionary periodical begun in 1820.
[2] 'Dr. Tornhippson' was also most probably a *Blackwood's* joke—see p. 284, note 2, above.

your readers. Don Juan is a sealed book to the ladies of our time, (to say no more,) and you will be doing them a great favour in thus affording a few extracts, upon the 'Family Bowdler'[1] principle, from a work, which, as a whole, they have no chance of seeing; or, if they did see it, of reading three pages in it without blushing to the back-bone. This will be a benefit.

2dly, Another great benefit will be this, that you will, by doing as I suggest, restore the line, which in former days always distinguished YOU from what Plutarch calls, 'the rest of the hunters;' and which I was very sorry to see my worthy friend Timothy Tickler, of all men in the world, doing his best to erase and obliterate. You will shew the world that you are still the old Christopher—too manly to deny anything that you feel, too just to confound together two questions essentially separate and distinct—the question of *moral tendency*, and that of *intellectual power*.

3dly, By vindicating your character as to this matter, you will give your own voice a chance of being really listened to by this singular man when you happen to address him in the words of admonition. A man like Byron will feel when any one calls him a devil for a piece of blackguardism; but he will only laugh at being called a dunce for a piece of brilliancy, even by YOU. That there is a prodigious deal of blackguardism in these three cantos, who can deny? What can be more so than to attack THE KING, as this Lord does, with low, vile, personal buffooneries—bottomed in utter falsehood, and expressed in crawling malice? Nothing, nothing. What can be more exquisitely worthy of contempt than the savage imbecility of these eternal tirades against the Duke of Wellington? What more pitiable than the state of mind that can find any gratification in calling such a man as Southey by nicknames that one would be ashamed of applying to a coal-heaver? What can be so abject as this eternal trampling upon the dust of Castlereagh? Shame! shame! shame! Byron ought to know, that all men of all parties (for Cockneys are not men, and saloop-parties are not parties,) unite in regarding all these things, but especially the first and the last, as insults to themselves, and as most miserable degradations of HIM. But he ought to be told this in a sensible manner. He ought not to be treated as if he were a driveller, or capable of being mistaken for one even for a moment; but he ought to be told plainly, distinctly, solemnly, and with a total negation of all humbug, that he is a writer of extraordinary talents—that Don Juan contains the outline of an extraordinary poem— and that he is voluntarily ruining both himself and his production.

[1] Thomas Bowdler was an expurgator who published his *Family Shakespeare* in 1818.

I observe some of the Monthly idiots talk of 'Don Juan' as if it were a by-job of Lord Byron's—a thing that he just takes up now and then, when he is (I must quote their own sweet words) 'relaxing from the fatigues of more serious literary exertions.' This I look upon as trash of the first water. It is very likely—indeed I have no doubt of it—that a canto of Don Juan costs Lord Byron much less trouble than a 'Werner' or a 'Cain.' In like manner, I daresay, one of Voltaire's lumbering tragedies cost Voltaire ten times more fatigue than ten Zadigs, Taureau Blancs, or Princesses of Babylon, would have done. In like manner, I have no doubt Wordsworth's 'Convention of Cintra' pamphlet cost him much more trouble than his 'Ruth,' or his 'Song for Brougham Castle,' or his 'Hart-leap Well.' In like manner, I have no doubt the Monthly List of Deaths, Marriages, Births, Bankruptcies, Patents, and Promotions, costs you more trouble than the 'Leading Article.' But this is not the way to judge of these things. Almost any one canto of Juan—certainly any one of these three—contains more poetry and more genius than any three of Byron's recent tragic attempts have done. The worthy I have been dishing probably opines that Lord Byron dashes off a canto of the Don after a tragedy, just as he himself *does* an article for 'My Grandmother,' after he has finished his sermon for next Sunday.

I shall now beg leave to 'relax from the fatigue of this serious literary exertion' over a tumbler of gin-twist; and, wishing mine Editor many similar relaxations, remain his most humble servant,

M. ODoherty.

Kilkenny, Sept. 12.

IV
Keats

Reviews of Keats's 'Poems' of 1817

Champion

March 9, 1817, p. 78. The author was probably John Hamilton Reynolds: see J. M. Turnbull, 'Keats, Reynolds, and The Champion', *London Mercury, XIX (1929), 384–94, and Hyder E. Rollins, 'Keats's Elgin Marbles Sonnets',* University of Missouri Studies, XXI (1946) 163–66.

Here is a little volume filled throughout with very graceful and genuine poetry. The author is a very young man, and one, as we augur from the present work, that is likely to make a great addition to those who would overthrow that artificial taste which French criticism has long planted amongst us. At a time when nothing is talked of but the power and the passion of Lord Byron, and the playful and elegant fancy of Moore, and the correctness of Rogers, and the sublimity and pathos of Campbell (these terms we should conceive are kept ready composed in the Edinburgh Review-shop) a young man starts suddenly before us, with a genius that is likely to eclipse them all. He comes fresh from nature,—and the originals of his images are to be found in her keeping. Young writers are in general in their early productions imitators of their favourite poet; like young birds that in their first songs, mock the notes of those warblers, they hear the most, and love the best: but this youthful poet appears to have tuned his voice in solitudes,—to have sung from the pure inspiration of nature. In the simple meadows he has proved that he can

> '——See shapes of light, aerial lymning,
> And catch soft floating from a faint heard hymning.'

We find in his poetry the glorious effect of summer days and leafy spots on rich feelings, which are in themselves a summer. He relies directly and wholly on nature. He marries poesy to genuine simplicity.

He makes her artless,—yet abstains carefully from giving her an un-comely homeliness:—that is, he shows she can be familiar with nature, yet perfectly strange to the habits of common life. Mr. Keats is fated, or 'we have no judgment in an honest face;' to look at natural objects with his mind, as Shakespeare and Chaucer did,—and not merely with his eye as nearly all modern poets do;—to clothe his poetry with a grand intellectual light,—and to lay his name in the lap of immortality. Our readers will think that we are speaking too highly of this young poet,—but luckily we have the power of making good the ground on which we prophecy so hardily. We shall extract largely from his volume:—It will be seen how familiar he is with all that is green, light, and beautiful in nature;—and with what an originality his mind dwells on all great or graceful objects. His imagination is very powerful,—and one thing we have observed with pleasure, that it never attempts to soar on undue occasions. The imagination, like the eagle on the rock, should keep its eye constantly on the sun,—and should never be started heavenward, unless something magnificent marred its solitude. Again, though Mr. Keats' poetry is remarkably abstracted, it is never out of reach of the mind; there are one or two established writers of this day who think that mystery is the soul of poetry—that artlessness is a vice—and that nothing can be graceful that is not metaphysical,—and even young writers have sunk into this error, and endeavoured to puzzle the world with a confused sensibility. We must however hasten to the consideration of the little volume before us, and not fill up our columns with observations, which extracts will render un-necessary.

The first poem in the book[1] seems to have originated in a ramble in some romantic spot, 'with boughs pavillioned.' The poet describes a delightful time, and a little world of trees,—and refreshing streams,—and hedges of filberts and wild briar, and clumps of woodbine

'———taking the wind
Upon their summer thrones.'

and flowers opening in the early sunlight. He connects the love of poetry with these natural luxuries.

'For what has made the sage or poet write,
But the fair paradise of Nature's light?'

This leads him to speak of some of our olden tales; and here we must

[1] 'I stood tip-toe.'

298

extract the passages describing those of Psyche, and Narcissus. The first is exquisitely written.

> 'So felt he, who first told, how Psyche went
> On the smooth wind to realms of wonderment;
> What Psyche felt, and Love, when their full lips
> First touch'd; what amorous and fondling nips
> They gave each other's cheeks; with all their sighs,
> And how they kist each other's tremulous eyes;
> The silver lamp—the ravishment—the wonder—
> The darkness—loneliness—the fearful thunder;
> Their woes gone by, and both to heaven upflown,
> To bow for gratitude before Jove's throne.'

The following passage is not less beautiful,

[Lines 163–80 are quoted.]

This Poem concludes with a brief but beautiful recital of the tale of Endymion,—to which indeed the whole poems seem to lean. The Address to the Moon is extremely fine.

[Lines 113–24 are quoted.]

'The Specimen of an induction to a poem,' is exceedingly spirited,— as is the fragment of a Tale of Romance immediately following it; but we cannot stay to notice them particularly. These four lines from the latter piece are very sweet.

> 'The side-long view of swelling leafiness,
> Which the glad setting sun in gold doth dress;
> Whence ever and anon the jay outsprings,
> And scales upon the beauty of its wings.'

The three poems following, addressed to Ladies, and the one to Hope are very inferior to their companions;—but Mr. Keats informs us they were written at an earlier period than the rest. The imitation of Spenser is rich. The opening stanza is a fair specimen.

[The first stanza of 'Imitation of Spenser' is quoted.]

The two Epistles to his friends, and one to his brother are written with great ease and power. We shall extract two passages, both equally beautiful.

[Lines 31–52 of the Epistle 'To George Felton Mathew' are quoted.]

The next passage is from the opening of the poet's letter to a friend.[1]

'Oft have you seen a swan superbly frowning,
And with proud breast his own white shadow crowning;
He slants his neck beneath the waters bright,
So silently, it seems a beam of light
Come from the galaxy: anon he sports,—
With outspread wings the Naiad Zephyr courts,
Or ruffles all the surface of the lake
In striving from the chrystal face to take
Some diamond water drops, and them to treasure
In milky nest, and sip them off at leisure.
But not a moment can he there insure them,
Nor to such downy rest can he allure them;
For down they rush as though they would be free,
And drop like hours into eternity.
Just like that bird am I in loss of time,
Whene'er I venture on the stream of rhyme;
With shatter'd boat, oar snapt, and canvass rent,
I slowly sail, scarce knowing my intent;
Still scooping up the water with my fingers,
In which trembling diamond never lingers.'

Except in a little confusion of metaphor towards the end, the above passage is exquisitely imagined and executed.

A few Sonnets follow these epistles, and, with the exception of Milton's and Wordsworth's, we think them the most powerful ones in the whole range of English poetry. We extract the first in the collection, with the assurance that the rest are equally great.

['To My Brother George' is quoted.]

We have been highly pleased with that Sonnet[2] which speaks—

'Of fair hair'd Milton's eloquent distress,
And all his love for gentle Lycid drown'd;—
Of lovely Laura in her light green dress,
And faithful Petrarch gloriously crown'd.'

But the last poem in the volume, to which we are now come, is the most powerful and the most perfect. It is entitled 'Sleep and Poetry.' The poet past a wakeful night at a brother poet's house, and has in this piece embodied the thoughts which passed over his mind. He gives his

[1] Epistle 'To Charles Cowden Clarke'.
[2] Sonnet IX, 'Keen, fitful gusts'.

opinion of the Elizabethan age,—of the Pope's school,—and of the poetry of the present day. We scarcely know what to select,—we are so confused with the beauties. In speaking of poetry, we find the following splendid passage:—

[Lines 71–84 are quoted.]

The following passage relating to the same, is even greater. It is the very magic of imagination.

[Lines 125–37 are quoted.]

We have not room to extract the passages on Pope and his followers, who,

> '——With a puling force,
> Sway'd them about upon a rocking horse,
> And thought it Pegasus.'

Nor can we give those on the modern poets. We shall conclude our extracts with the following perfect and beautiful lines on the busts and pictures which hung around the room in which he was resting.

[Lines 381–95 are quoted.]

We conclude with earnestly recommending the work to all our readers. It is not without defects, which may be easily mentioned, and as easily rectified. The author, from his natural freedom of versification, at times passes to an absolute faultiness of measure:—This he should avoid. He should also abstain from the use of compound epithets as much as possible. He has a few of the faults which youth must have; —he is apt occasionally to make his descriptions over-wrought,—But on the whole we never saw a book which had so little reason to plead youth as its excuse. The best poets of the day might not blush to own it.

We have had two Sonnets presented to us, which were written by Mr. Keats, and which are not printed in the present volume. We have great pleasure in giving them to the public,—as well on account of their own power and beauty, as of the grandeur of the subjects; on which we have ourselves so often made observations.

['To Haydon, with a Sonnet on seeing the Elgin Marbles' and 'On seeing the Elgin Marbles for the first time' are quoted.]

European Magazine

LXXI (May 1817), 434–37. The author was identified at the end of the review by the initials G.F.M., or George Felton Mathew. He was a friend of Keats; one of the Epistles in the Poems *was addressed to him.*

There are few writers more frequent or more presumptuous in their intrusions on the public than, we know not what to call them, versifiers, rhymists, metre-ballad mongers, what you will but poets. The productions of some among them rise, like the smoke of an obscure cottage, clog the air with an obtrusive vapour, and then fade away into oblivion and nothingness. The compositions of others equally ephemeral, but possessing, perhaps, a few eccentric features of originality, come upon us with a flash and an explosion, rising into the air like a rocket, pouring forth its short-lived splendour and then falling, like Lucifer, *never to rise again.*

The attention of the public, indeed, has been so frequently arrested and abused by these exhalations of ignorance, perverted genius, and presumption, that 'poems' has become a dull feature upon a title page, and it would be well for the more worthy candidates for regard and honour, particularly at this physiognomical, or, rather craniological period, could the spirit of an author be reflected there with more expressive fidelity.[1] A quotation from, and a wood-engraving of *Spenser,* therefore, on the title page of Mr. Keats's volume, is very judiciously and appropriately introduced as the poetical beauties of the volume we are about to review, remind us much of that elegant and romantic writer.

For the grand, elaborate, and abstracted music of nature our author has a fine ear, and now and then catches a few notes from passages of that never-ending harmony which God made to retain in exaltation and purity the spirits of our first parents. In 'places of Nestling-green for poets made,' we have this gentle address to Cynthia:

[Lines 116–24 of 'I stood tip-toe' are quoted.]

And also in his last poem, concerning sleep, the following interrogations and apostrophes are very pleasing:

[Lines 1–11 of 'Sleep and Poetry' are quoted.]

---

[1] Studies in phrenology and craniology were very popular in the period. See the *Edinburgh Review,* XXV (June 1815), 227–68, and the *Quarterly Review,* XIII (April 1815), 159–78.

The volume before us indeed is full of imaginations and descriptions equally delicate and elegant with these; but, although we have looked into it with pleasure, and strongly recommend it to the perusal of all lovers of real poetry, we cannot, as another critic has injudiciously attempted, roll the name of Byron, Moore, Campbell and Rogers, into the milky way of literature, because Keats is pouring forth his splendors in the Orient. We do not imagine that the fame of one poet, depends upon the fall of another, or that our morning and our evening stars necessarily eclipse the constellations of the meridian.

Too much praise is more injurious than censure, and forms that magnifying lens, through which, the faults and deformities of its object are augmented and enlarged; while true merit looks more lovely beaming through the clouds of prejudice and envy, because it adds to admiration and esteem the association of superior feelings.

We cannot then advance for our author equal claim to public notice for maturity of thought, propriety of feeling, or felicity of style. But while we blame the slovenly independance of his versification, we must allow that thought, sentiment, and feeling, particularly in the active use and poetical display of them, belong more to the maturity of summer fruits than to the infancy of vernal blossoms; to that knowledge of the human mind and heart which is acquired only by observation and experience, than to the early age, or fervid imagination of our promising author. But if the gay colours and the sweet fragrance of bursting blossoms be the promise of future treasures, then may we prophecy boldly of the future eminence of our young poet, for we have no where found them so early or so beautifully displayed as in the pages of the volume before us.

The youthful architect may be discovered in the petty arguments of his principal pieces. These poetical structures may be compared to no gorgeous palaces, no solemn temples; and in his enmity to the French school, and to the Augustan age of England, he seems to have a principle, that plan and arrangement are prejudicial to natural poetry.

The principal conception of his first poem is the same as that of a contemporary author, Mr. Wordsworth, and presumes that the most ancient poets, who are the inventors of the Heathen Mythology, imagined those fables chiefly by the personification of many appearances in nature; just as the astronomers of Egypt gave name and figure to many of our constellations, and as the late Dr. Darwin ingeniously illustrated the science of Botany in a poem called 'the Loves of the Plants.'[1]

[1] See note 1, p. 6, above.

After having painted a few 'places of nestling green, for poets made' thus Mr. Keats:

[Lines 163–80 of 'I stood tip-toe' are quoted.]

In the fragment of a Tale of Romance, young Calidore is amusing himself in a little boat in the park, till, hearing the trumpet of the warder, which announces the arrival of his friends at the castle, he hastens home to meet them: in after times we presume he is to become the hero of some marvellous achievements, devoting himself, like Quixotte, to the service of the ladies, redressing wrongs, dispelling the machinations of evil genii, encountering dragons, traversing regions aerial, terrestrial, and infernal, setting a price upon the heads of all giants, and forwarding them, trunkless, like 'a cargo of famed cestrian cheese,' as a dutiful tribute to the unrivalled beauty of his fair Dulcenea del Toboso. This fragment is as pretty and as innocent as childishness can make it, save that it savours too much,—as indeed do almost all these poems,—of the foppery and affectation of Leigh Hunt!

We shall pass over to the last of some minor pieces printed in the middle of the book, of superior versification, indeed, but of which, therefore, he seems to be partly ashamed, from a declaration that they were written earlier than the rest. These lines are spirited and powerful:

> 'Ah! who can e'er forget so fair a being?
> Who can forget her half retiring sweets?
> God she is like a milk-white lamb that bleats
> For man's protection. Surely the All-seeing,
> Who joys to see us with his gifts agreeing,
> Will never give him pinions, who intreats
> Such innocence to ruin; who vilely cheats
> A dove-like bosom. * * *!'[1]

There are some good sonnets; that on first looking into Chapman's Homer, although absurd in its application, is a fair specimen:

[The sonnet is quoted in full.]

'Till I heard Chapman speak out loud and bold' however, is a bad line—not only as it breaks the metaphor—but as it blows out the whole sonnet into an unseemly hyperbole. Consistent with this sonnet is a passage in his 'Sleep and Poetry.'

[Lines 181–206 are quoted.]

[1] Lines 29–36 of 'Woman! when I behold thee'.

These lines are indeed satirical and poignant, but levelled at the author of Eloise, and of Windsor Forest; of the Essays and the Satires, they will form no sun, no centre of a system; but like the moon exploded from the South Sea, the mere satellite will revolve only around the head of its own author, and reflect upon him an unchanging face of ridicule and rebuke. Like Balaam's ass before the angel, offensive only to the power that goads it on.

We might transcribe the whole volume were we to point out every instance of the luxuriance of his imagination, and the puerility of his sentiments. With these distinguishing features, it cannot be but many passages will appear abstracted and obscure. Feeble and false thoughts are easily lost sight of in the redundance of poetical decoration.

To conclude, if the principal is worth encountering, or the passage worth quoting, he says:

> 'Let there nothing be
> More boist'rous than a lover's bended knee:
> Nought more ungentle than the placid look
> Of one who leans upon a closed book;
> Nought more untranquil than the grassy slopes
> Between two hills.—All hail delightful hopes!
> As she was wont, the imagination
> Into most lovely labyrinths will be gone,
> And they shall be accounted Poet Kings
> Who simply tell the most hearteasing things.
> O may these joys be ripe before I die.'[1]

Though he well adds:

> 'Will not some say that I presumptuously
> Have spoken? that from hastening disgrace
> 'Twere better far to hide my foolish face?'

Let not Mr. Keats imagine that the sole end of poesy is attained by those

> 'Who strive with the bright golden wing
> Of genius, to flap away each sting
> Thrown by the pitiless world.'[2]

But remember that there is a sublimer height to which the spirit of the muse may soar; and that her arm is able to uphold the adamantine

[1] Lines 259–69 of 'Sleep and Poetry'.
[2] Lines 63–65 of the Epistle 'To George Felton Mathew'.

shield of virtue, and guard the soul from those insinuating sentiments, so fatally inculcated by many of the most popular writers of the day, equally repugnant both to reason and religion, which, if they touch us with their poisoned points, will contaminate our purity, inoculate us with degeneracy and corruption, and overthrow among us the dominion of domestic peace and public liberty.

Religion and the love of virtue are not inconsistent with the character of a poet: they should shine like the moon upon his thoughts, direct the course of his enquiries, and illuminate his reflections upon mankind. We consider that the specimens here presented to our readers, will establish our opinion of Mr. Keats's poetical imagination; but the mere luxuries of imagination, more especially in the possession of the proud egotist of diseased feelings and perverted principles, may become the ruin of a people—inculcate the falsest and most dangerous ideas of the condition of humanity—and refine us into the degeneracy of butterflies that perish in the deceitful glories of a destructive taper. These observations might be considered impertinent, were they applied to one who had discovered any incapacity for loftier flights—to one who could not appreciate the energies of Milton or of Shakspeare—to one who could not soar to the heights of poesy,—and ultimately hope to bind his brows with the glorious sunbeams of immortality.

G.F.M.

Eclectic Review

2d ser. VIII (Sept. 1817), 267–75. The author was Josiah Conder, a minor poet, bookseller, and editor of the Eclectic *from 1814 to 1836. Authority for this attribution is the marked staff copies of the* Eclectic *now in the London Library.*

There is perhaps no description of publication that comes before us, in which there is for the most part discovered less of what is emphatically denominated *thought*, than in a volume of miscellaneous poems. We do not speak of works which obviously bear the traits of incapacity in the Author. Productions of this kind abound in more than one department of literature; yet in some of those which rank at the very lowest degree of mediocrity, there is occasionally displayed a struggling effort of mind to do its best, which gives an interest and a character to what possesses no claims to originality of genius, or to intrinsic value. But poetry is that one class of written compositions, in which the business of expression seems often so completely to engross the Author's attention, as to suspend altogether that exercise of the rational faculties which we term *thinking*; as if in the same limited sense as that in which we speak of the arts of music and painting, poetry also might be termed an art; and in that case indeed the easiest of arts, as requiring less previous training of faculty, and no happy peculiarity either in the conformation of the organs, or in the acquired delicacy of the perceptions. So accustomed however are we to find poetry thus characterized, as consisting in the mysteries of versification and expression, so learnedly treated of in all the 'Arts of Poetry' extant, from Horace down to Mr. Bysshe, that it is not surprising that the generality of those who sit down to write verses, should aim at no higher intellectual exertion, than the melodious arrangement of 'the cross readings of memory.'[1] Poetry is an art, and it is an elegant art: and so is the writing of prose, properly speaking, an art likewise; and they are no otherwise distinguishable from each other, than as being different styles of composition suited to different modes of thought. Poetry is the more ornate, but not, perhaps, in its simpler forms, the more artificial style of the two: the purpose, however, to which it is directed, requires a more minute elaboration of expression, than prose. But what should we think of a person's professedly sitting down to write prose, or to read prose composition, without reference to any subject, or to the quality of the thoughts, without any definite object but the amusement afforded by the euphonous collocation of sentences? As a school exercise, the employment, no doubt, would be beneficial; but were the writer to proceed still further, and publish his prose, not for any important or interesting sentiment conveyed in his work, but as presenting polished specimens of the beautiful art of prose-writing, it would certainly be placed to the account of mental aberration.

On what ground, then, does the notion rest, that poetry is a something so sublime, or that so inherent a charm resides in words and syllables arranged in the form of verse, that the value of the composition is in any degree independent of the meaning which links together the sentences? We admit that rhythm and cadence, and rhymed couplets, have a pleasurable effect upon the ear, and more than this, that words have in themselves a power of awakening trains of association, when the ideas which they convey are very indistinct, and do not constitute or account for the whole impression. It may be added, that the perception of skill or successful art, is also attended with pleasurable emotions; and this circumstance forms, in addition to what we have already mentioned, a powerful ingredient in the whole combination of effect produced by genuine poetry: but that the mere art of setting

[1] Edward Bysshe published *The Art of English Poetry* in 1702.

words to the music of measure, should come to be regarded as the chief business of poetry, and the ultimate object of the writer, is so whimsical a prejudice, that after a brief exposition of the fact, it may be worth while to inquire a little into its cause.

As to the fact, it would be travelling too far out of the record, to make this notice of a small volume of poems, a pretence for instituting an examination of all the popular poets of the day. Suffice it to refer to the distinct schools into which they and their imitators, as incurable mannerists, are divided, as some evidence that mode of expression has come to form too much the distinguishing characteristic of modern poetry. Upon an impartial estimate of the intellectual quality of some of those poems which rank the highest in the public favour, it will be found to be really of a very humble description. As works of genius, they may deservedly rank high, because there is as much scope for genius in the achievements of art as in the energies of thought; but as productions of mind, in which respect their real value must after all be estimated, they lay the reader under small obligations. Wordsworth is by far the deepest thinker of our modern poets, yet he has been sometimes misled by a false theory, to adopt a puerile style of composition; and it is remarkable, that the palpable failure should be charged on his diction, which is attributable rather to the character of the thought, themselves; they were not adapted to any form of poetical expressions inasmuch as they are not worth being expressed at all. Scott, of all our leading poets, though the most exquisite artist, occupies the lowest rank in respect to the intellectual quality of his productions. Scarcely an observation or a sentiment escapes him, in the whole compass of his poetry, that even the beauty of expression can render striking or worth being treasured up by the reader for after reference. The only passages recurred to with interest, or cited with effect, are those admirable specimens of scenic painting in which he succeeds beyond almost every poet, in making one see and hear whatever he describes. But when we descend from such writers as confessedly occupy the first rank, to the [hoi polloi] of their imitators, respectable as many of them are, and far above mediocrity considered as artists, the characters of sterling thought, of intellect in action, become very faint and rare. It is evident that, in their estimation, to write poetry is an achievement which costs no laborious exercise of faculty; is an innocent recreation rather, to which the consideration of any moral purpose would be altogether foreign.

Now, on turning from the polished versification of the elegant *artists* of the present day, to the rugged numbers of our early poets, the most obvious feature in the refreshing contrast is, the life and the

vividness of thought diffused over their poetry. We term this originality, and ascribe the effect either to their pre-eminent genius, or to the
early age in which they flourished, which forced upon them the toil of
invention. But originality forms by no means a test of intellectual pre-
eminence; and we have proof sufficient, that originality does not necessarily depend on priority of time. Provided the person be capable of
the requisite effort of abstraction, nothing more is necessary in order
to his attaining a certain degree of originality, than that his thoughts
should bear the stamp of individuality, which is impressed by self-
reflective study. In the earlier stages of the arts, we behold mind acting
from itself, through the medium of outward forms, consulting its own
purpose as the rule of its working, and referring to nature as its only
model. But when the same arts have reached the period of more refined
cultivation, they cease to be considered as means through which to
convey to other minds the energies of thought and feeling: the productions of art become themselves the ultimate objects of imitation,
and the mind is acted upon by them instead of acting through them
from itself. Mind cannot be imitated; art can be: and when imitative
skill has brought an art the nearest to perfection, it is then that its
cultivation is the least allied to mind: its original purpose, as a mode of
expression, becomes wholly lost in the artificial object,—the display
of skill.

We consider poetry as being in the present day in this very predicament; as being reduced by the increased facilities of imitation, to an
elegant art, and as having suffered a forcible divorce from thought.
Some of our young poets have been making violent efforts to attain
originality, and in order to accomplish this, they have been seeking
with some success for new models of imitation in the earlier poets,
presenting to us as the result, something of the quaintness, as well as
the freedom and boldness of expression characteristic of those writers,
in the form and with the effect of novelties. But after all, this specious
sort of originality lies wholly in the turn of expression; it is only the
last effort of the cleverness of skill to turn eccentric, when the perfection of correctness is no longer new. We know of no path to
legitimate originality, but one, and that is, by restoring poetry to its
true dignity as a vehicle for noble thoughts and generous feelings,
instead of rendering meaning the mere accident of verse. Let the comparative insignificance of art be duly appreciated, and let the purpose
and the meaning be considered as giving the expression all its value;
and then, so long as men think and feel for themselves, we shall have
poets truly and simply original.

We have no hesitation in pronouncing the Author of these Poems, to be capable of writing good poetry, for he has the requisite fancy and skill which constitute the talent. We cannot, however, accept this volume as any thing more than an immature promise of possible excellence. There is, indeed, little in it that is positively good, as to the quality of either the thoughts or the expressions. Unless Mr. Keats has designedly kept back the best part of his mind, we must take the narrow range of ideas and feelings in these Poems, as an indication of his not having yet entered in earnest on the business of intellectual acquirement, or attained the full development of his moral faculties. To this account we are disposed to place the deficiencies in point of sentiment sometimes bordering upon childishness, and the nebulous character of the meaning in many passages which occur in the present volume. Mr. Keats dedicates his volume to Mr. Leigh Hunt, in a sonnet which, as possibly originating in the warmth of gratitude, may be pardoned its extravagance; and he has obviously been seduced by the same partiality, to take him as his model in the subsequent poem, to which is affixed a motto from the 'Story of Rimini.' To Mr. Hunt's poetical genius we have repeatedly borne testimony, but the affectation which vitiates his style must needs be aggravated to a ridiculous excess in the copyist. Mr. Hunt is sometimes a successful imitator of the manner of our elder poets, but this imitation will not do at second hand, for ceasing then to remind us of those originals, it becomes simply unpleasing.

Our first specimen of Mr. Keats's powers, shall be taken from the opening of the poem alluded to.

[Lines 1–60 of 'I stood tip-toe' are quoted.]

There is certainly considerable taste and sprightliness in some parts of this description, and the whole poem has a sort of summer's day glow diffused over it, but it shuts up in mist and obscurity.

After a 'specimen of an induction to a poem,' we have next a fragment, entitled Calidore, which, in the same indistinct and dreamy style, describes the romantic adventure of a Sir Somebody, who is introduced 'paddling o'er a lake,' edged with easy slopes and 'swelling leafiness,' and who comes to a castle gloomy and grand, with halls and corridor, where he finds 'sweet-lipped ladies,' and so forth; and all this is told with an air of mystery that holds out continually to the reader the promise of something interesting just about to be told, when, on turning the leaf, the Will o' the Wisp vanishes, and leaves him in darkness. However ingenious such a trick of skill may be, when the writer is too indolent, or feels incompetent to pursue his story, the production cannot claim to be read a second time; and it may therefore be questioned, without captiousness, whether it was worth printing for the sake of a few good lines which ambitiously aspired to overleap the portfolio.

The 'epistles' are much in the same style, *all about* poetry, and seem to be the first efflorescence of the unpruned fancy, which must pass away before any thing like genuine excellence can be produced. The sonnets are perhaps the best things in the volume. We subjoin one addressed 'To my brother George.'

[The entire sonnet is quoted.]

The 'strange assay' entitled Sleep and Poetry, if its forming the closing poem indicates that it is to be taken as the result of the Author's latest efforts, would seem to shew that he is indeed far gone, beyond the reach of the efficacy either of praise or censure, in affectation and absurdity. We must indulge the reader with a specimen.

[Lines 270–93 are quoted.]

We must be allowed, however, to express a doubt whether its [poetry's] nature has been as clearly perceived by the Author, or he surely would never have been able to impose even upon himself as poetry the precious nonsense which he has here decked out in rhyme. Mr. Keats speaks of

> 'The silence when some rhymes are coming out,
> And when they're come, *the very pleasant rout;*'

and to the dangerous fascination of this employment we must attribute this half-awake rhapsody. Our Author is a very facetious rhymer. We have *Wallace* and *solace*, *tenderness* and *slenderness*, *burrs* and *sepulchres*, *favours* and *behaviours*, *livers* and *rivers*;—and again,

> '*Where we may soft humanity put on,*
> And sit and rhyme, and think on *Chatterton.*'

Mr. Keats has satirized certain *pseudo* poets, who,

> 'With a puling infant's force,
> Sway'd about upon a rocking horse,
> And thought it Pegasus.'

Satire is a two-edged weapon: the lines brought irresistibly to our imagination the Author of these poems in the very attitude he describes. Seriously, however, we regret that a young man of vivid imagination

and fine talents, should have fallen into so bad hands, as to have been
flattered into the resolution to publish verses, of which a few years
hence he will be glad to escape from the remembrance. The lash of a
critic is the thing the least to be dreaded, as the penalty of premature
publication. To have committed one's self in the character of a versifier,
is often a formidable obstacle to be surmounted in after-life, when
other aims require that we should obtain credit for different, and what
a vulgar prejudice deems opposite qualifications. No species of authorship is attended by equal inconvenience in this respect. When a man
has established his character in any useful sphere of exertion, the fame
of the poet may be safely sought as a finish to his reputation. When
he has shewn that he can do something else besides writing poetry,
then, and not till then, may he safely trust the public with his secret.
But the sound of a violin from a barrister's chamber, is not a more
fatal augury than the poet's lyre strummed by a youth whose odes are
as yet all addressed to Hope and Fortune.

But perhaps the chief danger respects the individual character, a
danger which equally attends the alternative of success or failure.
Should a young man of fine genius, but of half-furnished mind, succeed
in conciliating applause by his first productions, it is a fearful chance
that his energies are not dwarfed by the intoxication of vanity, or that
he does not give himself up to the indolent day-dream of some splendid
achievement never to be realized. Poetical fame, when conceded to
early productions, is, if deserved, seldom the fruit of that patient self-
cultivation and pains-taking, which in every department of worthy
exertion are the only means of excellence; and it is but the natural
consequence of this easy acquisition of gratification, that it induces a
distaste for severer mental labour. Should, however, this fatal success
be denied, the tetchy aspirant after fame is sometimes driven to seek
compensation to his mortified vanity, in the plaudits of some worthless
coterie, whose friendship consists in mutual flattery, or in community
in crime, or, it may be, to vent his rancour in the satire of envy, or in
the malignity of *patriotism*.

Exceptions, brilliant exceptions, are to be found in the annals of
literature, and these make the critic's task one of peculiar delicacy. The
case has occurred, when a phlegmatic Reviewer, in a fit of morning
spleen, or of after-dinner dulness, has had it in his power to dash to
the ground, by his pen, the innocent hopes of a youth struggling for
honourable distinction amid all the disadvantages of poverty, or to
break the bruised reed of a tender and melancholy spirit; but such an
opportunity of doing mischief must of necessity be happily rare. Instances have also been, in which the performances of maturer life have

fully redeemed the splendid pledge afforded by the young Author, in his first crude and unequal efforts, with which he has had to thank the stern critic that he did not rest self-satisfied. Upon the latter kind of exceptions, we would wish to fix Mr. Keats's attention, feeling perfectly confident, as we do, that the patronage of the friend he is content to please, places him wholly out of the danger of adding to the number of those who are lost to the public for want of the smile of praise.

Mr. Keats has, however, a claim to leave upon our readers the full impression of his poetry; and we shall therefore give insertion to another of his sonnets, which we have selected as simple and pleasing:

['Happy is England' is quoted in full.]

Edinburgh Magazine

2d ser. I (Oct. 1817), 254–57. The reviewer is unknown.

Of the author of this small volume we know nothing more than that he is said to be a very young man, and a particular friend of the Messrs Hunt, the editors of the Examiner, and of Mr Hazlitt. His youth accounts well enough for some injudicious luxuriancies and other faults in his poems; and his intimacy with two of the wittiest writers of their day, sufficiently vouches both for his intellect and his taste. Going altogether out of the road of high raised passion and romantic enterprise, into which many ordinary versifiers have been drawn after the example of the famous poets of our time, he has attached himself to a model more pure than some of these, we imagine; and, at the same time, as poetical as the best of them. 'Sage, serious' *Spencer*, the most melodious and mildly fanciful of our old English poets, is Mr Keats's favourite. He takes his motto from him,—puts his head on his title-page,—and writes one of his most luxurious descriptions of nature in his measure. We find, indeed, *Spencerianisms* scattered through all his other verses, of whatsoever measure or character. But, though these things sufficiently point out where Mr K. has caught his inspiration, they by no means determine the general character of his manner, which partakes a great deal of that *picturesqueness* of fancy and licentious brilliancy of epithet which distinguish the early Italian novelists and amorous poets. For instance, those who know the careless, sketchy, capricious, and yet archly-thoughtful manner of *Pulci* and *Ariosto*, will understand what we mean from the following specimens, better than from any laboured or specific assertion of ours.

[Lines 61–68 and 87–106 of 'I stood tip-toe' and lines 110–42 of the Epistle 'To My Brother George' are quoted.]

This is so easy, and so like the ardent fancies of an aspiring and poetical spirit, that we have a real pleasure in quoting, for the benefit of our readers, another fragment of one of Mr Keats's *epistles*:

[Lines 1–14 of the Epistle 'To Charles Cowden Clarke' are quoted.]

All this is just, and brilliant too,—though rather ambitious to be kept up for any length of time in a proper and fitting strain. What follows appears to us the very pink of the smart and flowing conversational style. It is truly such elegant *badinage* as should pass between scholars and gentlemen who can feel as well as judge.

[Lines 109–33 of the Epistle 'To Charles Cowden Clarke' are quoted.]

These specimens will be enough to shew that Mr K. has ventured on ground very dangerous for a young poet;—calculated, we think, to fatigue his ingenuity, and try his resources of fancy, without producing any permanent effect adequate to the expenditure of either. He seems to have formed his poetical predilections in exactly the same direction as Mr Hunt; and to write, from personal choice, as well as emulation, at all times, in that strain which can be most recommended to the favour of the general readers of poetry, only by the critical ingenuity and peculiar refinements of Mr Hazlitt. That style is vivacious, smart, witty, changeful, sparkling, and learned—full of bright points and flashy expressions that strike and even seem to please by a sudden boldness of novelty,—rather abounding in familiarities of conception and oddnesses of manner which shew ingenuity, even though they be perverse, or common, or contemptuous. The writers themselves seem to be persons of considerable taste, and of comfortable pretensions, who really appear as much alive to the socialities and sensual enjoyments of life, as to the contemplative beauties of nature. In addition to their familiarity, though,—they appear to be too full of conceits and sparkling points, ever to excite any thing more than a cold approbation at the long-run—and too fond, even in their favourite descriptions of nature, of a reference to the factitious resemblances of society, ever to touch the heart. Their verse is straggling and uneven, without the lengthened flow of blank verse, or the pointed connection of couplets. They aim laudably enough at force and freshness, but are not so careful of the inlets of vulgarity, nor so self-denying to the temptations of indolence, as to make their force a merit. In their admiration of some of our elder writers, they have forgot the fate of

Withers and Ben Jonson, and May: And, without forgetting that Petrarch and Cowley are hardly read, though it be decent to profess admiration of them,—they seem not to bear in mind the appalling doom which awaits the faults of mannerism or the ambition of a sickly refinement. To justify the conclusions of their poetical philosophy, they are brave enough to sacrifice the sympathetic enthusiasm of their art, and that common fame which recurs to the mind with the ready freshness of remembered verse,—to a system of which the fruits come, at last, to make us exclaim with Lycidas,

'*Numeros* memini, si verba tenerem.'[1]

If Mr Keats does not forthwith cast off the uncleannesses of this school, he will never make his way to the truest strain of poetry in which, taking him by himself, it appears he might succeed. We are not afraid to say before the good among our readers, that we think this true strain dwells on features of manly singleness of heart, or feminine simplicity and constancy of affection,—mixed up with feelings of rational devotion, and impressions of independence spread over pictures of domestic happiness and social kindness,—more than on the fiery and resolute, the proud and repulsive aspects of misnamed humanity. It is something which bears, in fact, the direct impress of natural passion,—which depends for its effect on the shadowings of unsophisticated emotion, and takes no merit from the refinements of a metaphysical wit, or the giddy wanderings of an untamed imagination,—but is content with the glory of stimulating, rather than of oppressing, the sluggishness of ordinary conceptions.

It would be cold and contemptible not to hope well of one who has expressed his love of nature so touchingly as Mr K. has done in the following sonnets:

['O Solitude! if I must with thee dwell' and 'To one who has been long in city pent' are quoted in full.]

Another sonnet, addressed to Mr Haydon the painter, appears to us very felicitous. *The thought*, indeed, of the first eight lines is altogether admirable; and the whole has a veritable air of Milton about it which has not been given, in the same extent, to any other poet except Wordsworth.

[The entire sonnet is quoted.]

---

[1] 'The melody I remember, if only I could remember the words.' Virgil *Eclogues* ix.45.

We are sorry that we can quote no more of these sweet verses which have in them so deep a tone of moral energy, and such a zest of the pathos of genius. We are loth to part with this poet of promise, and are vexed that critical justice requires us to mention some passages of considerable affectation, and marks of offensive haste, which he has permitted to go forth into his volume. 'Leafy luxury,' 'jaunty streams,' 'lawny slope,' 'the moon-beamy air,' 'a sun-beamy tale;' these, if not namby-pamby, are, at least, the 'holiday and lady terms' of those poor affected creatures who write verses 'in spite of nature and their stars.'—

> 'A little noiseless noise among the leaves,
> Born of the very sigh that silence heaves.'[1]

This is worthy only of the Rosa Matildas whom the strong-handed Gifford put down.[2]

> 'To possess but a span of the hour of leisure,'[3]

> 'No sooner had I stepped into these pleasures.'[4]

These are two of the most unpoetical of Mr K.'s lines,—but they are not single. We cannot part, however, on bad terms with the author of such a glorious and Virgilian conception as this:

> 'The moon lifting her silver rim
> Above a cloud, and with a gradual swim
> Coming into the blue with all her light.'[5]

A striking natural vicissitude has hardly been expressed better by Virgil himself,—though the severe simpleness of his age, and the compact structure of its language, do so much for him in every instance:

> 'Ipse Pater, mediâ nimborum in nocte, coruscâ
> Fulmina molitur dextra.'[6]

---

[1] Lines 11–12 of 'I stood tip-toe'.

[2] William Gifford, later editor of the *Quarterly Review*, wrote two satires against the Della Cruscan school of English poets in the late eighteenth century. Anna (not Rosa) Matilda was a pseudonym for Mrs Hannah Cowley, a member of the school.

[3] Line 27 of 'To Some Ladies'.

[4] Line 97 of 'To Charles Cowden Clarke'.

[5] Lines 113–15 of 'I stood tip-toe'.

[6] 'The Father, enthroned in midnight cloud, hurls from a flashing right hand his lightning'. Virgil *Georgics* i.328, 329, trans. C. Day Lewis.

Review of Keats's 'Poems' of 1817 and 'Endymion'

Blackwood's Magazine

III (Aug. 1818), 519-24. The author was John Gibson Lockhart, a writer, lawyer, and later editor of the Quarterly Review; *see Alan L. Strout,* A Bibliography of Articles in Blackwood's Magazine 1817-1825 *(Lubbock, Texas, 1959), p. 43. This review was actually the fourth number of a series, the Cockney School of Poetry.*

————OF KEATS,

THE MUSES' SON OF PROMISE, AND WHAT FEATS
HE YET MAY DO, &c.

CORNELIUS WEBB.[1]

Of all the manias of this mad age, the most incurable, as well as the most common, seems to be no other than the *Metromanie.* The just celebrity of Robert Burns and Miss Baillie has had the melancholy effect of turning the heads of we know not how many farm-servants and unmarried ladies; our very footmen compose tragedies, and there is scarcely a superannuated governess in the island that does not leave a roll of lyrics behind her in her band-box. To witness the disease of any human understanding, however feeble, is distressing; but the spectacle of an able mind reduced to a state of insanity is of course ten times more afflicting. It is with such sorrow as this that we have contemplated the case of Mr John Keats. This young man appears to have received from nature talents of an excellent, perhaps even of a superior order—talents which, devoted to the purposes of any useful profession,

[1] The motto poem to the 'Cockney School' Series was possibly part of a eulogistic poem by Cornelius Webb, a sometime member of the Hampstead set. See J. R. MacGillivray, *Keats, A Bibliography and Reference Guide* (Toronto, 1949), pp. xix-xx.

must have rendered him a respectable, if not an eminent citizen. His friends, we understand, destined him to the career of medicine, and he was bound apprentice some years ago to a worthy apothecary in town. But all has been undone by a sudden attack of the malady to which we have alluded. Whether Mr John had been sent home with a diuretic or composing draught to some patient far gone in the poetical mania, we have not heard. This much is certain, that he has caught the infection, and that thoroughly. For some time we were in hopes, that he might get off with a violent fit or two; but of late the symptoms are terrible. The phrenzy of the 'Poems' was bad enough in its way; but it did not alarm us half so seriously as the calm, settled, imperturbable drivelling idiocy of 'Endymion.' We hope, however, that in so young a person, and with a constitution originally so good, even now the disease is not utterly incurable. Time, firm treatment, and rational restraint, do much for many apparently hopeless invalids; and if Mr Keats should happen, at some interval of reason, to cast his eye upon our pages, he may perhaps be convinced of the existence of his malady, which, in such cases, is often all that is necessary to put the patient in a fair way of being cured.

The readers of the Examiner newspaper were informed, some time ago, by a solemn paragraph, in Mr Hunt's best style, of the appearance of two new stars of glorious magnitude and splendour in the poetical horizon of the land of Cockaigne. One of these turned out, by and by, to be no other than Mr John Keats. This precocious adulation confirmed the wavering apprentice in his desire to quit the gallipots, and at the same time excited in his too susceptible mind a fatal admiration for the character and talents of the most worthless and affected of all the versifiers of our time. One of his first productions was the following sonnet, *'written on the day when Mr Leigh Hunt left prison.'* It will be recollected, that the cause of Hunt's confinement was a series of libels against his sovereign, and that its fruit was the odious and incestuous 'Story of Rimini.'

[The entire sonnet is quoted. The following phrases are italicized by the reviewer: Kind Hunt, In Spenser's halls, With daring Milton.]

The absurdity of the thought in this sonnet is, however, if possible, surpassed in another, *'addressed to Haydon'* the painter, that clever, but most affected artist, who as little resembles Raphael in genius as he does in person, notwithstanding the foppery of having his hair curled over his shoulders in the old Italian fashion. In this exquisite piece it will be observed, that Mr Keats classes together WORDSWORTH, HUNT, and HAYDON, as the three greatest spirits of the age, and that he alludes to himself, and some others of the rising brood of Cockneys, as likely to attain hereafter an equally honourable elevation. Wordsworth and Hunt! what a juxta-position! The purest, the loftiest, and, we do not fear to say it, the most classical of living English poets, joined together in the same compliment with the meanest, the filthiest, and the most vulgar of Cockney poetasters. No wonder that he who could be guilty of this should class Haydon with Raphael, and himself with Spenser.

[The entire sonnet is quoted. Lines 5–6 and 13–15 are italicized by the reviewer.]

The nations are to listen and be dumb! and why, good Johnny Keats? because Leigh Hunt is editor of the Examiner, and Haydon has painted the judgment of Solomon, and you and Cornelius Webb, and a few more city sparks, are pleased to look upon yourselves as so many future Shakspeares and Miltons! The world has really some reason to look to its foundations! Here is a *tempestas in matulâ* with a vengeance. At the period when these sonnets were published, Mr Keats had no hesitation in saying, that he looked on himself as '*not yet* a glorious denizen of the wide heaven of poetry,' but he had many fine soothing visions of coming greatness, and many rare plans of study to prepare him for it. The following we think is very pretty raving.

[Lines 89–121 of 'Sleep and Poetry' are quoted.]

Having cooled a little from this 'fine passion,' our youthful poet passes very naturally into a long strain of foaming abuse against a certain class of English Poets, whom, with Pope at their head, it is much the fashion with the ignorant unsettled pretenders of the present time to undervalue. Begging these gentlemen's pardon, although Pope was not a poet of the same high order with some who are now living, yet, to deny his genius, is just about as absurd as to dispute that of Wordsworth, or to believe in that of Hunt. Above all things, it is most pitiably ridiculous to hear men, of whom their country will always have reason to be proud, reviled by uneducated and flimsy striplings, who are not capable of understanding either their merits, or those of any other *men of power*—fanciful dreaming tea-drinkers, who, without logic enough to analyse a single idea, or imagination enough to form one original image, or learning enough to distinguish between the written language of Englishmen and the spoken jargon of Cockneys, presume to talk with contempt of some of the most exquisite spirits the world ever produced, merely because they did not happen to exert their faculties in laborious affected descriptions of flowers seen in window-pots, or cascades heard at Vauxhall; in short, because they chose to be wits, philosophers, patriots, and poets, rather than to found the Cockney school of versification, morality, and politics, a century before its time. After blaspheming himself into a fury against Boileau, &c. Mr Keats comforts himself and his readers with a view of the present more promising aspect of affairs; above all, with the ripened glories of the poet of Rimini. Addressing the manes of the departed chiefs of English poetry, he informs them, in the following clear and touching manner, of the existence of 'him of the Rose,' &c.

> 'From a thick brake,
> Nested and quiet in a valley mild,
> Bubbles a pipe; fine sounds are floating wild
> About the earth. Happy are ye and glad.'

From this he diverses into a view of 'things in general.' We smile when we think to ourselves how little most of our readers will understand of what follows.

[Lines 248–76 of 'Sleep and Poetry' are quoted. The rhyme-words *thorns* and *fawns* are italicized by the reviewer.]

From some verses addressed to various amiable individuals of the other sex, it appears, notwithstanding all this gossamer-work, that Johnny's affections are not entirely confined to objects purely etherial. Take, by way of specimen, the following prurient and vulgar lines, evidently meant for some young lady east of Temple-bar.

[Lines 23–40 of 'To ****' are quoted. The rhyme-words *higher* and *Thalia* are italicized by the reviewer.]

Who will dispute that our poet, to use his own phrase (and rhyme),

> 'Can mingle music fit for the soft *ear*
> Of Lady *Cytherea*.'

So much for the opening bud; now for the expanded flower. It is time to pass from the juvenile 'Poems,' to the mature and elaborate 'Endymion, a Poetic Romance.' The old story of the moon falling in love with a shepherd, so prettily told by a Roman Classic, and so exquisitely enlarged and adorned by one of the most elegant of German poets, has been seized upon by Mr John Keats, to be done with as might seem good unto the sickly fancy of one who never read a single line either of Ovid or of Wieland. If the quantity, not the quality, of the verses dedicated to the story is to be taken into account, there can be no doubt that Mr John Keats may now claim Endymion entirely to himself. To say the truth, we do not suppose either the Latin or the German poet would be very anxious to dispute about the property of the hero of the 'Poetic Romance.' Mr Keats has thoroughly appropriated the character, if not the name. His Endymion is not a Greek shepherd, loved by a Grecian goddess; he is merely a young Cockney rhymester, dreaming a phantastic dream at the full of the moon. Costume, were it worth while to notice such a trifle, is violated in every page of this goodly octavo. From his prototype Hunt, John Keats has acquired a sort of vague idea, that the Greeks were a most tasteful people, and that no mythology can be so finely adapted for the purposes of poetry as theirs. It is amusing to see what a hand the two Cockneys make of this mythology; the one confesses that he never read the Greek Tragedians, and the other knows Homer only from Chapman; and both of them write about Apollo, Pan, Nymphs, Muses, and Mysteries, as might be expected from persons of their education. We shall not, however, enlarge at present upon this subject, as we mean to dedicate an entire paper to the classical attainments and attempts of the Cockney poets. As for Mr Keats' 'Endymion,' it has just as much to do with Greece as it has with 'old Tartary the fierce;' no man, whose mind has ever been imbued with the smallest knowledge or feeling of classical poetry or classical history, could have stooped to profane and vulgarise every association in the manner which has been adopted by this 'son of promise.' Before giving any extracts we must inform our readers, that this romance is meant to be written in English heroic rhyme. To those who have read any of Hunt's poems, this hint might indeed be needless. Mr Keats has adopted the loose, nerveless versification, and Cockney rhymes of the poet of Rimini; but in fairness to that gentleman, we must add, that the defects of the system are tenfold more conspicuous in his disciple's work than in his own. Mr Hunt is a small poet, but he is a clever man. Mr Keats is a still smaller poet, and he is only a boy of pretty abilities, which he has done every thing in his power to spoil.

The poem sets out with the following exposition of the reasons which induced Mr Keats to compose it.

[Lines 1–35 of *Endymion* are quoted. *Therefore* in line 34 is italicized by the reviewer. Then there follows a brief summary of the story of Book I and part of Book II with long quotations interspersed.]

But we find that we really have no patience for going over four books filled with such amorous scenes as these, with subterraneous journeys equally amusing, and submarine processions equally beauti-

ful; but we must not omit the most interesting scene of the whole
piece.

[Lines 707–41 of Book II are quoted. After the line 'O fountain'd
hill! Old Homer's Helicon!' the reviewer italicized 'That thou wouldst
spout a little streamlet o'er / These sorry pages . . .'.]

After all this, however, the 'modesty,' as Mr Keats expresses it, of the
Lady Diana prevented her from owning in Olympus her passion for
Endymion. Venus, as the most knowing in such matters, is the first to
discover the change that has taken place in the temperament of the
goddess. 'An idle tale,' says the laughter-loving dame,

> 'A humid eye, and steps luxurious,
> When these are new and strange, are ominous.'

The inamorata, to vary the intrigue, carries on a romantic intercourse
with Endymion, under the disguise of an Indian damsel. At last, however, her scruples, for some reason or other, are all overcome, and the
Queen of Heaven owns her attachment.

> 'She gave her fair hands to him, and behold,
> Before three swiftest kisses he had told,
> They vanish far away!—Peona went
> Home through the gloomy wood in wonderment.'

And so, like many other romances, terminates the 'Poetic Romance' of
Johnny Keats, in a patched-up wedding.

We had almost forgot to mention, that Keats belongs to the Cockney
School of Politics, as well as the Cockney School of Poetry.

It is fit that he who holds Rimini to be the first poem, should believe
the Examiner to be the first politician of the day. We admire consistency, even in folly. Hear how their bantling has already learned to
lisp sedition.

[Lines 1–22 of Book III are quoted.]

And now, good-morrow to 'the Muses' son of Promise;' as for 'the
feats he yet may do,' as we do not pretend to say, like himself, 'Muse of
my native land am I inspired,' we shall adhere to the safe old rule of
pauca-verba. We venture to make one small prophecy, that his bookseller will not a second time venture £50 upon any thing he can write.
It is a better and a wiser thing to be a starved apothecary than a starved

poet; so back to the shop Mr John, back to 'plasters, pills, and oint-ment boxes,' &c. But, for Heaven's sake, young Sangrado, be a little more sparing of extenuatives and soporifics in your practice than you have been in your poetry.

Reviews of Keats's 'Endymion'

Quarterly Review

XIX (April 1818), 204–08. The author was John Wilson Croker, First Secretary of the Admiralty, a scholar, a poet, and a mainstay of the Quarterly: *see Hill Shine and Helen C. Shine,* The Quarterly Review under Gifford *(Chapel Hill, N.C., 1949), pp. 61–62. The issue in which the review appeared was published in Sept. 1818 (ibid., p. 60).*

Reviewers have been sometimes accused of not reading the works which they affected to criticise. On the present occasion we shall antici-pate the author's complaint, and honestly confess that we have not read his work. Not that we have been wanting in our duty—far from it—indeed, we have made efforts almost as super-human as the story itself appears to be, to get through it; but with the fullest stretch of our perseverance, we are forced to confess that we have not been able to struggle beyond the first of the four books of which this Poetic Romance consists. We should extremely lament this want of energy, or whatever it may be, on our parts, were it not for one consolation—namely, that we are no better acquainted with the meaning of the book through which we have so painfully toiled, than we are with that of the three which we have not looked into.

It is not that Mr. Keats, (if that be his real name, for we almost doubt that any man in his senses would put his real name to such a rhapsody,) it is not, we say, that the author has not powers of language, rays of fancy, and gleams of genius—he has all these; but he is un-happily a disciple of the new school of what has been somewhere called Cockney poetry; which may be defined to consist of the most incongruous ideas in the most uncouth language.

Of this school, Mr. Leigh Hunt, as we observed in a former Number, aspires to be the hierophant. Our readers will recollect the pleasant recipes for harmonious and sublime poetry which he gave us in his preface to 'Rimini,' and the still more facetious instances of his harmony and sublimity in the verses themselves; and they will recollect above all the contempt of Pope, Johnson, and such like poetasters and pseudo-critics, which so forcibly contrasted itself with Mr. Leigh Hunt's self-complacent approbation of

> ————'all the things itself had wrote,
> Of special merit though of little note.'

This author is a copyist of Mr. Hunt; but he is more unintelligible, almost as rugged, twice as diffuse, and ten times more tiresome and absurd than his prototype, who, though he impudently presumed to seat himself in the chair of criticism, and to measure his own poetry by his own standard, yet generally had a meaning. But Mr. Keats had advanced no dogmas which he was bound to support by examples; his nonsense therefore is quite gratuitous; he writes it for its own sake, and, being bitten by Mr. Leigh Hunt's insane criticism, more than rivals the insanity of his poetry.

Mr. Keats's preface hints that his poem was produced under peculiar circumstances.

'Knowing within myself (he says) the manner in which this Poem has been produced, it is not without a feeling of regret that I make it public.— What manner I mean, will be *quite clear* to the reader, who must soon perceive great inexperience, immaturity, and every error denoting a feverish attempt, rather than a deed accomplished.'—*Preface*, p. vii.

We humbly beg his pardon, but this does not appear to us to be *quite so clear*—we really do not know what he means—but the next passage is more intelligible.

'The two first books, and indeed the two last, I feel sensible are not of such completion as to warrant their passing the press.'—*Preface*, p. vii.

Thus 'the two first books' are, even in his own judgment, unfit to appear, and 'the two last' are, it seems, in the same condition—and as two and two make four, and as that is the whole number of books, we have a clear and, we believe, a very just estimate of the entire work.

Mr. Keats, however, deprecates criticism on this 'immature and feverish work' in terms which are themselves sufficiently feverish; and we confess that we should have abstained from inflicting upon him any of the tortures of the '*fierce hell*' of criticism, which terrify his imagination, if he had not begged to be spared in order that he might write more; if we had not observed in him a certain degree of talent which deserves to be put in the right way, or which, at least, ought to be warned of the wrong; and if, finally, he had not told us that he is of an age and temper which imperiously require mental discipline.

Of the story we have been able to make out but little; it seems to be mythological, and probably relates to the loves of Diana and Endymion; but of this, as the scope of the work has altogether escaped us, we cannot speak with any degree of certainty; and must therefore content ourselves with giving some instances of its diction and versification:—and here again we are perplexed and puzzled.—At first it appeared to us, that Mr. Keats had been amusing himself and wearying his readers with an immeasurable game at *bouts-rimés*; but, if we recollect rightly, it is an indispensable condition at this play, that the rhymes when filled up shall have a meaning; and our author, as we have already hinted, has no meaning. He seems to us to write a line at random, and then he follows not the thought excited by this line, but that suggested by the *rhyme* with which it concludes. There is hardly a complete couplet inclosing a complete idea in the whole book. He wanders from one subject to another, from the association, not of ideas but of sounds, and the work is composed of hemistichs which, it is quite evident, have forced themselves upon the author by the mere force of the catchwords on which they turn.

We shall select, not as the most striking instance, but as that least liable to suspicion, a passage from the opening of the poem.

> ————'Such the sun, the moon,
> Trees old and young, sprouting a shady boon
> For simple sheep; and such are daffodils
> With the green world they live in; and clear rills
> That for themselves a cooling covert make
> 'Gainst the hot season; the mid forest brake,
> Rich with a sprinkling of fair musk-rose blooms:
> And such too is the grandeur of the dooms
> We have imagined for the mighty dead; &c. &c.'—pp. 3, 4.

Here it is clear that the word, and not the idea, *moon* produces the simple sheep and their shady *boon*, and that 'the *dooms* of the mighty dead' would never have intruded themselves but for the '*fair musk-rose blooms.*'

> 'For 'twas the morn: Apollo's upward fire
> Made every eastern cloud a silvery pyre
> Of brightness so unsullied, that therein

> A melancholy spirit well might win
> Oblivion, and melt out his essence fine
> Into the winds: rain-scented eglantine
> Gave temperate sweets to that well-wooing sun;
> The lark was lost in him; cold springs had run
> To warm their chilliest bubbles in the grass;
> Man's voice was on the mountains; and the mass
> Of nature's lives and wonders puls'd tenfold,
> To feel this sun-rise and its glories old.'—p. 8.

Here Apollo's *fire* produces a *pyre*, a silvery pyre of clouds, *wherein* a spirit might *win* oblivion and melt his essence *fine*, and scented *eglantine* gives sweets to the *sun*, and cold springs had *run* into the *grass*, and then the pulse of the *mass* pulsed *tenfold* to feel the glories *old* of the new-born day, &c.

One example more.

> 'Be still the unimaginable lodge
> For solitary thinkings; such as dodge
> Conception to the very bourne of heaven,
> Then leave the naked brain: be still the leaven,
> That spreading in this dull and clodded earth
> Gives it a touch ethereal—a new birth.'—p. 17.

Lodge, dodge—heaven, leaven—earth, birth; such, in six words, is the sum and substance of six lines.

We come now to the author's taste in versification. He cannot indeed write a sentence, but perhaps he may be able to spin a line. Let us see. The following are specimens of his prosodial notions of our English heroic metre.

> 'Dear as the temple's self, so does the moon,
> The passion poesy, glories infinite.'—p. 4.
> 'So plenteously all weed-hidden roots.'—p. 6.
> 'Of some strange history, potent to send.'—p. 18.
> 'Before the deep intoxication.'—p. 27.
> 'Her scarf into a fluttering pavilion.'—p. 33.
> 'The stubborn canvass for my voyage prepared———.'—p. 39.
> ' "Endymion! the cave is secreter
> Than the isle of Delos. Echo hence shall stir
> No signs but sigh-warm kisses, or light noise
> Of thy combing hand, the while it travelling cloys
> And trembles through my labyrinthine hair." '—p. 48.

By this time our readers must be pretty well satisfied as to the meaning of his sentences and the structure of his lines: we now present them with some of the new words with which, in imitation of Mr. Leigh Hunt, he adorns our language.

We are told that 'turtles *passion* their voices,' (p. 15); that 'an arbour was *nested*,' (p. 23); and a lady's locks '*gordian'd* up,' (p. 32); and to supply the place of the nouns thus verbalized Mr. Keats, with great fecundity, spawns new ones; such as 'men-slugs and human *serpentry*,' (p. 41); the '*honey-feel* of bliss,' (p. 45); 'wives prepare *needments*,' (p. 13)—and so forth.

Then he has formed new verbs by the process of cutting off their natural tails, the adverbs, and affixing them to their foreheads; thus, 'the wine out-sparkled,' (p. 10); the 'multitude up-followed,' (p. 11); and 'night up-took,' (p. 29). 'The wind up-blows,' (p. 32); and the 'hours are down-sunken,' (p. 36).

But if he sinks some adverbs in the verbs he compensates the language with adverbs and adjectives which he separates from the parent stock. Thus, a lady 'whispers *pantingly* and close,' makes '*hushing* signs,' and steers her skiff into a '*ripply* cove,' (p. 23); a shower falls '*refreshfully*,' (p. 45); and a vulture has a '*spreaded* tail,' (p. 44).

But enough of Mr. Leigh Hunt and his simple neophyte.—If any one should be bold enough to purchase this 'Poetic Romance,' and so much more patient, than ourselves, as to get beyond the first book, and so much more fortunate as to find a meaning, we entreat him to make us acquainted with his success; we shall then return to the task which we now abandon in despair, and endeavour to make all due amends to Mr. Keats and to our readers.

Baldwin's London Magazine

I (April 1820), 380–89. A headnote says that the review is 'from a correspondent'. The author was P. G. Patmore, a minor author and friend of Hazlitt and Lamb. Authority for this attribution is T. Rowland Hughes, 'The London Magazine' (Ph.D. dissertation, Oxford University, 1931). Reference is there made to 'John Taylor's MS note to his own copy'.

That the periodical criticism of the present day, *as* criticism, enjoys but a slender portion of public respect,—except among mere book-buyers and blue-stockings,—cannot be denied. It would be unjust not to confess that it has its uses. But, in return, it has its reward. The public, and public critics, mutually serve and despise each other; and if both, for the most part, know that this is the case, the latter are too politic to complain of injustice, and the former too indolent to resent it. Each party is content to accept the evil with the good.

But a feeling much stronger than that of contempt has attached itself to this part of the public press, in consequence of certain attempts of modern criticism to blight and wither the maturity of genius; or—still worse—to change its youthful enthusiasm into despair, and thus tempt it to commit suicide; or—worst of all—to creep to its cradle, and strangle it in the first bloom and beauty of its childhood. To feel that all this has been attempted, and most of it effected, by modern critic-ism, we need only pronounce to ourselves the names of Chatterton and Kirke White among the dead, of Montgomery, and Keats, and Words-worth among the living;—not to mention Byron, Shelley, Hunt, &c. It is only necessary to refer, in particular, to the first four of these names; for the others, with an equal share of poetic 'ambition,' have less of 'the illness does attend it;'—less of its over-refined and morbid sensibility.

The miraculous boy, Chatterton, might have been alive, glorying in, and glorifying himself, his country, and his age, at this day, if he had not encountered a shallow-thoughted and cold-blooded critic: for though he was one of the true 'children of the sun' of poetry, his more than human power was linked to more than human weakness. Poor Kirke White, too! different as they were in almost every thing—the one a star, the other a flower—yet both received their light and beauty from the same sun, and both participated in the same fate. To think that the paltry drudge of a bookseller should be permitted to trample in the dirt of a review such an amaranthine flower as this—worthy as it was, to have bloomed in the very Eden of Poetry!—And what had the brilliant, and witty, and successful creator of a new era in criticism to do with the plaintive and tender Montgomery?—If he was too busy or too happy to discover any music in sighs, or any beauty in tears, at least he might have been too philosophical, or too good-natured, to laugh at them. Suppose the poet did indulge a little too much in the 'luxury of grief,'—if it was weakness, at least it was not hypocrisy; and there was small chance of its infecting either the critic or his readers—so that he exhibited little either of skill or courage in going out of his way to pick a quarrel with it. The poet, with all his fine powers, has scarcely yet recovered from the effects of that visitation; and the critic, with all his cleverness, never will.

It would lead us too far from our present purpose,—and indeed does not belong to it,—to do more than refer to the exploits of the same work against the early attempts of the two writers who at present share the poetic throne of the day. Whatever else they might want, these attacks had at least boldness; and they could do little mischief, for the objects of them were armed at all points against the assault. It is not to these latter, but to such as those on Kirke White and Montgomery, and a late one on the work which we are about to notice, that the periodical criticism of the day owes that resentment and indignation which is at present felt against it, by the few whose praise (in matters of literature) is not censure. To make criticism subservient to pecuniary or ambitious views is poor and paltry enough; but there is some natural motive, and therefore some excuse, for this: but to make it a means of depressing true genius, and defrauding it of its dearest reward—its fair fame— is unnaturally, because it is gratuitously, wicked. It is a wickedness, however, that might safely be left to work out its own punishment, but that its anonymous offspring too frequently do their mischievous bidding for a time, and thus answer the end of their birth.

In thinking of these things we are tempted to express an opinion which perhaps it would be more prudent to keep to ourselves,—viz. that poetical criticism is, for the most part, a very superfluous and impertinent business; and is to be tolerated at all only when it is written in an unfeigned spirit of admiration and humility. We must therefore do ourselves the justice to disclaim, for once, any intention of writing a regular critique in the present instance. Criticism, like every thing else, is very well in its place; but, like every thing else, it does not always know where that is. Certainly a poet, properly so called, is beyond its jurisdiction;—for *good* and *bad*, when applied to poetry, are words without a meaning. One might as well talk of good or bad virtue. That which *is* poetry must be good. It may differ in kind and in degree, and therefore it may differ in value; but if it *be* poetry, it is a thing about which criticism has no concern, any more than it has with other of the highest productions of Fine Art. The sublimities of Michael Angelo are beyond the reach of its ken—the divine forms of Raphael were not made to be meddled with by its unhallowed fingers —the ineffable expressions of Corregio must not be sullied by its earthy breath. These things were given to the world for something better than to be written and talked about; and they have done their bidding hitherto, and will do it till they cease to exist. They have opened a perpetual spring of lofty thoughts and pure meditations; they have blended themselves with the very existence, and become a living principle in the hearts of mankind;—and they are, now, no more fit to be touched and tampered with than the stars of heaven—for like them

Levan di terra al cielo nostr' intelletto.[1]

[1] 'They raise our mind from earth to heaven.'

We will not shrink from applying these observations, prospectively, to the young poet whose work we are about to notice. Endymion, if it be not, technically speaking, a poem, is poetry itself. As a *promise*, we know of nothing like it, except some things of Chatterton. Of the few others that occur to us at the moment, the most remarkable are Pope's Pastorals, and his Essay on Criticism;—but these are proofs of an extraordinary precocity, not of genius, but of taste, as the word was understood in his day; and of a remarkably early acquaintance with all the existing common-places of poetry and criticism. It is true that Southey's Joan of Arc, and Campbell's Pleasures of Hope, were both produced before their authors were one-and-twenty. But Joan of Arc, though a fine poem, is diffuse, not from being rich, but from being diluted; and the Pleasures of Hope is a delightful work—but then it *is* a work—and one cannot help wishing it had been written at thirty instead of twenty.

Endymion is totally unlike all these, and all other poems. As we said before, it is not *a poem* at all. It is an ecstatic dream of poetry—a flush —a fever—a burning light—an involuntary out-pouring of the spirit of poetry—that will not be controuled. Its movements are the starts and boundings of the young horse before it has felt the bitt—the first flights of the young bird, feeling and exulting in the powers with which it is gifted, but not yet acquainted with their use or their extent. It is the wanderings of the butter-fly in the first hour of its birth; not as yet knowing one flower from another, but only that all *are* flowers. Its similitudes come crowding upon us from all delightful things. It is the May-day of poetry—the flush of blossoms and weeds that start up at the first voice of spring. It is the sky-lark's hymn to the day-break, involuntarily gushing forth as he mounts upward to look for the fountain of that light which has awakened him. It is as if the muses had steeped their child in the waters of Castaly, and we beheld him emerging from them, with his eyes sparkling and his limbs quivering with the delicious intoxication, and the precious drops scattered from him into the air at every motion, glittering in the sunshine, and casting the colours of the rainbow on all things around.

Almost entirely unknown as this poem is to general readers, it will perhaps be better to reserve what we have further to say of its characteristics, till we have given some specimens of it. We should premise this, however, by saying, that our examples will probably exhibit almost as many faults as beauties. But the reader will have anticipated this from the nature of the opinion we have already given—at least if we have succeeded in expressing what we intended to express. In fact, there is scarcely a passage of any length in the whole work, which does not exhibit the most glaring faults—faults that in many instances amount almost to the ludicrous: yet positive and palpable as they are, it may be said of them generally, that they are as much collateral evidences of poetical power, as the beauties themselves are direct ones. If the poet had had time, or patience, or we will even say taste, to have weeded out these faults as they sprang up, he could not have possessed the power to create the beauties to which they are joined. If he had waited to make the first half dozen pages of his work faultless, the fever—the ferment of mind in which the whole was composed would have subsided for ever. Or if he had attempted to pick out those faults afterwards, the beauties must inevitably have gone with them—for they are inextricably linked together.

The title of Endymion will indicate the subject of it. It is, in one word, the story of the mutual loves of Endymion and the Moon,—including the trials and adventures which the youthful shepherd was destined to pass through, in order to prepare and fit him for the immortality to which he at last succeeds.

It is not part of our plan to follow the poet and his hero—for they go hand in hand together—through their adventures; for, as a tale, this work is nothing. There is no connecting interest to bind one part of it to another. Almost any two parts of it might be transposed, without disadvantage to either, or to the whole. We repeat, it is not a poem, but a dream of poetry; and while many of its separate parts possess that vivid distinction which frequently belongs to the separate parts of a dream, the impression it leaves as a whole is equally indistinct and confused.—The poet begins by noticing the delightful associations we are accustomed to attach to beautiful thoughts and objects, and continues,

> ———therefore 'tis that I
> Will trace the story of Endymion.
> The very music of his name has gone
> Into my being.

Then, after dallying a little with the host of beautiful images which are conjured up by that name, he exclaims

> And now at once, adventuresome, I send
> My herald thought into a wilderness.

These two lines are very characteristic. It is the bold boy plunging for the first time into the stream, without knowing or caring whither it may carry him. The story, such as it is, commences with the description of a procession and festival, in honour of the god Pan. The following are parts of this description:

[Lines 107–21, 135–52, and 175–81 of Book I are quoted.]

The following are parts of a hymn to Pan, sung by a chorus of shepherds. We direct the reader's attention to the imagery as well as the rhythm of these extracts in particular. They are, likewise, almost entirely free from the writer's characteristic faults.

[Lines 232–46, 279–92, 321–25, and 442–52 of Book I are quoted with brief interlocking comments.]

Nothing can be more exquisitely beautiful than this—nothing more lulling-sweet than the melody of it.—And let us here, once for all, direct the readers' attention to the rhythm of the various extracts we lay before them; and add that, upon the whole, it combines more freedom, sweetness, and variety than are to be found in that of any other long poem written in the same measure, without any exception whatever. In the course of more than four thousand lines it never cloys by sameness, and never flags. To judge of the comparative extent of this praise, turn at random to Pope's Homer, or even Dryden's Virgil and read two or three pages. Sweetness and variety of music in the versification of a young writer, are among the most authentic evidences of poetical power. These qualities are peculiarly conspicuous in Shakspeare's early poems of Lucrece, and Venus and Adonis. It should be mentioned, however, that in the work before us, these qualities seem to result from—what shall we say?—a fine natural ear? —from any thing, however, rather than system—for the verse frequently runs riot, and loses itself in air. It is the music of the happy wild-bird in the woods—not of the poor caged piping-bullfinch.

The following description of the impressions Endymion receives from various external objects,—on awaking from an Elysian dream of love, and finding that it was *but* a dream,—is finely passionate and natural:

[Lines 682–705 of Book I are quoted.]

Peona succeeds in rousing her brother from the listless trance into which he has fallen, and he again feels the true dignity of his being, and its mysterious bridal with the external forms and influences of Nature. The following strikes us as being exceedingly fine, notwithstanding some obvious faults in the diction.—It is the very faith, the religion, of imaginative passion.

———Hist, when the airy stress
Of music's kiss impregnates the free winds,
And with a sympathetic touch unbinds
Eolian magic from their lucid wombs:
Then old songs waken from enclouded tombs;
Old ditties sigh above their father's grave;
Ghosts of melodious prophecyings rave
Round every spot where trod Apollo's foot;
Bronze clarions awake, and faintly bruit,
Where long ago a giant battle was;
And, from the turf, a lullaby doth pass
In every place where infant Orpheus slept.
Feel we these things?—that moment have we stept
Into a sort of oneness, and our state
Is like a floating spirit's.

They who do not find poetry in this, may be assured that they will
look for it in vain elsewhere.

[The plot summary continues. Lines 49–51 of Book II are quoted.]

Through buried paths, where sleepy twilight dreams
The summer time away. One track unseams
A wooded cleft, and, far away, the blue
Of ocean fades upon him; then, anew,
He sinks adown a solitary glen,
Where there was never sound of mortal men,
Saving, perhaps, some snow-light cadences
Melting to silence, when upon the breeze
Some holy bark let forth an anthem sweet,
To cheer itself to Delphi.

'Snow-light cadences,' &c. may be a little fantastical, perhaps; but it
is very delicate and poetical, nevertheless. The passage in italics is also
very still and lonely.—The following delightful little picture of cool
quietude is placed in contrast to the restless fever of Endymion's
thoughts, when his winged conductor leaves him:—

[Lines 131–37 of Book II are quoted.]

After this he yields up his whole soul to the dominion of passion and
imagination, and they at last burst forth with an extatic address to his
unearthly mistress, the moon—though he does not yet know her as
such. The latter part of this address follows: and amidst numerous
faults, both of thought and diction, the reader will not fail to detect

much beauty. In the picture which follows the close of this address there is great power, and even sublimity.

[Lines 179–98 and 211–13 of Book II are quoted and the plot summary continues.]

It will be seen that here is a rich fund of materials, fitted for almost every variety and degree of poetical power to work upon. And if the young builder before us has not erected from them a regular fabric, which will bear to be examined by a professional surveyor, with his square and rule and plumb-line,—he has at least raised a glittering and fantastic temple, where we may wander about, and delightedly lose ourselves while gazing on the exquisite pictures which every here and there hang on its sun-bright walls—the statues and flower-vases which ornament its painted niches—the delicious prospects opening upon us from its arabesque windows—and the sweet airs and romantic music which come about us when we mount upon its pleasant battlements. And it cannot be denied that the fabric is at least as well adapted to the airy and fanciful beings who dwell in it, as a regular Epic Palace—with its grand geometrical staircases, its long dreary galleries, its lofty state apartments, and its numerous *sleeping-rooms*—is to its kings and heroes.

The whole of the foregoing extracts are taken from the first and the beginning of the second book. We had marked numerous others through the rest of the work; but the little space that we have left for quotations must be given to a few of the fancies, images, and detached thoughts and similes—the pictures, statues, flowers, &c.—which form the mere ornaments of the building, and are scattered here and there almost at random.

The little cabinet gems which follow may take their place in any collection. The first might have been cut out of a picture by Salvator:

> Echoing grottos, full of tumbling waves
> And moonlight. p. 25.

The next we can fancy to have formed a part of one of Claude's delicious skies. It is Venus ascending from the earth.

> ————At these words up flew
> The impatient doves, up rose the floating car,
> Up went the hum celestial. High afar
> The Latmian saw them 'minish into nought.

The third reminds us of a sublime picture of the Deluge, by Poussin. It is a lover who loses his mistress, he knows not how, and afterwards, while swimming, finds her dead body floating in the sea.

Upon a dead thing's face my hand I laid;
I look'd—'twas Scylla———
———Cold, O cold indeed
Were her fair limbs, *and like a common weed*
The sea-swell took her hair.

The fourth picture has all the voluptuous beauty of Titian:

Do not those curls of glossy jet surpass
For tenderness the arms so idly lain
Amongst them? Feelest not a kindred pain,
To see such lovely eyes in swimming search
After some warm delight, *that seems to perch*
Dovelike in the dim cell lying beyond
Their upper lids?

The following are a few of the wild flowers of Fancy that are scatter'd up and down.

When last the wintry gusts gave over strife
With the conquering sun of spring, and left the skies
Warm and serene, *but yet with moistened eyes*
In pity of the shatter'd infant buds.—
  A brook running between mossy stones
'Mong which it gurgled blythe adieus, to mock
Its own sweet grief at parting.
The little flowers felt his pleasant sighs,
And stirr'd them faintly.

LOVER'S TALK

———And then there ran
Two bubbling springs of talk from their sweet lips.

The following are a few of the detached thoughts which float about like clouds, taking their form and colour from the position and the medium through which they are seen.

SUPPOSED EMPLOYMENTS OF DISEMBODIED SPIRITS

———To nightly call
Vesper, the beauty-crest of summer weather;
To summon all the downiest clouds together
For the sun's purple couch:—
To tint her pallid cheek with bloom, who cons
Sweet poesy by moon-light.

A POET

————One who through this middle earth should pass
Most like a sojourning demi-god, *and leave*
His name upon the harp-string.

THE END OF UNREQUITED LOVE

And then the ballad of his sad life closes
With sighs, and an alas!

LOVE

————Awfully he stands,—
No sight can bear the lightning of his bow;
His quiver is mysterious, none can know
What themselves think of it.—
A scowl is sometimes on his brow, but who
Look full upon it feel anon the blue
Of his fair eyes run liquid through their souls.

REMEMBRANCE OF PAST YEARS

————Is it then possible
To look so plainly through them? to dispel
A thousand years with backward glance sublime?
To breathe away as 'twere all scummy slime
From off a crystal pool, to see its deep,
And one's own image from the bottom peep?

The following similes are as new as they are beautiful:

————his eyelids
Widened a little, as when Zephyr bids
A little breeze to creep between the fans
Of careless butterflies.
————As delicious wine doth, sparkling, dive
In nectar'd clouds and curls through water fair,
So from the arbour roof down swell'd an air
Odorous and enlivening.
————like taper-flame
Left sudden by a dallying breath of air,
He rose in silence.

One more cluster of beautiful thoughts, fancies, and images meeting together, and one example of a totally different style of composition,—and we have done with quotations. The first is part of an address to the Moon, by the poet in his own character:

[Lines 42 and 44–71 of Book III are quoted.]

If there be such a thing as inspiration, breathed forth by the forms and influences of the external world, and echoed back again from the inner shrine of the poet's breast—this is it. The image of the wren, is, in its kind, not to be surpassed in the whole circle of poetry.[1] We remember nothing equal to it, except Burns's morning picture, which is an exact companion to it, and probably suggested it.

> Just when the lark,
> 'Twixt light and dark,
> Awakens, by the daisy's side.

Our last extract shall be part of a song, supposed to be sung by an Indian maid, who has wandered far away from her own native streams:

[Lines 146–63, 182–87, and 279–90 of Book IV are quoted.]

This is, to be sure

> ————Silly sooth,
> And dallies with the innocence of grief;

but it is very touching and pathetic, nevertheless. Perhaps we like it the better from its reminding us (we do not very well know why) of two little elegies that are especial favourites with us,—one by Chatterton, beginning 'O sing unto my roundelay;'—and the other by Kirke White, 'Edwy, Edwy, ope thine eye!' It was perhaps suggested by Fletcher's divine song to Melancholy, in the Passionate Madman.

We cannot refrain from asking, Is it credible that the foregoing extracts are taken, almost at random, from a work in which a writer in the most popular—we will say *deservedly* the most popular—critical journal of the day, has been unable to discover any thing worthy to redeem it from mere contempt? Those who have the most respect for the Quarterly Review will feel most pain at seeing its pages disgraced by such an article as that to which we allude. Almost anywhere else it

[1]   . . . The nested wren
  Has thy fair face within its tranquil ken,
  And from beneath a sheltering ivy leaf
  Takes glimpses of thee . . . .

338

would have been harmless, and unworthy of particular notice; but *there* it cannot fail to gain a certain degree of credit from the company which it keeps. It would be foolish to doubt or to deny the extensive effect which such an article is likely to produce, appearing as it does in a work which is read by tens of thousands, nine-tenths of whom are not able to judge for themselves, and half of the other tenth will not take the trouble of doing so. Its chief mischief, however, is likely to take effect on the poet himself, whose work is the subject of it. Next to the necessity of pouring forth that which is within him, the strongest active principle in the mind of a young poet is the love of fame. Not fame weighed and meted out by the scales of strict justice. Not fame, properly so called. But *mere* fame—mere praise and distinction. He loves it for itself alone. During a certain period, this love exists almost in the form of an instinct in a poet's nature; and seems to be given him for the purpose of urging or leading him on to that 'hereafter' which is to follow. If it is not the food and support of his poetical life, it is at least the *stimulus* without which that life would be but too apt to flag and faulter in its appointed course. Woe to the lovers of poetry, when poets are content merely to *deserve* fame! Let that pest of the literary republic, the mere versifier, be derided and put down as a common nuisance. But let us, even for our own sakes, beware of with-holding from youthful poets the fame which they covet;—let us beware of heaping ridicule even upon their faults; lest, in revenge, they learn to keep to themselves the gift which was bestowed on them for the benefit of their fellow-beings, and be satisfied with finding in poetry 'its own reward.' But we willingly return to our more immediate subject. We at first intended to have accompanied the foregoing extracts by a few of a contrary description, shewing the peculiar faults and deficiencies of the work before us. But as, in the present instance, we disclaim any intention of writing a regular criticism, we feel that this would be superfluous. It is not our object to give a distinct idea of the work as a whole; and we repeat, it is not a fit one to be judged of by rules and axioms. We only wish to call the public notice to the great and remarkable powers which it indicates,—at the same time giving encouragement—as far as our sincere suffrage is of any value—to the poet himself; and bespeaking,—not favour,—but attention,—to any thing that he may produce hereafter. It is, therefore, surely sufficient —for it is saying a great deal—to confess that Endymion is as full of faults as of beauties. And it is the less needful to point out those faults, as they are exactly of such a description that any one who has a relish for the amusement may readily discover them for himself. They will not hide themselves from his search. He need only open a page at random, and they will look him boldly, but not impudently, in the face—for their parent is, as yet, too inexperienced himself to know how to teach them better.

The same reasons which make it unnecessary to point out the peculiar faults of this work, make it difficult, if not impossible, to state its peculiar beauties as a whole, in any other than general terms. And, even so, we may exhaust all the common-places of criticism in talking about the writer's active and fertile imagination, his rich and lively fancy, his strong and acute sensibility, and so forth,—without advancing one step towards characterising the work which all these together have produced: because, though the writer possesses all these qualities in an eminent degree, his poetical character has not yet taken up any tangible or determinate ground. So that, though we know of no poetical work which differs from all others more than Endymion does, yet its distinguishing feature is perhaps nothing more than that exuberant spirit of youth,—that transport of imagination, fancy, and sensibility—which gushes forth from every part, in a glittering shower of words, and a confused and shadowy pomp of thoughts and images, creating and hurrying each other along like waves of the sea. And there is no egotism in all this, and no affectation. The poet offers himself up a willing sacrifice to the power which he serves: not fretting under, but exulting and glorying in his bondage. He plunges into the ocean of Poetry before he has learned to stem and grapple with the waves; but they 'bound beneath him as a steed that knows its rider;' and will not let him sink. Still, however, while they bear him along triumphantly, it is, evidently at *their* will and pleasure, not at his. He 'rides on the whirlwind' safely; but he cannot yet 'direct the storm.'

We have spoken of this work as being richer in promise than any other that we are acquainted with, except those of Chatterton. It by no means follows that we confidently anticipate the fulfilment of that promise to its utmost extent. We are not without our fears that it may be like that flush of April blossoms which our fine soil almost always sends forth, but which our cloudy and uncertain skies as often prevent from arriving at maturity. Notwithstanding the many living poets that we possess, the times in which we live are essentially unpoetical; and powerful and resolute indeed must that spirit be, which, even in its youth, can escape their influence. When the transports of enthusiasm are gone by, it can hardly dare hope to do so. It must submit to let 'the years bring on the inevitable yoke.' This has been one strong inducement for us to notice the young writer before us; and we cannot conclude these slight and desultory remarks without entreating him not to be cast down or turned aside from the course which nature has marked out for him. He is and must be a poet—and he may be a great one. But let him never be tempted to disregard this first evidence of that power which at present rules over him—much less affect to do so: and least of all let him wish or attempt to make it any thing but what it is. Nothing can ever tame and polish this wild and wayward firstling, and make it fit to be introduced to 'mixed company;' but let him not therefore be ashamed to cherish and claim it for his own. He may live to see himself surrounded by a flourishing family, endowed with all sorts of polite accomplishments and able not only to make their own way in the world, but to further *his* fortunes too. But *this*—the firstborn of his hopes—the child of his youth—whatever he may say or think to the contrary—must ever be the favourite. He may admire those which are to come, and pride himself upon them; but he will never love them as he has loved this; he will never again watch over the infancy and growth of another with such full and unmixed delight: for *this* was born while his muse was his mistress, and he her rapturous lover. He will marry her by and bye—or perhaps he has already—and then he may chance to love her *better* than ever; but he will cease to be *her lover*.

Review of Keats's 'Endymion' and 'Lamia' Volume

Edinburgh Review

XXXIV (*Aug. 1820*), *203–13. The author was Francis Jeffrey: see Walter E. Houghton* (*ed.*), The Wellesley Index to Victorian Periodicals (*Toronto, 1966*), *p. 461.*

We had never happened to see either of these volumes till very lately—and have been exceedingly struck with the genius they display, and the spirit of poetry which breathes through all their extravagance. That imitation of our older writers, and especially of our older dramatists, to which we cannot help flattering ourselves that we have somewhat contributed, has brought on, as it were, a second spring in our poetry; —and few of its blossoms are either more profuse of sweetness or richer in promise, than this which is now before us. Mr Keats,—we understand, is still a very young man; and his whole works, indeed, bear evidence enough of the fact. They are full of extravagance and irregularity, rash attempts at originality, interminable wanderings, and excessive obscurity. They manifestly require, therefore, all the indulgence that can be claimed for a first attempt:—but we think it no less plain that they deserve it; for they are flushed all over with the rich lights of fancy, and so coloured and bestrewn with the flowers of poetry, that even while perplexed and bewildered in their labyrinths, it is impossible to resist the intoxication of their sweetness, or to shut our hearts to the enchantments they so lavishly present. The models upon which he has formed himself, in the Endymion, the earliest and by much the most considerable of his poems, are obviously the Faithful Shepherdess of Fletcher, and the Sad Shepherd of Ben Jonson;—the exquisite metres and inspired diction of which he has copied with great boldness and fidelity—and, like his great originals, has also contrived to impart to the whole piece that true rural and poetical air which breathes only in them and in Theocritus—which is at once homely and majestic, luxurious and rude, and sets before us the genuine sights and sounds and smells of the country, with all the magic and grace of Elysium. His subject has the disadvantage of being mythological; and in this respect, as well as on account of the raised and rapturous tone it consequently assumes, his poetry may be better compared perhaps to the Comus and the Arcades of Milton, of which, also, there are many traces of imitation. The great distinction, however, between him and these divine authors, is, that imagination in them is subordinate to reason and judgment, while, with him, it is paramount and supreme— that their ornaments and images are employed to embellish and recommend just sentiments, engaging incidents, and natural characters, while his are poured out without measure or restraint, and with no apparent design but to unburden the breast of the author, and give vent to the overflowing vein of his fancy. The thin and scanty tissue of his story is merely the light frame work on which his florid wreaths are suspended; and while his imaginations go rambling and entangling themselves everywhere, like wild honeysuckles, all idea of sober reason, and plan, and consistency, is utterly forgotten, and are 'strangled in their waste fertility.' A great part of the work indeed, is written in the strangest and most fantastical manner that can be imagined. It seems as if the author had ventured everything that occurred to him in the shape of a glittering image or striking expression—taken the first word that presented itself to make up a rhyme, and then made that word the germ of a new cluster of images—a hint for a new excursion of the fancy—and so wandered on, equally forgetful whence he came, and heedless whither he was going, till he had covered his pages with an interminable arabesque of connected and incongruous figures, that multiplied as they extended, and were only harmonized by the brightness of their tints, and the graces of their forms. In this rash and headlong career he has of course many lapses and failures. There is no work, accordingly, from which a malicious critic could cull more matter for ridicule, or select more obscure, unnatural, or absurd passages. But we do not take *that* to be our office;—and just beg leave, on the contrary, to say, that any one who, on this account, would represent the whole poem as despicable, must either have no notion of poetry, or no regard to truth.

It is, in truth, at least as full of genius as of absurdity; and he who does not find a great deal in it to admire and to give delight, cannot in

343

his heart see much beauty in the two exquisite dramas to which we have already alluded, or find any great pleasure in some of the finest creations of Milton and Shakespeare. There are very many such persons, we verily believe, even among the reading and judicious part of the community—correct scholars we have no doubt many of them, and, it may be, very classical composers in prose and in verse—but utterly ignorant of the true genius of English poetry, and incapable of estimating its appropriate and most exquisite beauties. With that spirit we have no hesitation in saying that Mr K. is deeply imbued—and of those beauties he has presented us with many striking examples. We are very much inclined indeed to add, that we do not know any book which we would sooner employ as a test to ascertain whether any one had in him a native relish for poetry, and a genuine sensibility to its intrinsic charm. The greater and more distinguished poets of our country have so much else in them to gratify other tastes and propensities, that they are pretty sure to captivate and amuse those to whom their poetry is but an hindrance and obstruction, as well as those to whom it constitutes their chief attraction. The interest of the stories they tell—the vivacity of the characters they delineate—the weight and force of the maxims and sentiments in which they abound—the very pathos and wit and humour they display, which may all and each of them exist apart from their poetry and independent of it, are quite sufficient to account for their popularity, without referring much to that still higher gift, by which they subdue to their enchantments those whose souls are attuned to the finer impulses of poetry. It is only where those other recommendations are wanting, or exist in a weaker degree, that the true force of the attraction, exercised by the pure poetry with which they are so often combined, can be fairly appreciated—where, without much incident or many characters, and with little wit, wisdom, or arrangement, a number of bright pictures are presented to the imagination, and a fine feeling expressed of those mysterious relations by which visible external things are assimilated with inward thoughts and emotions, and become the images and exponents of all passions and affections. To an unpoetical reader such passages always appear mere raving and absurdity—and to this censure a very great part of the volume before us will certainly be exposed, with this class of readers. Even in the judgment of a fitter audience, however, it must, we fear, be admitted, that, besides the riot and extravagance of his fancy, the scope and substance of Mr K.'s poetry is rather too dreary and abstracted to excite the strongest interest, or to sustain the attention through a work of any great compass or extent. He deals too much with shadowy and incomprehensible beings, and is too constantly rapt into

344

an extramundane Elysium, to command a lasting interest with ordinary mortals—and must employ the agency of more varied and coarser emotions, if he wishes to take rank with the seducing poets of this or of former generations. There is something very curious too, we think, in the way in which he, and Mr Barry Cornwall also, have dealt with the Pagan mythology, of which they have made so much use in their poetry. Instead of presenting its imaginary persons under the trite and vulgar traits that belong to them in the ordinary systems, little more is borrowed from these than the general conception of their conditions and relations; and an original character and distinct individuality is bestowed upon them, which has all the merit of invention, and all the grace and attraction of the fictions on which it is engrafted. The antients, though they probably did not stand in any great awe of their deities, have yet abstained very much from any minute or dramatic representation of their feelings and affections. In Hesiod and Homer, they are coarsely delineated by some of their actions and adventures, and introduced to us merely as the agents in those particular trans-actions; while in the Hymns, from those ascribed to Orpheus and Homer, down to those of Callimachus, we have little but pompous epithets and invocations, with a flattering commemoraton of their most famous exploits—and are never allowed to enter into their bosoms, or follow out the train of their feelings, with the presumption of our human sympathy. Except the love-song of the Cyclops to his Sea Nymph in Theocritus—the Lamentation of Venus for Adonis in Moschus—and the more recent Legend of Apuleius, we scarcely recol-lect a passage in all the writings of antiquity in which the passions of an immortal are fairly disclosed to the scrutiny and observation of men. The author before us, however, and some of his contemporaries, have dealt differently with the subject;—and, sheltering the violence of the fiction under the ancient traditionary fable, have created and imagined an entire new set of characters, and brought closely and minutely before us the loves and sorrows and perplexities of beings, with whose names and supernatural attributes we had long been familiar, without any sense or feeling of their personal character. We have more than doubts of the fitness of such personages to maintain a permanent interest with the modern public;—but the way in which they are here managed, certainly gives them the best chance that now remains for them; and, at all events, it cannot be denied that the effect is striking and graceful. But we must now proceed to our extracts.

The first of the volumes before us is occupied with the loves of Endymion and Diana—which it would not be very easy, and which we do not at all intend to analyze in detail.

[A brief summary of the opening of the poem is given and lines 169–81 of Book I are quoted.]

There is then a choral hymn addressed to the sylvan deity, which appears to us to be full of beauty; and reminds us, in many places, of the finest strains of Sicilian or English poetry. A part of it is as follows:

[Lines 232–41, 247–87, and 466–98 of Book I are quoted.]

He then tells her all the story of his love and madness; and is afterwards led away by butterflies to the haunts of Naiads, and by them sent down into enchanted caverns, where he sees Venus and Adonis, and great flights of Cupids, and wanders over diamond terraces among beautiful fountains and temples and statues, and all sorts of fine and strange things. All this is very fantastical: But there are splendid pieces of description, and a sort of wild richness on the whole. We cull a few little morsels. This is the picture of the sleeping Adonis.

[Lines 393–94, 403–14, and 418–27 of Book II are quoted.]

There is another and more classical sketch of Cybele.

[Lines 639–49 of Book II are quoted.]

In the midst of all these spectacles, he has, we do not very well know how, a ravishing interview with his unknown goddess; and, when she melts away from him, he finds himself in a vast grotto, where he overhears the courtship of Alpheus and Arethusa, and, as they elope together, discovers that the grotto has disappeared, and that he is at the bottom of the sea, under the transparent arches of its naked waters. The following is abundantly extravagant; but comes of no ignoble lineage, nor shames its high descent.

[Lines 119–36 of Book III are quoted and a brief summary of the rest of the story follows.]

We have left ourselves room to say but little of the second volume, which is of a more miscellaneous character. Lamia is a Greek antique story, in the measure and taste of Endymion. Isabella is a paraphrase of the same tale of Boccaccio, which Mr Cornwall has also imitated under the title of 'a Sicilian Story.' It would be worth while to compare the two imitations; but we have no longer time for such a task. Mr K. has followed his original more closely, and has given a deep pathos to several of his stanzas. The widowed bride's discovery of the murdered body is very strikingly given.

[Stanzas XLVII–XLVIII and LI–LII are quoted.]

346

The following lines from an ode to a Nightingale, are equally distinguished for harmony and feeling.

[Lines 15–28 and 63–70 are quoted.]

We must close our extracts with the following lively lines to Fancy.

[Lines 9–24 and 39–66 are quoted.]

There is a fragment of a projected Epic, entitled 'Hyperion,' on the expulsion of Saturn and the Titanian deities by Jupiter and his younger adherents, of which we cannot advise the completion: For, though there are passages of some force and grandeur, it is sufficiently obvious, from the specimen before us, that the subject is too far removed from all the sources of human interest, to be successfully treated by any modern author. Mr Keats has unquestionably a very beautiful imagination, and a great familiarity with the finest diction of English poetry; but he must learn not to misuse or misapply these advantages; and neither to waste the good gifts of nature and study on intractable themes, nor to luxuriate too recklessly on such as are more suitable.

Reviews of Keats's 'Lamia' Volume

Monthly Review

XCII (*July 1820*), *305–10. The reviewer is unknown.*

This little volume must and ought to attract attention, for it displays the ore of true poetic genius, though mingled with a large portion of dross. Mr. Keats is a very bold author, bold perhaps because (as we learn) he has yet but little more than touched the 'years of discretion;' and he has carried his peculiarities both of thought and manner to an extreme which, at the first view, will to many persons be very displeasing. Yet, whatever may be his faults, he is no *Della Crusca* poet; for, though he is frequently involved in ambiguity, and dressed in the affectation of quaint phrases, we are yet sure of finding in all that he writes the proof of deep thought and energetic reflection.[1] Poetry is now become so antient an art, and antiquity has furnished such a storehouse of expression and feeling, that we daily meet with new worshippers of the Muse who are content to repeat for the thousandth time her prescriptive language. If any one would deviate from this beaten track, and from those great landmarks which have so long been the guides of the world in all matters of taste and literary excellence, he will find that it requires no timid foot to strike into new paths, and must deem himself fortunate if he be not lost amid the intricacies of a region with which he is unacquainted. Yet, even should this be partially the case, the wild and beautiful scenery, which such an excursion is frequently the means of developing, is a fair remuneration for the inequalities and obstructions which he may chance to experience on his ramble. We must add that only by attempts like these can we discover the path of true excellence; and that, in checking such efforts by illiberal and ill-timed discouragement, we shut out the prospect of all improvement. Innovations of every kind, more especially in matters of

[1] See p. 316, note 2, above.

taste, are at first beheld with dislike and jealousy, and it is only by time and usage that we can appreciate their claims to adoption.

Very few persons, probably, will admire Mr. Keats on a short acquaintance; and the light and the frivolous never will. If we would enjoy his poetry, we must think over it; and on this very account, which is perhaps the surest proof of its merit, we are afraid that it will be slighted. Unfortunately, Mr. Keats may blame himself for much of this neglect; since he might have conceded something to established taste, or (if he will) established prejudice, without derogating from his own originality of thought and spirit. On the contrary, he seems to have written directly in despite of our preconceived notions of the *manner* in which a poet ought to write; and he is continually shocking our ideas of poetical decorum, at the very time when we are acknowledging the hand of genius. In this boldly running counter to old opinions, however, we cannot conceive that Mr. Keats merits either contempt or ridicule; the weapons which are too frequently employed when liberal discussion and argument would be unsuccessful. At all events, let him not be pre-judged without a candid examination of his claims.—A former work by this very young poet, (*Endymion*,) which escaped our notice, cannot certainly be said to have had a fair trial before the public; and now that an opportunity is afforded for correcting that injustice, we trust that the candour of all readers will take advantage of it.

For ourselves, we think that Mr. Keats is very faulty. He is often laboriously obscure; and he sometimes indulges in such strange intricacies of thought, and peculiarities of expression, that we find considerable difficulty in discovering his meaning. Most unluckily for him, he is a disciple in a school in which these peculiarities are virtues: but the praises of this small *coterie* will hardly compensate for the disapprobation of the rest of the literary world. Holding, as we do, a high opinion of his talents, especially considering his youth and few advantages, we regret to see him sowing the seeds of disappointment where the fruit should be honour and distinction. If his writings were the dull common-places of an every-day versifier, we should pass them by with indifference or contempt: but, as they exhibit great force and feeling, we have only to regret that such powers are misdirected.

The wild and high imagination of antient mythology, the mysterious being and awful histories of the deities of Greece and Rome, form subjects which Mr. Keats evidently conceives to be suited to his own powers: but, though boldly and skilfully sketched, his delineations of the immortals give a faint idea of the nature which the poets of Greece attributed to them. The only modern writer, by whom this spirit has been completely preserved, is Lord Byron, in his poem of 'Prometheus.' In this mould, too, the character of Milton's Satan is cast.

The fragment of *Hyperion,* the last poem in the volume before us, we consider as decidedly the best of Mr. Keats's productions; and the power of both heart and hand which it displays is very great. We think, too, that it has less conceit than other parts of the volume. It is the fable of the antient gods dethroned by the younger.

[Lines 1–14 and 22–36 of Book I of 'Hyperion' are quoted. Lines 10 and 35–36 are italicized by the reviewer.]

The appearance of Saturn among the Titans is splendidly told:

[Lines 105–28 of Book II are quoted. Lines 118–20 are italicized by the reviewer.]

The description of Hyperion also is really fine:

[Lines 371–91 of Book II are quoted.]

The story of Isabella, or the Pot of Basil, from Boccaccio, is the worst part of the volume; and Mr. Barry Cornwall's versification of this fable in his *Sicilian Story* is in some respects superior to Mr. Keats's attempt. The latter gentleman seems inclined, in this poem, to shew us at once the extent of his simplicity and his affectation; witness the following *tirade* against the mercantile pride of the brothers of Isabella:

> 'Why were they proud? Because their marble founts
>   Gush'd with more pride than do a wretch's tears?—
> Why were they proud? Because fair orange-mounts
>   Were of more soft ascent than lazar stairs?—
> Why were they proud? Because *red lin'd accounts*
>   Were richer than the songs of Grecian years?—
> Why were they proud? *again we ask aloud,*
> *Why in the name of Glory were they proud?*'

Mr. Keats displays no great nicety in his selection of images. According to the tenets of that school of poetry to which he belongs, he thinks that any thing or object in nature is a fit material on which the poet may work; forgetting that poetry has a nature of its own, and that it is the destruction of its essence to level its high being with the triteness of every-day life. Can there be a more pointed *concetto* than this address to the Piping Shepherds on a Grecian Urn?

> 'Heard melodies are sweet, but those *unheard*
>   Are sweeter; therefore, ye soft pipes, play on;

> Not to the sensual ear, but, more endear'd,
>   Pipe to the spirit *ditties of no tone:*'

but it would be irksome to point out all the instances of this kind which are to be found in Mr. K.'s compositions.

Still, we repeat, this writer is very rich both in imagination and fancy; and even a superabundance of the latter faculty is displayed in his lines 'On Autumn,' which bring the reality of nature more before our eyes than almost any description that we remember.

['To Autumn' is quoted in full.]

If we did not fear that, young as is Mr. K., his peculiarities are fixed beyond all the power of criticism to remove, we would exhort him to become somewhat less strikingly original,—to be less fond of the folly of too new or too old phrases,—and to believe that poetry does not consist in either the one or the other. We could then venture to promise him a double portion of readers, and a reputation which, if he persist in his errors, he will never obtain. Be this as it may, his writings present us with so many fine and striking ideas, or passages, that we shall always read his poems with much pleasure.

Examiner

July 30, 1820, pp. 494–95. The author was Charles Lamb: see Edmund Blunden, Leigh Hunt's 'Examiner' Examined (London, 1928), pp. 101–02. The review begins directly below.

[The following specimens of Mr. Keats's volume of poetry just published, and the happy comments that succeed, are by a critic in the *New Times*. The poet and the critic are worthy of each other,—a rare coincidence, when the first is good:—]

[Stanzas XXIV–XXVII of 'The Eve of St. Agnes' are quoted.]

Such is the description which Mr. Keats has given us with a delicacy worthy of *Christabel*, of a high-born damsel, in one of the apartments of an old baronial castle, laying herself down devoutly to dream, on the charmed Eve of St. Agnes; and like the radiance, which comes from those old windows upon the limbs and garments of the damsel, is the almost Chaucer-like painting, with which this poet illumines every subject he touches. We have scarcely any thing like it in modern description. It brings us back to ancient days, and

Beauty making-beautiful old rhyme.

The finest thing in the volume is the paraphrase of Boccaccio's story of the Pot of Basil. Two Florentine merchants, discovering that their sister Isabella has placed her affections upon Lorenzo, a young factor in their employ, when they had hopes of procuring for her a noble match, decoy Lorenzo, under pretence of a ride, into a wood, where they suddenly stab and bury him. The anticipation of the assassination is wonderfully conceived in one epithet, in the narration of the ride—

> So the two brothers, and their *murder'd* man,
>   Rode past fair Florence, to where Arno's stream
> Gurgles—

Returning to their sister, they delude her with a story of their having sent Lorenzo to look after their merchandise; but the spirit of her lover appears to Isabella in a dream, and discovers how and where he was stabbed, and the spot where they have buried him. To ascertain the truth of the vision, she sets out to the place, accompanied by her old nurse, ignorant as yet of her wild purpose. Her arrival at it, and digging for the body, is described in the following stanzas, than which there is nothing more awfully simple in diction, more nakedly grand and moving in sentiment in Dante, in Chaucer, or in Spenser:—

[Stanzas XLVI–XLVIII of 'Isabella' are quoted, followed by a summary of the rest of the story.]

It is a great while ago since we read the original; and in this affecting revival of it we do but

> *Weep again a long-forgotten woe.*

More exuberantly rich in imagery and painting is the story of the Lamia. It is of as gorgeous stuff as ever romance was composed of. Her first appearance in serpentine form—

> —a beauteous wreath with melancholy eyes—

her dialogue with Hermes, the *Star of Lethe,* as he is called by one of those prodigal phrases which Mr. Keats abounds in, which are each a poem in a word, and which in this instance lays open to us at once, like a picture, all the dim regions and their inhabitants, and the sudden coming of a celestial among them; the charming of her into woman's shape again by the God; her marriage with the beautiful Lycius; her magic palace, which those who knew the street, and remembered it

complete from childhood, never remembered to have seen before; the
few Persian mutes, her attendants,

> ———who that same year
> Were seen about the markets: none knew where
> They could inhabit;—

the high-wrought splendours of the nuptial bower, with the fading of
the whole pageantry, Lamia, and all, away, before the glance of Apollonius,—are all that fairy land can do for us. They are for younger
impressibilities. To us an ounce of feeling is worth a pound of fancy;
and therefore we recur again, with a warmer gratitude, to the story of
Isabella and the pot of basil, and those never cloying stanzas which we
have cited, and which we think should disarm criticism, if it be not in
its nature cruel; if it would not deny to honey its sweetness, nor to
roses redness, nor light to the stars in Heaven; if it would not bay the
moon out of the skies, rather than acknowledge she is fair.

Indicator

*Aug. 2, 1820, pp. 337–44; Aug. 9, 1820, pp. 345–52. The author was
Leigh Hunt: see Louis Landré, Leigh Hunt (Paris, 1936), II, 192.*

In laying before our readers an account of another new publication,
it is fortunate that the nature of the work again falls in with the character of our miscellany; part of the object of which is to relate the
stories of old times. We shall therefore abridge into prose the stories
which Mr. Keats has told in poetry, only making up for it, as we go,
by cutting some of the richest passages out of his verse, and fitting
them in to our plainer narrative. They are such as would leaven a
much greater lump. Their drops are rich and vital, the essence of a
heap of fertile thoughts.

The first story, entitled Lamia, was suggested to our author by a
passage in Burton's Anatomy of Melancholy, which he has extracted
at the end of it. We will extract it here, at the beginning, that the
readers may see how he has enriched it. Burton's relation is itself an
improvement on the account in Philostratus. The old book-fighter with
melancholy thoughts is speaking of the seductions of phantasmata.

[The passage of Burton's *Anatomy of Melancholy* given by Keats is
quoted in full. A plot summary begins and lines 35–41 are quoted.]

Mercury went looking about among the trees and grass,

> Until he found a palpitating snake,
> Bright, and cirque-couchant in a dusky brake.

The admiration, pity, and horror, to be excited by humanity in a brute shape, were never perhaps called upon by a greater mixture of beauty and deformity than in the picture of this creature. Our pity and suspicions are begged by the first word: the profuse and vital beauties with which she is covered seem proportioned to her misery and natural rights; and lest we should lose sight of them in this gorgeousness, the 'woman's mouth' fills us at once with shuddering and compassion.

> She was a gordian shape of dazzling hue,
> Vermillion-spotted, golden, green, and blue;
> Striped like a zebra, freckled like a pard,
> Eyed like a peacock, and all crimson-barr'd;
> And full of silver moons, that, as she breathed,
> Dissolv'd or brighter shone, or interwreathed
> Their lustries with the gloomier tapestries—
> So rainbow-sided, touch'd with miseries,
> She seem'd at once, some penanced lady elf,
> Some daemon's mistress, or the daemon's self.
> Upon her crest she wore a wannish fire
> Sprinkled with stars, like Ariadne's tiar:
> Her head was serpent, but ah, bitter-sweet!
> She had a woman's mouth with all its pearls complete:
> And for her eyes: what could such eyes do there,
> But weep, and weep, that they were born so fair?
> As Proserpine still weeps for her Sicilian air.

[A summary of the rest of the story is given, with brief quotations interspersed. The only comment made is that lines 122–24 of Part II are 'the very quintessence of the romantic'.]

Mr. Keats has departed as much from common-place in the character and moral of this story, as he has in the poetry of it. He would see fair play to the serpent, and makes the power of the philosopher an ill-natured and disturbing thing. Lamia though liable to be turned into painful shapes had a soul of humanity; and the poet does not see why she should not have her pleasures accordingly, merely because a philosopher saw that she was not a mathematical truth. This is fine and good. It is vindicating the greater philosophy of poetry. At the same time, we wish that for the purpose of his story he had not appeared to give into the common-place of supposing that Apollonius's sophistry must always prevail, and that modern experiment has done a deadly thing to poetry by discovering the nature of the rainbow, the air, &c.: that is to say, that the knowledge of natural history and physics, by shewing us the nature of things, does away the imaginations that once adorned them. This is a condescension to a learned vulgarism, which so excellent a poet as Mr. Keats ought not to have made. The world will always have fine poetry, as long as it has events, passions, affections, and a philosophy that sees deeper than this philosophy. There will be a poetry of the heart, as long as there are tears and smiles: there will be a poetry of the imagination, as long as the first causes of things remain a mystery. A man who is no poet, may think he is none, as soon as he finds out the physical cause of the rainbow; but he need not alarm himself:—he was none before. The true poet will go deeper. He will ask himself what is the cause of that physical cause; whether truths to the senses are after all to be taken as truths to the imagination; and whether there is not room and mystery enough in the universe for the creation of infinite things, when the poor matter-of-fact philosopher has come to the end of his own vision. It is remarkable that an age of poetry has grown up with the progress of experiment; and that the very poets, who seem to countenance these notions, accompany them by some of their finest effusions. Even if there were nothing new to be created,— if philosophy, with its line and rule, could even score the ground, and say to poetry 'Thou shalt go no further,' she would look back to the old world, and still find it inexhaustible. The crops from its fertility are endless. But these alarms are altogether idle. The essence of poetical enjoyment does not consist in belief, but in a voluntary power to imagine.

The next story, that of the Pot of Basil, is from Boccaccio. After the narrative of that great writer, we must make as short work of it as possible in prose. To turn one of his stories into verse, is another thing. It is like setting it to a more elaborate music. Mr. Keats is so struck with admiration of his author, that even while giving him this accompaniment, he breaks out into an apology to the great Italian, asking pardon for this

—Echo of him in the north-wind sung.

We might waive a repetition of the narrative altogether, as the public have lately been familiarized with it in the Sicilian Story of Mr. Barry Cornwall:

[A brief plot summary is given.]

Our author can pass to the most striking imaginations from the most delicate and airy fancy. He says of the lovers in their happiness,

> Parting they seemed to tread upon the air,
>   Twin roses by the zephyrs blown apart
> Only to meet again more close, and share
>   The inward fragrance of each other's heart.

These pictures of their intercourse terribly aggravate the gloom of what follows. Lorrenzo, when lured away to be killed, is taken un-knowingly out of his joys, like a lamb out of the pasture. The following masterly anticipation of his end, conveyed in a single word, has been justly admired:—

> So the two brothers and their *murder'd* man
>   Rode past fair Florence, to where Arno's stream
> Gurgles through straitened banks
>   They passed the water
> Into a forest quiet for the slaughter.

When Mr. Keats errs in his poetry, it is from the ill management of a good thing,—exuberance of ideas. Once or twice, he does so in a taste positively bad, like Marino[1] or Cowley, as in a line in his Ode to Psyche

> At tender eye-dawn of aurorean love;

but it is once or twice only, in his present volume. Nor has he erred much in it in a nobler way. What we allude to is one or two passages in which he over-informs the occasion or the speaker; as where the brothers, for instance, whom he describes as a couple of mere 'money-bags,' are gifted with the power of uttering the following exquisite metaphor:—

> 'To day we purpose, ay, this hour we mount
> To spur three leagues towards the Apennine:

[1] Giovan Battista Marino (1569-1626) was an Italian poet whose mythological poem *Adone* had a very long and thin plot and sensual and extravagant imagery.

Come down, we pray thee, ere the hot sun count
His dewy rosary on the eglantine.'

But to return to the core of the story.—Observe the fervid misery of the following.

[Stanzas XLVI–XLVIII are quoted.]

It is curious to see how the simple pathos of Boccaccio, or (which is the same thing) the simple intensity of the heroine's feelings, suffices our author more and more, as he gets to the end of his story. And he has related it as happily, as if he had never written any poetry but that of the heart. The passage about the tone of her voice,—the poor lost-witted coaxing,—the 'chuckle,' in which she asks after her Pilgrim and her Basil,—is as true and touching an instance of the effect of a happy familiar word, as any in all poetry. The poet bids his imagination depart,

[The last nineteen lines of the poem are quoted.]

The Eve of St. Agnes, which is rather a picture than a story, may be analysed in a few words. It is an account of a young beauty, who going to bed on the eve in question to dream of her lover, while her rich kinsmen, the opposers of his love, are keeping holiday in the rest of the house, finds herself waked by him in the night, and in the hurry of the moment agrees to elope with him. The portrait of the heroine, preparing to go to bed, is remarkable for its union of extreme richness and good taste; not that those two properties of description are naturally distinct; but that they are too often separated by very good poets, and that the passage affords a striking specimen of the sudden and strong maturity of the author's genius. When he wrote Endymion he could not have resisted doing too much. To the description before us, it would be a great injury either to add or diminish. It falls at once gorgeously and delicately upon us, like the colours of the painted glass. Nor is Madeline hurt by all her encrusting jewelry and rustling silks. Her gentle, unsophisticated heart is in the midst, and turns them into so many ministrants to her loveliness.

[Stanzas XXIV–XXVII are quoted.]

Is not this perfectly beautiful?

As a specimen of the Poems, which are all lyrical, we must indulge ourselves in quoting entire the Ode to a Nightingale. There is that mixture in it of real melancholy and imaginative relief, which poetry alone presents us in her 'charmed cup,' and which some over-rational critics have undertaken to find wrong because it is not true. It does not follow that what is not true to them, is not true to others. If the relief is real, the mixture is good and sufficing. A poet finds refreshment in his imaginary wine, as other men do in their real; nor have we the least doubt, that Milton found his grief for the loss of his friend King, more solaced by the allegorical recollections of Lycidas, (which were exercises of his mind, and recollections of a friend who would have admired them) than if he could have anticipated Dr. Johnson's objections, and mourned in nothing but broadcloth and matter of fact. He yearned after the poetical as well as social part of his friend's nature; and had as much right to fancy it straying in the wilds and oceans of romance, where it had strayed, as in the avenues of Christ's College where his body had walked. In the same spirit the imagination of Mr. Keats betakes itself, like the wind, 'where it listeth,' and is as truly there, as if his feet could follow it. The poem will be the more striking to the reader, when he understands what we take a friend's liberty in telling him, that the author's powerful mind has for some time past been inhabiting a sickened and shaken body, and that in the mean while it has had to contend with feelings that make a fine nature ache for its species, even when it would disdain to do so for itself;—we mean, critical malignity,—that unhappy envy, which would wreak its own tortures upon others, especially upon those that really feel for it already.

[The 'Ode to a Nightingale' is quoted in full.]

The Hyperion is a fragment,—a gigantic one, like a ruin in the desart, or the bones of the mastodon. It is truly of a piece with its subject, which is the downfall of the elder gods. It opens with Saturn, dethroned, sitting in a deep and solitary valley, benumbed in spite of his huge powers with the amazement of the change.

[The first forty-one lines are quoted.]

By degrees, the Titans meet in one spot, to consult how they may regain their lost empire; but Clymene the gentlest, and Oceanus the most reflective of those earlier deities, tell them that it is irrecoverable. A very grand and deep-thoughted cause is assigned for this by the latter. Intellect, he gives them to understand, was inevitably displacing a more brute power.

[Lines 182–90 and 202–15 of Book II are quoted.]

The more imaginative parts of the poem are worthy of this sublime moral. Hyperion, the God of the Sun, is the last to give way; but horror begins to visit his old beautitude with new and dread sensations. The living beauty of his palace, whose portals open like a rose, the awful phaenomena that announce a change in heaven, and his inability to bid the day break as he was accustomed,—all this part, in short, which is the core and inner diamond of the poem, we must enjoy with the reader.

[Lines 176–304 of Book I are quoted.]

The other Titans, lying half lifeless in their valley of despair, are happily compared to

> A dismal cirque
> Of Druid stones, upon a forlorn moor,
> When the chill rain begins at shut of eve
> In dull November, and their chancel vault,
> The Heaven itself, is blinded throughout night.

The fragment ends with the deification of Apollo. It strikes us that there is something too effeminate and human in the way in which Apollo receives the exaltation which his wisdom is giving him. He weeps and wonders somewhat too fondly; but his powers gather nobly on him as he proceeds. He exclaims to Mnemosyne, the Goddess of Memory,

> Knowledge enormous makes a God of me,
> Names, deeds, gray legends, dire events, rebellions,
> Majesties, sovran voices, agonies,
> Creations and destroying, all at once
> Pour into the wide hollows of my brain,
> And deify me, as if some blithe wine
> Or bright elixir peerless I had drunk,
> And so become immortal.

After this speech, he is seized with a glow of aspiration, and an intensity of pain, proportioned to the causes that are changing him; Mnemosyne upholds her arms, as one who prophesied; and

> At length
> Apollo shrieked;—and lo! from all his limbs
> Celestial * * * * * *

Here the poem ceases, to the great impatience of the poetical reader.

If any living poet could finish this fragment, we believe it is the author himself. But perhaps he feels that he ought not. A story which involves passion, almost of necessity involves speech; and though we may well enough describe beings greater than ourselves by comparison, unfortunately we cannot make them speak by comparison. Mr. Keats, when he first introduces Thea consoling Saturn, says that she spoke

> Some mourning words, which in our feeble tongue
> Would come in these like accents; O how frail
> To that large utterance of the early Gods!

This grand confession of want of grandeur is all that he could do for them. Milton could do no more. Nay, he did less, when according to Pope he made

> God the father turn a school divine.

The moment the Gods speak, we forget that they did not speak like ourselves. The fact is, they feel like ourselves; and the poet would have to make them feel otherwise, even if he could make them speak otherwise, which he cannot, unless he venture upon an obscurity which would destroy our sympathy: and what is sympathy with a God, but turning him into a man? We allow, that superiority and inferiority are, after all, human terms, and imply something not so truly fine and noble as the levelling of a great sympathy and love; but poems of the present nature, like Paradise Lost, assume a different principle; and fortunately perhaps, it is one which it is impossible to reconcile with the other.

We have now to conclude the surprise of the reader, who has seen what solid stuff these poems are made of, with informing him of what the book has not mentioned,—that they were almost all written four years ago, when the author was but twenty. Ay, indeed! cries a critic, rubbing his hands delighted (if indeed even criticism can do so, any longer); 'then that accounts for the lines you speak of, written in the taste of Marino.'—It does so; but, sage Sir, after settling the merits of those one or two lines you speak of, what accounts, pray, for a small matter which you leave unnoticed, namely, all the rest?—The truth is, we rather mention this circumstance as a matter of ordinary curiosity, than any thing else; for great faculties have great privileges, and leap over time as well as other obstacles. Time itself, and its continents, are things yet to be discovered. There is no knowing even how much duration one man may crowd into a few years, while others drag out their slender lines. There are circular roads full of hurry and scenery, and straight roads full of listlessness and barrenness; and travellers may arrive by both, at the same hour. The Miltons, who begin intellectually old, and still intellectual, end physically old, are indeed Methusalems; and may such be our author, their son.

Mr. Keats's versification sometimes reminds us of Milton in his blank verse, and sometimes of Chapman both in his blank verse and rhyme; but his faculties, essentially speaking, though partaking of the unearthly aspirations and abstract yearnings of both these poets, are altogether his own. They are ambitious, but less directly so. They are more social, and in the finer sense of the word, sensual, than either. They are more coloured by the modern philosophy of sympathy and natural justice. Endymion, with all its extraordinary powers, partook of the faults of youth, though the best ones; but the reader of Hyperion and these other stories would never guess that they were written at twenty. The author's versification is now perfected, the exuberances of his imagination restrained, and a calm power, the surest and loftiest of all power, takes place of the impatient workings of the younger god within him. The character of his genius is that of energy and voluptuousness, each able at will to take leave of the other, and possessing, in their union, a high feeling of humanity not common to the best authors who can less combine them. Mr. Keats undoubtedly takes his seat with the oldest and best of our living poets.

We have carried our criticism to much greater length than we intended; but in truth, whatever the critics might think, it is a refreshment to us to get upon other people's thoughts, even though the rogues be our contemporaries. Oh! how little do those minds get out of themselves, and what fertile and heaven-breathing prospects do they lose, who think that a man must be confined to the mill-path of his own homestead, merely that he may avoid seeing the abundance of his neighbours! Above all, how little do they know of us eternal, weekly, and semi-weekly writers! We do not mean to say that it is not very pleasant to run upon a smooth road, seeing what we like, and talking what we like; but we do say, that it is pleasanter than all, when we are tired, to hear what we like, and to be lulled with congenial thoughts and higher music, till we are fresh to start again upon our journey. What we would not give to have a better Examiner and a better Indicator than our own twice every week, uttering our own thoughts in a finer manner, and altering the world faster and better than we can alter it! How we should like to read our present number, five times bettered; and to have nothing to do, for years and years, but to pace the green lanes, forget the tax-gatherer, and vent ourselves now and then in a verse.

Baldwin's *London Magazine*

II (Sept. 1820), 315–21. The author was John Scott, a writer and editor of the London. *Authority for the attribution is T. Rowland Hughes, 'The London Magazine' (Ph.D. dissertation, Oxford University, 1931).*

We opened this volume with very considerable anxiety:—an anxiety partly occasioned by the unqualified praises of which the author has been the object,—but more owing to the abuse by which he has been assailed. Perhaps from the whole history of criticism, real and pretended, nothing more truly unprincipled than that abuse can be quoted; nothing more heartless, more vindictive,—more nefarious in design, more pitiful and paltry in spirit. We consider it one of the worst signs of these, the worst times which England, we are afraid, has ever seen, that the miserable selfishness of political party has erected itself into a literary authority, and established, by means of popular channels, the most direct and easy access to the public ear on literary questions. The provocation, we allow, is reciprocal: the vanity of the Examiner manifests just as great a deficiency in real candour as is apparent in the bitter spite of the Quarterly, or the merry ruffianism of Blackwood. But the distinct consciousness of depravity in the two latter, which must accompany them in many of their lucubrations, gives a blacker feature to their conduct. It would be well worthy, we think, of the great talents and lofty principles of the new Edinburgh Professor of Moral Philosophy,[1] to discuss ethically from his comfortable chair,—where he sits, the honour of Scotland, and fit substitute for Dugald Stewart, —the specific difference in moral guilt and personal degradation, which distinguishes the misrepresentations of a blind overweening vanity from those of a sordid and cunning worldly greediness. The young Scotchmen would listen attentively to the arguments of one so well-qualified to handle this point; and the lecture might have blessed effects on their future lives and fortunes.—But to the subject before us, from whence we are wandering.

Mr. Keats, though not a political writer, plunged at once, with what we shall take the liberty of calling a boyish petulance, and with an air of rather insulting bravado, into some very delicate subjects;—subjects on which, we have no hesitation to say, those very qualities of his mind which confer on his poetry its most characteristic beauties, incapacitate him fairly to pronounce. There have been, and it is possible there may be even now, great comprehensive intellects, which, to wealthy and voluptuous imaginations, add a far-sightedness sufficient

[1] John Wilson, a major contributor to *Blackwood's*.

to discern, and a magnanimity inducing them to acknowledge, the deep, internal, and inextricable connection between the pains and penalties of human nature, and its hopes and enjoyments: whose spirits dwell and play in 'the plighted clouds,'—but who understand enough of the philosophy of earthly existence to know, that as man must cultivate the ground by the sweat of his brow, so he must cultivate his faculties by self-denials and struggles of soul:—who perceive lurking in the common restraints of society, eternal principles of human nature— mysterious instincts, which, through the mortification of desire, the humiliation of feeling, and often in the absence of an active sense of justice or clear view of utility, conduct to the average *maximum*, such as it is, of human good and moral beauty. Such intellects are scornful of none of our necessities while they provide for our delights: in stimulating the strength of human nature, they do not mislead or neglect its weaknesses: they are impartial in their judgments, because their views are commanding, and their motives issue from lofty dispositions. They will not palter, or play false with what they see daily before them, because the conclusions it suggests may chance to reproach some of their own actions. They will have learnt, by degrees, to correct the unfavourable decisions which we are all naturally inclined to found on dissimilarity of habits, and opposition of tastes; and they will at length have been induced to convert these into reasons for self-suspicion, rather than grounds for accusing others. Following human life into its various walks; contemplating it fairly and kindly in all its aspects, they will have been compelled to conclude, that it is not self-abandonment to the favourite themes of touching description, and to those pursuits which seem to lead most directly to the indulgence and excitement of a reflective sensibility, that exclusively proves the fine construction and delicate movements of the mind. In the labyrinth of the world they will have found that appearances are not guides;— that a face cast up towards the moon does not more certainly infer an amiable or susceptible disposition, than a contracted brow cast down over a ledger of bad debts. Selfishness, it will have struck them, is often most active in the whirlwind of passion; and it will have occurred to them that, in the estimation of intelligences altogether superior to this worldly turmoil, fainting away over a fair bosom does not, unless accompanied by other symptoms, prove much more in favour of the refinement of the transported person than clasping a money-bag, or ogling a haunch of venison. A man may smell to a rose, or walk out to admire an effect of sun-set, and yet not have half that complication of the warmer affections stirring within him, which shall move a tradesman of the Strand, seated with his wife, children, and shopman,

363

in his back parlour;—and the said tradesman may take out a writ against a dilatory customer, in no worse spirit than that in which one author pursues another for literary defalcation. It is well to let the imagination contemplate splendours hanging over past times; the soul must stretch itself somehow out of its cramps: but this may be done without committing crying, positive injustice towards the present. It may be allowable in poetry to treat ancient thieves with the respect due to true men; but the poet has no business, more than the police officer, to treat true men, his neighbours, as thieves. If Maid Marian were to come back, and complain in our hearing, as she does in Mr. Keats's poetry—

> ———Strange! that honey
> Can't be got without hard money—

we would ask her what there is strange in this? and whether it is not quite as well to get things by hard money as by hard blows? and whether more injustice be included in the inequality of purses—a consequence of society—than in that inequality of arms, which is an effect of nature? Of course, we would not have thus selected, for the purpose of argument, a passage bearing an air of pleasantry, if we did not think that Mr. Keats's sensibility is diseased in this respect—that his spirit is impregnated with a flippant impatience, (irritated and justified by a false philosophy) of the great phenomena of society, and the varieties of human nature, which hurts his poetry quite as much as it corrupts his sentiments—and which is altogether unworthy of the grandeur of his powers. There are some stanzas introduced into his delicious tale of 'Isabel—poor simple Isabel,' in this volume, which, we think, dreadfully mar the musical tenderness of its general strain. They are no better than extravagant school-boy vituperation of trade and traders; just as if lovers did not trade,—and that, often in stolen goods—or had in general any higher object than a barter of enjoyment! These stanzas in Mr. Keats's poem, when contrasted with the larger philosophy of Boccaccio, and his more genial spirit, as exemplified with reference to the very circumstances in question, are additionally offensive. Instead of tirading against the brothers as 'money-bags,' 'Baalites of pelf,' 'ledger-men,'—and asking, 'why, in the name of glory, were they proud?' Boccaccio describes the honour of the family as actually injured by Lorenzo, whom they employed—he shows us the elder brother, on discovering his sister's dishonour, afflicted with grief and perplexity, and passing a sleepless night on his bed—he even compliments the discretion of this member of the family—and it is thus naturally, and faithfully, and feelingly introduced, that he leads up the dreadful catastrophe to its consumation in Italian revenge, and the broken-heartedness of widowed love. Does the pathos of the tale suffer by thus looking fairly into the face of human nature? Do we pity the lovers less; do we sympathize less with Isabel's bitter tears, because we have both sides of the case thus placed before us? No—our sympathies, being more fairly excited, are more keenly so: the story is in fine keeping, as a painter would say: the effect of truth overpowers us: we weep the more because we feel that human frailty provides for human suffering, and that the best impulses of the heart are not removed from the liability of producing the extremities of agony and of crime. Mr. Keats, we are sure, has a sensibility sufficiently delicate to feel this beauty in Boccaccio: why then has he substituted for it, in his own composition, a boisterous rhapsody, which interrupts the harmony of the sorrowful tale,—repels sympathy by the introduction of caricature,—and suggests all sorts of dissenting, and altercating prejudices and opinions? His device is a clumsy one: Boccaccio's delicate and true. That most beautiful Paper, (by a correspondent of course) in our last number, on the 'ledger-men,' of the South Sea House, is an elegant reproof of such short-sighted views of character; such idle hostilities against the realities of life.[1] How free from intolerance of every sort must the spirit be, that conceived that paper,— or took off so fair and clear an impression from facts! It would not be prone to find suggestion of invective in the sound of Sabbath bells, as Mr. Keats has done in a former work. The author of Endymion and Hyperion must delight in that Paper;—and, to give another example of what we mean, he must surely feel the gentle poetical beauty which is infused into the star-light tale of Rosamund Grey, through its vein of 'natural piety.'[2] What would that tale be without the Grandmother's Bible? How eclipsed would be the gleaming light of such a character as Rosamund's, in a re-modelled state of society, where it should be the fashion for wives to be considered as dainties at a pic-nic party, each man bringing his own with him—but ready to give and take with those about him! Creeds here are out of the question altogether;—we only speak with reference to the wants and instincts of the human soul. We mention these things, not because we desire to see Mr. Keats playing the hypocrite, or enlisted as a florid declaimer on the profitable side of things; but because, with our admiration of his powers, we are loath to see him irrecoverably committed to a flippant and false system of reasoning on human nature;—because to his picturesque imagination,

[1] Lamb's 'The South-Sea House'.
[2] A short novel by Lamb.

we wish that he would add a more pliable, and, at the same time, a more magnanimous sensibility. Nor need his philosophy be a whit more condescending to what is grovelling and base. Let him write, as much as he pleases, in the bold indignant style of Wordsworth's glorious Sonnet!

The world is too much with us!

Here the poet speaks—not the malcontent;—it is not mortification, but inspiration he feels;—it is not classes of men, but crawling minds he anathematizes. We must positively give this magnificent Sonnet entire, now we have accidentally been brought to it by the current of our writing. It cannot be deemed out of place any where—for it is a high animation to noble thoughts.

[The sonnet is quoted in full.]

From what we have said, in the way of objection to the fashion of Mr. Keats's thinking, on certain important questions, it will easily be seen that he has very much, and very incautiously exposed himself to attack;—and his chivalry, as it will be guessed, has done him but little service in his contest with the wind-mills in Albemarle-street.[1] These things, that go furiously with the breeze of the time, have beaten his lance out of its rest, battered his helmet, and over-turned in the dirt himself and his steed. It is impossible,—however we may regret the extravagant course his Knight-errantry has taken,—not to feel our wishes and sympathies on the side of the knight of the Sorrowful countenance in this encounter. His spirit is a gallant one; his brain is full of high feats; his heart beats in real devotion to a Dulcinea whom he has clad with fine attributes in his imagination, though, certainly, we believe her to be much less a lady than he imagines her. His delusion, however, is the offspring of a romantic temperament; whereas his maulers are but things of brute matter, machines for grinding grist; —'plates hung on pins to turn with the wind,'—acquiring a murderous power from their specific levity.

The injustice which has been done to our author's works, in estimating their poetical merit, rendered us doubly anxious, on opening his last volume, to find it likely to seize fast hold of general sympathy, and thus turn an overwhelming power against the paltry traducers of a talent, more eminently promising in many respects, than any that the present age has been called upon to encourage. We have not found it

[1] The location of the publishing house of John Murray, who published the *Quarterly Review*.

to be quite all that we wished in this respect—and it would have been very extraordinary if we had, for our wishes went far beyond reasonable expectations. But we have found it of a nature to present to common understandings the poetical power with which the author's mind is gifted, in a more tangible and intelligible shape than that in which it has appeared in any of his former compositions. It is, therefore, calculated to throw shame on the lying, vulgar spirit, in which this young worshipper in the temple of the Muses has been cried-down; whatever questions it may still leave to be settled as to the kind and degree of his poetical merits. Take for instance, as a proof of the justice of our praise, the following passage from an Ode to the Nightingale:—it is distinct, noble, pathetic, and true: the thoughts have all chords of direct communication with naturally-constituted hearts: the echoes of the strain linger about the depths of human bosoms.

[Stanzas VII and VIII are quoted. Lines 65–67 are italicized by the reviewer.]

Let us take also a passage of another sort altogether—the description of a young beauty preparing for her nightly rest, overlooked by a concealed lover, in which we know not whether most to admire the magical delicacy of the hazardous picture, or its consummate, irresistible attraction. 'How sweet the moonlight sleeps upon this bank,' says Shakspeare; and sweetly indeed does it fall on the half undressed form of Madeline:—it has an exquisite moral influence, corresponding with the picturesque effect.

[Stanzas XXIII and XXV–XXVIII are quoted. Lines 201–02, 222–25, and 229–31 are italicized by the reviewer.]

One more extract,—again varying entirely the style of the composition. It shall be taken from a piece called Hyperion; one of the most extraordinary creations of any modern imagination. Its 'woods are ruthless, dreadful, deaf, and dull:' the soul of dim antiquity hovers, like a mountain-cloud, over its vast and gloomy grandeur: it carries us back in spirit beyond the classical age; earlier than 'the gods of the Greeks;' when the powers of creation were to be met with visible about the young earth, shouldering the mountains, and with their huge forms filling the vallies. The sorrows of this piece are 'huge;' its utterance 'large;' its tears 'big.'—Alas, centuries have brought littleness since then,—otherwise a crawling, reptile of office, with just strength enough to leave its slimy traces on the pages of a fashionable Review, could never have done a real mischief to the poet of the Titans! It is but a fragment we have of Hyperion: an advertisement tells us that 'the

367

poem was intended to have been of equal length with Endymion, *but the reception given to that work discouraged the author from proceeding.*' Let Mr. Croker read the following sublime and gorgeous personification of Asia, and be proud of the information thus given him—and of that superior encouragement to which it is owing that we have his Talavera in a complete state![1]

[Lines 52–63 of Book II are quoted. Lines 56–60 are italicized by the reviewer.]

This is not the extract, however, which we were about to make: it was the opening of the poem we thought of. The dethronement of Saturn by Jupiter, and the later gods taking the places of the early powers of heaven and earth, form its subject. We seem entering the awful demesne of primeval solitude as the poet commences:

[The first seventy-one lines of Book I are quoted. Lines 1–7, 10, 13–17, 24, 31–33, and 37–41 are italicized by the reviewer.]

Will not our readers feel it as a disgrace attaching to the character of the period, that a dastardly attempt should have been made to assassinate a poet of power equal to these passages: that one should come like a thief to steal his 'precious diadem;'—a murder and a robbery 'most foul and horrible?' Cold-blooded conscious dishonesty, we have no hesitation to say, must have directed the pen of the critic of Endymion in the Quarterly Review: making every allowance for the callousness of a worldly spirit, it is impossible to conceive a total insensibility to the vast beauties scattered profusely over that dis-ordered, ill-digested work. The author provokes opposition, as we have already fully said: not unfrequently he even suggests angry cen-sure. We cannot help applying the word *insolent*, in a literary sense, to some instances of his neglectfulness, to the random swagger of occasional expressions, to the bravado style of many of his sentiments. But, coupling these great faults with his still greater poetical merits, what a fine, what an interesting subject did he offer for perspicacious, honourable criticism! But he was beset by a very dog-kennel; and he must be more than human if he has not had his erroneous tendencies hardened in him in consequence.

What strike us as the principal faults of his poetry, impeding his popularity, we would venture thus to specify.

[1] John Wilson Croker was the author of the review of Keats's *Endymion* in the *Quarterly Review*, which is reprinted in this edition. His *The Battles of Talavera*, a poem first published in 1809, was frequently reprinted.

1. His frequent obscurity and confusion of language. As an instance of the latter, we may mention, that he attaches the epithet of '*leaden-eyed*,' to despair, considered as a quality or sentiment. Were it a personification of despair, the compound would be as finely applied, as, under the actual circumstances, it is erroneously so. There are many, many passages too, in his last volume, as well as in his earlier ones, from which we are not able, after taking some pains to understand them, to derive any distinct notion or meaning whatever.

2. He is too fond of running out glimmerings of thoughts, and indicating distant shadowy fancies: he shows, also, a fondness for dwelling on features which are not naturally the most important or prominent. His imagination coquets with, and mocks the reader in this respect; and plain earnest minds turn away from such tricks with disgust. The greatest poets have always chiefly availed themselves of the plainest and most palpable materials.

3. He affects, in bad taste, a quaint strangeness of phrase; as some folks affect an odd manner of arranging their neckcloths, &c. This 'shows a most pitiful ambition.' We wish Mr. Keats would not talk of *cutting mercy with a sharp knife to the bone*; we cannot contemplate the *skeleton* of mercy. Nor can we familiarize ourselves pleasantly with the *dainties made to still an infant's cries*: the latter is indeed a very round about way of expression,—and not very complimentary either, we think. Young ladies, who know, of course, little or nothing of the economy of the nursery, will be apt, we imagine, to pout at this periphrasis, which puts their charms on a level with baby-corals!

But we are by this time tired of criticism; as we hope our readers are:—let us then all turn together to the book itself. We have said here what we have deemed it our duty to say: we shall there find what it will be our delight to enjoy.

British Critic

2nd ser. XIV (Sept. 1820), 257–64. The reviewer is unknown. This is a very rare example of a Review reversing its position and apologizing for a previous criticism.

If there be one person in the present day, for whom we feel an especial contempt, it is Mr. Examiner Hunt; and we confess that it is not easy for us to bring our minds to entertain respect for any one whose taste, whether in morals, in poetry, or politics, is so exceedingly corrupt as that person's must be supposed to be, who is willing to take such a man for his model. It was for this reason that Mr. Keats fell under our lash, so severely, upon the occasion of his poem of Endymion. Upon recurring to the poem, we are not unwilling to admit, that it possesses more merit, than upon a first perusal of it we were able to perceive, or rather than we were in a frame of mind to appreciate. We can hardly doubt as to that poem having been corrected by our modern Malvolio, and projected by his advice and under his superintendence;—so full was it, of all the peculiarities of that ingenious gentleman's ideas. The effect of this upon Mr. Keats's poetry, was like an infusion of ipecacuanha powder in a dish of marmalade. It created such a sickness and nausea, that the mind felt little inclination to analyse the mixture produced, and to consider, whether after all, the dose might not have been mixed with some ingredients that were in themselves agreeable. In the poems before us, the same obstacle to a dispassionate judgment, is still to be encountered—not perhaps to so great a degree, as upon the former occasion, but still in such a degree, as to reflect great praise, we think, upon our impartiality for the commendation which we feel willing to bestow.

We cannot approve of the morality of the principal poems in this little collection. One of them is from Boccaccio, and the others upon exactly the same sort of subjects as the Florentine too generally chose. However, there is nothing in the details of either poem, that would appear calculated to wound delicacy, and this, in cases whether the temptation to the contrary may be supposed to have existed, is certainly deserving of praise.

The first tale is in two parts, and called Lamia. The subject of it is taken from the following passage in Burton's 'Anatomy of Melancholy;' and we extract it as conveying a very agreeable fiction, and which loses none of its merit in the hands of Mr. Keats.

[The passage of Burton's *Anatomy of Melancholy* given by Keats is quoted in full.]

We shall now present our readers with some specimens of the manner in which our poet has dressed up the materials here afforded him; and we think those which we shall give, will prove that Mr. Keats is really a person of no ordinary genius; and that if he will only have the good sense to take advice, making Spenser or Milton his model of poetical diction, instead of Mr. Leigh Hunt, he need not despair of attaining to a very high and enviable place in the public esteem.—The poem opens with a description of Hermes seeking a nymph, of whom he was enamoured. In the course of his pursuit through the woods, he is addressed by a voice which issues from a creature in the form of a serpent, who tells him that she is a woman in love with a youth of Corinth, and that if he will restore her, as he is able to do, to her natural shape, she will give him accounts of the nymph whom he seeks. This being premised, the reader will be able to enter into the beauty of the following specimen of the manner in which this part of the poem is managed, and from thence to form some judgment of the whole.

[Lines 1–37, 93–111, 134–45, and 261–87 are quoted with interlocking comments.]

The Lamia then accompanies the youth to Corinth; and the remainder of the story displays the same richness of fancy, only as the scene becomes less peculiarly poetical, the interest, in consequence, is not sustained. The next tale is from Boccaccio, and possesses less merit; nor is there much to admire in the 'Eve of St. Agnes;' but the last poem, which is unfinished, and is called 'Hyperion,' contains some very beautiful poetry, although the greater part of it appears not to have been executed with much success; nor do we think that Mr. Keats has evinced any want of taste in leaving it incomplete; for it is plainly projected upon principles that would infallibly lead to failure, even supposing the subject were not, which we think it is, somewhat above the pitch of Mr. Keats's peculiar genius, which lies altogether in the region of fancy and description. The fable of the poem seems to be, the wars of the Titans: Saturn is described sitting alone, in despair for the loss of his celestial dominions, and afterwards Thea and Coelus, and others belonging to the Saturnian dynasty in heaven, are severally introduced. The opening of this poem struck us as very beautiful indeed.

[The first fifty lines are quoted.]

We pass over the speech which ensues; but the following lines, which come immediately after it, are, we think, strikingly fine.

[Lines 72–92 are quoted.]

We think that the specimens which we have now given of Mr. Keats's talents, are quite decisive as to his poetical powers. That a man who can write so well, should produce such absurd lines, and fall into such ridiculous modes of expression, as are to be met with in almost every page, is really lamentable. An example or two will be sufficient to convince our readers of the forbearance which we have exerted, in giving these poems the praise which is their due; for if we were to strike a balance between their beauties and absurdities, many would probably be disposed to doubt as to which side the scale inclined.

Thus we are told that

> '———charmed God
> Began an oath, and through the serpent's ears it ran
> *Warm, tremulous, devout, psalterian.*' P. 10

In another place the Lamia, as we are told,

> 'Writh'd about, convuls'd with *scarlet* pain:
> A deep *volcanian* yellow took the place
> Of all her *milder-mooned* body's grace.' P. 12.

We hear also of 'a clear pool, wherein she *passioned*, to see herself escaped.' P. 14. And likewise of this same person's pacing about 'in a pale contented sort of discontent.' P. 35. In another poem, we have the following exquisite nonsense to describe a kiss:

> 'So said, his erewhile timid lips grew bold,
> And *poesied* with her's in *dewy rhyme.*' P. 53.

Thus likewise we hear of *pleasuring* a thing, and *mirrorring* a thing; of doing a thing *fearingly* and *fairily*; of *leafits*; of walking '*silken* hush'd and *chaste*;' and innumerable other such follies, which are really too contemptible to criticise.[1] If all this nonsense is mere youthful affectation, perhaps as Mr. Keats gets more sense, he will learn to see it in its true light; such innovations in language are despicable in themselves, and disgusting to the imagination of every man of virtue and taste, from having been originally *conceited*, as Mr. Keats would say, in the brain of one of the most profligate and wretched scribblers that we can remember to have ever either heard or read of.

---

[1] The criticism of the last example given derives from a misreading of lines 185–87 of 'The Eve of St. Agnes':

> Safe at last,
> Through many a dusky gallery, they gain
> The maiden's chamber, silken, hush'd and chaste.

It should be noted, however, that the syntax of the passage is confusing.

New Monthly Magazine

XIV (*Sept. 1820*), *245–48. The reviewer is unknown.*

These poems are very far superior to any which their author has previously committed to the press. They have nothing showy, or extravagant, or eccentric about them; but are pieces of calm beauty, or of lone and self-supported grandeur. There is a fine freeness of touch about them, like that which is manifest in the old marbles, as though the poet played at will his fancies virginal, and produced his most perfect works without toil. We have perused them with the heartiest pleasure—for we feared that their youthful author was suffering his genius to be enthralled in the meshes of sickly affectation—and we rejoice to find these his latest works as free from all offensive peculiarities—as pure, as genuine, and as lofty, as the severest critic could desire.

'Lamia,' the first of these poems, is founded on the following passage in Burton's Anatomy of Melancholy, which is given as a note at its close:

[The passage of Burton's *Anatomy of Melancholy* given by Keats is quoted in full.]

The poem commences with the descent of Mercury to Crete, in search of a nymph of whom he is enamoured. We give the opening passage, as it will enable the reader to feel the airy spirit with which the young poet sets forth on his career.

[Lines 1–26 of Part I, 115–16, 119–45 and 199–220 of Part II are quoted with a brief summary of the story.]

There is, in this poem, a mingling of Greek majesty with fairy luxuriance, which we have not elsewhere seen. The fair shapes stand clear in their antique beauty, encircled with the profuse magnificence of romance, and in the thick atmosphere of its golden lustre!

'Isabella' is the old and sweet tale of the Pot of Basil, from Boccaccio, which forms the groundwork of Barry Cornwall's delicious Sicilian story. It is here so differently told, that we need not undertake the invidious task of deciding which is the sweetest. The poem of Mr. Keats has not the luxury of description, nor the rich love-scenes, of Mr. Cornwall; but he tells the tale with a naked and affecting simplicity which goes irresistibly to the heart. The following description of Isabella's visit with her old nurse to her lover's grave, and their digging for the head, is as wildly intense as any thing which we can remember.

[Stanzas XLIV–XLVIII are quoted.]

'The Eve of St. Agnes' is a piece of consecrated fancy, which shews how a young lover, in the purity of heart, went to see his gentle mistress, the daughter of a baron, as she laid herself in her couch to dream in that holy season—and how she awoke and these lovers fled into the storm—while the father and his guests were oppressed with strange night-mare, and the old nurse died smitten with the palsy. A soft religious light is shed over the whole story. The following is part of the exquisite scene in the chamber:

[Stanzas XXIV–XXVIII are quoted.]

'Hyperion, a fragment,' is in a very different style. It shews us old Saturn after the loss of his empire, and the Titans in their horrid cave, meditating revenge on the usurper, and young Apollo breathing in the dawn of his joyous existence. We do not think any thing exceeds in silent grandeur the opening of the poem, which exhibits Saturn in his solitude:

[The first twenty-one lines are quoted.]

The picture of the vast abode of Cybele and the Titans—and of its gigantic inhabitants, is in the sublimest style of Æschylus. Lest this praise should be thought extravagant we will make room for the whole.

[Lines 5–81 of Book II are quoted.]

We now take leave of Mr. Keats with wonder at the gigantic stride which he has taken, and with the good hope that, if he proceeds in the high and pure style which he has now chosen, he will attain an exalted and a lasting station among English poets.

Monthly Magazine

L (*Sept. 1820*), *166. The reviewer is unknown.*

We have read with pleasure a volume of *Poems*, lately published by Mr. Keats, the author of Endymion. There is a boldness of fancy and a classical expression of language in the poetry of this gentleman, which, we think, entitle him to stand equally high in the estimation of poetic opinion, as the author of Rimini, or as he (Barry Cornwall) of the Dramatic Scenes. Our pleasure, however, was not unmingled with sentiments of strong disapprobation. The faults characteristic of his school, are still held up to view with as much affectation, by Mr. K. as if he were fearful of not coming in for his due share of singularity, obscurity, and conceit. But though of the same genus, his poetic labours are specifically different from those of his fellow labourers in the same vineyard.—There is more reach of poetic capacity, more depth and intenseness of thought and feeling, with more classical power and expression, than what we discover in the writings of his master, or of his fellow pupil Mr. Cornwall. It is likewise more original poetry than theirs. Mr. C. is compounded of imitation—of Shakspeare, and of Mr. Leigh Hunt. Mr. H. is a familiar copier of Dryden, with the manner, only a more sparkling one, but without the pathos, of Crabbe. Mr. K., on the contrary, is always himself, and as long as *fair* originality shall be thought superior to good imitation, he will always be preferred. The Poems consist of various Tales, *Lamia, Isabella, The Eve of St. Agnes,* of which we think the first is the best. *Hyperion,* however, is the most powerful.

V
Shelley

Reviews of Shelley's 'Alastor'

British Critic

2d ser. V (May 1816), 545–46. The reviewer is unknown.

If this gentleman is not blessed with the inspiration, he may at least console himself with the madness of a poetic mind. In the course of our critical labours, we have been often condemned to pore over much profound and prosing stupidity; we are therefore not a little delighted with the nonsense which mounts, which rises, which spurns the earth, and all its dull realities; we love to fly with our author to a silent nook.

> 'One silent nook
> Was there. Even on the edge of that vast mountain
> Upheld by knotty roots and fallen rocks
> It overlooked in its serenity
> The dark earth and the bending vault of stars.'

Tolerably high this aforesaid nook, to overlook the stars: but

> 'Hither the poet came. His eyes beheld
> Their own wan light through the reflected lines
> Of his thin hair, distinct in the dark depths
> Of that still fountain.'

Vastly intelligible. Perhaps, if his poet had worn a wig, the case might have been clearer: for then it might have thrown some light on the passage from the ancient legend.

> 'By the side of a soft flowing stream
> An elderly gentleman sat;
> On the top of his head was his wig,
> On the top of his wig was his hat.'

But this aforesaid hair is endowed with strange qualities.

> 'his scattered hair
> Sered by the autumn of strange suffering,
> Sung dirges in the wind.'

This can only be interpreted by supposing, that the poet's hair was en-twined in a fiddle-stick, and being seared with 'the autumn of strange sufferings,' *alias* rosin, 'scraped discords in the wind,' for so the last line should evidently be read. But, soft—a little philosophy, for our poet is indubitably a vast philosopher.

> 'Seized by the sway of the *ascending* stream
> With dizzy swiftness round, and round, and round
> Ridge after ridge the straining boat arose,
> Till on the verge of the extremest curve
> Where through an opening of the rocky bank
> The waters overflow, and a smooth spot
> Of glassy quiet 'mid those battling tides
> Is left, the boat paused shuddering.'

A very animated boat this; something resembling that of the Irish-man, which must needs know its way to Greenwich, because it had been down the stream so often. We cannot do sufficient justice to the creative fancy of our poet. A man's hair singing dirges, and a boat pausing and shuddering, are among the least of his inventions; nature for him reverses all her laws, the streams ascend. The power of the syphon we all know, but it is for the genius of Mr. Shelley to make the streams run up hill. But we entreat the pardon of our readers for dwell-ing so long upon this *ne plus ultra* of poetical sublimity.

Blackwood's Magazine

VI (Nov. 1819), 148–54. The author was John Gibson Lockhart, a writer, lawyer, and later editor of the Quarterly Review: *see Alan L. Strout,* A Bibliography of Articles in Blackwood's Magazine 1817–1825 *(Lubbock, Texas, 1959), p. 61.*

We believe this little volume to be Mr Shelley's first publication;[1] and

[1] *Alastor* was Shelley's first major poem published under his own name. It should be noted that this review appeared over three years after the publication of the poem.

such of our readers as have been struck by the power and splendour of genius displayed in the Revolt of Islam, and by the frequent tenderness and pathos of 'Rosalind and Helen,' will be glad to observe some of the earliest efforts of a mind destined, in our opinion, under due discipline and self-management, to achieve great things in poetry. It must be encouraging to those who, like us, cherish high hopes of this gifted but wayward young man, to see what advances his intellect has made within these few years, and to compare its powerful, though still imperfect display, in his principal poem with its first gleamings and irradiations throughout this production almost of his boyhood. In a short preface, written with all the enthusiasm and much of the presumption of youth, Mr Shelley gives a short explanation of the subject of 'Alastor; or, the Spirit of Solitude,' which we cannot say throws any very great light upon it, but without which, the poem would be, we suspect, altogether unintelligible to ordinary readers. Mr Shelley is too fond of allegories; and a great genius like his should scorn, now that it has reached the maturity of manhood, to adopt a species of poetry in which the difficulties of the art may be so conveniently blinked, and weakness find so easy a refuge in obscurity.

[The first paragraph of the Preface is quoted.]

Our readers will not expect, from this somewhat dim enunciation, at all times to see the drift of this wild poem; but we think they will feel, notwithstanding, that there is the light of poetry even in the darkness of Mr Shelley's imagination. Alastor is thus first introduced to our notice.

[Lines 67–82 are quoted.]

He is then described as visiting volcanoes, lakes of bitumen, caves winding among the springs of fire, and starry domes of diamond and gold, supported by crystal columns, and adorned with shrines of pear and thrones of chrysolite—a magnificent pilgrimage no doubt, and not the less so on account of its being rather unintelligible. On completing his mineralogical and geological observations, and on re-ascending from the interior of our earth into the upper regions, his route is, to our taste, much more interesting and worthy of a poet.

[Lines 106–28 are quoted.]

During the soul-rapt enthusiasm of these mystic and magnificent wanderings, Alastor has no time to fall in love; but we are given to understand that, wherever he roams, he inspires it. There is much beauty in this picture.

[The story is sketched out and in the process, the following lines are quoted: Lines 129–44, 151–72, 239–47, 272–90, 305–07, 397–412, 420–68, 488–92, 502–14, 533–39, and 572–76. The description in lines 420–68, 'though too much labored, in the unsatisfied prodigality of opulent youth, is, beyond doubt, most highly poetical'. The address to the stream in lines 502–14 'contains a wild, and solemn, and mysterious foreboding of dissolution'. The image in 533–39 is said to be 'very fine'.]

There is scarcely any part of the Poem which does not partake of a character of extravagance—and probably many of our readers may have felt this to be the case in our extracts, even more than ourselves. Be this as it may, we cannot but think that there is great sublimity in the death scene.

[Lines 632–71 are quoted.]

Several of the smaller poems contain beauties of no ordinary kind— but they are almost all liable to the charge of vagueness and obscurity! —Mr Shelley's imagination is enamoured of dreams of death; and he loves to strike his harp among the tombs.

['On Death' is quoted in full.]

There breathes over the following scene, a spirit of deep, solemn, and mournful repose.

['A Summer Evening Churchyard' is quoted in full.]

Long as our extracts have been, we must find room for one more, from a strange and unintelligible fragment of a poem, entitled 'The Daemon of the World.' It is exceedingly beautiful.

[The first forty-seven lines are quoted.]

We beg leave, in conclusion, to say a few words about the treatment which Mr Shelley has, in his poetical character, received from the public. By our periodical critics he has either been entirely overlooked, or slightingly noticed, or grossly abused. There is not so much to find fault with in the mere silence of critics; but we do not hesitate to say, with all due respect for the general character of that journal, that Mr Shelley has been infamously and stupidly treated in the Quarterly Review. His Reviewer there, whoever he is,[1] does not shew himself a man of such lofty principles as to entitle him to ride the high horse in company with the author of the Revolt of Islam. And when one com-

---

[1] The critique of Shelley's *Revolt of Islam* in the *Quarterly Review*, XXI (April 1819), 460–71, was written by John Taylor Coleridge, nephew of Samuel Taylor Coleridge.

pares the vis inertiae of his motionless prose with the 'eagle-winged raptures' of Mr Shelley's poetry, one does not think indeed of Satan reproving Sin, but one does think, we will say it in plain words and without a figure, of a dunce rating a man of genius. If that critic does not know that Mr Shelley is a poet, almost in the very highest sense of that mysterious word, then, we appeal to all those whom we have enabled to judge for themselves, if he be not unfit to speak of poetry before the people of England. If he does know that Mr Shelley is a great poet, what manner of man is he who, with such conviction, brings himself, with the utmost difficulty, to admit that there is any beauty at all in Mr Shelley's writings, and is happy to pass that admission off with an accidental and niggardly phrase of vague and valueless commendation. This is manifest and mean—glaring and gross injustice on the part of a man who comes forward as the champion of morality, truth, faith, and religion. This is being guilty of one of the very worst charges of which he accuses another; nor will any man who loves and honours genius, even though that genius may have occasionally suffered itself to be both stained and led astray, think but with contempt and indignation and scorn of a critic who, while he pretends to wield the weapons of honour, virtue, and truth, yet clothes himself in the armour of deceit, hypocrisy, and falsehood. He *exults* to calumniate Mr Shelley's moral character, but he *fears* to acknowledge his genius. And therefore do we, as the sincere though sometimes sorrowing friends of Mr Shelley, scruple not to say, even though it may expose us to the charge of personality from those from whom alone such a charge could at all affect our minds, that the critic shews himself by such conduct as far inferior to Mr Shelley as a man of worth, as the language in which he utters his falsehood and uncharitableness shews him to be inferior as a man of intellect.

In the present state of public feeling, with regard to poets and poetry, a critic cannot attempt to defraud a poet of his fame, without paying the penalty either of his ignorance or his injustice. So long as he confines the expression of his envy or stupidity to works of moderate or doubtful merit, he may escape punishment; but if he dare to insult the spirit of England by contumelious and scornful treatment of any one of her gifted sons, that contumely and that scorn will most certainly be flung back upon himself, till he be made to shrink and to shiver beneath the load. It is not in the power of all the critics alive to blind one true lover of poetry to the splendour of Mr Shelley's genius—and the reader who, from mere curiosity, should turn to the Revolt of Islam to see what sort of trash it was that so moved the wrath and the spleen and the scorn of the Reviewer, would soon feel, that to understand the greatness of the poet, and the littleness of his traducer, nothing more was necessary than to recite to his delighted sense any six successive stanzas of that poem, so full of music, imagination, intellect, and passion. We care comparatively little for injustice offered to one moving majestical in the broad day of fame—it is the injustice done to the great, while their greatness is unknown or misunderstood that a generous nature most abhors, in as much as it seems more basely wicked to wish that genius might never lift its head, than to envy the glory with which it is encircled.

There is, we firmly believe, a strong love of genius in the people of this country, and they are willing to pardon to its possessor much extravagance and error—nay, even more serious transgressions. Let both Mr Shelley and his critic think of that—let it encourage the one to walk onwards to his bright destiny, without turning into dark or doubtful or wicked ways—let it teach the other to feel a proper sense of his own insignificance, and to be ashamed, in the midst of his own weaknesses and deficiencies and meannesses, to aggravate the faults of the highly-gifted, and to gloat with a sinful satisfaction on the real or imaginary debasement of genius and intellect.

And here we ought, perhaps, to stop. But the Reviewer has dealt out a number of dark and oracular denunciations against the Poet, which the public can know nothing about, except that they imply a charge of immorality and wickedness. Let him speak out plainly, or let him hold his tongue. There are many wicked and foolish things in Mr Shelley's creed, and we have not hitherto scrupled, nor shall we henceforth scruple to expose that wickedness and that folly. But we do not think that he believes his own creed—at least, that he believes it fully and to utter conviction—and we doubt not but the scales will yet all fall from his eyes. The Reviewer, however, with a face of most laughable horror, accuses Mr Shelley in the same breath of some nameless act of atrocity, and of having been rusticated, or expelled, or warned to go away from the University of Oxford! He seems to shudder with the same holy fear at the violation of the laws of morality and the breaking of college rules. He forgets that in the world men do not wear caps and gowns as at Oriel or Exeter. He preaches not like Paul—but like a Proctor.

Once more, then we bid Mr Shelley farewell. Let him come forth from the eternal city, where, we understand, he has been sojourning,—in his strength, conquering and to conquer. Let his soul watch his soul, and listen to the voice of its own noble nature—and there is no doubt that the future will make amends for the past, whatever its errors may have been—and that the Poet may yet be good, great, and happy.

Review of Shelley's 'Rosalind and Helen'

Monthly Review

XC (Oct. 1819), 207–09. The reviewer is unknown.

We are here presented with another specimen of the modern school of *poetical metaphysics*. Indistinct, however, and absolutely unmeaning, as Mr. Shelley usually is, he has, in his lucid intervals, a power of composition that raises him much above many of his fellows. We regret, indeed, to see so considerable a portion of real genius wasted in merely desultory fires; and still more do we lament to observe such extensive infidelity in the mind of a writer who is evidently capable of better things. The practical influence, which his scepticism would seem to have on the poet, is a subject of sincere commiseration. We can overlook a few general sallies of a thoughtless nature: but, when a man comes to such a degree of perverseness, as to represent the vicious union of two individuals of different sexes as equally sacred with the nuptial tie, we really should be wanting in our duty not to reprobate so gross an immorality.

> 'We will have rites our faith to bind,
> But our church shall be the starry night,
> Our altar the grassy earth outspread,
> And our priest the muttering wind.'

So speaks the modern *Helen*; who seems about as chaste as her antient namesake and prototype; and this is not the only passage in which such sentiments are clothed in the author's best garb of words, or put into the mouth of some interesting and amiable being.

When this writer speaks of the 'bloody faith,' we well know *what*

385

faith he means; and to charge the wicked abuses of darker ages, and of false professors of religion, on *the spirit itself* of the mildest of creeds, is no common degree of audacity. We shall not, however, waste any valuable time on an author who, we fear, is quite incorrigible in this respect; and we shall rather turn to his poetical merits; which, with the drawback of obscurity overclouding almost all that he writes, are, on some occasions, of no common stamp.

The following description of a delightful journey, taken by a lover (just released from prison) with his happy love, certainly manifests much force and feeling:

[Lines 936–77 are quoted.]

We would, in a friendly manner, admonish this poet to *stop in time.*

The death of Lionel is very striking, but occasionally disfigured by extravagant *conceits*, and throughout pervaded by *mysticism.*

In the lines written among the Euganēan Hills, (as Mr. Shelley barbarously calls them,—*Euganĕâ quantumvis molliar agnâ,*[1]) a spirited, handsome, and deserved compliment is paid to Lord Byron. We extract the best part of it. The poet is addressing Venice:

[Lines 194–205 are quoted.]

A sublime volley of bombast is uttered by the hero, in defiance of his gaolers, at p. 47.:

[Lines 894–901 of *Rosalind and Helen* are quoted.]

Yield, Nathanaël Lee! and hide thy diminish'd head![2]

[1] 'So much softer than an Euganean Lamb.' Juvenal *Satires* viii.15. The reference is here made to the pronunciation of the word *Euganean.*

[2] Nathaniel Lee (1653?–92) was a playwright whose works are noted for their bombast.

Review of Shelley's 'The Cenci'

British Review

XVII (*June 1821*), *380–89. The reviewer is unknown.*

The Cenci is the best, because it is by far the most intelligible, of Mr. Shelley's works. It is probably indebted for this advantage to the class of compositions to which it belongs. A tragedy must have a story, and cannot be conducted without men and women: so that its very nature imposes a check on the vagabond excursions of a writer, who imagines that he can find the perfection of poetry in incoherent dreams or in the ravings of bedlam. In speaking of the Cenci, however, as a tragedy, we must add, that we do so only out of courtesy and in imitation of the example of the author, whose right to call his work by what name he pleases we shall never dispute. It has, in fact, nothing really dramatic about it. It is a series of dialogues in verse; and mere versified dialogue will never make a drama. A drama must, in the course of a few scenes, place before us such a succession of natural incidents, as shall lead gradually to the final catastrophe, and develope the characters and passions of the individuals, for whom our interest or our sympathy is to be awakened: these incidents give occasion to the dialogue, which, in its turn, must help forward the progression of events, lay open to us the souls of the agents, move our feelings by the contemplation of their mental agitations, and sooth us with the charms of poetical beauty. It is from the number and nature of the ends which the poet has to accomplish, as compared with the means which he employs, that the glory and difficulty of the dramatic art arise. If the only object of a writer is to tell a story, or to express a succession of various feelings, the form of dialogue, far from adding to the arduousness of the task, is the easiest that can be adopted. It is a sort of drag net, which enables him to introduce and find a place for every thing that his wildest reveries suggest to him.

The fable of the Cenci is taken from an incident which occurred at Rome towards the end of the sixteenth century. An aged father committed the most unnatural and horrible outrages on his daughter; his wife and daughter avenged the crime by procuring the assassination of the perpetrator, and became in their turns the victims of public justice. The incident is still recollected, and often related at Rome. Hence Mr. Shelley infers, 'that it is, in fact, a tragedy which has already received, from its capacity of awakening and sustaining the sympathy of man, approbation and success.' It is remembered and related, because it is extraordinary—because it is horrible—because it is, in truth, *undramatic*. A murder, attended with circumstances of peculiar atrocity, is scarcely ever forgotten on the spot where it happened; but it is not for that reason a fit subject for dramatic poetry. The catastrophe of Marrs' family will be long recollected in London; the assassination of Fualdes will not soon be forgotten in Rhodes; yet who would ever dream of bringing either event upon the stage? Incestuous rape, murder, the rack, and the scaffold, are not the proper materials of the tragic Muse: crimes and punishments are not in themselves dramatic, though the conflict of passions which they occasion, and from which they arise, often is so. The pollution of a daughter by a father—the murder of a father by his wife and daughter, are events too disgusting to be moulded into any form capable even of awakening our interest. Mr. Shelley himself seems to have been aware of this. 'The story of the Cenci,' says he, 'is indeed eminently fearful and monstrous; any thing like a dry exhibition of it on the stage would be insupportable. The person who would treat such a subject must increase the ideal, and diminish the actual, horror of the events, so that the pleasure which arises from the poetry, which exists in these tempestuous sufferings and crimes, may mitigate the pain of the contemplation of the moral deformity from which they spring.' Without presuming to comprehend these observations completely (for we know not what poetry exists in rape and murder, or what pleasure is to be derived from it), we are sure, that whatever may be thought as to the possibility of overcoming by any management the inherent defects of the tale, Mr. Shelley, far from having even palliated its moral and its dramatic improprieties, has rendered the story infinitely more horrible and more disgusting than he found it, and has kept whatever in it is most revolting constantly before our eyes. A dialogue in which Cenci makes an open confession to a Cardinal of a supreme love of every thing bad merely for its own sake, and of living only to commit murder—a banquet given by him to the Roman nobility and dignitaries, to celebrate an event of which he has just received the news,—the death of two of his sons—and declarations of gratuitous uncaused hatred against all his relations, not excepting that daughter whom he resolves to make the victim of his brutal outrage for no other reason than because his imagination is unable to devise any more horrible crime, fill up the first two acts. Cenci has accomplished the deed of horror before the opening of the third act, in which the resolution to murder him is taken. In the fourth he again comes before us, expressing no passion, no desire, but pure abstract depravity and impiety. The murder follows, with the immediate apprehension of the members of the family by the officers of justice. The last act is occupied with the judicial proceedings at Rome. Cenci is never out of our sight, and, from first to last, he is a mere personification of wickedness and insanity. His bosom is ruffled by no passion; he is made up exclusively of inveterate hatred, directed not against some individuals, but against all mankind, and operating with a strength proportioned to the love which each relation usually excites in other men. There is no mode of expressing depravity in words which Mr. Shelley has not ransacked his imagination to ascribe to this wretch. His depravity is not even that of human nature; for it is depravity without passion, without aim, without temptation: it is depravity seeking gratification, first, in the perpetration of all that is most repulsive to human feelings, and next in making a display of its atrocity to the whole world. The following dialogue, for example, (and it is one of the gentler passages of the play) takes place in the presence of, and is in part addressed to, the Roman nobles and cardinals assembled at a banquet:—

[Lines 21–89 of Act I, scene iii, are quoted.]

The first time he alludes to the deed, which constitutes the substance of the plot, is in the following words addressed to a cardinal:—

> '———I am what your theologians call
> Hardened; which they must be in impudence,
> So to revile a man's peculiar taste.
>
> *   *   *   *   *   *   *   *   *
>
> *But that there yet remains a deed to act*
> *Whose horror might make sharp an appetite*
> *Duller than mine—I'd do—I know not what.*'—(P. 6, 7.)

After the unnatural outrage has been committed, he aims at something still more extravagent in inquity:—

> 'Might I not drag her by the golden hair?
> Stamp on her? Keep her sleepless, till her brain

Be overworn? Tame her with chains and famine?
Less would suffice. *Yet so to leave undone*
What I most seek! No, 'tis her stubborn will,
Which, by its own consent, shall stoop as low
As that which drags it down.'—(P. 56.)

His wife tries to terrify him by pretending that his death has been announced by a supernatural voice; his reply is in these words:

'————Why—such things are—
No doubt divine revealings may be made.
'Tis plain I have been favoured from above,
For when I cursed my sons, they died. Aye—so
As to the right or wrong, that's talk—repentance,
Repentance is an easy moment's work,
And more depends on God than me. Well—well,
I must give up the greater point, which was
To poison and corrupt her soul.'—(P. 57, 58.)

Such blasphemous ravings cannot be poetry, for they are neither sense nor nature. No such being as Cenci ever existed; none such could exist. The historical fact was in itself disgustingly shocking; and, in Mr. Shelley's hands, the fable becomes even more loathsome and less dramatic than the fact. It is true that there are tragedies of the highest order (the Œdipus Tyrannus for instance) where the catastrophe turns upon an event from which nature recoils; but the deed is done unwittingly; it is a misfortune, not a crime; it is kept back as much as possible from our view; the hopes, and fears, and sufferings of the parties occupy our thoughts, and all that is revolting to purity of mind is only slightly hinted at. Here the deed is done with premeditation; it is done from a wanton love of producing misery; it is constantly obtruded upon us in its most disgusting aspect; the most hateful forms of vice and suffering, preceded by involuntary pollution and followed by voluntary parricide, are the materials of this miscalled tragedy. They who can find dramatic poetry in such representations of human life must excuse us for wondering of what materials their minds are composed. Delineations like these are worse than unpoetical; they are unholy and immoral. But 'they are as lights,' if we believe Mr. Shelley, 'to make apparent some of the most dark and secret caverns of the human heart.' No, no; they teach nothing; and, if they did, knowledge must not be bought at too high a price. There is a knowledge which is death and pollution. Is knowledge any compensation for the injury sustained by being made familiar with that which ought to be to us all as if it were not? If such feelings, such ideas, exist in the world, (we cannot believe they do, for the Cenci of the Roman tradition is very different from the Cenci of Mr. Shelley) let them remain concealed. Our corporeal frames moulder into dust after death: are putrefying bodies, therefore, to be exposed in the public ways, that, forsooth, we may know what we are to be hereafter? The ties of father and daughter, of husband and wife, ought not to be profaned as they are in this poem. It is in vain to plead, that the delineations are meant to excite our hatred; they ought not to be presented to the mind at all; still less, pressed upon it long and perseveringly.

The technical structure of the piece is as faulty as its subject matter is blameable. The first two acts serve only to explain the relative situation of the parties, and do not in the least promote the action of the play; the fifth, containing the judicial proceedings at Rome, is a mere excrescence. The whole plot, therefore, is comprised in the incestuous outrage and in the subsequent assassination of the perpetrator; the former enormity occurs in the interval between the second act and the third; the latter in the fourth act. Thus the play has, properly speaking, no plot except in the third and fourth acts. But the incurable radical defects of the original conception of this drama render a minute examination of its structure superfluous.

The language is loose and disjointed; sometimes it is ambitious of simplicity, and it then becomes bald, inelegant, and prosaic. Words sometimes occur to which our ears are not accustomed; thus an 'unappealable God' means a God from whom there is no appeal. We have a great deal of confused and not very intelligible imagery. A crag is 'huge as despair;' Cenci

> '———Bears a gloom duller
> Than the earth's shade or interlunar air:'

And he describes his soul as a scourge, which will not be demanded of him till *the lash be broken in its last and deepest wound:*

> 'My soul, which is a scourge, will I resign
> Into the hands of him who wielded it;
> Be it for its own punishment or theirs,
> He will not ask it of me till the lash
> Be broken in its last and deepest wound;
> Until its hate be all inflicted.'—(P. 58.)

We extract the following lines, because we have heard them much admired:—

> '———If there should be
> No God, no Heaven, no Earth in the void world;
> The wide, grey, lampless, deep, unpeopled world!
> If all things then should be—my father's spirit,
> His eye, his voice, his touch, surrounding me;
> The atmosphere and breath of my dead life!
> If sometimes, as a shape more like himself,
> Even the form which tortured me on earth,
> Masked in grey hairs and wrinkles, he should come
> And wind me in his hellish arms, and fix
> His eyes on mine, and drag me down, down, down!
> For was he not alone omnipotent
> On Earth, and ever present? Even tho' dead,
> Does not his spirit live in all that breathe,
> And work for me and mine still the same ruin,
> Scorn, pain, despair?' (P. 99, 100.)

We confess that to us this seems metaphysical jargon in substance, dressed out in much flaunting half-worn finery.

The following is another of the admired passages in this tissue of versified dialogue:—

[Lines 6–38 of Act III, scene i, are quoted.]

We say nothing of the conceit of misery killing its own father [line 37], because we wish to direct our observations, not to the imperfections of particular passages, but to the general want of fidelity to nature which pervades the whole performance. In the crowd of images here put into the mouth of Beatrice, there is neither novelty, nor truth, nor poetical beauty. Misery like hers is too intensely occupied with its own pangs to dwell so much on extraneous ideas. It does not cause the pavement to sink, or the wall to spin round, or the sunshine to become black; it does not stain the heaven with blood; it does not change the qualities of the air, nor does it clothe itself in a mist which glues the limbs together, eats into the sinews, and dissolves the flesh; still less does it suppose itself dead. This is not the language either of extreme misery or of incipient madness; it is the bombast of a declamation, straining to be energetic, and falling into extravagant and unnatural rant.

[Lines 78–111 of Act IV, scene i, are quoted.]

This passage exemplifies the furious exaggeration of Mr. Shelley's caricatures, as well as of the strange mode in which, throughout the whole play, religious thoughts and atrocious deeds are brought together. There is something extremely shocking in finding the truths, the threats, and the precepts of religion in the mouth of a wretch, at the very moment that he is planning or perpetrating crimes at which nature shudders. In this intermixture of things, sacred and impure, Mr. Shelley is not inconsistent if he believes that religion is in Protestant countries hypocrisy, and that it is in Roman Catholic countries 'adoration, faith, submission, penitence, blind admiration; not a rule for moral conduct, and that it has no necessary connexion with any one virtue.'—(Preface, p. 13.) Mr. Shelley is in an error: men act wrongly in spite of religion; but it is because they have no steady belief of it, or because their notions of it are erroneous, or because its precepts do not occur to them at the moment some vicious passion prevails. A Christian murderer does not amuse his fancy with the precepts and denunciations of his faith at the very moment of perpetrating the deed.

The moral errors of this book prevent us from quarrelling with its literary sins.

Reviews of Shelley's 'Prometheus Unbound'

Gold's *London Magazine*

II (Sept. 1820), 306–07, (Oct. 1820), 382–91. The reviewer is unknown.

This book has made its appearance so extremely late in the month, that, although we profess to give as early and as satisfactory notices of new works as are any where to be met with, it has fairly puzzled even our most consummate ingenuity. 'Something must be done, and that right quickly, friend Bardolph'; this is our opinion as well as honest Jack Falstaff's; and with this quotation we buckle to our task. Of 'Prometheus Unbound,' the principal poem in this beautiful collection, we profess to give no account. It must be reserved for our second series, as it requires more than ordinary attention. The minor pieces are stamped throughout with all the vigorous peculiarities of the writer's mind, and are everywhere strongly impregnated with the alchymical properties of genius. But what we principally admire in them is their strong and healthy freshness, and the tone of interest that they elicit. They possess the fever and flush of poetry; the fragrant perfume and sunshine of a summer's morning, with its genial and kindly benevolence. It is impossible to peruse them without admiring the peculiar property of the author's mind, which can doff in an instant the cumbersome garments of metaphysical speculations, and throw itself naked as it were into the arms of nature and humanity. The beautiful and singularly original poem of The Cloud will evince proofs of our opinion, and show the extreme force and freshness with which the writer can impregnate his poetry.

['The Cloud' is quoted in full. The review of *Prometheus Unbound*, in the next issue, follows.]

394

This is one of the most stupendous of those works which the daring and vigorous spirit of modern poetry and thought has created. We despair of conveying to our readers, either by analysis or description, any idea of its gigantic outlines, or of its innumerable sweetnesses. It is a vast wilderness of beauty, which at first seems stretching out on all sides into infinitude, yet the boundaries of which are all cast by the poet; in which the wildest paths have a certain and noble direction; and the strangest shapes which haunt its recesses, voices of gentleness and of wisdom. It presents us with the oldest forms of Greek mythology, informed with the spirit of fresh enthusiasm and of youngest hope; and mingles with these the creatures of a new mythology, in which earth, and the hosts of heaven, spirits of time and of eternity, are embodied and vivified, to unite in the rapturous celebration of the reign of Love over the universe.

This work is not, as the title would lead us to anticipate, a mere attempt to imitate the old tragedy of the Greeks. In the language, indeed, there is often a profusion of felicitously compounded epithets; and in the imagery, there are many of those clear and lucid shapes, which distinguish the works of Æschylus and of Sophocles. But the subject is so treated, that we lose sight of persons in principles, and soon feel that all the splendid machinery around us is but the shadow of things unseen, the outward panoply of bright expectations and theories, which appear to the author's mind instinct with eternal and eternally progressive blessings. The fate of Prometheus probably suggested, even to the heroic bard by whom it was celebrated in older time, the temporary predominance of brute force over intellect; the oppression of right by might; and the final deliverance of the spirit of humanity from the iron grasp of its foes. But, in so far as we can judge from the mighty fragment which time has spared, he was contented with exhibiting the visible picture of the magnanimous victim, and with representing his deliverance, by means of Hercules, as a mere personal event, having no symbolical meaning. In Mr. Shelley's piece, the deliverance of Prometheus, which is attended by the dethroning of Jupiter, is scarcely other than a symbol of the peaceful triumph of goodness over power; of the subjection of might to right; and the restoration of love to the full exercise of its benign and all-penetrating sympathies. To represent vividly and poetically this vast moral change, is, we conceive, the design of this drama, with all its inward depths of mystical gloom, its pregnant clouds of imagination, its spiry eminences of icy splendour, and its fair regions overspread by a light 'which never was by sea or land,' which consecrates and harmonizes all things.

To the ultimate prospect exhibited by that philosophical system which Mr. Shelley's piece embodies, we have no objection. There is nothing pernicious in the belief that, even on earth, man is destined to attain a high degree of happiness and of virtue. The greatest and wisest have ever trusted with the most confiding faith to that nature, with whose best qualities they were so richly gifted. They have felt that in man were undeveloped capabilities of excellence; stores of greatness, suffered to lie hidden beneath basest lumber; sealed up fountains, whence a brighter day might loosen streams of fresh and ever-living joys. In the worst and most degraded minds, vestiges of goodness are not wanting; some old recollections of early virtue; some feeling of wild generosity or unconquerable love; some divine instinct; some fragments of lofty principle; some unextinguishable longings after nobleness and peace, indicate that there is good in man which can never yield to the storms of passion or the decays of time. On these divine instances of pure and holy virtue; on history; on science; on imagination; on the essences of love and hope; we may safely rest, in the expectation that a softer and tenderer light will ultimately dawn on our species. We further agree with Mr. Shelley, that Revenge is not the weapon with which men should oppose the erring and the guilty. He only speaks in accordance with every wise writer on legislation, when he deprecates the infliction of one vibration of *unnecessary* pain on the most criminal. He only echoes the feeling of every genuine Christian, when he contends for looking with deep-thoughted pity on the vicious, or regarding them tenderly as the unfortunate, and for striving 'not to be overcome of evil, but to overcome evil with good.' He only coincides with every friend of his species, when he deplores the obstacles which individuals and systems have too often opposed to human progress. But when he would attempt to realize in an instant his glorious visions; when he would treat men as though they are now the fit inhabitants of an earthly paradise; when he would cast down all restraint and authority as enormous evils; and would leave mankind to the guidance of passions yet unsubdued, and of desires yet unregulated, we must protest against his wishes, as tending fearfully to retard the good which he would precipitate. Happy, indeed, will be that time, of which our great philosophical poet, Wordsworth, speaks, when love shall be an 'unclouded light, and joy its own security.' But we shall not hasten this glorious era by destroying those forms and dignities of the social state, which are essential to the restraint of the worst passions, and serviceable to the nurture of the kindliest affections. The stream of human energy is gathering strength; but it would only be scattered in vain, were we rashly to destroy the boundaries which now confine it in its deep channel; and it can only be impeded by the impatient attempt to strike the shores with its agitated waters.

Although there are some things in Mr. Shelley's philosophy against which we feel it a duty thus to protest, we must not suffer our difference of opinion to make us insensible to his genius. As a poem, the work before us is replete with clear, pure, and majestical imagery, accompanied by a harmony as rich and various as that of the loftiest of our English poets. The piece first exhibits a ravine of icy rocks in the Indian Caucasus, where Prometheus is bound to the precipice, and Panthea and Ione sit at his feet to soothe his agonies. He thus energetically describes his miseries, and calls on the mountains, springs, and winds, to repeat to him the curse which he once pronounced on his foe, whom he now regards only with pity:

[Lines 31–73 of Act I, scene i, are quoted.]

The voices reply only in vague terms, and the Earth answers that they dare not tell it; when the following tremendous dialogue follows:

[Lines 131–86 of Act I, scene i, are quoted; and the brief summary of the story continues, with lines 262–302 of Act I, scene i, quoted in the process.]

Mercury next enters with the Furies sent by Jupiter to inflict new pangs on his victim. This they effect, by placing before his soul pictures of the agonies to be borne by that race for whom he is suffering. The Earth afterwards consoles him, by calling up forms who are rather dimly described as

> ———'Subtle and fair spirits,
> Whose homes are the dim caves of human thought,
> And who inhabit, as birds wing the wind,
> Its world surrounding ether.'——

We give part of their lovely chaunt in preference to the ravings of the Furies, though these last are intensely terrible:

[Lines 708–51 of Act I, scene i, are quoted; and the brief summary of the story continues, with lines 196–206 of Act II, scene i, and lines 1–63 of Act II, scene ii, quoted in the process. The Spirits of the Wood in the last quotation are said to describe 'magnificently' the recesses of the forest.]

Asia and Panthea follow the sounds into the realm of Demogorgon, into whose cave they descend from a pinnacle among the mountains.

o

Here Asia, after an obscure metaphysical dialogue, sets forth the blessing bestowed by Prometheus on the world in the richest colouring, and
asks the hour of his freedom. On this question the rocks are cloven and
the Hours are seen flying in the heavens. With one of these the sisters
ascend in the radiant Car; and Asia becomes encircled with lustre,
which inspires Panthea thus rapturously to address her:—

[Lines 16–47 of Act II, scene v, are quoted.]

Another voice is heard in the air, and Asia bursts into the following
strain, which is more liquidly harmonious, and of a beauty more
ravishing and paradisaical, than any passage which we can remember
in modern poetry:—

> 'My soul is an enchanted boat,
> Which, like a sleeping swan, doth float
> Upon the silver waves of thy sweet singing;
> And thine doth like an angel si
> Beside the helm conductingi
> Whilst all the winds with melody are ringing.
> It seems to float ever, for ever,
> Upon that many-winding river,
> Between mountains, woods, abysses,
> A paradise of wildernesses!
> Till, like one in slumber bound,
> Borne to the ocean, I float down, around,
> Into a sea profound, of ever-spreading sound:
> Meanwhile thy spirit lifts its pinions
> In music's most serene dominions;
> Catching the winds that fan that happy heaven.
> And we sail on, away, afar,
> Without a course, without a star,
> But, by the instinct of sweet music driven;
> Till through Elysian garden islets
> By thee, most beautiful of pilots,
> Where never mortal pinnace glided,
> The boat of my desire is guided:
> Realms where the air we breathe is love,
> Which in the winds on the waves doth move,
> Harmonizing this earth with what we feel above.
>
> We have pass'd Age's icy caves,
> And Manhood's dark and tossing waves,
> And Youth's smooth ocean, smiling to betray.
> Beyond the glassy gulph's we flee
> Of shadow-peopled infancy,

Through Death and Birth, to a diviner day;
A paradise of vaulted bowers,
Lit by downward-gazing flowers,
And watery paths that wind between
Wildernesses calm and green,
Peopled by shapes too bright to see,
And rest, having beheld; somewhat like thee;
Which walk upon the sea, and chaunt melodiously!'

In the third act, Jupiter is dethroned by Demogorgon, and Prometheus is unchained by Hercules. The rest of the Drama is a celebration of the joyous results of this triumph, and anticipations of the reign of Love. Our readers will probably prefer reposing on the exquisite description given by Prometheus of the cave which he designs for his dwelling, to expatiating on the wide and brilliant prospects which the poet discloses:—

[Lines 10–56 of Act III, scene iii, are quoted.]

We have left ourselves no room to expatiate on the minor Poems of this volume. The 'Vision of the Sea' is one of the most awful pictures which poetry has set before us. In the 'Ode to Liberty,' there are passages of a political bearing, which, for the poet's sake, we heartily wish had been omitted. It is not, however, addressed to minds whom it is likely to injure. In the whole work there is a spirit of good— of gentleness, humanity, and even of religion, which has excited in us a deep admiration of its author, and a fond regret that he should ever attempt to adorn cold and dangerous paradoxes with the beauties which could only have been produced by a mind instinctively pious and reverential.

Quarterly Review

XXVI (Oct. 1821), 168–80. The author was W. S. Walker, a Cambridge Fellow and Shakespearian critic: see Hill Shine and Helen C. Shine, The Quarterly Review under Gifford *(Chapel Hill, N.C., 1949), p. 76. The issue containing the review was published in December 1821 (ibid., p. 75).*

A great lawyer of the present day is said to boast of practising three different modes of writing: one which any body can read; another which only himself can read; and a third, which neither he nor any body else can read. So Mr. Shelley may plume himself upon writing in three different styles: one which can be generally understood; another which can be understood only by the author; and a third which is absolutely and intrinsically unintelligible. Whatever his command may be of the first and second of these styles, this volume is a most satisfactory testimonial of his proficiency in the last.

If we might venture to express a general opinion of what far surpasses our comprehension, we should compare the poems contained in this volume to the visions of gay colours mingled with darkness, which often in childhood, when we shut our eyes, seem to revolve at an immense distance around us. In Mr. Shelley's poetry all is brilliance, vacuity, and confusion. We are dazzled by the multitude of words which sound as if they denoted something very grand or splendid: fragments of images pass in crowds before us; but when the procession has gone by, and the tumult of it is over, not a trace of it remains upon the memory. The mind, fatigued and perplexed, is mortified by the consciousness that its labour has not been rewarded by the acquisition of a single distinct conception; the ear, too, is dissatisfied: for the rhythm of the verse is often harsh and unmusical; and both the ear and the understanding are disgusted by new and uncouth words, and by the awkward, and intricate construction of the sentences.

The predominating characteristic of Mr. Shelley's poetry, however, is its frequent and total want of meaning. Far be it from us to call for strict reasoning, or the precision of logical deductions, in poetry; but we have a right to demand clear, distinct conceptions. The colouring of the pictures may be brighter or more variegated than that of reality; elements may be combined which do not in fact exist in a state of union; but there must be no confusion in the forms presented to us. Upon a question of mere beauty, there may be a difference of taste. That may be deemed energetic or sublime, which is in fact unnatural or bombastic; and yet there may be much difficulty in making the difference sensible to those who do not preserve an habitual and exclusive intimacy with the best models of composition. But the question of meaning, or no meaning, is a matter of fact on which common sense, with common attention, is adequate to decide; and the decision to which we may come will not be impugned, whatever be the want of taste, or insensibility to poetical excellence, which it may please Mr. Shelley, or any of his coterie, to impute to us. We permit them to assume, that they alone possess all sound taste and all genuine feeling of the beauties of nature and art: still they must grant that it belongs only to the judgment to determine, whether certain passages convey any signification or none; and that, if we are in error ourselves, at least we can mislead nobody else, since the very quotations which we must adduce as examples of nonsense, will, if our charge be not well founded, prove the futility of our accusation at the very time that it is made. If, however, we should completely establish this charge, we look upon the question of Mr. Shelley's poetical merits as at an end; for he who has the trick of writing very showy verses without ideas, or without coherent ideas, can contribute to the instruction of none, and can please only those who have learned to read without having ever learned to think.

The want of meaning in Mr. Shelley's poetry takes different shapes. Sometimes it is impossible to attach any signification to his words; sometimes they hover on the verge between meaning and no meaning, so that a meaning may be obscurely conjectured by the reader, though none is expressed by the writer; and sometimes they convey ideas, which, taken separately, are sufficiently clear, but, when connected, are altogether incongruous. We shall begin with a passage which exhibits in some parts the first species of nonsense, and in others the third.

> 'Lovely apparitions, dim at first,
> Then radiant, as the mind, arising bright
> From the embrace of beauty, whence the forms
> Of which these are the phantoms, casts on them
> The gathered rays which are reality,
> Shall visit us, the immortal progeny
> Of painting, sculpture, and wrapt poesy,
> And arts, tho' unimagined, yet to be.'—p. 105.

The verses are very sonorous; and so many fine words are played off upon us, such as, *painting, sculpture, poesy, phantoms, radiance, the embrace of beauty, immortal progeny*, &c. that a careless reader, influenced by his habit of associating such phrases with lofty or agreeable ideas, may possibly have his fancy tickled into a transient feeling of satisfaction. But let any man try to ascertain what is really said, and he will immediately discover the imposition that has been practised. From beauty, or the embrace of beauty, (we know not which, for ambiguity of phrase is a very frequent companion of nonsense,) certain forms proceed: of these forms there are phantoms; these phantoms are dim; but the mind arises from the embrace of beauty, and casts on them the gathered rays which are reality; they are then baptized by the name of immortal progeny of the arts, and in that character proceed to visit Prometheus. This *galimatias* (for it goes far beyond simple nonsense) is rivalled by the following description of something that is done by a cloud.

> 'I am the daughter of earth and water,
> And the nursling of the sky;

I pass through the pores of the oceans and shores,
  I change, but I cannot die.
For after the rain, when with never a stain
  The pavilion of heaven is bare,
And the winds and sunbeams with their convex gleams,
  Build up the blue dome of air.
I silently laugh at my own cenotaph,
  And out of the caverns of rain,
Like a child from the womb, like a ghost from the tomb,
  I arise, and unbuild it again.'—pp. 199, 200.[1]

There is a love-sick lady, who 'dwells under the glaucous caverns of ocean,' and *'wears the shadow of Prometheus' soul,'* without which (she declares) she cannot *go to sleep*. The rest of her story is utterly incomprehensible; we therefore pass on to the *debut* of the Spirit of the earth.

'And from the other opening in the wood
Rushes, with loud and whirlwind harmony,
A sphere, which is as many thousand spheres,
Solid as chrystal, yet through all its mass
Flow, as through empty space, music and light:
Ten thousand orbs involving and involved,
Purple and azure, white, green, and golden,
Sphere within sphere; and every space between
Peopled with unimaginable shapes,
Such as ghosts dream dwell in the lampless deep,
Yet each inter-transpicuous, and they whirl
Over each other with a thousand motions,
Upon a thousand sightless axles spinning,
And with the force of self-destroying swiftness,
Intensely, slowly, solemnly, roll on,
Kindling with mingled sounds, and many tones,
Intelligible words and music wild.
With mighty whirl the multitudinous orb
Grinds the bright brook into an azure mist
Of elemental subtlety, like light;
And the wild odour of the forest flowers,
The music of the living grass and air,
The emerald light of leaf-entangled beams
Round its intense yet self-conflicting speed,
Seem kneaded into one aërial mass
Which drowns the sense.'

[1] Lines 73–84 of 'The Cloud'.

We have neither leisure nor room to develope all the absurdities here accumulated, in defiance of common sense, and even of grammar; whirlwind harmony, a solid sphere which is as many thousand spheres, and contains ten thousand orbs or spheres, with inter-transpicuous spaces between them, whirling over each other on a thousand sightless (alias invisible) axles; self-destroying swiftness; intelligible words and wild music, kindled by the said sphere, which also grinds a bright brook into an azure mist of elemental subtlety; odour, music, and light, kneaded into one aërial mass, and the sense drowned by it!

> 'Oh quanta species! et cerebrum non habet.'[1]

One of the personages in the Prometheus is Demogorgon. As he is the only agent in the whole drama, and effects the only change of situation and feeling which befals the other personages; and as he is likewise employed to sing or say divers hymns, we have endeavoured to find some intelligible account of him. The following is the most perspicuous which we have been able to discover:—

> '———A mighty power, which is as darkness,
> Is rising out of earth, and from the sky,
> Is showered like night, and from within the air
> Bursts, *like eclipse which had been gathered up*
> *Into the pores of sun-light.*'—p. 149.

Love, as might be expected, is made to perform a variety of very extraordinary functions. It fills 'the void annihilation of a sceptred curse' (p. 140); and, not to mention the other purposes to which it is applied, it is in the following lines dissolved in air and sun-light, and then folded round the world.

> '———The impalpable thin air,
> And the all circling sun-light were transformed,
> As if the sense of love dissolved in them,
> Had folded itself round the sphered world.'—p. 116.

Metaphors and similes can scarcely be regarded as ornaments of Mr. Shelley's compositions; for his poetry is in general a mere jumble of words and heterogeneous ideas, connected by slight and accidental associations, among which it is impossible to distinguish the principal object from the accessory. In illustrating the incoherency which prevails in his metaphors, as well as in the other ingredients of his verses,

---

[1] 'Oh, what beauty, but no brains!'

we shall take our first example, not from that great storehouse of the obscure and the unintelligible—the Prometheus, but from the opening of a poem, entitled, 'A Vision of the Sea,' which we have often heard praised as a splendid work of imagination.

> '——The rags of the sail
> Are flickering in ribbons within the fierce gale:
> From the stark night of vapours the dim rain is driven,
> And when lightning is loosed, like a deluge from heaven,
> She sees the black trunks of the water-spouts spin,
> And bend, as if heaven was raining in,
> Which they seem'd to sustain with their terrible mass
> As if ocean had sunk from beneath them: they pass
> To their graves in the deep with an earthquake of sound,
> And the waves and the thunders made silent around
> Leave the wind to its echo.'—p. 174.

At present we say nothing of the cumbrous and uncouth style of these verses, nor do we ask who this 'she' is, who sees the water-spouts; but the funeral of the water-spouts is curious enough: 'They pass to their graves with an earthquake of sound.' The sound of an earthquake is intelligible, and we suspect that this is what Mr. Shelley meant to say: but an earthquake of sound is as difficult to comprehend as a cannon of sound, or a fiddle of sound. The same vision presents us with a battle between a tiger and a sea-snake; of course we have—

> '——The whirl and the splash
> As of some hideous engine, whose brazen teeth smash
> The thin winds and soft waves into thunder; the screams
> And hissings crawl fast o'er the smooth ocean streams,
> Each sound like a centipede.'—p. 180.

The comparison of sound to a centipede would be no small addition to a cabinet of poetical monstrosities: but it sinks into tame commonplace before the engine, whose brazen teeth pound thin winds and soft waves into thunder.

Sometimes Mr. Shelley's love of the unintelligible yields to his preference for the disgusting and the impious. Thus the bodies of the dead sailors are thrown out of the ship:

> 'And the sharks and the dog-fish their grave-cloths unbound,
> And were glutted, like Jews, with this manna rained down
> From God on their wilderness.'—p. 177.

Asia turns her soul into an enchanted boat, in which she performs a wonderful voyage:

'My soul is an enchanted boat,
  Which, like a sleeping swan, doth float
Upon the silver waves of thy sweet singing:
  And thine doth like an angel sit
  Beside the helm conducting it,
Whilst all the winds with melody are ringing.
  It seems to float ever, for ever,
  Upon that many-winding river,
  Between mountains, woods, abysses,
  A paradise of wildernesses!
Till, like one in slumber bound,
Borne to the ocean, I float down, around,
Into a sea profound, of ever-spreading sound:
  Meanwhile thy spirit lifts its pinions
  In music's most serene dominions;
Catching the winds that fan the happy heaven.
  And we sail on, away, afar,
  Without a course, without a star,
By the instinct of sweet music driven;
  Till through Elysian garden islets
  By thee, most beautiful of pilots,
  Where never mortal pinnace glided,
  The boat of my desire is guided.'—p. 94.

The following comparison of a poet to a cameleon has no more meaning than the jingling of the bells of a fool's cap, and far less music.

'Poets are on this cold earth,
  As camelions might be,
Hidden from their early birth
  In a cave beneath the sea;
Where light is camelions change:
    Where love is not, poets do:
    Fame is love disguised; if few
Find either never think it strange
That poets range.'—p. 186.

Sometimes to the charms of nonsense those of doggerel are added. This is the conclusion of a song of certain beings, who are called 'Spirits of the human mind:'

'And Earth, Air, and Light,
And the Spirit of Might,

> Which drives round the stars in their fiery flight;
> And Love, Thought, and Breath,
> The powers that quell Death,
> Wherever we soar shall assemble beneath.
> And our singing shall build
> In the void's loose field
> A world for the Spirit of Wisdom to wield;
> We will take our plan
> From the new world of man,
> And our work shall be called the Promethean.'—p. 130.

Another characteristic trait of Mr. Shelley's poetry is, that in his descriptions he never describes the thing directly, but transfers it to the properties of something which he conceives to resemble it by language which is to be taken partly in a metaphorical meaning, and partly in no meaning at all. The whole of a long poem, in three parts, called 'the Sensitive Plant,' the object of which we cannot discover, is an instance of this. The first part is devoted to the description of the plants. The sensitive plant takes the lead:

> 'No flower ever trembled and panted with bliss,
> In the garden, the field, or the wilderness,
> Like a doe in the noon-tide with love's sweet want,
> As the companionless sensitive plant.'—p. 157.

Next come the snow-drop and the violet:

> 'And their breath was mixed with fresh odour, sent
> From the turf, *like the voice and the instrument.*'

The rose, too,

> '————Unveiled the depth of her glowing breast,
> Till, fold after fold, *to the fainting air*
> *The soul of her beauty and love lay bare.*'

The hyacinth is described in terms still more quaint and affected:

> 'The hyacinth, purple, and white, and blue;
> Which flung from *its bells a sweet peal anew,*
> Of music so delicate, soft, and intense,
> It was felt like an odour within the sense.'

It is worth while to observe the train of thought in this stanza. The bells of the flower occur to the poet's mind; but ought not bells to ring a peal? Accordingly, by a metamorphosis of the odour, the bells of the hyacinth are supposed to do so: the fragrance of the flower is first converted into a peal of music, and then the peal of music is in the last line transformed back into an odour. These are the tricks of a mere poetical harlequin, amusing himself with

'The clock-work tintinnabulum of rhyme.'

In short, it is not too much to affirm, that in the whole volume there is not one original image of nature, one simple expression of human feeling, or one new association of the appearances of the moral with those of the material world.

As Mr. Shelley disdains to draw his materials from nature, it is not wonderful that his subjects should in general be widely remote from every thing that is level with the comprehension, or interesting to the heart of man. He has been pleased to call 'Prometheus Unbound' a lyrical drama, though it has neither action nor dramatic dialogue. The subject of it is the transition of Prometheus from a state of suffering to a state of happiness; together with a corresponding change in the situation of mankind. But no distinct account is given of either of these states, nor of the means by which Prometheus and the world pass from the one to the other. The Prometheus of Mr. Shelley is not the Prometheus of ancient mythology. He is a being who is neither a God nor a man, who has conferred supreme power on Jupiter. Jupiter torments him; and Demogorgon, by annihilating Jupiter's power, restores him to happiness. Asia, Panthea, and Ione, are female beings of a nature similar to that of Prometheus. Apollo, Mercury, the Furies, and a faun, make their appearance; but have not much to do in the piece. To fill up the *personae dramatis*, we have voices of the mountains, voices of the air, voices of the springs, voices of the whirlwinds, together with several echos. Then come spirits without end: spirits of the moon, spirits of the earth, spirits of the human mind, spirits of the hours; who all attest their super-human nature by singing and saying things which no human being can comprehend. We do not find fault with this poem, because it is built on notions which no longer possess any influence over the mind, but because its basis and its materials are mere dreaming, shadowy, incoherent abstractions. It would have been quite as absurd and extravagant in the time of Æschylus, as it is now.

It may seem strange that such a volume should find readers, and still more strange that it should meet with admirers. We are ourselves surprized by the phenomenon: nothing similar to it occurred to us, till we recollected the numerous congregations which the incoherencies of an itinerant Methodist preacher attract. These preachers, without any connected train of thought, and without attempting to reason, or to attach any definite meaning to the terms which they use, pour out a deluge of sonorous words that relate to sacred objects and devout feelings. These words, connected as they are with all that is most venerable in the eyes of man, excite a multitude of pious associations in the hearer, and produce in him a species of mental intoxication. His feelings are awakened, and his heart touched, while his imagination and understanding are bewildered; and he receives temporary pleasure, sometimes even temporary improvement, at the expense of the essential and even permanent depravation of his character. In the same way, poetry like that of Mr. Shelley presents every where glittering constellations of words, which taken separately have a meaning, and either communicate some activity to the imagination, or dazzle it by their brilliance. Many of them relate to beautiful or interesting objects, and are therefore capable of imparting pleasure to us by the associations attached to them. The reader is conscious that his mind is raised from a state of stagnation, and he is willing to believe, that he is astounded and bewildered, not by the absurdity, but by the originality and sublimity of the author.

It appears to us much more surprizing, that any man of education should write such poetry as that of 'Prometheus Unbound,' than, that when written, it should find admirers. It is easy to read without attention; but it is difficult to conceive how an author, unless his intellectual habits are thoroughly depraved, should not take the trouble to observe whether his imagination has definite forms before it, or is gazing in stupid wonder on assemblages of brilliant words. Mr. Shelley tells us, that he imitates the Greek tragic poets: can he be so blinded by self-love, as not to be aware that his productions have not one feature of likeness to what have been deemed classical works, in any country or in any age? He, no doubt, possesses considerable mental activity; for without industry he could never have attained to so much facility in the art of throwing words into fantastical combinations: is it not strange that he should never have turned his attention from his verses to that which his verses are meant to express? We fear that his notions of poetry are fundamentally erroneous. It seems to be his maxim, that reason and sound thinking are aliens in the dominions of the Muses, and that, should they ever be found wandering about the foot of Parnassus, they ought to be chased away as spies sent to discover the nakedness of the land. We would wish to persuade him, if possible, that the poet is distinguished from the rest of his species, not by wanting what other men have, but by having what other men want. The reason of the poet ought to be cultivated with as much care as that of the philosopher, though the former chooses a peculiar field for its exercise, and associates with it in its labours other faculties that are not called forth in the mere investigation of truth.

But it is often said, that though the poems are bad, they at least show poetical power. Poetical power can be shown only by writing good poetry, and this Mr. Shelley has not yet done. The proofs of Mr. Shelley's genius, which his admirers allege, are the very exaggeration, copiousness of verbiage, and incoherence of ideas which we complain of as intolerable. They argue in criticism, as those men do in morals, who think debauchery and dissipation an excellent proof of a good heart. The want of meaning is called sublimity, absurdity becomes venerable under the name of originality, the jumble of metaphor is the richness of imagination, and even the rough, clumsy, confused structure of the style, with not unfrequent violations of the rules of grammar, is, forsooth, the sign and effect of a bold overflowing genius, that disdains to walk in common trammels. If the poet is one who whirls round his reader's brain, till it becomes dizzy and confused; if it is his office to envelop he knows not what in huge folds of a clumsy drapery of splendid words and showy metaphors, then, without doubt, may Mr. Shelley place the Delphic laurel on his head. But take away from him the unintelligible, the confused, the incoherent, the bombastic, the affected, the extravagant, the hideously gorgeous, and 'Prometheus', and the poems which accompany it, will sink at once into nothing.

But great as are Mr. Shelley's sins against sense and taste, would that we had nothing more to complain of! Unfortunately, to his long list of demerits he has added the most flagrant offences against morality and religion. We should abstain from quoting instances, were it not that we think his language too gross and too disgusting to be dangerous to any but those who are corrupted beyond the hope of amendment. After a revolting description of the death of our Saviour, introduced merely for the sake of intimating, that *the religion he preached is the great source of human misery and vice*, he adds,

> —'Thy name I will not speak,
> It hath become a curse.'

Will Mr. Shelley, to excuse this blasphemy against the name '*in which all the nations of the earth shall be made blessed*,' pretend, that these are the words of Prometheus, not of the poet? But the poet himself hath told us, that his Prometheus is meant to be 'the type of the highest perfection of moral and intellectual excellence.' There are other passages, in which Mr. Shelley speaks directly in his own person. In what he calls an ode to Liberty, he tells us that she did

> —'groan, not weep,
> When from its sea of death to kill and burn
> The Galilaean serpent forth did creep
> And made thy world an undistinguishable heap.'—p. 213.

And after a few stanzas he adds,

> 'O, that the free would stamp the impious name
>   Of ******[1] into the dust! or write it there,
> So that this blot upon the page of fame
>   Were as a serpent's path, which the light air
> Erases, and that the flat sands close behind!
>   Ye the oracle have heard:
>   Lift the victory-flashing sword,
> And cut the snaky knots of this foul Gordian word,
>   Which weak itself as stubble, yet can bind
>   Into a mass, irrefragably firm,
>   The axes and the rods which awe mankind;
>   The sound has poison in it, 'tis the sperm
> Of what makes life foul, cankerous, and abhorred;
>   Disdain not thou, at thine appointed term,
>   To set thine armed heel on this reluctant worm.
> O, that the wise from their bright minds would kindle
>   Such lamps within the dome of this dim world,
> That the pale name of PRIEST might shrink and dwindle
>   Into the hell from which it first was hurled,
> A scoff of impious pride from fiends impure;
>   Till human thoughts might kneel alone
>   Each before the judgement-throne
> Of its own awless soul, or of the power unknown!'—p. 218.

At present we say nothing of the harshness of style and incongruity of metaphor, which these verses exhibit. We do not even ask what is or

---

[1] Leigh Hunt in a later article in the *Examiner* claimed that the substitution of six asterisks in the quotation for four in the text was a deliberate attempt on the part of the reviewer to deceive the reader into thinking that the omitted word was *Christ* rather than *King*, as it stood in manuscript (see Newman I. White, *The Unextinguished Hearth* [Durham, North Carolina, 1938], pp. 310–11).

In view of the reference to 'the Galilaean serpent' in the previous quotation, however, the added asterisks would seem to have been an unnecessary trick. There is, furthermore, nothing in the passage itself that would suggest that any word but *Christ* was intended.

can be meant by *the kneeling of human thought before the judgment-throne of its own awless soul*: for it is a praiseworthy precaution in an author, to temper irreligion and sedition with nonsense, so that he may avail himself, if need be, of the plea of lunacy before the tribunals of his country. All that we now condemn, is the wanton gratuitous impiety thus obtruded on the world. If any one, after a serious investigation of the truth of Christianity, still doubts or disbelieves, he is to be pitied and pardoned; if he is a good man, he will himself lament that he has not come to a different conclusion; for even the enemies of our faith admit, that it is precious for the restraints which it imposes on human vices, and for the consolations which it furnishes under the evils of life. But what is to be said of a man, who, like Mr. Shelley, wantonly and unnecessarily goes out of his way, not to reason against, but to revile Christianity and its author? Let him adduce his arguments against our religion, and we shall tell him where to find them answered: but let him not presume to insult the world, and to profane the language in which he writes, by rhyming invectives against a faith of which he knows nothing but the name.

The real cause of his aversion to Christianity is easily discovered. Christianity is the great prop of the social order of the civilized world; this social order is the object of Mr. Shelley's hatred; and, therefore, the pillar must be demolished, that the building may tumble down. His views of the nature of men and of society are expressed, we dare not say explained, in some of those '*beautiful idealisms of moral excellence*,' (we use his own words,) in which the 'Prometheus' abounds.

'The painted veil, by those who were, called life, which mimicked, as with colours idly spread, all men believed and hoped, is torn aside; the loathsome mask has fallen, the man remains sceptreless, free, uncircumscribed, but man equal, unclassed, tribeless, and nationless, exempt from awe, worship, degree, the king over himself; just, gentle, wise: but man passionless; no, yet free from guilt or pain, which were for his will made or suffered them, nor yet exempt, tho' ruling them like slaves, from chance and death, and mutability, the clogs of that which else might oversoar the loftiest star of unascended heaven, pinnacled dim in the intense inane.'—p. 120.

Our readers may be puzzled to find out the meaning of this paragraph; we must, therefore, inform them that it is not prose, but the conclusion of the third act of Prometheus verbatim et literatim. With this information they will cease to wonder at the absence of sense and grammar; and will probably perceive, that Mr. Shelley's poetry is, in sober sadness, *drivelling prose run mad*.

With the prophetic voice of a misgiving conscience, Mr. Shelley objects to criticism. 'If my attempt be ineffectual, (he says) let the punishment of an unaccomplished purpose have been sufficient; let none trouble themselves to heap the dust of oblivion upon my efforts.' Is there no respect due to common sense, to sound taste, to morality, to religion? Are evil spirits to be allowed to work mischief with impunity, because, forsooth, the instruments with which they work are contemptible? Mr. Shelley says, that his intentions are pure. Pure! They be so in his vocabulary; for, (to say nothing of his having unfortunately mistaken nonsense for poetry, and blasphemy for an imperious duty,) vice and irreligion, and the subversion of society are, according to his system, pure and holy things; Christianity, and moral virtue, and social order, are alone impure. But we care not about his intentions, or by what epithet he may choose to characterize them, so long as his works exhale contagious mischief. On his own principles he must admit, that, in exposing to the public what we believe to be the character and tendency of his writings, we discharge a sacred duty. He professes to write in order to reform the world. The essence of the proposed reformation is the destruction of religion and government. Such a reformation is not to our taste; and he must, therefore, applaud us for scrutinizing the merits of works which are intended to promote so detestable a purpose. Of Mr. Shelley himself we know nothing, and desire to know nothing. Be his private qualities what they may, his poems (and it is only with his poems that we have any concern) are at war with reason, with taste, with virtue, in short, with all that dignifies man, or that man reveres.

Review of Shelley's 'Queen Mab'

Monthly Magazine

LI (*June 1821*), *460–61. The reviewer is unknown.*

A poem entitled *Queen Mab*, by Mr. Percy Bysshe Shelley, was printed and distributed among his friends, about seven years ago; but has at length been published. The text of the work is in measured lines, of unequal length, which being divided into parcels, by means of Roman numerals, have the appearance of so many odes, but without rhyme. It is in the Thalaba style, which has been so bepraised by the poetasters of the present day. 'He,' says Dr. Johnson, 'that thinks himself capable of astonishing, may write blank verse; but those that hope only to please, must condescend to rhyme.' The Author before us does, indeed, endeavour to *astonish*, by the extravagance of his paradoxes, and the incongruity of his metaphors; and may, therefore, claim the right to print his lines of such various lengths as may suit his own whim or the taste of his compositor. It is a continuous declamation without either 'rhyme or reason,' and the speaker may pause where he will without injury to the sense or interruption to the monotonous flow of the harangue. The notes occupy much more space than the text; and consist chiefly of extracts from various authors, in favour of Atheism, the equalization of property, and the unrestrained intercourse of the sexes! The French, Latin, and Greek passages, which were left in their original dress in the gratuitous edition, are here translated for the benefit of the mere English reader. Advocates, as we are, for a very extended freedom of the press, we fear commenting further on this work, lest we should, unintentionally, assist in that *powerful* criticism, to which, we fear, it will soon be subjected. We have observed, of late, a seeming design to lure the unwary author to his destruction. The public journals, not even excepting the Quarterly Review, have lauded Mr. Shelley as a poet,—as a genius of the highest order! The

413

other panders of corruption speak of his 'powerful talents'! What can all this flattery mean, if it be not to decoy the witless bird, and to catch him in the snare? Either this is the case, or our Critics are a set of dunces, who cannot distinguish between sublimity and bombast,—between poetry and 'prose run mad.'

Review of Shelley's 'Adonais'

Literary Chronicle

Dec. 1, 1821, pp. 751–54. The reviewer is unknown.

Through the kindness of a friend, we have been favoured with the latest production of a gentleman of no ordinary genius, Mr. Bysshe Shelley. It is an elegy on the death of a youthful poet of considerable promise, Mr. Keats, and was printed at Pisa. As the copy now before us is, perhaps, the only one that has reached England, and the subject is one that will excite much interest, we shall print the whole of it.

It has been often said, and Mr. Shelley repeats the assertion, that Mr. Keats fell a victim to his too great susceptibility of a severe criticism on one of his poems. How far this may have been the case we know not. Cumberland[1] used to say, that authors should not be thin skinned, but shelled like the rhinoceros; but poor Keats was of too gentle a disposition for severity, and to a mind of such exquisite sensibility, we do not wonder that he felt keenly the harsh and ungenerous attack that was made upon him. Besides, we are not without instances of the effects of criticism on some minds.—Hawkesworth[2] died of criticism: when he published his account of the voyages in the South Seas, for which he received £6000, an innumerable host of enemies attacked it in the newspapers and magazines; some pointed out blunders in matters of science, and some exercised their wit in poetical translations and epigrams. It was, says Dr. Kippis, 'a fatal undertaking, and which, in its consequences, deprived him of presence of mind and of life itself.'

[1] Richard Cumberland was the editor of the *London Review* (1809), which dropped the anonymity of its reviews. Cumberland was himself said to be very sensitive to criticism.

[2] John Hawkesworth published *An Account of the Voyages undertaken by order of his present Majesty for making Discoveries in the Southern Hemisphere* in 1773.

Tasso was driven mad by criticisms; his susceptibility and tenderness of feeling were so great, that when his sublime work, 'Jerusalem Delivered,' met with unexpected opposition, the fortitude of the poet was not proof against the keenness of disappointment. He twice attempted to please his ignorant and malignant critics, by recomposing his poem; and, during the hurry, the anguish, and the irritation attending these efforts, the vigour of a great mind was entirely exhausted, and, in two years after the publication of his work, the unhappy bard became an object of pity and of terror.

Even the mild Newton, with all his philosophy, was so sensible to critical remarks, that Whiston tells us he lost his favour, which he had enjoyed for twenty years, for contradicting Newton in his old age; for, says he, no man was of 'a more fearful temper.' Whiston declares that he would never have thought proper to have published his work against Newton's Chronology during the life of the great philosopher, 'because,' says he, 'I knew his temper so well, that I should have expected it would have killed him.'

We have never been among the very enthusiastic admirers of Mr. Keats's poetry, though we allow that he possessed considerable genius; but we are decidedly averse to that species of literary condemnation, which is often practised by men of wit and arrogance, without feeling and without discrimination.

Mr. Shelley is an ardent admirer of Keats; and though he declares his repugnance to the principles of taste on which several of his earlier compositions were modelled, he says that he considers 'the fragment of Hyperion as second to nothing that was ever produced by a writer of the same years.' Mr. Shelley, in the preface, gives some details respecting the poet:—

[All but the first paragraph of the Preface is quoted.[1]]

Of the beauty of Mr. Shelley's elegy we shall not speak; to every poetic mind, its transcendant merits must be apparent.

[The entire poem is quoted.]

[1] [To Shelley's comment that Keats had 'been hastened from the stage of life, no less by those on whom he had wasted the promise of his genius . . .', was appended the following footnote: 'We do not know to whom Mr. Shelley alludes; but we believe we may say that the city of London does not boast a bookseller more honourable in his dealings, or more liberal to rising genius or indigent merit than the publishers of Mr. Keats's poems.—Ed.']

Review of Shelley's
'Posthumous Poems'

Edinburgh Review

XL (*July 1824*), *494–514. The author was William Hazlitt: see Walter E. Houghton* (*ed.*), The Wellesley Index to Victorian Periodicals (*Toronto, 1966*), *p. 466.*

Mr Shelley's style is to poetry what astrology is to natural science— a passionate dream, a straining after impossibilities, a record of fond conjectures, a confused embodying of vague abstractions,—a fever of the soul, thirsting and craving after what it cannot have, indulging its love of power and novelty at the expense of truth and nature, associating ideas by contraries, and wasting great powers by their application to unattainable objects.

Poetry, we grant, creates a world of its own; but it creates it out of existing materials. Mr Shelley is the maker of his own poetry—out of nothing. Not that he is deficient in the true sources of strength and beauty, if he had given himself fair play (the volume before us, as well as his other productions, contains many proofs to the contrary): But, in him, fancy, will, caprice, predominated over and absorbed the natural influences of things; and he had no respect for any poetry that did not strain the intellect as well as fire the imagination—and was not sublimed into a high spirit of metaphysical philosophy. Instead of giving a language to thought, or lending the heart a tongue, he utters dark sayings, and deals in allegories and riddles. His Muse offers her services to clothe shadowy doubts and inscrutable difficulties in a robe of glittering words, and to turn nature into a brilliant paradox. We thank him—but we must be excused. Where we see the dazzling beacon-lights streaming over the darkness of the abyss, we dread the quicksands and the rocks below. Mr Shelley's mind was of 'too fiery a

417

quality' to repose (for any continuance) on the probable or the true—
it soared 'beyond the visible diurnal sphere,' to the strange, the improbable, and the impossible. He mistook the nature of the poet's
calling, which should be guided by involuntary, not by voluntary impulses. He shook off, as an heroic and praise-worthy act, the trammels
of sense, custom, and sympathy, and became the creature of his own
will. He was 'all air,' disdaining the bars and ties of mortal mould. He
ransacked his brain for incongruities, and believed in whatever was
incredible. Almost all is effort, almost all is extravagant, almost all is
quaint, incomprehensible, and abortive, from aiming to be more than
it is. Epithets are applied, because they do not fit: subjects are chosen,
because they are repulsive: the colours of his style, for their gaudy,
changeful, startling effect, resemble the display of fire-works in the
dark, and, like them, have neither durability, nor keeping, nor discriminate form. Yet Mr Shelley, with all his faults, was a man of genius;
and we lament that uncontrollable violence of temperament which
gave it a forced and false direction. He has single thoughts of great
depth and force, single images of rare beauty, detached passages of
extreme tenderness; and, in his smaller pieces, where he has attempted
little, he has done most. If some casual and interesting idea touched
his feelings or struck his fancy, he expressed it in pleasing and unaffected verse: but give him a larger subject, and time to reflect, and he
was sure to get entangled in a system. The fumes of vanity rolled volumes of smoke, mixed with sparkles of fire, from the cloudy tabernacle
of his thought. The success of his writings is therefore in general in
the inverse ratio of the extent of his undertakings; inasmuch as his
desire to teach, his ambition to excel, as soon as it was brought into
play, encroached upon, and outstripped his powers of execution.

   Mr Shelley was a remarkable man. His person was a type and shadow
of his genius. His complexion, fair, golden, freckled, seemed transparent with an inward light, and his spirit within him

> ———'so divinely wrought,
> That you might almost say his body thought.'

He reminded those who saw him of some of Ovid's fables. His form,
graceful and slender, drooped like a flower in the breeze. But he was
crushed beneath the weight of thought which he aspired to bear, and
was withered in the lightning-glare of a ruthless philosophy! He mistook
the nature of his own faculties and feelings—the lowly children of the
valley, by which the skylark makes its bed, and the bee murmurs, for
the proud cedar or the mountain-pine, in which the eagle builds its

418

eyry, 'and dallies with the wind, and scorns the sun.'—He wished to make of idle verse and idler prose the frame-work of the universe, and to bind all possible existence in the visionary chain of intellectual beauty—

> 'More subtle web Arachne cannot spin,
> Nor the fine nets, which oft we woven see
> Of scorched dew, do not in th' air more lightly flee.'

Perhaps some lurking sense of his own deficiencies in the lofty walk which he attempted, irritated his impatience and his desires; and urged him on, with winged hopes, to atone for past failures, by more arduous efforts, and more unavailing struggles.

With all his faults, Mr Shelley was an honest man. His unbelief and his presumption were parts of a disease, which was not combined in him either with indifference to human happiness, or contempt for human infirmities. There was neither selfishness nor malice at the bottom of his illusions. He was sincere in all his professions; and he practised what he preached—to his own sufficient cost. He followed up the letter and the spirit of his theoretical principles in his own person, and was ready to share both the benefit and the penalty with others. He thought and acted logically, and was what he professed to be, a sincere lover of truth, of nature, and of human kind. To all the rage of paradox, he united an unaccountable candour and severity of reasoning: in spite of an aristocratic education, he retained in his manners the simplicity of a primitive apostle. An Epicurean in his sentiments, he lived with the frugality and abstemiousness of an ascetick. His fault was, that he had no deference for the opinions of others, too little sympathy with their feelings (which he thought he had a right to sacrifice, as well as his own, to a grand ethical experiment)—and trusted too implicitly to the light of his own mind, and to the warmth of his own impulses. He was indeed the most striking example we remember of the two extremes described by Lord Bacon as the great impediments to human improvement, the love of Novelty, and the love of Antiquity. 'The first of these (impediments) is an extreme affection of two extremities, the one Antiquity, the other Novelty; wherein it seemeth the children of time do take after the nature and malice of the father. For as he devoureth his children, so one of them seeketh to devour and suppress the other; while Antiquity envieth there should be new additions, and Novelty cannot be content to add, but it may deface. Surely the advice of the Prophet is the true direction in this matter: *Stand upon the old ways, and see which is the right and good way, and walk therein.* Antiquity deserveth that reverence, that men should make a stand thereupon, and discover what is the best way; but when the discovery is well taken, then to take progression. And to speak truly, *Antiquitas seculi Juventas mundi.* These times are the ancient times, when the world is ancient, and not those which we count ancient, *ordine retrogrado,* by a computation backwards from ourselves.' (ADVANCEMENT OF LEARNING, Book I. p. 46.)—Such is the text: and Mr Shelley's writings are a splendid commentary on one half of it. Considered in this point of view, his career may not be uninstructive even to those whom it most offended; and might be held up as a beacon and warning no less to the bigot than the sciolist. We wish to speak of the errors of a man of genius with tenderness. His nature was kind, and his sentiments noble; but in him the rage of free inquiry and private judgment amounted to a species of madness. Whatever was new, untried, unheard of, unauthorized, exerted a kind of fascination over his mind. The examples of the world, the opinion of others, instead of acting as a check upon him, served but to impel him forward with double velocity in his wild and hazardous career. Spurning the world of realities, he rushed into the world of nonentities and contingencies, like air into a *vacuum.* If a thing was old and established, this was with him a certain proof of its having no solid foundation to rest upon: if it was new, it was good and right. Every paradox was to him a self-evident truth; every prejudice an undoubted absurdity. The weight of authority, the sanction of ages, the common consent of mankind, were vouchers only for ignorance, error, and imposture. Whatever shocked the feelings of others, conciliated his regard; whatever was light, extravagant, and vain, was to him a proportionable relief from the dulness and stupidity of established opinions. The worst of it however was, that he thus gave great encouragement to those who believe in all received absurdities, and are wedded to all existing abuses: his extravagance seeming to sanction their grossness and selfishness, as theirs were a full justification of his folly and eccentricity. The two extremes in this way often meet, jostle,—and confirm one another. The infirmities of age are a foil to the presumption of youth; and 'there the antics sit,' mocking one another—the ape Sophistry pointing with reckless scorn at 'palsied eld,' and the bed-rid hag, Legitimacy, rattling her chains, counting her beads, dipping her hands in blood, and blessing herself from all change and from every appeal to common sense and reason! Opinion thus alternates in a round of contradictions: the impatience or obstinacy of the human mind takes part with, and flies off to one or other of the two extremes 'of affection' and leaves a horrid gap, a blank sense and feeling in the middle, which seems never likely to be filled up, without a total change in our mode of proceeding. The martello-towers with which we are to repress, if we cannot destroy, the systems of fraud and oppression should not be castles in the air, or clouds in the verge of the horizon, but the enormous and accumulated pile of abuses which have arisen out of their own continuance. The principles of sound morality, liberty and humanity, are not to be found only in a few recent writers, who have discovered the secret of the greatest happiness to the greatest numbers, but are truths as old as the creation. To be convinced of the existence of wrong, we should read history rather than poetry: the levers with which we must work out our regeneration are not the cobwebs of the brain, but the warm, palpitating fibres of the human heart. It is the collision of passions and interests, the petulance of party-spirit, and the perversities of self-will and self-opinion that have been the great obstacles to social improvement—not stupidity or ignorance; and the caricaturing one side of the question and shocking the most pardonable prejudices on the other, is not the way to allay heats or produce unanimity. By flying to the extremes of scepticism, we make others shrink back and shut themselves up in the strongholds of bigotry and superstition—by mixing up doubtful or offensive matters with salutary and demonstrable truths, we bring the whole into question, fly-blow the cause, risk the principle, and give a handle and a pretext to the enemy to treat all philosophy and all reform as a compost of crude, chaotic, and monstrous absurdities. We thus arm the virtues as well as the vices of the community against us; we trifle with their understandings, and exasperate their self-love; we give to superstition and injustice all their old security and sanctity, as if they were the only alternatives of impiety and profligacy, and league the natural with the selfish prejudices of mankind in hostile array against us. To this consummation, it must be confessed that too many of Mr Shelley's productions pointedly tend. He makes no account of the opinions of others, or the consequences of any of his own; but proceeds—tasking his reason to the utmost to account for every thing, and discarding every thing as mystery and error for which he cannot account by an effort of mere intelligence—measuring man, providence, nature, and even his own heart, by the limits of the understanding—now hallowing high mysteries, now desecrating pure sentiments, according as they fall in with or exceeded those limits; and exalting and purifying, with Promethean heat, whatever he does not confound and debase.

Mr Shelley died, it seems, with a volume of Mr Keats's poetry grasped with one hand in his bosom! These are two out of four poets, patriots and friends, who have visited Italy within a few years, both of whom have been soon hurried to a more distant shore. Keats died young; and 'yet his infelicity had years too many.' A canker had blighted the tender bloom that o'erspread a face in which youth and genius strove with beauty. The shaft was sped—venal, vulgar, venomous, that drove him from his country, with sickness and penury for companions, and followed him to his grave. And yet there are those who could trample on the faded flower—men to whom breaking hearts are a subject of merriment—who laugh loud over the silent urn of Genius, and play out their game of venality and infamy with the crumbling bones of their victims! To this band of immortals a third has since been added!—a mightier genius, a haughtier spirit, whose stubborn impatience and Achilles-like pride only Death could quell. Greece, Italy, the world, have lost their poet-hero; and his death has spread a wider gloom, and been recorded with a deeper awe, than has waited on the obsequies of any of the many great who have died in our remembrance. Even detraction has been silent at his tomb; and the more generous of his enemies have fallen into the rank of his mourners. But he set like the sun in his glory; and his orb was greatest and brightest at the last; for his memory is now consecrated no less by freedom than genius. He probably fell a martyr to his zeal against tyrants. He attached himself to the cause of Greece, and dying, clung to it with a convulsive grasp, and has thus gained a niche in her history; for whatever *she* claims as hers is immortal, even in decay, as the marble sculptures on the columns of her fallen temples!

The volume before us is introduced by an imperfect but touching Preface by Mrs Shelley, and consists almost wholly of original pieces, with the exception of *Alastor, or the Spirit of Solitude*, which was out of print; and the admirable Translation of the *May-day Night*, from Goethe's Faustus.

Julian and Maddalo (the first Poem in the collection) is a Conversation or Tale, full of that thoughtful and romantic humanity, but rendered perplexing and unattractive by that veil of shadowy or of glittering obscurity, which distinguished Mr Shelley's writings. The depth and tenderness of his feelings seems often to have interfered with the expression of them, as the sight becomes blind with tears. A dull, waterish vapour, clouds the aspect of his philosophical poetry, like that mysterious gloom which he has himself described as hanging over the Medusa's Head of Leonardo da Vinci. The metre of this poem, too, will not be pleasing to every body. It is in the antique taste of the rhyming parts of Beaumont and Fletcher and Ben Jonson—blank verse in its freedom and unbroken flow, falling into rhymes that appear altogether accidental—very colloquial in the diction—and sometimes sufficiently prosaic. But it is easier showing than describing it. We give the introductory passage.

[Lines 1–33, 53–111, and 132–40 are quoted.]

The march of these lines is, it must be confessed, slow, solemn, sad: there is a sluggishness of feeling, a dearth of imagery, an unpleasant glare of lurid light. It appears to us, that in some poets, as well as in some painters, the organ of colour (to speak in the language of the adepts) predominates over that of form; and Mr Shelley is of the number. We have every where a profusion of dazzling hues, of glancing splendours, of floating shadows, but the objects on which they fall are bare, indistinct, and wild. There is something in the preceding extract that reminds us of the arid style and matter of Crabbe's versification, or that apes the labour and throes of parturition of Wordsworth's blank-verse. It is the preface to a story of Love and Madness—of mental anguish and philosophic remedies—not very intelligibly told, and left with most of its mysteries unexplained, in the true spirit of the modern metaphysical style—in which we suspect there is a due mixture of affectation and meagreness of invention.

This poem is, however, in Mr Shelley's best and *least mannered* manner. If it has less brilliancy, it has less extravagance and confusion. It is in his stanza-poetry, that his Muse chiefly runs riot, and baffles all pursuit of common comprehension or critical acumen. The *Witch of Atlas*, the *Triumph of Life*, and *Marianne's Dream*, are rhapsodies or allegories of this description; full of fancy and of fire, with glowing allusions and wild machinery, but which it is difficult to read through, from the disjointedness of the materials, the incongruous metaphors and violent transitions, and of which, after reading them through, it is impossible, in most instances, to guess the drift or the moral. They abound in horrible imaginings, like records of a ghastly dream;—life, death, genius, beauty, victory, earth, air, ocean, the trophies of the past, the shadows of the world to come, are huddled together in a strange and hurried dance of words, and all that appears clear, is the passion and paroxysm of thought of the poet's spirit. The poem entitled the *Triumph of Life*, is in fact a new and terrific *Dance of Death*; but it is thus Mr Shelley transposes the appellations of the commonest things, and subsists only in the violence of contrast. How little this poem is deserving of its title, how worthy it is of its author, what an example of the waste of power, and of genius 'made as flax,' and devoured by its own elementary ardours, let the reader judge from the concluding stanzas.

[Lines 480–514 and 523–34 are quoted.]

Any thing more filmy, enigmatical, discontinuous, unsubstantial than this, we have not seen; nor yet more full of morbid genius and vivifying soul. We cannot help preferring *The Witch of Atlas* to *Alastor, or the Spirit of Solitude*; for, though the purport of each is equally perplexing and undefined, (both being a sort of mental voyage through the un-explored regions of space and time), the execution of the one is much less dreary and lamentable than that of the other. In the 'Witch,' he has indulged his fancy more than his melancholy, and wantoned in the felicity of embryo and crude conceits even to excess.

[Lines 161–64 and 169–76 are quoted.]

We give the description of the progress of the 'Witch's' boat as a slight specimen of what we have said of Mr Shelley's involved style and imagery.

> 'And down the streams which clove those mountains vast,
>   Around their inland islets, and amid
> The panther-peopled forests, whose shade cast
>   Darkness and odours, and a pleasure hid
> In melancholy gloom, the pinnace past:
>   By many a star-surrounded pyramid
> Of icy crag cleaving the purple sky,
> And caverns yawning round unfathomably.
> . . . .
> 'And down the earth-quaking cataracts which shiver
>   Their snow-like waters into golden air,
> Or under chasms unfathomable ever
>   Sepulchre them, till in their rage they tear
> A subterranean portal for the river,
>   It fled—the circling *sunbows* did upbear
> Its fall down the hoar precipice of spray,
> Lighting it far upon its lampless way.'

This we conceive to be the very height of wilful extravagance and mysticism. Indeed it is curious to remark every where the proneness to the marvellous and supernatural, in one who so resolutely set his face against every received mystery, and all traditional faith. Mr Shelley must have possessed, in spite of all his obnoxious and indiscreet scepti-cism, a large share of credulity and wondering curiosity in his composi-tion, which he reserved from common use, and bestowed upon his own inventions and picturesque caricatures. To every other species of im-posture or disguise he was inexorable; and indeed it is his only anti-pathy to established creeds and legitimate crowns that ever tears the veil from his *ideal* idolatries, and renders him clear and explicit. Indignation makes him pointed and intelligible enough, and breathes into his verse a spirit very different from his own boasted spirit of Love.

The *Letter to a Friend in London* shows the author in a pleasing and familiar, but somewhat prosaic light; and his *Prince Athanase, a Fragment*, is, we suspect, intended as a portrait of the writer. It is amiable, thoughtful, and not much over-charged. We had designed to give an extract, but from the apparently personal and doubtful interest attached to it, perhaps it had better be read altogether, or not at all. We rather choose to quote a part of the *Ode to Naples*, during her brief revolution, —in which immediate and strong local feelings have at once raised and pointed Mr Shelley's style, and 'made of light-winged toys of feathered cupid,' the flaming ministers of Wrath and Justice.

[Lines 52–58, 77–90, and 102–76 are quoted.]

This Ode for Liberty, though somewhat turbid and overloaded in the diction, we regard as a fair specimen of Mr Shelley's highest powers —whose eager animation wanted only a greater sterness and solidity to be sublime.' The poem is dated *September* 1820. Such were then the author's aspirations. He lived to see the result,—and yet Earth does not roll its billows over the heads of its oppressors! The reader may like to contrast with this the milder strain of the following stanzas, addressed to the same city in a softer and more desponding mood.

[Lines 1–18 and 28–45 of 'Stanzas written in Dejection, near Naples are quoted.]

We pass on to some of Mr Shelley's smaller pieces and translations, which we think are in general excellent and highly interesting. His *Hymn of Pan* we do not consider equal to Mr Keats's sounding lines in the Endymion. His *Mont Blanc* is full of beauties and of defects; but it is akin to its subject, and presents a wild and gloomy desolation. GINEVRA, a fragment founded on a story in the first volume of the 'Florentine Observer,' is like a troublous dream, disjointed, painful, oppressive, or like a leaden cloud, from which the big tears fall, and the spirit of the poet mutters deep-toned thunder. We are too much subject to these voluntary inflictions, these 'moods of mind,' these effusions of 'weakness and melancholy,' in the perusal of modern poetry. It has shuffled off, no doubt, its old pedantry and formality; but has at the same time lost all shape or purpose, except that of giving vent to some morbid feeling of the moment. The writer thus discharges a fit of the spleen or a paradox, and expects the world to admire and be satisfied. We are no longer annoyed at seeing the luxuriant growth of nature and fancy clipped into arm-chairs and peacocks' tails; but there is danger of having its stately products choked with unchecked underwood, or weighed down with gloomy nightshade, or eaten up with personality, like ivy clinging round and eating into the sturdy oak! The *Dirge*, at the conclusion of this fragment, is an example of the manner in which this craving after novelty, this desire 'to elevate and surprise,' leads us to 'overstep the modesty of nature,' and the bounds of decorum.

'Ere the sun through heaven once more has roll'd,
The rats in her heart
Will have made their nest,
And the worms be alive in her golden hair,
While the spirit that guides the sun,
Sits throned in his flaming chair,
    She shall sleep.'

The 'worms' in this stanza are the old and traditional appendages of the grave;—the 'rats' are new and unwelcome intruders; but a modern artist would rather shock, and be disgusting and extravagant, than produce no effect at all, or be charged with a want of genius and originality. In the unfinished scenes of Charles I., (a drama on which Mr Shelley was employed at his death) the *radical* humour of the author breaks forth, but 'in good set terms' and specious oratory. We regret that his premature fate has intercepted this addition to our historical drama. From the fragments before us, we are not sure that it would be fair to give any specimen.

The TRANSLATIONS from Euripedes, Calderon, and Goethe in this Volume, will give great pleasure to the scholar and to the general reader. They are executed with equal fidelity and spirit. If the present publication contained only the two last pieces in it, the *Prologue in Heaven*, and the *May-day Night* of the Faust (the first of which Lord Leveson Gower has omitted, and the last abridged, in his very meritorious translation of that Poem), the intellectual world would receive it with an *All Hail*! We shall enrich our pages with a part of the *May-day Night*, which the Noble Poet has deemed untranslateable.

[Lines 146–89, 211–22, and 244–70 of scene ii are quoted.]

The preternatural imagery in all this medley is, we confess, (comparatively speaking) meagre and monotonous; but there is a squalid nudity, and a fiendish irony and scorn thrown over the whole, that is truly edifying. The scene presently after proceeds thus.

[Lines 371–403 of scene ii are quoted.]

The latter part of the foregoing scene is to be found in both translations; but we prefer Mr Shelley's, if not for its elegance, for its simplicity and force. Lord Leveson Gower has given, at the end of his volume, a translation of Lessing's Faust, as having perhaps furnished the hint for the larger production. There is an old tragedy of our own, founded on the same tradition, by Marlowe, in which the author has treated the subject according to the spirit of poetry, and the learning of his age. He has not evaded the main incidents of the fable (it was not the fashion of the dramatists of his day), nor sunk the chief character in glosses and episodes (however subtle or alluring), but has described Faustus's love of learning, his philosophic dreams and raptures, his religious horrors and melancholy fate, with appropriate gloom or gorgeousness of colouring. The character of the old enthusiastic inquirer after the philosopher's stone, and dealer with the Devil, is nearly lost sight of in the German play: its bold development forms the chief beauty and strength of the old English one. We shall not, we hope, be accused of wandering too far from the subject, if we conclude with some account of it in the words of a contemporary writer.

[A quotation (concerning *Dr Faustus*) of about a page from Hazlitt's own *The Dramatic Literature of the Age of Elizabeth* is given (*The Complete Works of William Hazlitt*, ed. P. P. Howe [London, 1931], VI, 202–03).]

Selected Further Reading

General

Amarasinghe, Upali. *Dryden and Pope in the Early Nineteenth Century.* Cambridge, 1962.

Cox, R. G. 'The Great Reviews', *Scrutiny*, VI (1937), 2–20, 155–75.

Dudek, Louis. *Literature and the Press.* Toronto, 1960.

Elliot, Arthur R. D. 'Reviews and Magazines in the Early Years of the Nineteenth Century'. In *The Cambridge History of English Literature*, ed. A. W. Ward and A. R. Waller, Vol. XII, Chap. vi, Cambridge, 1915.

Elton, Oliver. 'The Official Reviewers'. In *The Survey of English Literature 1780–1830.* 2 vols, London, 1912.

Graham, Walter. *English Literary Periodicals.* New York, 1930.

Hayden, John O. *The Romantic Reviewers 1802–24.* Chicago, 1969. [Contains an extended bibliography.]

—— 'Coleridge, the Reviewers, and Wordsworth', *Studies in Philology*, LXVIII (1971), 105–19.

Hodgart, Patricia, and Theodore Redpath, eds. *Romantic Perspectives.* London, 1964.

Jack, Ian. *English Literature 1815–1832.* Oxford, 1963.

Saintsbury, George. *A History of Nineteenth Century Literature (1780–1895).* London, 1896.

Strout, Alan L., ed. *John Bull's Letter to Lord Byron.* Norman, Okla., 1947.

Wain, John, ed. *Contemporary Reviews of Romantic Poetry.* London, 1953.

Ward, W. S. *Index and Finding List of Serials Published in the British Isles 1789–1832.* Lexington, Ky., 1953.

On Individual Periodicals

Annual Review

Robberds, J. W. *Memoir of the Life and Writings of the Late William Taylor*

429

of Norwich. 2 vols. London, 1843. [See also for information on the *Monthly Review*, *Critical Review* and *Monthly Magazine.*]

Blackwood's Magazine

Oliphant, Margaret. *Annals of a Publishing House.* 2 vols. Edinburgh, 1897.

Strout, Alan L. *A Bibliography of Articles in Blackwood's Magazine, 1817–1825.* Texas Tech. College Library Bulletin No. 5, Lubbock, Texas, 1959. [Contains further bibliography on *Blackwood's.*]

British Critic

Mineka, F. E. *The Dissidence of Dissent.* Chapel Hill, N.C., 1944.

British Review

Roberts, Rev. Arthur. *The Life, Letters, and Opinions of William Roberts.* London, 1850.

Ward, W. S. 'Lord Byron and "My Grandmother's Review" ', *Modern Language Notes*, LXIV (1949), 25–29.

Champion

Hughes, T. Rowland. 'John Scott, Author, Editor, and Critic', *London Mercury*, XXI (1930), 518–28. [See also for information on the *London Magazine.*]

Critical Review

Roper, Derek. 'The Politics of the *Critical Review*, 1756–1817', *Durham University Journal*, n.s. XXII (1961), 117–22.

Eclectic Review

Holland, John, and James Everett. *Memoirs of the Life and Writings of James Montgomery.* 7 vols. London, 1854–56.

Ryland, J. E. *The Life and Correspondence of John Foster.* 2 vols. London, 1846.

Edinburgh Review

Bagehot, Walter. 'The First Edinburgh Reviewers.' In *Literary Studies.* 2 vols. London, 1879.

Bald, R. C. 'Francis Jeffrey as a Literary Critic', *Nineteenth Century and After*, XCVII (1925), 201–05.

Clive, John. *Scotch Reviewers: The Edinburgh Review 1802–1815.* Cambridge, Mass., 1957. [Contains further bibliography on the *Edinburgh.*]

Constable, Thomas. *Archibald Constable and His Literary Correspondents.* 3 vols. Edinburgh, 1873.

Crawford, Thomas. *The Edinburgh Review and Romantic Poetry (1802–1829).*

Auckland University College Bulletin No. 47, English Series No. 8, 1955.

Derby, R. 'The Paradox of Jeffrey: Reason versus Sensibility', *Modern Language Quarterly*, VII (1946), 489–500.

'The *Edinburgh Review* (1802–1902)', *Edinburgh Review*, CXLV (1902), 275–318.

Greig, James A. *Francis Jeffrey of the Edinburgh Review*. Edinburgh, 1948.

Houghton, Walter E., ed. *The Wellesley Index to Victorian Periodicals 1824–1900*. Toronto, 1966. [Contains attributions of articles in the *Edinburgh* from 1802.]

Hughes, M. Y. 'The Humanism of Francis Jeffrey', *Modern Language Review*, XVI (1921), 243–51.

Stephen, Sir Leslie. 'The First Edinburgh Reviewers.' In *Hours in a Library*. 3 vols. London, 1892.

Examiner

Blunden, Edmund, ed. *Leigh Hunt's 'Examiner' Examined*. London, 1928.

Literary Gazette

Jerdan, William. *Autobiography*. 4 vols. London, 1852–53.

Baldwin's *London Magazine*

Bauer, Josephine. *The London Magazine 1820–1829*. Copenhagen, 1953. [Contains further bibliography on the *London*.]

Blunden, Edmund. *Keats's Publisher, a Memoir of John Taylor*, London, 1940.

Morgan, Peter F. 'Taylor and Hessey: Aspects of their Conduct of the *London Magazine*', *Keats–Shelley Journal*, VII (1958), 61–68.

Monthly Magazine

Carnall, Geoffrey. 'The Monthly Magazine', *Review of English Studies*, n.s. V (1954), 158–64.

Monthly Review

Nangle, B. C. *The Monthly Review, Second Series*. Oxford, 1955.

New Monthly Magazine

Redding, Cyrus. *Fifty Years Recollections Literary and Personal*. 3 vols. London, 1858.

Quarterly Review

Brightfield, M. F. *John Wilson Croker*. Berkeley, 1940.

'The Centenary of the "Quarterly Review"', *Quarterly Review*, CCX and CCXI (1909), 731–84, 279–324.

Clark, R. B. *William Gifford, Tory Satirist, Critic, and Editor*. New York, 1930.

Graham, Walter. *Tory Criticism in the Quarterly Review 1809–1853*. New York, 1921,

Shine, Hill, and Helen Chadwick Shine. *The Quarterly Review under Gifford; Identification of Contributors 1809–1824*. Chapel Hill, N.C., 1949. [Contains further bibliography on the *Quarterly*.]

Smiles, Samuel. *A Publisher and His Friends: Memoir and Correspondence of John Murray*. 2 vols. London, 1891.

On Reviewing of Individual Writers

Byron

Chew, S. C. *Byron in England: His Fame and After-Fame*. New York, 1924.

Rutherford, Andrew, ed. *Byron: The Critical Heritage*. London and New York, 1970.

Coleridge

Graham, Walter. 'Contemporary Critics of Coleridge', *PMLA*, XXXVIII (1923), 278–89.

Jackson, J. R. de J., ed. *Coleridge: The Critical Heritage*. London and New York, 1970.

Keats

Briggs, Harold E. 'Keats's Conscious and Unconscious Reactions to Criticisms of *Endymion*', *PMLA*, LX (1945), 1106–29.

MacGillivray, J. R. *John Keats: A Bibliography and Reference Guide*. Toronto, 1949.

Marsh, George L., and Newman I. White. 'Keats and the Periodicals of His Time', *Modern Philology*, XXXII (1934), 37–53.

Shelley

Marsh, George L. 'The Early Reviews of Shelley', *Modern Philology*, XXVII (1929), 73–95.

Strout, Alan L. 'Maga, Champion of Shelley', *Studies in Philology*, XXIX (1932), 95–119.

White, Newman I. *The Unextinguished Hearth*. Durham, N.C., 1938.

Wordsworth

Beatty, J. M., Jr. 'Lord Jeffrey and Wordsworth', *PMLA*, XXXVIII (1923), 221–35.

Daniel, Robert. 'Jeffrey and Wordsworth: The Shape of Persecution', *Sewanee Review*, L (1942), 195–213.

Logan, J. V. *Wordsworthian Criticism: A Guide and Bibliography*. Columbus, Ohio, 1947.

Noyes, R. *Wordsworth and Jeffrey in Controversy*. Bloomington, Ind., 1941.

Raysor, Thomas M. 'The Establishment of Wordsworth's Reputation', *Journal of English and Germanic Philology*, LIV (1955), 61–71.

Smith, Elsie, ed. *An Estimate of Wordsworth by His Contemporaries 1793–1822*. Oxford, 1932.

Strout, Alan L. 'John Wilson, "Champion" of Wordsworth', *Modern Philology*, XXXI (1934), 383–94.